Sister act with Judy Garland

SOPHIE TUCKER
HOT REMEDY
...VE Got to be
...VED To be
HEALTHY

Walter
Huston
Ted
Friend
Raymond
Massey
Jimmy
Walker

Some of These Days

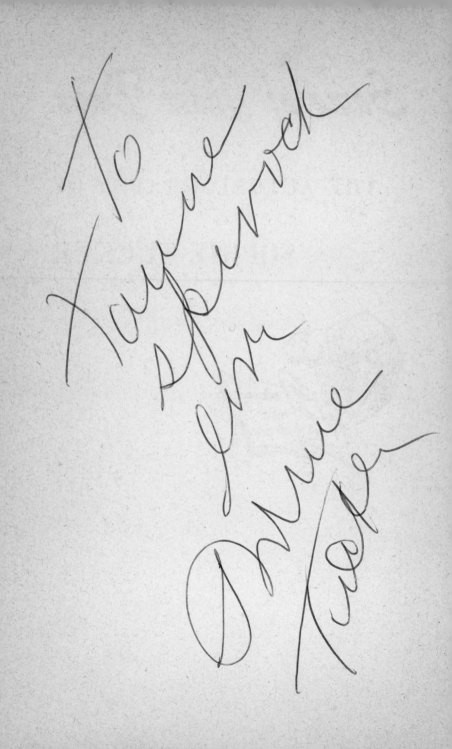

Some of These Days

THE AUTOBIOGRAPHY OF

SOPHIE TUCKER

THIS BOOK WAS WRITTEN IN COLLABORATION WITH DOROTHY GILES

*Photographs used on endpapers by courtesy of Shea, Boston;
White Studio, New York; Apeda, New York; Scherer, New
York; Murray Korman, New York;
Maurice Seymour, Chicago.*

CONTENTS

Some of These Days

CHAPTER 1: *That Abuza Kid*

"You'll have to bind it in asbestos."

The rumble coming over the wires wasn't bombs bursting on Washington; it was J. Edgar Hoover having himself a belly laugh. "So the last of the Red-hot Mamas is about to tell all! Whose ears are going to be red?"

"You'll be surprised at a lot of it," I fired back.

"It takes a lot to surprise me."

"Just the same, G-man, take this from me, you ain't heard nothing yet."

Again the rumble. "I'm listening. Go to it, Sophie. And put me down for a copy. For years I've been waiting to be told how you learned the facts of life."

"Just for that," I boomed at him, "I *will!*"

So here goes.

I was born on the road.

Not on the Orpheum, the Pantages, Keith, or any of the other circuits I've traveled since. The road I mean is the long, rutted track that leads away from Russia across Poland to the Baltic. Mama was jolting over that road in one of the big, canvas-covered wagons that used to carry poor emigrants bound for America. Somewhere along the way—Mama never could remember exactly where—she leaned over and tapped the driver on the shoulder.

"You'll have to let me get down," she said, and groaned.

He took a look at her, then pulled up the horses. The other emigrants helped her and my brother Philip, then not two years old, to get out. They handed down Mama's bundle. Then the wagon drove on, leaving the scared little boy and the woman in labor alone in the country road.

Fortunately there was a house near by, and people in it with hearts as big and warm as the feather bed they put Mama in, and where I was promptly born. I never was late for a show in my life.

Poor little Mama! She was only seventeen, and up to then she had never been more than a few miles from her native village. She knew no language except Yiddish and Russian, and nothing of America.

But Mama had guts; *dreistige,* as we Jewish people say. She could always do what she had to do, or what she thought was her duty. Her duty now was to get to Papa as fast as she could and before the money he had sent her was used up.

Besides other worries, which now included me, there was the problem of her name. When she and Papa, who came from South Russia, were married she had become Mrs. Kalish. Then Papa ran away from his military service to go to America. Somewhere along the way he fell in with an Italian named Charles Abuza, also A.W.O.L. The two palled up. Then Abuza fell sick and died. Papa, who had a terror of the Russian authorities reaching out and grabbing him and shipping him to Siberia for life, prudently helped himself to the Italian's papers and moniker.

Don't ask me what the United States Immigration officers made of an Italian who couldn't speak anything but Russian and Yiddish; but it was as "Charles Abuza" that Papa got into this country, and found a job in Boston.

Papa never did get over his fear of the Russians and what they would do to him if they caught him. Years after he had taken out second papers and had voted for Teddy Roosevelt, the sight of a tall, military-looking man coming down the street was enough to send him scuttling up the stairs to hide under the bed.

I was three months old when I made my first appearance in Boston. There is no record that I stopped the show. Boston went on its usual way for the eight years we lived there. Though I learned English in Boston, no one has ever admired my Harvard accent.

One thing, though, I've carried all my life that I got in those early years: a long, red welt across my fanny. A reminder of a washday when Mama got flustered and sat me down hard on a red-hot poker.

The year I was eight Papa bought a business in Hartford and we moved there. There were now four Abuza kids—Philip, me, Anna, and Moses. The new restaurant was on Front Street overlooking the Connecticut River and the docks. It was an exciting street for a kid: all kinds of people coming and going at all hours, big trucks loading and unloading at the piers, boat whistles and bells sounding all day. Every spring the river rose and overflowed the lower part of the town. Then business along the water front was done in boats. One year Philip and I rented a rowboat and ran a jitney ferry for the restaurant customers.

We did a good business. Mama's cooking got to be famous among the drummers and the show people who made Hartford. I still have one of the menus:

DINNER . . . 0.25

CHOICE OF	Pickled Herring or Chopped Liver. Friday special, *Gefüllte fish*.
CHOICE OF SOUP . . .	Bean, Rice, Barley, Pea, Cabbage, Noodle, Borsch, Kasha.
CHOICE OF MEAT . . .	Pot Roast, Veal, Boiled Beef, Hamburger.

EXTRA FIFTY-CENT DINNER: Steak, Chicken, or Duck.

CHOICE OF VEGETABLES	Potatoes, boiled, mashed, fried; Green Peas, Carrots, Sauerkraut, Lettuce and Tomatoes, Dill Pickles and Tomatoes.
CHOICE OF DESSERT . .	Prunes, Apricots, Apple Pie, Lemon Meringue Pie. Special delicacies: Noodle and Carrot Puddings, Potato Kugel.

TEA . . .	BLACK COFFEE	SODA POP
BEER, 0.15 a Bottle.		WHISKY, 0.25 a Drink.

This was a bargain to the customers, but to us in the kitchen it meant hard work and long hours. There never was any money to hire help. Not at a quarter a meal. Fortunately, Philip was extremely handy for a boy; many a Monday morning he has hung out a fine line of washing before starting for school. And I was always big and strong for my age.

I went to the Brown School up the street. I loved school. Not because I was a student, but because school meant being free from the restaurant and with other children of my own age. The teachers were always kind to me. I guess they felt sorry for me, as one of the poor Jewish children of the neighborhood who had to work hard at home.

"So-o-phie."
No answer
"SO-O-O-PHIE."
The noise on Front Street went right on regardless of Mama standing on the stoop outside Abuza's Home Restaurant, looking first one way then the

other along Hartford's water front, trying to shout above the rattle of the big beer wagons going down to the docks.

"SOPHIE ABUZA!"

That did it. The tangle of youngsters around Silversmith's peddler's cart unraveled to let out a bulky nine-year-old in a faded gingham dress that was too short and too skimpy over her behind. Above the dress was a mop of bright yellow curls. Each hand clutched a ripe banana.

"You, Sophie Abuza, come here this minute."

"Yes, Mama."

When Mama spoke that way you paid attention. You dropped whatever it was you were doing on your own, gave your skirt a hitch to bring it farther down over your knees, pushed the hair out of your eyes, and started. What's more, you hurried. Mama wouldn't stand being kept waiting. Not when she had something she wanted you to do.

And she usually had. There never was any unemployment problem around Abuza's Home Restaurant, what with the customers dropping in at all hours, whenever the boats or the trains got in, and eating their way through the five courses from borsch to blintze they got for a quarter. There were always tables to scrub, trays to carry, vegetables to peel, errands to run, dishes to wash. . . .

Dishes. . . .

If I had a dollar for every greasy dish I've washed I'd be the richest woman in show business today.

Hell, you may say. What kind of a start-off is that for the story of the Last of the Red-hot Mamas? Where's the glamor? And the sex appeal? There's no *oomph* to dishwashing.

Are you telling me? I've done my best to think up some other opening lines, but anything else would be fake. And this is a true story. I'm telling it just the way it came off. It's what really happened to that Abuza kid. . . .

There may be things in the story that you don't expect. And maybe some you will wish had been left out. But that's life, isn't it?

If experience is any sort of teacher, then I've had plenty of education. When I came into show business vaudeville was in its heyday. There wasn't a town of any pretension to size that didn't have at least one house where you could see stars such as Lillian Russell, May Irwin, Eva Tanguay, Anna Held, Trixie Friganza, Marie Dressler (then singing her famous "Heaven Will Protect the Working-girl"), George M. Cohan, Weber and Fields, Louis Mann, Montgomery and Stone, Conroy and Le Maire (two great blackface comedians who gave me a lot of pointers for my own coon shouting), Bert

Williams, one of the most talented artists that ever appeared on the American stage, W. C. Fields, Will Rogers, and many more. Fields was doing a juggling act when I played on the same bill with him at the Hathaway Theatre in Lynn, Massachusetts, back in May 1908. He was rated then as the headliner of the week, and he has never let go that position in all these years.

All the cities had their own stock companies as well. And pretty good they were, too, judging from the actors who went from them to the "legit" theaters on Broadway.

Besides big-time and small-time vaudeville, "legit," and stock companies there was burlesque. For ten months out of every year dozens of burlesque shows played steadily, two shows a day, seven days a week, in all but the few states that banned Sunday shows. These companies made millions for their owners.

Oh, show business was flourishing. In those days, if you wanted to tap your foot to a swell new tune, or learn a new song or laugh away your worries, you went to a show. You didn't just sit home and twiddle a button and pick up a hash of war news, laxative ads, recipes, boogie-woogie, the Lone Ranger, and Whodunits.

You can see that my story has to be the story of show business during the past thirty years. Show business has been my life. I wouldn't have had any other. It is the life I always wanted. Back in those days when Mama would call me in to wash the dishes I used to prop open the door into the restaurant so I could listen to the talk of the actors who always made a beeline for our place to get the best twenty-five-cent meal east of the Hudson.

"If I ever get out of this," I'd mutter, wringing out the dishcloth, "I'm going in show business myself some of these days."

It seemed as if our family finances always followed the thermometer. Invariably, as the weather got colder, we got poorer. Papa made a few, and futile, efforts to break the hoodoo. Once he fell for some slick sales talk and bought a place in New York, on Allen Street near Delancey, where the El roared overhead. He went down to look the place over and saw it full of customers eating their heads off. He paid down his money and moved us down to New York, only to discover that the customers had all been planted there to sell a yokel a gold brick. Friends had to come to our rescue, and we trailed back to Hartford to start over again there.

Another winter Papa got the idea of adding a delicatessen as a side line to the restaurant. He broke through the front parlor, set up a counter and me behind it. Most of the customers were workingmen who had no women-folks to put up lunches for them. They would turn up very early in the morning before they started on their shifts. For me this meant getting up at 3 A.M. to wipe the frost off the salami and bolognas and slice bread for sandwiches.

That was the coldest winter I remember. There were many mornings when I had to wrap my feet and stuff the front of my dress with newspapers to keep out the biting cold. After the delicatessen customers were attended to, there were the housework, errands to run, vegetables to peel for the big pots of soup, before I grabbed my books and started for school. Along about eleven o'clock drowsiness would sweep over me. I would fall asleep behind my géography until the big book clattered to the floor and woke me up.

There was one period in school when I never had any trouble keeping awake for: the singing lesson. I had the strongest voice of any girl in the school, and I was always a quick study. Just hearing a song a couple of times, and I had it. The teacher usually called on me to lead the singing. And did that make me feel proud?

At that time the great popular song hit was "Just Break the News to Mother." Everybody sang it, including me. At suppertime, when the restaurant tables were well filled and the place steamy with the plates of hot food, I would stand up in the narrow space by the door and sing the tear-jerker with all the drama I could put into it. At the end of the last chorus, between me and the onions, there wasn't a dry eye in the house.

Later, when I went round to wait on the tables, a lot of the customers would slip me an extra tip, "for the entertainment."

Sometimes, if the door stood open, passers-by would stop to listen. "Come right in," I would invite them, with an eye to business. "You won't find another restaurant in town that gives you a grand meal and entertainment for a quarter."

Because some of them did come in, and because those tips I made and turned over to Mama gave her some extra much-needed dollars, her objections to my making a show of myself were tuned off. To the Abuzas, with four pairs of growing feet to keep in shoes and six mouths to feed, every dime meant something.

"Vell, mein Dolly"—Papa would rub his hands together approvingly when they were alone in their room—"what a girl is that Sophie! You see, someday, with that great big voice of hers, she'll make big money for us."

"If you and your *schlemihls* don't put us in the poorhouse first."

"Now, Mama, what's with you? I got a family to support, ain't I? Do you think money grows on trees here in America any more than in Russia? It's like I tell you, you got to make it the way you can."

"You don't have to make it *those* ways," meaningly. "That I should marry a man who . . ."

Swiftly, cunningly, Papa would save himself from the row he could see coming. "Maybe we should give Sophie a musical education. What do you think? Tonight I was talking to a fellow, an actor he is, and he was saying a girl like Sophie could maybe get into show business."

"Show business? Do you want our daughter should travel around with those *paskudnicks* (worthless people)? Our Sophie should marry a good husband. A *parnusa gaber* (good provider), like her mother didn't know enough to get for herself."

And so on and on, till Papa would pull the blanket over his head and pretend to snore.

However, some of his suggestions took effect on Mama, for when she heard about a secondhand baby grand that was going for twenty-five dollars she bought it for me. The piano was moved into the big front room upstairs over the restaurant and a teacher was engaged to teach me at a quarter a lesson. Every afternoon when I came home from school Mama shooed me upstairs to practice.

But I couldn't twist my stubby fingers, that were red and rough from dishwashing, around scales and arpeggios. And I couldn't sit on that wobbly piano stool (at eleven I overflowed it), when I could hang out the front window and holler down at the other kids playing hopscotch and shinny under the horses' noses and the wheels of the big drays.

When Mama didn't hear the piano going she would come up to find out the reason why. She tried smacks first, then she warmed that poker mark on my seat. When that didn't keep me on the piano stool she stopped the lessons. Finally, when an opportunity came, she sold the piano.

It was years before she stopped rubbing it in on me that she lost five dollars on the deal.

CHAPTER 2: *What Price Personality?*

MR. EMERSON, the music teacher at the Brown School, was talking to one of the grade teachers. As I passed by I heard him say: "Sophie Abuza has personality."

What was "personality"?

I knew a lot of words that weren't in the spelling books, but most of those had only four letters. This was a new one to me. Going home from school I asked Dora Diwinski, who lived in our block and was my girl friend. But Dora was stumped too.

It began to look bad. After supper I asked Mama: "What does 'personality' mean?"

The word that was to make Dale Carnegie famous was beyond Mama. She had neither the English nor the patience to explain it.

"Personality, is it? What next? You should get to the dishwashing, and not fill your head with craziness."

It wasn't that Mama was unkind or didn't love you that made her snap you up like that. All of us, even Moses who had now started to school, knew that. We knew if Mama was cranky it was because she was tired from standing in the kitchen all day. Her back ached and her feet were killing her. And she had worries. Phil and I, being the older ones, understood more about the worries.

The biggest worry was the card games that went on in the big room on the top floor. There was nothing in that room but an old round kitchen table that had some green pool-table cloth tacked over the top and a lot of battered chairs. Often the room would be filled with men in their shirt sleeves, the air thick with smoke and sour with the stench of stale beer and rotgut whisky. That was another of Mama's worries.

Papa wouldn't let any of us into that room, but you couldn't get him out of it so long as a game was going on. Upstairs, the pinochle sessions would run on for hours. One game, I remember, ran steadily for four days and nights. Poker games usually started on Saturdays and would last through till Monday or, if some players with real money came along, till Tuesday. When there was a big game on, the lines in Mama's forehead got deeper and deeper. Phil or I would be sent out to stand guard at the corner and keep an eye out for any strange coppers. We knew all the regulars on our beat, like Big Dan Ahearn. Big Dan was one of our best friends. We didn't have to worry about *him*.

It wasn't just the money Papa lost on the card games that made Mama sore. Most of all she hated the kind of people who often came to the house: hard-faced men, who talked out of the side of their mouths, bums, and pimps. Besides the restaurant, we ran a rooming house upstairs. A lot of fine traveling men and people in show business used to stay with us when their work brought them to Hartford. But Papa's card-playing customers were a different sort; they were the sporty set of the neighborhood.

Without understanding all that was wrong I felt that the card games and the gamblers and their girls constituted a danger which Mama was terribly afraid of. I knew these goings-on made her angry. I could hear her scolding Papa at night in their room which was next to the one where Anna and I slept. I knew, too, that Papa's gambling kept us poor. If he had a run of good luck he would branch out, as when he took over the Boston Hotel on State Street. Then the luck deserted him, and pretty soon we were back in the old neighborhood, and I was out on the corner with a wash boiler full of sweet corn to sell, a penny an ear.

Sometimes, during the summers, Papa would rent the soft-drink concession at Riverside Park where the crowds went on Saturdays and Sundays. That would be my job, opening the bottles of soda pop from the time the park opened in the morning till the cops chased the stragglers home. It was tough on the dogs, but I loved it. I loved the crowds, out for a good time. I loved the bands. I was friends with the peanut man and the old Greek who sold popcorn and balloons to the kids.

It never occurred to me to be sorry for myself. I hated having to work in the restaurant when I wanted to be out playing with the other children in the block. But I accepted that, along with some of the other things that went on, as something that was unavoidable if you were poor. Everyone I knew had to work hard to get along, some at one trade, some at another. All around us were families going through terrible struggles. Poor as we were, Mama always managed to have something to give away to the ones who were worse off than we were. Scraps of food were carefully saved to be carried to some woman whose husband was out of work and whose children would have gone to bed hungry but for Mama's charity. Old clothes that had passed from Phil to Moe, or from me to Anna, were repatched and darned and handed on to other children. Nothing was ever wasted or thrown away. Oftentimes a knock would come at the back door, and there would stand a woman with a shawl over her head, or an old man, bearded and long-haired under his black skullcap. There would be whispers, and then Mama would dig down into her petticoat pocket and bring out her worn leather purse. She would count out some silver or even a dollar or two to buy coal or medicine or to satisfy a landlord. A lot of the money I earned singing went that way. I turned the tips over to Mama as a matter of course and, true to her own nature, she used as little of them as possible for ourselves and as much as possible for those she considered really poor. That was another reason why she hated those card games upstairs. If Papa hadn't gambled away the earnings, she would have had more to give to the needy and desperate.

Knowing this, I used to try to think up ways of drawing more customers to the restaurant. I took to hanging around the stage doors of the three theaters in town, waiting for the actors to leave. I would go up to them and hold out one of our menus. "Follow me," I'd say, "and I'll take you where you can get the best meal in town for the least money."

When any of them did turn up at our place I took it as a personal triumph, and I would lay myself out to make them like it and come again. That was really how I started singing in the restaurant, hoping to draw more customers. None of our competitors offered entertainment with meals.

The show people were appreciative. They seemed to like my singing, especially when I would sing their own hits and try to mimic them. Some of the customers would give me a quarter, or even fifty cents. Once or twice it was as much as a dollar. They gave me their songs, too, writing down the words for me on a scrap of paper. I couldn't have read the notes if I had had them. And I had no need of them. I was born with a quick and true ear. The songs were the smash hits of those days, "Wait Till the Sun Shines, Nellie," and "On a Sunday Afternoon," and another of Harry Von Tilzer's, "I'd Leave Ma Happy Home for You."

Some of the dimes I made singing in the restaurant went for seats for Dora and me at the Saturday matinees at Poli's Vaudeville Theatre, or at the Hartford Opera House. Among the vaudevillians our favorites were the Howard brothers, Willie and Eugene, and the Empire City Quartette, featuring Harry Cooper. All these used to come to our place to eat whenever they made Hartford.

Sometimes one of the companies of Jewish actors would come to Hartford for a one-night stand. Then they always came to our place to eat, and when we ran the hotel, they would stay all night with us. In the restaurant I waited on the great Jacob Adler, Mr. and Mrs. Boris Thomashefsky, Madame Lipsky, and that grand Jewish comedian, Margoulis. The thrill I got when I took an order from Bertha Kalich! She was my ideal Jewish artist. After she went on the English-speaking stage I never saw her except across the footlights. When I was in London in 1926, I went down to Whitechapel one night for a real Jewish meal and there in the restaurant was Madame Kalich. We had a long talk after I told her I was the little girl who used to carry the big plates of food in Abuza's Restaurant back in Hartford.

Jacob Adler and Boris Thomashefsky both tried to get my family to let me go with one of the Jewish companies. But I wasn't keen for it. I had seen how hard it was to make the Jewish plays a success even for one night. It used to be up to Papa to sell the tickets. Many times he was left, holding the bag, with hundreds of seats, meals, and sleeping rooms given free because of no business. I had noticed that this sort of thing didn't happen with the regular American shows.

Going to shows with Dora taught me a lot of new songs and I began to work up business to go with them. Later I would try out some of the ideas I got from these shows on the customers in the restaurant and at the amateur concerts in Riverside Park where they gave prizes for the most popular acts. I was shy about going up on the stage in the park. I was going on thirteen, and already I weighed one hundred and forty-five pounds. I was gawky and self-conscious. But Anna, who was pretty and dark, had a lovely singing voice. I didn't mind going on the stage to accompany her (with one finger). I thought, sitting on the piano stool, my size didn't matter. She and I carried off a lot of prizes.

Gradually, at the concerts I began to hear calls for "the fat girl." "Let the fat girl do her stuff," and "give us the fat girl." Then I would jump up from the piano stool, forgetting all about my size, and work to get all the laughs I could get. That was when I began to say to myself that maybe in show business size didn't matter if you could sing and could make people laugh.

That was what really started me thinking seriously about going in show business. I said to myself: suppose you could earn a living by singing and making people laugh, wouldn't that be better than spending your life drudging in a kitchen? I thought about Mama, and the years she had slaved at the stove and the sink. I knew I would do anything to get away from that. As the idea took hold of me I began to ask the actors who came to our restaurant how to get into show business.

Mama heard me, of course. Ever since I showed my first interest in the theater she had been warning me to keep away from all that.

"Don't have anything to do with traveling men, or with show people. There are too many grifters and grafters among them. They have no real homes; no sense of responsibility. That kind don't care what they do on the road." According to Mama, show people were no better than the gypsies who used to wander through Russia, thieving and making trouble—as well as music—in every village. She and Papa, to whom she confided her fears about me, took to watching me like hawks.

That spring everybody sang or whistled "Bedelia." The big girls had peek-aboo waists. Mama wouldn't let me have one. "A good girl don't go around showing everybody what she has got." The shad started running up the Connecticut, and something else came stealing up the river valley with the warm April mists—something that gets you when you are going on sixteen and big for your age.

I sat hunched up on the back stoop in the evening, after the kitchen work was done, and gave myself over to the luxury of thinking about Sophie Abuza.

In two months I was to graduate from school. Then what? I didn't seem any nearer my dream of getting into show business than I had been six months before, and Mama and Papa were set and determined that I should not make that dream come true. Mama was already talking about when I should get married. To her mind, marriage, having babies, and helping her husband get ahead were career enough for any woman. I couldn't make her understand that it wasn't a career that I was after. It was just that I wanted a life that didn't mean spending most of it at the cookstove and the kitchen sink.

"After you are through school," Mama said, "then you must look around for a good, steady young man and get married."

I propped my elbows on my knees and my cheeks on my two clenched fists and considered the proposition. I didn't see how I was going to do any looking around when most of my time was spent in the restaurant, and Mama always discouraged me from making friends with the men customers. I had never been to a dance, or a picnic, or a straw ride. Always, I had to hurry home from school to help with the work. There were plenty of boys and girls in our neighborhood and they were friendly with me. Just the same, when they would be starting out for some fun they never asked me to go along with them. It was only when I had some money—money I had earned singing, or even some I stole out of the restaurant cashbox—and offered to stand treat to sodas or seats at Poli's or at a circus or one of the patent-medicine shows that pitched their tents in the vacant lots on the edge of town, that I was popular. Popularity was so sweet I wasn't above stealing money from Mama to buy a taste of it now and then.

Something inside my chest gave a big, unhappy thump. More than anything in the world I wanted to be *wanted*.

From the house came Mama's voice calling: "Sophie, Sophie. A customer is here. What are you sitting out there mooning at?"

I started to get up when I happened to look up the street and saw Louis Tuck coming. Louis lived just across from us. He was a wonderful dancer and had the reputation of being a "card." All the girls in the block were crazy about Louis. They used to hang around hoping he would ask them to go to the park to have a soda or something.

"Hello, Soph," Louis said, and stopped by the fence.

"Hello," I said back. I couldn't help smiling, Louis was so easy to look at. Maybe it was that that made Louis smile too.

"Listen," he said, "there's going to be a dance tomorrow night. How would you like to go?"

"With you?"

' Sure. Want to?"

'Sure," I gulped. Still I couldn't believe my own ears. Louis Tuck asking *me!* To go to a dance with *him!* I was waiting for the catch.

"Okay," said Louis. "Be ready around nine."

I nodded.

Mama's voice sounded again, nearer now. "Sophie! Where are you, Sophie?"

"So long," Louis said, and was around the corner before Mama opened the screen door.

"I'm coming," I hollered, scrambling up. I still couldn't believe any of it had happened. And to me.

The dance was wonderful; as, I suppose, every girl's first dance is. Part of the fun for me was seeing the jealousy of some of the other girls because Louis was with me. That spurred me on to laugh and joke and dance better than I thought I could. I guess Louis enjoyed himself, too, because after that evening he began coming round to the house, stopping by nearly every evening when he came home from work. Mama looked anxious. Then she heard from the neighbors that Louis's family liked me, and she let up on the scoldings. Still she didn't approve of my going out with him, not while there was work to be done at home.

June came, and graduation. I led the singing. Later I marched up the aisle in my starched white dress that Mama had made to get my diploma. Mr. Ames, the principal, handed it to me saying: "For Sophie Abuza, the girl with the personality."

There was that word again. Why couldn't he have said: "The smartest girl in the class"? That, I felt, would have meant something worth while. But I didn't bother too much about it because that night Louis said to me: "Look, kid, let's you and me go over to Holyoke next Saturday afternoon and get married. Then you won't have to work so hard, and we'll have lots of fun."

We made all the plans that night. I would tell Mama that I was meeting Dora Diwinski to go to a matinee, as we usually did on Saturdays. Louis would knock off work after lunch. We would meet at the railroad station. Holyoke was only a little over an hour's run from Hartford. We would go there, be married, and get back early, and act as though nothing had happened.

It all went through as we planned until suddenly we were back in Hartford, and I was scared stiff. How was I going to face Mama? What was I going to say? Louis was no help.

"Go on and tell them right out," he said, giving me a little push. "If you don't, then I will."

We are walking down Market Street. I can see Papa come out on the stoop, looking both ways along the street. Looking for me, of course. Wondering why I don't get home from the matinee. Then Mama . . .

Louis and I get to the stoop. I can see Mama's face, and Papa's. Are they mad? Here it is two whole hours after the time I should be home to help in the kitchen. Mama starts in to give me what's on her mind. Then Louis butts in.

"Listen," he says, "Sophie and I have got something to tell you. We were married this afternoon."

That was all. Mama shut her mouth with a snap and just looked at us both. Papa's jaw sort of hung open, but he didn't say a word. The silence was terrible. I began to cry. Then Mama turned and went into the house, still without one word to me. Papa followed her. We didn't know what to do, so Louis and I went in too.

"Aren't you going to say something, Mama?" I sobbed.

Mama was never one to do a lot of talking, but when she said anything you could bet it was to the point. She shot her words right at you. Now she stood in front of Louis who, even if he was six feet tall, looked like a little boy she was getting ready to spank. Her glasses had slipped down one side of her nose the way they always did when she was upset about something. One eye glared at Louis over the steel rim.

"Sophie is a good girl," Mama said. "No scandal has ever touched her. Nobody must know anything about this until after you and she are properly married. We will have a fine Orthodox wedding, as becoming our eldest daughter and us as a fine family in the community. I am sure"—she fixed Louis with her eye—"your family would wish the same."

None of us thought of not agreeing to this. If Mama said a thing it went, especially if she said it that way. Louis gave me a sick kind of grin.

"So long, Soph," he said, and left.

Mama turned to me. "What does he work at?"

I told her: "He drives a beer wagon."

"How much does he earn?"

"I don't know."

She looked at me as though she had no more patience left.

"Do you think it was right to go to Holyoke with him before you found out if he is able to support you?"

I could only answer with the truth: "I wanted to get out of the kitchen and have some fun."

Mama clicked her tongue against her front teeth.

"It's done," she said. "You have made your bed, and you must lie on it. But not"—she gave me the kind of look she used to give me when she was going to lick me—"not until after we have a proper Orthodox wedding. And now, Sophie Abuza, you can start to get supper ready."

I heard her going upstairs. I was all alone in the kitchen. Holyoke, and what had happened there that afternoon, seemed like a dream. Here I was, back in the kitchen with a pile of greasy pots and pans staring me in the face. Then I remembered Louis and what he had promised: "Marry me, and we'll have fun."

I started to cakewalk up and down the kitchen, singing (only low, so Mama wouldn't hear), *"I'd leave my happy home for you-oo-oo-oo."*

CHAPTER 3: *New York—One Way*

MAMA WAS SATISFIED with the wedding, I think. She should have been; Louis's family and all the *mishpocha* (all the relatives) on both sides and the neighbors were suitably impressed, you could see. Like every girl of our people, I had my "hope chest," which Mama had started for her daughters as soon as she reached this country. From that day on, true to the traditions of our people, whenever she bought a piece of linen for her own house, she also bought a piece for the daughters' "hope chests." All through my childhood the chests had been filling up to be ready for the day when Anna and I would be getting married.

When it came to the wedding ceremony and supper, everything was of the best. Mama was known in the community as a fine caterer. The ceremony was held in Germania Hall. I wore a real wedding dress of white dotted swiss, with a veil and a train.

"You should be proud this day, Mrs. Abuza," the women all said to Mama, "with two such fine daughters. One so big and blonde and handsome, and the other so dark and pretty. May Anna get as fine a husband as Sophie!"

"Yes, please God! Thank you," Mama would say, and lift one aching foot at a time off the floor under her long black satin skirt to rest it.

Even I was so impressed by all the preparations and the trousseau and the presents that I forgot about wanting to go into show business. I began to think getting married was the most important thing in life.

I have never been able to figure out how Mama got together the money for all this, let alone for the wedding itself, and the banquet for one hundred guests that followed the ceremony. I remember Papa used to say to us kids—and maybe he wasn't joshing, at that—"Your mother has a habit of going through my pants whenever I take a nap."

We set up housekeeping in an apartment on Park Street: four rooms and bath, rent fifteen dollars a month. I couldn't believe it was me, living in such luxury, with all the wedding presents, and my trousseau filling the closet in the bedroom. At first I was busy going over the presents, exchanging the duplicates for things we needed, but soon I had time hanging on my hands. It seemed only right as soon as Louis had gone to work and I had done my own housework to run over and give Mama a hand. I would dash home to get Louis's dinner for him, then back to Mama's for the afternoon. Often, if there were a lot of customers, I helped her in the evenings too.

Usually when I started home Mama would have a package of food ready for me to take with me. Those packages were a help, let me tell you. Louis's wages were fifteen dollars a week. With what we paid for rent and the installments on the furniture we bought on time, there wasn't much left over for two healthy appetites. Mama would ask me if we were putting something by. Gosh, how could we, out of sixty bucks a month?

You can see it coming, can't you? The inevitable moment that brings down the curtain on the first act of all the newlywed dramas, when the young husband's pay check won't stretch to cover the payments on the marriage bed and the near-oriental rugs and the grocery-store bill. The moment when little wifie throws herself face down on the old-rose silk bedspread and sobs into the pillow: "And I'm going to have a *ba-a-a-by.*"

It happened with us, just as it has happened to a million others. And the same old solution occurred to us that has seemed such a bright idea to so many—to save rent and board by going home to live with the folks.

It was my folks we selected for the honor. At the time the street in front of the old restaurant was being torn up, and Papa decided to move. The new place was much bigger. I really was needed to help Mama. Anna was in school, and Mama and I were determined she should have a chance at a real education. Moe, too, who wanted to study law someday. And Mama wasn't so well as she had been. The doctor said she had diabetes.

"You can help me in the kitchen," Mama said. "That will pay for your and Louis's board. Out there your size won't matter."

For I was huge. No wonder Louis would rather go places without me. I couldn't blame him when I looked at myself. He was paid to drive a truck, not drag one along on his arm after working hours. And I was sick a lot of the time, besides.

The same old pattern, you see.

Even though we weren't paying anything for our living there still seemed to be nothing to put by at the end of the month. Louis had always prided himself in being known as a classy dresser. Now he was catching up on those months when he had had to pay it all out in rent and housekeeping bills. My trousseau hung in the closet as good as new while I went around in a calico wrapper. I looked like that native woman in *Rain,* the wife of the hotelkeeper.

Our son was born on the fifth of February. He was the first grandchild and a fine, sturdy boy; naturally the family made much of him. On the eighth day we had the Orthodox *"briss"* with all the relatives invited.

Now that the furniture was all paid for and I was well again I wanted my own home. I said so to Louis.

But Louis couldn't see any reason for changing. He kept telling me that sixty dollars a month wasn't enough to keep us by ourselves.

"You should get a job that pays more," I came back.

Still Louis couldn't see it my way. I know now it wasn't that he was mean or cruel; only selfish and easy-going. He was always good-tempered; never a cross or ugly word. But he lacked responsibility, and I had made the mistake of taking all responsibility off his shoulders just when it would have strengthened him to carry it. "Marry me, and you won't have to work so hard. We'll have lots of fun," was what he had said to me. Instead of this I was right back in the restaurant working to keep him and me and our child.

After a bit I shut up. I was never one to nag. Like Mama, I said what I had to say.

I suppose me keeping quiet made Louis think I'd forgotten or given up. He was contented. It didn't take much to satisfy his needs. He thought I should be contented too.

I began to think about singing, the only way I knew to earn money. I went into the restaurant again to entertain the customers and picked up some money that way. Louis didn't like it, though. When he objected I came back with my old argument: "Get a job that pays better so you can support me and Son."

That spring the Howard Brothers came through in vaudeville. They said my voice was better than it used to be. Having the baby had matured me. "You shouldn't stick around here waiting on table and washing dishes," Willie said. "You could make good money in show business, Sophie." Harry Cooper, of the Empire City Quartette, when he heard me, said the same thing. "Get out. You can use your voice to better advantage than singing in the restaurant."

I took time to think it over. I didn't say anything to a soul, not even to Mama. After all, she had always lectured me that a woman should keep her troubles with her husband to herself. "You don't see me hanging out the window gossiping with the neighbors, do you?"

A week or so later, when Louis came home from work, I put it to him. "Since before the baby came I have asked you to find another job that pays more so we can be independent of my family. I've told you time and time again I don't want to wind up running a restaurant, looking after you and the family the way Mama has, and be a slave in the kitchen all my life. I haven't nagged you, or argued. I've only asked you to do what is right by yourself, your son, and by me.

"Either you get another job so you can support Son and me, or"—I looked him straight in the eye so he could see I meant every word of it—"if I stay on here and work as I am doing to keep Son and myself, then you and I separate."

"Ah, now, Soph . . ."

"I mean it," I said. "You and I must separate before it gets too late. I'm still young, and I'm not going to throw my life away."

He saw I meant it, and though he tried to make up to me I didn't give in. I'm like that, once I make up my mind. Finally, Louis packed up his things and went to New Haven to live with his sister.

Mama and Papa were horrified. "When a girl marries, she marries for better or for worse," they said. "You can't do a thing like this. It's not right. Remember you've got a child now. You can't please yourself."

Yes, I thought, looking at Mama, that is how *you* figured it out. And look at the life you've had. Not for me. I'm getting out while there's time. I'm not afraid of work. I'll support my baby and myself. But I won't spend my life in a kitchen and keep a husband doing it, the way you have. Not while

I have a voice. And what's more, if I make good at all, *and I will,* you're not going to stand over the cookstove much longer, either.

It sounded very fine to talk about getting out. But how? How did a person get started in show business? I'd looked over all the opportunities in Hartford. No one there had any confidence in my ability. There wasn't a soul who would have backed me to show. It looked as though I would have to go to New York to get my start. That took money. The first thing, therefore, was to get together a bank roll.

After that all the money I made singing in the restaurant or at amateur nights in the park went into a box locked away in my bottom bureau drawer. Each time I put a dollar in the box I'd think: that's to get you into show business.

Oh, I missed Louis. There were nights when I cried myself to sleep. Lonely. If only he had kept his promise to me: "We'll have fun." It was fun I wanted, not kitchen work.

Mama failed a lot that summer. The hot weather wore her down. It used to gripe me seeing her in that steaming hot kitchen, on her feet all day, cooking, waiting on customers, washing up. The doctor wanted her to go to New York to consult a specialist, the first physician in this country to use insulin.

"Go on," I told her. "I can run the place."

"All right," she agreed. "Then when I get back you can have two weeks' vacation. Anna and I will mind the baby."

This just fitted my plans. I'd had my eye on the calendar for weeks, figuring how to make it. While Mama was away I had the dressmaker go over all my clothes so everything was in order. Twenty times I counted the bills in the box. I, Sophie Tuck, had one hundred dollars of my own. I was set and raring to go.

Then Mama came home from New York. "Now, Sophie, you take two weeks off. Where will you go?"

"I think I'll go to New Haven," I said.

I could see Mama was thinking: New Haven. That's where Louis's sister lives. That's where he is staying. Maybe they'll get together again.

"That'll be fine," she encouraged me. "Enjoy yourself. If you stay two weeks you'll come home in time to help prepare for the High Holidays."

"Yes," I said.

But in my heart I knew I wasn't coming back. Not that year. Not until I had made good. I was going to buy my ticket one way—no return.

Anna held Son up to the window to wave "Day-day."

I took one quick backward look over my shoulder, then I started to run for the streetcar. My suitcase bumped into my legs and my big, top-heavy hat slid down my pompadour over one eye.

I had to run. Otherwise the choke in my throat and the smart in my eyes would have gotten me. I'd have thrown the suitcase into the gutter and gone back for good. I had to shut my heart against the pull of that cute little baby face at the window and those fat little hands waving to me. I had to remember that behind them was that kitchen which was what I was really running away from. I had to say over and over: it's only by getting out, making something of yourself, making real money, that you can do the most for Son and for Mama who has done so much for you.

Sophie, this was the best day's work you ever did. And the hardest.

The Howard Brothers were playing at Poli's in New Haven that week. I'd gotten their itinerary from Willie when they came through Hartford earlier in the season. For weeks I'd been counting on making my getaway in time to catch them there.

I checked my suitcase in the railroad station and made a beeline for the theater. I bet the most surprised man in the world was Willie Howard when he came out of the stage door after his turn and found me.

"Soph, what's happened?"

"I've left home," I said. "I'm going in show business like you always said I should. I came right on here to find you and Gene."

"Go on home," he said.

"Not me," I told him.

"Then go to New York," was Willie's advice. "Take the next train. For God's sake, Sophie, get out of this town while we're here." To make sure I did, he went with me to the station.

He told me to go and see the song writers in Tin Pan Alley and get them to teach me some songs. He wrote down the name and address of Harry Von Tilzer and Ben Bernstein, who were the most popular music publishers at that time. "Tell them I sent you to them. Tell them I said you were good. And now, for God's sake, get aboard that train."

When I was settled in my seat I took my handkerchief and rubbed the dust off a corner of the window so I could wave to Willie. But already he was beating it away from that station platform. He never once looked back.

The hour-and-a-half ride from New Haven to New York wasn't too long for all I had to do. First there was a letter to be written to Mama, telling her I had suddenly decided to go on and have a look at New York, where we had relatives.

Next, I decided I would *not* go to my cousins' at all. If I did, I could not give all my time and attention to getting into show business. I would not even look them up. I would go to a hotel and start out at once making the rounds of Tin Pan Alley as the Howard Brothers suggested.

The hotel was a dingy small one on Forty-second Street across from the station. I got a room for a dollar and a half a day with a window looking into a court into which a sooty rain was falling. It hurt my sense of economy to waste a day's room rent staying indoors, but I thought that was better than turning up at the music publishers' looking like a drowned rat. But what if it rained for a week? I figured out the expense and shivered. I simply had to get started before my hundred dollars was gone.

Next day the sun shone, and I sang as I dressed to go out. I had the card Willie Howard had given me, and I copied the addresses of other firms from the phone book. I was going to "do" Tin Pan Alley.

I started with Von Tilzer, using Willie Howard's card as an introduction. Then—in 1906—Harry Von Tilzer was the leading song writer in this country. One after another, he had produced such smash hits as "Wait Till the Sun Shines, Nellie," "A Bird in a Gilded Cage," "What You Goin' to Do When the Rent Comes 'Round?" "Good-bye, Eliza Jane," "On a Sunday Afternoon," "Down Where the Wurzburger Flows," and a dozen more. Later he was to produce "All Alone," "Under the Yum Yum Tree," "I Love My Wife but Oh! You Kid!" and the perennial favorite, "I Want a Girl Just Like the Girl That Married Dear Old Dad."

Von Tilzer heard me, said "H'mm" a couple of times, and finally told me to drop in again someday. That was that. I took the next address on my list, and the next, going down the sheet of paper and getting about the same response everywhere. Nobody in Tin Pan Alley seemed impressed by me.

The next day I started out and did the same thing all over again. I sat for a while in each office, hearing the pianos going on all sides, catching snatches of tunes and lyrics, just enough to tantalize me. Singers came and went. Some got no better treatment than I; for others doors were opened right away. On the third day I made the rounds again. I didn't know what else to do. Maybe, I thought desperately, they'll get so tired seeing me sitting here they'll give me a song just to get rid of me.

At the end of a week I knew I must make some new plans. First I wrote a letter home. I still like its *chutsba* (nerve).

DEAREST FOLKS,

I have decided to go into show business. I have decided that I can do big things and have definitely made up my mind that you will never stand behind a stove and cook any more, and every comfort that I can bring you both I am going to do, and I know I can do it, if you will let me alone. Don't come to take me back home. Take care of Son and I will make you proud of me some of these days.

Love to all,
SOPHIE.

This posted, I counted my money and then set about finding a cheaper place to live. The way it looked, it was going to take me some time to make good on the promises in that letter. Funny, isn't it, how I used that phrase "Some of These Days"?

I found a room for five dollars a week, which included breakfast, on Second Avenue near St. Mark's Place. I lived there for several weeks while I tried all the doors in Tin Pan Alley without success. Meanwhile my funds were running low. I knew I must save every fifty cents. I grudged every cent I had to spend on food. One evening it occurred to me perhaps I could sing in one of the restaurants in the neighborhood and earn a meal that way. Around on Eighth Street was the Café Monopol. I went in and said to the proprietor: "I'm hungry, and I haven't any money. I'm a singer. If I sing for your customers tonight will you give me my dinner?"

He thought for a moment. "What kind of songs do you sing?" he demanded.

"Popular songs," I told him. "I'll sing what the customers ask for. I used to do that in a restaurant in Hartford, my home town."

"All right," he agreed. Then he asked my name.

I had my mail sent to Mrs. Louis Tuck, care of General Delivery, as of course that was my name. But "Mrs. Tuck" didn't sound right for a singer. "Sophie Tucker," I told him.

Right like that a career was born.

CHAPTER 4: *Smartening Up to Broadway*

THE CAFÉ MONOPOL'S CUSTOMERS liked me. They applauded and called for more songs. I could see the proprietor thought he had made a good bargain.

"Come round again some evening," he told me. "I'll be glad to give you your dinner again and have you entertain the customers."

I thanked him. That was something—an ace in the hole. But I knew I couldn't go there too often. I would have to hunt around for some other restaurants and make the same offer. And I did.

Every morning I turned out of bed and marched myself up to the music publishers' and got the pianists to go over new songs with me. I was singing for my supper, but I was getting a lot more than just the big plate of hot food—gosh, but it tasted good too—the waiter set in front of me after my act. I was getting hep to myself, and I was making friends for Sophie Tucker.

Success in show business depends on your ability to make and keep friends. You'll notice that the entertainers who last are the ones who aren't standoffish and high-hat. To hold your audience you've got to give something of yourself across the footlights. And that something has got to be genuine, sincere. You can fake it for a season or two maybe. Then the public gets wise and gives you the razzberry. And you're done. Washed up!

Of course back in those weeks of the fall of 1906 I had not had the experience to teach me this. What I did have was an honest-to-God anxiety about getting some work that would pay in dollars as well as roast-beef medium. I could never get far from the thought of that canvas money bag I wore strapped around my waist, which was getting lighter and lighter every week. If something didn't open up for me pretty soon, a day was coming when I wouldn't be able to meet my landlady on the stairs.

The people I got to know around Second Avenue were encouraging. When I asked them if they knew any places that had paid entertainers they told me that many of the rathskellers uptown employed singers.

"You ought to go up to the German Village," I was told. "That's a big joint, three floors and crowded all night. They must use fifteen to twenty singers there all the time."

The German Village was then one of New York's hot spots. It was on Fortieth Street, just off Broadway, and it got the theater crowds. It was a high-class "beer garden" patterned after those in Europe, with continuous musical entertainment up to dawn.

One evening I set out to have a look at the Village. To save carfare, I walked. Every nickel counted.

It was one of those mild, muggy nights you get in New York in the fall, when you smell the harbor and the garbage scows being towed out to the dumping ground; when you taste coal smoke and gas with every breath you draw. It's nights like those that make you feel lonely. The lights in the houses you pass seem to glow sweeter and cozier. At other times you look up at the house fronts and know the people living there have their troubles, just the same as you. They're worrying about the rent, and Papa being out of work, and that fellow Mary has started going with. They're nagging each other and scrapping and cheating, the way folks do all over the world, a lot of the time. They aren't really any better off than you. But try giving yourself that line on one of those lonesome nights. It just doesn't go down. You're positive life picked you to get the seltzer water in the pants.

That's the frame of mind I was in by the time I made Thirty-fourth Street. My feet were too big for my shoes and I was feeling sorry for myself all over.

Up Broadway from Thirty-fourth Street I began to notice something: girls standing on the corners and in doorways, loitering along, all waiting for something to happen. Then I saw it happen: a man came along, gave the girls the once-over, picked one of them, said something, and then the two went off together down a side street. It wasn't always the men who spoke first; a girl would sidle up to a man, tuck her hand inside his arm, whisper something. Then maybe that couple would go off together. There, in the Tenderloin, the streetwalkers were plying their trade as openly as the push-cart sellers did their business down around Hester Street.

I thought about the girls the men used to bring to our hotel in Hartford. Maybe some of them had come from tramping the Broadway beat. I'd never given them much thought till now. Now I began to wonder how they started hustling in the first place. Were they girls like me who had come to New York to make good in show business or some other line, and who hadn't been able to make a go of it? Maybe they, too, had written their folks a boasting letter saying they wanted to be let alone, and then couldn't go back on their boasts. Was it the ultimate grim necessity of getting something to eat and a roof over their heads that sent them on the streets to sell themselves half a dozen times a night? Or was it the lonesomeness that got them down? I was having my own taste of *that*.

Was this what I had to look forward to?

Asking myself that seemed to make the bottom of my stomach fall out.

A man edged up to me and took hold of my elbow. I shook him off. I was going to the German Village to ask for a job. I told myself: you're going to *make* them take you on. A block, and another man suggested with a leer: "How about it, girlie?" I pulled away and walked faster. When a third man stopped square in front of me, looking me over, I shoved him with such force he fell into the gutter. I brought up at the door of the German Village breathless and red in the face.

It *was* a big place. The three floors were all lighted up. Out on the sidewalk you could hear the laughter and singing. I opened the door and went in. A table near the entrance was vacant, so I sat down there. When the waiter came up expectantly I told him I wanted to see the manager.

"Mr. Jumbo? All right, I'll tell him."

Alone, I took a good look around. The tables on that floor were well filled.

and from the noise that came up from the rathskeller business there was good. The people around me looked like spenders; big parties, out for a good time. A girl stood up to sing. I watched and listened critically. Just what did it take to make good in a place like this?

I didn't see the drunk till he leaned across my table, breathing into my face. "Come on upstairs, kid," he hiccoughed. "You're a nice-looking country girl. I'll be nice to you."

Zingo. I hopped to my feet, hauled off, and let him have a right to the jaw. It sent him backward out the door and flat onto the sidewalk. There was a yell, the sound of running feet, a police whistle. Outside a crowd gathered. Inside the people at the tables stood up, craning their necks. The music faltered. The manager and a flock of waiters came rushing from a back room. A policeman shouldered through the crowd and into the room.

"Hey, what's all this?"

I burst into tears. Everybody started talking at once, pointing at me.

"He insulted me," I sputtered, mad and scared at the same time.

"What are you doing here?" The manager—a big chucker-out, "Mr. Jumbo" just suited him—looked threatening.

"I'm a great singer," I fired at him. "I came here tonight to ask for a job and that man insulted me."

Mr. Jumbo got the policeman into a corner and began talking very hard. They kept looking me over. I didn't realize it, but with my hair-do and the kind of dress I wore, I looked just what I was, a big, gawky country girl, and not more than seventeen. Then Jumbo came over to me. He was sorry, he said, that I'd been insulted. As for my getting a job there, I was much too young. They only took girls over twenty. There was a police law against hiring girls any younger than that. Before I knew it I was out the door.

Walking uptown I had said to myself if I landed a job I could afford a nickel to ride home. Now there was nothing for it but to let my feet do the work. I started down Broadway. There were the girls. How easy to join them, to saunter idly, ready to look meaningly into the next man's face. If I didn't find some work that paid pretty soon I might have to come to this. If every place turned me down, what was I to do?

"I'll wash dishes first," I swore to myself. "I'll go back to the cookstove and the sink if I must. Not on the streets!" And quick as lightning my mind added: "And I shan't wash dishes again, either. I came to this town to get into show business, and I'm going to get there. I told the folks I was going to. I've got to make good on that promise. There must be a way."

Jumbo had said I was too young. I couldn't help my age, but what about my appearance? It made me sore to remember that that drunk had called me a "nice-looking country girl."

I began to look closely at the girls sauntering along Broadway. They all looked well dressed. Nothing of the country girl about any of *them*. I took to looking into the shop windows, sizing up the clothes, comparing them with my own. There was a hell of a lot of difference. I guessed, if you wanted to go places in New York, you had to look like New York.

I had my nose glued to a plate-glass window trying to read the price tag on a plaid taffeta suit when a hand tapped me on the shoulder. I swung round. My God! Another cop.

He looked me over, tear marks on my face and all. "What are you doing here?" he demanded. "Where are you from? You don't look like a New Yorker. You don't belong in this neighborhood."

"You're darn right," I said, and told him: "I come from Hartford and I'm trying to get a job." I started to tell him about my experience at the German Village but he cut in:

"Go on home. Don't hang around here. Nice girls don't come this way after dinnertime."

I thanked him, took the way he pointed, east to Sixth Avenue, and beat it for St. Mark's Place and bed. Chased off Broadway. Why? As far as I could see it, for looking like a country girl, and no older than I really was.

For the rest of the walk I thought things over, backwards and forwards. It was pretty plain that if I was ever going to get a toe hold on that magic thoroughfare I'd have to change my style of dress. I would have to put up my hair, look older. I didn't have the word for it, but that night I tumbled to the idea—"New Yorkish."

Sophie Tucker was going to have to look and act as if she belonged to Broadway.

Something else I tumbled to in the course of that night's walk: you could buy clothes on time.

The next day I hunted me an outfit that looked smart. It cost ten dollars. I peeled one dollar off the thin roll in my money belt and paid it down, pledging myself to pay a dollar a week until I was clear. Now, I *had* to get work that paid.

Back in my room I practiced ways of doing my hair to make me look at least five years older. When I was satisfied with my appearance I walked up Broadway again, to Times Square. I kept an eye out for that policeman, betting with myself he wouldn't know me in my new get-up, but he wasn't anywhere about.

On the upper west corner of Forty-second Street and Seventh Avenue, fronting the Square, was Hammerstein's, "The Variety House of the World." Naturally I'd heard of it. An act was made if it was booked there. A good seat at a matinee at Hammerstein's cost seventy-five cents. I hung around outside the theater, reading the names billed and studying the photographs of that week's headliners. I didn't recognize a single one who ever played Hartford.

Meanwhile I was having a fierce argument with myself.

"You know you haven't any business spending money," I said to myself. "You're down to your last ten dollars right now. Wait till you get a job before you take in any shows."

And myself answered back: "How are you going to learn anything about show business if you don't go and see shows? You haven't any time to waste finding out all you can about it."

Myself won. I marched up to the window, plunked down three quarters, and went in.

I never have minded paying for what I get, but it's my nature to want my money's worth. I got it out of that seventy-five cents. I was early for the matinee, so I took the opportunity to go all over the theater, up in the gallery, peering into the boxes, staring at the crowds gathering at the bar. I touched the walls and the gilded pillars and ran my hand over the upholstery. I sniffed the unmistakable smell of theater. I would have given another seventy-five cents to be able to get backstage. And again I said to myself: "Someday I'll sing here. Someday my name SOPHIE TUCKER will be billed outside. I've got to make good. I simply have to."

Now the house was filling: mostly women, all so smart looking. They came in couples or four or five together, all laughing and chatting. It seemed as though I was the only single ticket in the whole lower floor. If only I knew somebody. If I just had a friend to pal around with, the way Dora Diwinski and I used to back home.

The curtain went up. The orchestra played; so many men in the pit. I shut my eyes and saw Harry Tighe, the pianist who furnished all the music at Poli's Vaudeville in Hartford. Then the lady next to me dropped her program. I quickly picked it up, handed it back, smiling.

"Thanks," she said.

"Thank *you*," I replied.

She looked surprised. "Why do you thank me?"

"Because," I told her, "it makes me feel good to have someone speak to me."

She smiled again and offered me some candy. I would have said some more only then the show came on.

The usual acrobatic troupe opened the show. The women around me, I noticed, were not interested. The second act was a musical family; the third a monologuist. He was funny, and the women liked him. The fourth act was a sketch. Some star had streamlined her play to a twenty-minute act. She was very British, but she had a beautiful figure and she dressed smartly. The women fell hard for her; they were all talking about her figure and her gown. To me every act was great.

Some more acts, and then the intermission. Everyone went out to the bar— everyone but me. But I wasn't lonely. I was too busy digesting all I had seen and learned that afternoon. I thought: there's no two ways about it, you've got to dress smart. Then the women in the audience rave about you. If you ever get on the stage, think of your clothes, look smart. It helps put you over.

When my neighbor came back to her seat she spoke again: "I'm sorry I didn't ask you to come and have a drink with us girls. I didn't realize you were all alone."

"Yes," I said, "this is my first show in New York. I'm in show business myself. I'm a singer, and I'm just looking things over before I get started in New York."

Chutsba? You said it. But I got away with it. Mrs. Abe Bernstein looked impressed. When the show was out she gave me her name and address— Second Avenue at Tenth Street, my own neighborhood—and invited me to have dinner with her and her husband the next evening.

That's how I made my first friend in New York. And what friends the Bernsteins were to me. I had no intention of letting them know how I was fixed, but I hadn't been in their home an hour or met the whole family before I broke down and blubbered like a kid. Homesick. It all came out, the lie I'd told, and how I was down to my last few cents and everything. Mr. and Mrs. Bernstein made me go back to my room and pack up and move in with them. They took me to their hearts, and from then on they helped me until I began to earn.

When I told them my experience at the German Village, and being turned down because I was too young:

"Go on back there," my new friends advised. "Wear your new clothes. Make them listen to you sing. You'll get there, Sophie, if you keep on trying."

When I went back, about half past seven one evening, the manager, "Mr. Jumbo," was not in yet. They told me the proprietor, Mr. Buchalter, was there. Would he do?

Was I in luck? Jumbo would have been sure to recognize me even in my New York clothes. Yes, I would see the proprietor.

"I'm a singer," I told him.

"Sorry," he said. "I have more singers in the place now than I can use."

"But, Mr. Buchalter, how can you say you don't need me when you haven't heard me sing? Maybe I sing better than some of the girls you have now. Please hear me, then if I don't satisfy, tell me to go."

He sized me up quickly. "How old are you?"

"Twenty-three," I said without a quiver.

The door behind him opened. Was that Jumbo? If so, I'm sunk. But it wasn't Jumbo. It was the proprietor's wife. She looked me over.

"What does she want?" she asked her husband.

I told her myself. "Look," I said. "To give you an idea what I can do, the songs I sing, I can accompany myself on this piano." The Buchalters sat down and, playing the air with one finger, I sang for them "Good-bye, Mr. Greenback." As a performance it was pretty poor, but I figured if I sang loud and showed off what a powerful voice I had, it would do me the most good. When I finished, before they could get a word in, I said: "If I don't get a job tonight I'll have to go out on the 'Broadway Beat,' as the last of my greenbacks is gone. I've been in New York over six weeks trying to get work."

That night, it was a Tuesday, early in November 1906, I went to work at the German Village at a salary of fifteen dollars a week. Mr. Buchalter sent me up to the second floor, which was where the beginners pushed off. Four girls and four boys worked on the stand with me. Our room was filled only when the rathskeller and the street floor were capacity. Then the overflow was sent upstairs.

I was ready to start my first song when I looked up and saw Mr. Jumbo in the doorway. He didn't recognize me at first, but when the song was over he came across the room and said, frowning, "Don't I know you?"

Tell him the truth, I thought quickly. Be friendly. If he likes your work he'll put in a good word for you downstairs. I told him what I had done to make myself look older, and that the boss liked my singing and had hired me. "Don't tell," I said.

He winked. "Good luck, kid. Use your head. And look out for that punch in your right."

"I'll save it for my songs," I promised.

Work at the German Village was hard; every night I sang fifty to one hundred songs. Working at a salary of fifteen dollars a week, it was up to a singer to make friends, to find out the customers' favorite songs, and be ready to sing them on request. For this the customers usually tipped us from fifty cents to a dollar. This money, earned by the eight singers and two pianists, was pooled and split up after work.

Every week when we were paid, a money order went off to Mama. "Take good care of Son for me. . . . Get yourself something you need. . . . Pretty soon I'll be sending more. . . . Love, Sophie. . . ." The balance which I kept went for room, board, and clothes. I'd taken a room uptown to be near the Village. The Bernsteins, who had seen me through the bad times, were delighted that I was getting ahead.

The rest of the money I made at the Village, from the tips, went for clothes. I had to look nice every night. The Village wasn't stylish like the Haymarket Café, where evening dress was the rule. We singers wore shirt-waists and skirts. When I saw the other girls smile and tip each other the wink at my plain white linen shirtwaists I went out and bought myself a couple of lace peekaboos that would have turned Mama's hair white. Oh yes, I was smartening up to Broadway.

One night a singer on the street floor didn't show up. Jumbo called me down to take her place. Here there was a different clientele. The customers never gave fifty cents if you sang a song for them; it was always a dollar or more. In the rathskeller, I was told, even more money was spent. Miss Flossie Crane, known as "The Girl with the Man's Voice," who was the lead-ing singer downstairs, made as much as two hundred dollars a week. That bit of gossip started me to scheme and plan to get into the rathskeller.

Meanwhile, the weekly money orders were getting bigger. "Didn't I say I'd do it? Get Son a pair of red shoes. . . . Get Anna a new dress. . . . Go on believing in me. . . . Love, Sophie. . . ."

Every day I haunted the music publishers'. The boys there were getting to know me, "The big girl from the German Village." Sometimes they saved songs for me. "Try this, Soph. It's your stuff." They would say: "I dropped into the Village last night. You were *great!*" Or (and honestly, I liked this even better), "I heard you last night. That song, 'My Mariutch,' you're not getting all you can get out of it. Try it like this"—going through the music for me to sing:

*"My Mariutch she mak-a de hootch-a-ma-kootch down at Coney Isle.
She make me smile. She go lik-a dis, lik-a dat, lik-a dis.
She mak-a such a dance and never move-a de feet, that's a funny style. . . ."*

"Got something new, boys?" was my invariable greeting. Something new. That was what the customers liked. New songs, new business. From those days to this my motto has been: "Get something new. Keep fresh. Don't get stale, singing the same songs."

I still had my heart set on getting to work in the rathskeller. It wasn't only that that was where the big money was made (though the thought of pulling down as much as two hundred a week acted on me like the rattle of dice to a gambler). The rathskeller was where a lot of big people in show business came. I would hear about them: "Who do you think is downstairs tonight? Erlanger, Dillingham, Ziegfeld, Hammerstein." Once, I remember, the word went around, Caruso was there.

It looked as if I'd have to make my chance myself. Accordingly, two or three nights after our room cleared and closed I went down to the rathskeller and sat around. I sat until the scrub women came with their pails and chased me out. Then one night—or early one morning—there was a party in the rathskeller that had heard me sing upstairs, and asked for me. That song brought me ten dollars. I put it into the box of the other singers. Before that night's work was done I had put in more than seventy-five dollars.

Maybe there's a fate in such things. Anyway, it was just a few days after that that Flossie Crane left to go to headline Hammerstein's. I moved downstairs. Soon I was cutting in on one hundred to one hundred and fifty dollars a week. The money orders to Hartford grew proportionately: "Hire some help in the restaurant. . . . Make Papa go to the dentist. . . . Take five dollars out of this and bring the baby to New York for a day so I can see him. . . . Love, Soph."

Gradually I became friends with the girls who made their living from the men who came to the Village. What impressed me most about these girls was that every one of them supported a family back home, or a child somewhere. In addition—and this I found surprising—each girl had some man to whom she gave her money regularly. What the strong tie was between her and the man—who, as she told you frankly, had a string of other girls doing the same thing for him—I never could make out. These men came around regularly for their pay. I used to see them. After a while the girls got in the way of peeling a few bills off their takings and passing them over to me so the men wouldn't know they were holding out on them. Usually, before the night's work was over, I had one hundred dollars or so crammed into my stockings. I kept my mouth shut about it, and no one ever knew the little drama that went on in the ladies' room each night.

The next afternoon the girls would drop round to my room for their money from which they sent money orders home. They made no bones about their profession; to them, hustling was just a business. Just the same, they didn't recommend it. What I've found out is that the closer you get to vice the less gilt and glamor you find there is to it. "You're lucky," they would tell me, "you've got a voice. Why don't you get into show business and not stick around a joint like the Village?"

That was what I asked myself twenty times a day. But how?

Meanwhile, any ideas I may have had that I was on to Broadway received a jolt. I was living in an old brown-stone front on Broadway at Thirty-sixth Street. The house was run by a French couple. I had a hall bedroom for which I paid two dollars a week. By my agreeing to wash the dishes, the landlady gave me my breakfast. I thought myself in luck.

One morning about four, right after I had gone to bed, there was a commotion in the street outside, police, and men and girls in all stages of undress being dragged out of the house and pushed into the patrol wagon. A heavy knock came at my door. A voice ordered: "Get up. Get out of there." It didn't do any good my telling the cop I was the singer at the German Village and had just come home and gone to bed, virtuously and alone. I was made to get into my street clothes and sent out onto the sidewalk to the waiting wagon.

"Listen," I protested, "I don't know any of these people. I don't belong in this crowd."

One blue-coated figure separated itself from the rest and came over to stare at me. "Say, sister, I know you. . . ." Believe it or not, it was the cop who had chased me off Broadway that night six months earlier.

"That's right, Sergeant," he told the one in authority. "I'll swear this one is O.K. She's a kid from the country. She don't belong with this crowd. She sings up at the German Village. I've heard her."

The cops let me off on that recommendation. I hunted around and found a new boardinghouse. Meanwhile, I gave a lot of thought to my work at the German Village. I was making money there, but I had a hunch the place wouldn't stay open much longer. McClellan had just been re-elected on a reform ticket and he was pledged to clean up the Tenderloin. I didn't read the political news, but I heard the hustlers talking about the police net that was closing in on them. It was common gossip that a lot of the rathskellers in that part of town would soon be padlocked.

I could probably get a job singing in some more conservative café, but that wasn't what I wanted. I wanted to get into show business. I knew I never would be satisfied until I did.

Chapter 5: *Blackface*

The boys at the music publishers' put me on to it. I heard them talking: "Up at the 125th Street Theatre, corner of Third Avenue, Chris Brown is running big amateur nights." These, by report, weren't anything like the amateur nights in the Bowery theaters where they put a hook around the neck of a performer who failed to please the audience and pulled her screaming off the stage while the crowd roared with laughter. Chris Brown's "amateur nights" were more like tryouts.

"Big doings. The producers and booking agents are up there every week scouting for talent."

Enough said. When the next amateur night came round Sophie Tucker asked off from work at the Village and lined up with fifty or more in front of Chris Brown.

"What do you do?"

"Sing."

"All right." He took the envelope I handed him that had my songs in it and ran them over, selecting half a dozen. "Try these." The pianist beat out the tunes and I did my best with them, keeping my eye glued to Chris Brown, lolling back in his shirt sleeves, hands on hips, chewing a cigar. He looked bored as hell, but when I finished he nodded. "O.K. Use the first three we tried. You can go on."

My chance had come.

I stumbled out of the door conscious of the envious looks of the others who had been turned down or who were lined up waiting a chance to be heard. I felt dizzy; hot and then cold. Behind me came Chris Brown's voice, calling to an assistant: "This one's so big and ugly the crowd out front will razz her. Better get some cork and black her up. She'll kill 'em."

The assistant took me in hand. He got some ordinary corks from liquor bottles, lit a match, burned the corks, and smeared my face, ears, and neck. I was in street clothes—a tailored suit. He gave me a pair of black cotton gloves, tied a red bandanna over my hair; with lipstick he painted me a grotesque grinning mouth. "All right, you're on."

A shove sent me from the wings onto the stage. The footlights and the cork in my eyes made me blink. Beyond the lights was a sea of faces filling pit and gallery. I heard a roar of laughter. They'd been booing and cat-calling a performer off the stage a few minutes ago. I'd heard and seen what that crowd could do to an act they didn't like. . . . "She's so big and ugly, they'll razz her," Brown had said. What would they do to me? I felt sick and frightened inside. Then the pianist thumped out the opening chords and gave me a signal. That jolted me out of my stage fright.

What the hell? That crowd couldn't scare me now. I knew I could sing. Working at the Village, I'd learned some of the tricks to get a crowd warmed up, liking me. Those tough guys in the gallery were no tougher than a lot of the people at the German Village. Let her go!

The three songs weren't enough. The audience wouldn't let me go till I had sung three more. Oh, they liked me all right. Take that, Mr. Chris Brown. I was a hit.

In the dressing room I struggled to get the burnt cork off. There was no one to help me, to tell me how to get the nasty mess out of my ears and eyes. Everyone had gone. The doorman found me crying. "Use soap and water," he advised.

The burnt cork stuck in my ears and in the roots of my hair. It had ruined my best white shirtwaist. But that wasn't why I cried. I knew I'd been the hit of that night's show. And yet none of that weighed against Chris Brown's verdict: "too big and ugly." If he was right, what chance had I, now or ever?

I left the theater, still grimy (it was days before I felt really clean), and mounted the steps of the Third Avenue El. It was nearly 1 A.M. and the platform was deserted. No, there at the far end was a man. He looked vaguely familiar. I walked down toward him. Yes, it was the one I'd seen in Chris Brown's office; someone said he was Joe Woods, one of our best-known booking agents.

I marched up to him. "Listen," I said, "I'm the girl they blacked up tonight. You heard me sing. Did you like me? Do you think you could book me?"

He thought a minute, then he pulled out one of his cards. "Come round to my office tomorrow and I'll let you know."

Joe Woods booked me on the small-time circuit at a salary of fifteen to twenty dollars a week in New York; twenty-five dollars a week when out of town. I'd been pulling down four and five times that at the Village, but I didn't care. This, at last, was show business.

"You'll have to black up," he ordered.

He told the girl in his office to get a dress out of the wardrobe. At that time Joe put out acts of his own, costumed them, drew down the salary, and paid the performers what he had contracted them for. The dress was of white satin.

"It'll look good with blackface," said Joe. "You can pay a dollar a week rental until you've paid off the twenty-five bucks it cost me." By the terms of my contract I was also to pay him 5 per cent of my salary for booking me.

"Let me leave off the black," I pleaded. "Try me out the way I am and see if I don't go over." But he wouldn't hear of it.

That's how I became a blackface singer. "World-renowned Coon Shouter" was how Joe put it on his notices. On the Park Circuit I was also billed as "Sophie Tucker, the Ginger Girl, Refined Coon Singer" (may the stiff-necked frozen faces who now and then have objected to the songs I sing take count of that one!). And on my first New York date in December 1907 as "Sophie Tucker, Manipulator of Coon Melodies."

When I started out on the Park Circuit I wore the white satin dress Joe Woods sold me, and used burnt cork for make-up. But the difficulty of keeping the dress clean was too great. I soon changed to a high-yellow make-up and rented a black velvet dress which gave a contrast. I kept to the gloves, however. It made a good stunt at the end of my act to peel off a glove and wave to the crowd to show I was a white girl.

My first date was in Meriden, Connecticut; not many miles from Hartford and the folks, but it might as well have been a thousand. I was working on a fast schedule—my next date was in Cohoes, New York—and no one I knew owned a car in those days to take me home between shows. I didn't let them know I was playing Meriden for fear they would come to the theater and see me. I couldn't bear to have them know I went on in blackface.

The Park Circuit kept actors working from June until Labor Day. We played the smaller cities in New York, New Jersey, Pennsylvania, and Ohio, with one-week or three-day stands in each place. Ina Claire played the same circuit with me that summer. She was billed as a mimic and did impersonations of headliners and famous personages. I remember her mother traveled with her. We usually put up at the same boardinghouse, near the Park, which catered regularly to actors. I paid five dollars a week for my room, sent five dollars home, and then stretched the balance of that twenty-five-dollar salary (minus 5 per cent to Joe Woods) to cover all my other expenses. Every night I hung out my washing, darned my black lisle stockings (three pairs for a dollar), and dropped into bed dog-tired.

If I said a prayer it was: "God, please make me a headliner!"

In each place I played I would ask the manager for a return date before I left. "I promise to have new songs," I would tell him. And when I got a return engagement I kept my word. Something new, that was what counted with audiences. After a few months I found the managers were asking the office if I had any open time. Meanwhile, I learned that by playing return engagements quickly the audiences remembered me. When my name went up on the announceator or on the big placards at the side of the stage, there would be a welcoming round of applause.

In addition to the dates in the theaters, Joe booked me for Sunday shows for clubs and conventions. I got five to ten dollars for these performances. That little bit extra helped the budget a lot.

There weren't many single women playing the small-time circuits then. Most of the single women in show business were headliners or playing in shows on the Park Circuit. The six or seven acts that formed the bill usually broke down into something like this: a young dancer, mimic, or singer traveling with her mother; the dance team (married or living together); the acrobatic troupe—a family of Mama, Papa, and the kids; the comedian (single, or with a wife and family settled somewhere); the sketch—usually three actors, a husband and wife and one single woman; a musical family; the two hoofers—both single and playing the girls in every town.

On every bill I was always alone. None of the others knew whether I was married or single. I had a way of keeping my business to myself. A big, husky girl, carrying her own suitcase, attending to her own railroad tickets, boarding places, looking out for herself, as capable and independent as a man. ("Look out for that skirt. She can cuss like a man too.") The hoofers, comedians, monologuists never asked me to go out to dinner or to take a walk between shows. None of them ever said: "She's a good scout, let's take her along." Or even: "She's a good-looking broad; let's make her."

Maybe Chris Brown was right: "Too big and too ugly." I thought about that a lot.

I realize now that one reason I found it hard to make friends with the others was that in my early years I had had so little fun and companionship. I wanted them, just as I wanted them when I was a kid and used to steal dimes out of the cash box to buy popularity with the other boys and girls in our block. But I didn't seem to know how to win them. I knew I didn't want to drift into the ways I saw a lot of acts getting into, doubling up to save room rent. And many of the men I saw around the theaters seemed too much like those I'd run into at the German Village. They wanted a woman not for what they could give her but for what they could get out of her. Hadn't I put an end to my own married life to escape *that*?

If I was lonesome (and I was), if sometimes I cried myself to sleep, hearing plenty goings-on in the next room, I could always put my energy into getting ahead, making good. I didn't mean to stay on small-time forever. I'd keep my nose clean and plug away and get to be a headliner. It wasn't just the big money I was after, though that counted, of course. I *had* to take care of Son, give him an education and a start in life. And I *had* to take Mama out of the kitchen. I'd sworn to do both those things, and, by God, I was going through with them. But there was something else egging me on: the will to succeed, whatever it cost.

So I stuck to my work, always the first one to get to the theater and the last one to leave; dressing for my act early so I could stand in the wings and watch the acts ahead of me; noticing what they did, how they worked, the tricks they pulled to get laughs. I'm a born noticer, I guess. For one thing I had no money to spend in the towns I played.

Every Monday morning I was at the post office as soon as it opened to send off my money orders. One went to Joe Woods, commission on my week's salary and a dollar for the white satin dress. The other money order went to Mama. It wasn't much now. It had been hard explaining to the folks why the money orders which ran to sixty and seventy dollars a week sometimes while I was at the Village had dwindled to five or ten. They couldn't see any sense to throwing over a job that paid so well for one that barely kept me. I might have thought it nuts myself if I hadn't cared more about the future than the present; if I hadn't been so hell-bent on getting somewhere in show business.

I played my first New York date at the Music Hall on 116th Street on December 9, 1906. The Bernsteins came and brought their friends to give me a reception.

I had other rooters too. Back in the days when I roomed on Second Avenue and used to sing at the Monopol and other cafés in that neighborhood for a meal I got to know a lot of the boys who handled papers for the *Evening World* which was printed near by. Several times I entertained the paper boys at their club. They never forgot me. When I sent them word I would be at the Music Hall at 116th Street a lot of them turned up and gave me a big hand. For years these boys who handled the big bundles of papers fresh off the presses were my strong supporters whenever I played in one of the New York houses.

With what curiosity I watched the flicker of the motion picture which opened the bill. It was murky and jerky. The spots where the reel had been cut and patched showed. Some of the cuts didn't match; legs and arms appeared from nowhere. The poorest act on the bill, I thought.

For once my hunch failed me. I didn't tumble to the fact that I was witnessing the birth of an era that was to bring about the death of vaudeville.

Here, had I known it, was the first bomb of the blitz that was to black out the small-time and big-time houses everywhere. Even at that time there were several picture theaters in the city, little houses that showed one-act slapstick comedy scenes and popular songs flashed on the screen and sung by a singer on the stage.

The little ten-cent theater owned by Marcus Loew, Adolph Zukor, and Nicholas Schenck at 116th Street and Lenox Avenue was one of these houses. I was often engaged to sing there. All they showed was a one-reel slapstick comedy and me in blackface for the ten afternoon shows, and whiteface for the ten night shows. Twenty shows a day for a salary of twenty dollars a week. I would get to the theater for the first show at noon and sit there until the lights went out a little before midnight. Marcus Loew would bring me my food in between shows. He was very fond of me, even aside from the fact that he knew I brought in the dimes when I was singing there. He changed his singers weekly, but I played more return dates than any of the others.

He was a stanch friend to me, giving me kindly advice and always pleased when I would show him the money orders that went home every week. It was a tribute to those days when he called on me to help him open the first Loew Picture Theatre, which was in Boston. He used to say I was his good-luck charm. I never remember Marcus coming into any city on business that he didn't ask, "Is Sophie Tucker playing in town?" And if I was, then there would be a note asking me to meet him for supper after work. His interest was always keen. Was I happy? Was I saving my money? Was I still looking after the family? His theaters were always open to me to play at any time, from the days when I was a small-salaried performer up to the days after I had climbed into the big-money brackets.

Joe Woods and I got to be great friends. Whenever I was in New York—and I was playing the small-time houses in the city and near-by towns that winter—I would drop into his office and have long talks with him.

"The thing is, you've got guts," he would say, cocking his crossed feet up on the desk and leaning back in his chair looking at me as though he was trying to find out how I got that way. "And that's what it takes in this business."

"You watch me, Joe. I'll make it. I'll be in the big brackets yet."

"That's it, kid. Stick to it."

"Got any new dates for me?" anxiously.

"Jeez! What a glutton for work."

Ragging me, of course. One reason Joe liked me was that I was one of his acts that wanted to work all the time, anywhere, and his best commission payer.

"Well, have you? Hell! What have I got a booking agent for? Listen, Joe, I've got to eat."

"It wouldn't hurt you any to lose twenty-thirty pounds." Then he grinned. "I was just going to tell you. I can book you on the New England Circuit. Thirty-five per. All good houses. You'll be number two on a seven-act bill. It looks as if you'll be out all summer."

For a year I had been playing the small-time houses—three-day and one-week stands. I'd learned a lot since I left the German Village. I had a stage wardrobe now: two dresses, one of red velvet, the other black, a pair of high-heeled black patent-leather pumps, a black wig, black lisle hose, and two pairs of black cotton gloves. Also a tube of brown paste, a can of brown powder, black pencil for eyebrows, and a red lipstick. Into the same grip were packed my street clothes: two suits, one black and one brown, three white shirtwaists, two sets of underwear (cotton and linen mixture, no silk), six handkerchiefs (from the Five-and-Ten), two cotton wrappers (a quarter apiece—one for the dressing room, the other for the boardinghouse), two pairs of black cotton bloomers, and six ribbed sweat shirts (ten cents each).

The only things I splurged on were three fancy frames for Mama's, Papa's, and Son's pictures. These went with me everywhere. The minute I opened my grip the photographs went on my dressing table. They're there now, only in handsome blue cloisonné frames that were given me in London.

The rest of my luggage consisted of a hatbox with a black and a brown hat in it and a music case to carry my orchestrations.

Even in the most awful theaters—and some of them were terrible, dirty, vermin-infested old firetraps—my dressing room was always clean and neat. A clean runner on the shelf; make-up in boxes. No mess on the floor. I always got a great kick out of hearing others on the bill and the stage crew admire its order. My biggest expense was towels and laundry. (No kleenex then.) The brown make-up stained the six towels I carried with me. Nearly every other week I had to buy new ones. I did my own washing every night before dropping into bed, and my ironing the first thing in the morning.

The New England Circuit of the Hathaway theaters played Malden, Brockton, Lynn, Lowell, Worcester, New Bedford, Fall River, and Providence; also the small-time houses in Boston. I was number two of a seven-act bill in all these houses. The billing of all acts was done at the main office in New York.

The team of Conroy and Le Maire, blackface comedians, were the head-liners on the bill. It was my first experience in a theater with a headliner. Now to watch and learn.

After the Monday matinee George Le Maire sent for me to come to the greenroom—the theater manager's office, hung with photographs of per-formers dating back to Jenny Lind, which was the only place in the theater for actors to meet. My heart went down into my boots. I was scared to death that Le Maire was going to have me taken off the bill because his act was blackface too. Of course we didn't conflict because I sang coon songs while he and Conroy were a straight comedy team. Still you never can tell where an actor's jealousy begins.

"Kid," he said, "you've got a bad make-up on."

"What's the matter with it?" I stammered.

"It don't mean anything." And he went on to explain. "Up North they don't know anything about the high yellow. Here you're either black or white. Now you sit down, and I'm going to show you how to put on a perfect blackface make-up."

And he did.

No one could have been kinder or more encouraging to a beginner than he was to me. I would see him standing in the wings watching my act. When I came off he was always quick to compliment and encourage me. It was he, too, who advised me how to build up my program. First the bright number ("to get the audience to like you"); second, the dramatic song ("to rouse their interest"); third, the novelty ("that's to start them laughing"); fourth, the fast ragtime number ("by this time they'll be ready to applaud and keep time with you").

"Don't overfeed the audience," George Le Maire was always preaching to me. "Leave them hungry. Make 'em yell for more."

My act was allowed ten to twelve minutes. If the house kept applauding and wanted an encore, I would come off to the wings and ask the stage man-ager what to do. If George Le Maire was standing there, he would yell, "Go out. Ask them what they want. If you've got it, if you know it, sing it."

I started doing this, and soon I was averaging eight to ten songs a show. My greatest difficulty was convincing the audience I was a white girl. My Southern accent had got to be as thick and smooth as molasses. When I would pull off one of my gloves and show that I was white there'd be a sort of surprised gasp, then a howl of laughter. That season I started interpolating Jewish words in some of my songs, just to give the audience a kick.

All the songs I used then were straight singing songs. No tricks, no fancy arrangements, no talking songs such as I do now. I made it my job to learn all the new popular numbers as they came out and to have these with me. Then it was easy to ask the orchestra leader to turn to whatever song the audience asked for. If the music went wrong, I would keep right on. If the mistake was so bad I had to stop, I would tell the audience, "Sorry. That's my fault. Let me try it again." Or, "I didn't learn that one right." Or, "I tried something new and it didn't work out." Taking the blame to myself—and not laying it onto the leader—laughing my way out of the difficulties, made the audience more friendly. They liked me better because I didn't grouch. After a while I caught onto the trick of starting the song myself and letting the orchestra come in after two or three measures.

I got so I could kid with the front spotlight man if the light wasn't the right color. I'd holler up to the gallery where he was working the lights: "Say, boy, I'm a nice girl and I look just awful in that red or green spot. Please put a white one on me." My voice was so powerful everybody knew he heard me, and the audience would laugh, and I'd get the white spot. After the show the electrician would come and ask me to go over the cues again, he wanted to get the lights right. The orchestra leader would come and ask me to go over the music again, so there would be no more mistakes. By taking the blame to myself, if anything went wrong, I made them friendly to me.

From the first bill I played I noticed something. An act would go on and something would go wrong. The light cues would be wrong or something would happen to the music. The act would come off ready to tear everybody's hair, cursing, fuming. Between the ravings he would run out to smile and bow and wave to the audience. Maybe he thought he could smooth it over that way. Now what I noticed was that the acts that did this invariably lost the audience before they were through. The energy they put into being mad backstage took something out of their work. Besides this, they got the crew and the musicians down on them. Even a headliner can't afford to make enemies of the stage crew and the orchestra.

Right then I said to myself, no matter what happens, I'll never fuss backstage.

That season I played the New England and small-time circuits. I started a practice of giving the stage crew a dollar every week to buy smokes. Another dollar went weekly to the orchestra leader, "to buy a cigar." Those two dollars bit into my thirty-five per, but they paid in the end. I found when I came back to play those houses again that I had good friends who were ready to help me put my act across.

That same season I found out how important the publicity man of the theater is. I kept the names of the publicity men in all the houses I played. I would write them from time to time, sending them new photographs and the names of my new songs. The photographs were another heavy expense, but I knew I had to have them. The public got tired of the same old poses. *Something new*. That rule governs every department of show business.

About this time I started to keep an address book, putting down the names of everyone I met who was connected with show business or who showed an interest in me. I would drop them cards from time to time to keep that interest alive. When I was booked to play their town again I would let them know in advance and tell them to be sure to come and see me.

I have continued to do this through all my years in show business. That book now has over five thousand names in it.

I was working too hard to be lonely. And I suppose the determination to get ahead, to have my name up in electric lights over the theater someday, made up for some of the discomforts and inconveniences. Every morning I would rush to get all the papers to read the notices. I cut these out and pasted them into a ledger I bought at the Five-and-Ten. I have a trunk full of those ledgers now. The clippings go back to my first appearances in blackface, when Joe Woods booked me on small-time.

CHAPTER 6: *Bad Girl*

ALL THAT SEASON as I played the New England and the Park circuits and the small-time houses around Boston I had been looking forward to a date in Boston itself. In the back of my mind was the hope that the newspapers would make a feature of me—"Home-town Girl Comes HOME in Triumph," or something of that sort. Maybe I figured I was going to be written up like Paul Revere.

Well, Boston didn't bite. The headliners on the bill got all the breaks. I was just an "also ran," with not a line about me.

After the opening matinee I jammed on my hat and started out to let Boston know that Sophie Tucker was in town. We had a lot of relatives living there. Even if some of them had not seen me since I was out of diapers, and would need some telling to understand that Sophie Tucker, the Coon Shouter at the Bijou, was Charles Abuza's Sophie, I made up my mind to give it a whirl. I hadn't an idea where all of them lived. The only address I had was that of Mama's sister, who had come to my wedding. I decided to start with her and get her and her family to do the rest.

I laid it on thick. None of them knew anything about show business so they couldn't know how much was truth and how much *chutsba*. The aunt and cousins listened wide-eyed while I told them that if I brought people into the theater I would get to be a star. And if people applauded long and loud the management would raise my salary.

"Please come tonight," I begged, "and get the *mishpocha* and everyone else you can think of to come and give me a hand."

The rest of Boston may have been uninterested in the career of Sophie Tucker, once Sophie Abuza of 22 Salem Street, but my relatives weren't. They turned out in droves. They talked me up with the neighbors and got them to come along. Before the week was over I was getting an enthusiastic reception when the card with my name on it went up on the stage. And talk about calls for encores!

I had the satisfaction of knowing that the relatives liked my act. They boasted to their neighbors about their cousin or niece who was on at the Bijou that week. I made them proud. Fortunately, I was booked to move out of town before they could come round and ask how big a raise they had helped me get.

Being with the Boston relatives started up all my hunger for my own people again. All I had seen of them in two years was when Mama or Papa or Anna brought Son down to New York for a day when I could spend it with them. When I played my last New England date I decided I would go home for my first visit. I knew I couldn't take the train for New York and let it carry me past Son and Mama. I had to see them.

I wrote Joe Woods that I was going to Hartford for a few days. If he had any bookings for me he could wire me there, collect.

Mama's hair had turned so white. So had Papa's. Why, they were *old!*

It was only two years since I had left home. Then Mama stood erect. Now she stooped over. Her feet were bothering her more than ever.

Son was toddling. Talking too. He came to my arms—he was always an affectionate baby—but he kept turning his little head around to look for Sister Anna. Anna was his mama now. I was just a visitor. He put his arms round my neck and hugged and kissed me, then he squirmed to get down to toddle back to Sis.

My brothers, Philip and Moses, welcomed me. I never was a bad egg at home. Philip was married to my old school chum, Leah Zwillinger, and had a job in the post office. Moses was in high school. He wanted to study law. Anna was in high school, too, and doing the work around the house that I used to do, besides taking care of Son.

Nothing was changed very much. Business wasn't too good. The restaurant made just a bare living for the family. Upstairs, the pinochle and poker games were still going on. Mama was still scolding about them. I knew my weekly money orders were helping her to hold things together, but of course lately they hadn't been large. It wasn't the way it was while I worked at the German Village.

Everything was so quiet. Finally it got on my nerves.

"Where is everybody?" I demanded. "Why don't the neighbors come in? Don't they know I'm back?"

Nobody said anything. I caught a few looks. Mama got up and went out in the kitchen. I pushed back my chair and followed her.

"Listen," I said. "What's the matter anyhow? Is everybody down on me, or what?"

Mama's face was working as if she was going to cry. Her glasses slid down one side of her nose the funny way they always did when she was worked up over anything.

"Tell me," I insisted. "What is the matter?"

She told me then. The neighbors had never forgiven me for going away, leaving my child and my family. They said only a bad woman would do such a thing. I must be a bad woman—a whore, in the unvarnished language of the Scriptures. They had said so to Mama dozens of times.

I could feel myself starting to choke with anger.

"They said things like that to you?"

She nodded. The tears were running down under the crooked glasses. Right then and there I learned how much evil the minds of some good people can hold. I thought over those two years during which I had worked as hard and lived as straight as I did when I was at home. I thought of the lonely times, and what it had taken to save the money to send home in my weekly letters. I'd been in tough joints, such as the German Village and that French couple's boardinghouse, and I had seen and heard a lot of evil. But nowhere, it seemed to me, had I come across such cruelty as this that the "good" people had used on Mama.

I brazened it out for a day. I went out to walk along the block, determined to make the neighbors speak to me. The women turned their backs. The men stared and tittered. The kids ran after me yelling, "Look, she's got paint on her face. She's no good."

I saw Anna, white-faced, shamed, sneaking home from school. I saw the children pointing their fingers at Son. "His mother's a bad woman; she ran away and left him. She's on the stage."

I couldn't take it.

That night, out in the kitchen, I threw my arms around Mama, both of us crying. "I'm getting out on the first train in the morning," I said. "I'll never come back to this town again until I'm a big success, a headliner at Poli's. They won't dare say things about me then. And before that happens, you're going to be out of this kitchen for good. You're going to have your own home, in some other part of town where nobody can say terrible things like that to you. Moe's going to Yale if he wants to. And Son's going to have the best education this country has got to give. And Anna"—Anna, who was mothering my child for me—"Anna's to have the grandest wedding in the world."

I kept my word to the last letter. I never went back to Hartford until May 1913, when I headlined the bill at Poli's at five hundred dollars for the week.

But quite a lot of things happened before that.

First, I'm back in New York dashing around to see if Joe Woods has anything for me. He hasn't. He is now putting out acts of his own and isn't booking anything else. It's up to me to find another agent right away.

Before I do that I look in on the boys in Tin Pan Alley. Maybe they can give me some pointers. They know everybody in show business.

"Hello, Soph. Listen to my new rag."

"Listen to this one, Sophie. It's your stuff."

> "... Ain't it funny,
> When you look for money,
> All you get is sympathy...."

"Play it through for me again."

Hat on back of head, cigarette on lip, working that little battered old upright for all it's got, he teaches it to me. It's a grand song; just my meat.

"Put my photograph on the cover of that one," I tell him. "Remember, and save it for me. I'm going to introduce it."

"Okay, sister. Got a date?"

"Not yet," I have to admit. "But I'm going to have one any day now."

"Good luck, Soph."

I *had* to get work. My funds were getting low and I still smarted from the lash of that experience in Hartford.

Hanging around the music publishers' you got to see a lot of other show people. Whenever two or three of them got together the first questions invariably were: "Where are you playing?" "Have you got a date?" "Who's booking you now?" Something else I kept hearing was: "If I could get a date at Tony Pastor's," or, importantly, "I'm playing Tony Pastor's next week."

I asked Fred Fisher, the song writer, about it. "Which booking agent is the best one to get me on at Tony Pastor's?"

"Hell, you don't need a booking agent to get you a date there," said Fred. "Tony Pastor's a great showman. He books his own acts. If he likes you, he makes a place for you on the bill." Those thin, restless hands that created so many swell songs strummed a few chords. "Why don't you go down to Fourteenth Street and see Tony for yourself?"

"I will," I said.

I'd heard of Tony Pastor ever since the days when I used to run errands for the show people who came to eat in our restaurant. He was almost a legend, the little Italian whose father played in the orchestra at the old Park Theatre and who got his own start, at the age of eight, singing in the minstrel shows aboard Commodore Vanderbilt's ferryboats. Barnum heard him and signed him on as a boy prodigy.

Later Tony had his own theater, on lower Broadway first, then on the Bowery, which was the center of show business in New York. Finally he moved to Fourteenth Street, next door to Tammany Hall. It was he who made that street New York's melody lane.

Tony had ambitions. He also had the right idea. Back in the hoopskirt era few women went to shows. It wasn't considered proper or refined. And probably most of the shows weren't. The old man went and got a big kick out of it, but he wouldn't have taken the missis along on a dare. Maybe Tony Pastor foresaw that this country was going feminist. Maybe he just figured shrewdly that if you could sell five tickets to a family you made more money than by selling just one. Anyway, he got the bright idea of putting on shows that women would want to come to. The motion-picture industry has been built up on the same idea.

To get the women coming he gave away prizes of groceries, coal, dress patterns, dishes. (Well, now we have Beano and Screeno and Banknites, if you call that progress.) He advertised clean shows that were first-rate entertainment. He scoured this country and Europe for talent. A great friend to the actors, Tony probably "made" more headliners than any other one person who has figured in show business in this country. It was at Tony

Pastor's that Pat Rooney got his start and started "Sweet Rosie O'Grady" to fame. It was there that the British female baritone Helene Mora introduced "Say Au Revoir, but Not Good-bye," and Vesta Victoria wowed the galleries with "Daddy Wouldn't Buy Me a Bow-wow," and Emma Carus used her soon-to-be-famous opening line, "I'm not pretty, but I'm good to my family." Flora and May Irwin, Nat Goodwin, Gus Williams, Eddie Foy, and a dozen others who were stars when I was starting out were proud to tell that they were among Tony's finds. To be playing at Tony Pastor's was what "playing the Palace" came to be a few years later in the sunset of vaudeville.

Tony never missed one of his own shows. He just about lived at the theater.

He was a little fellow, and the first thing you felt about him was his great kindness. He didn't freeze up and dare you to thaw him out. He acted as though he was as keen to find a new act that was good as the act was to prove itself a hit. I had taken my book of notices with me to show where I had worked and how I had gone over. I told him I had just played the New England Circuit and the audiences had seemed to like me.

He looked me over, his forehead wrinkling the way a monkey's does when it sees something new. "You're the first kid I ever interviewed that didn't tell me she knocked 'em dead."

"I hope to someday," I said.

"What do you do now?"

"Well, I can sing a nice song. And, Mr. Pastor, I've got some new songs that are better than any I've been using. I work in blackface." I added that last quickly, thinking he might be of Chris Brown's way of thinking; "Too big and too ugly."

"H'mm," he said. "What do you get?"

Something inside me whispered: "If you tell him thirty-five, he'll offer you only twenty-five. You're pretty near down to your last dollar right now."

"Fifty," I told him, and never batted an eyelash.

He looked through his list of acts, me not daring to breathe, my knees wobbling, praying.

Finally, "I can use you next week," he said, "for forty dollars. I have a big show on, and I can't pay more than that."

If Tony Pastor thought I was going to sniff at forty bucks and a chance in his theater he got the surprise of his life. I threw my arms around him and hugged him and kissed him. I was blubbering, and the tears ran all over him.

"My God," he gasped, trying to wriggle loose. "What are you? A cyclone?"

When he had come up for air and straightened his collar, he grinned at me. "Go next door and get your contract. Only don't try that act on the fellow in there. I need him."

I was walking on air.

I breezed into the music publishers'. "Listen, boys, what do you know? I'm booked at Tony Pastor's." Irving Berlin was the first I told the good news. He was one of the Tin Pan Alley boys I'd gotten to know through scouting for songs to sing in my blackface act. Several times he put me onto something good.

I selected my songs: "All I Get Is Sympathy," "Why Was I Ever Born Lazy?" "Rosie, My Dusky Georgia Rosie," and half a dozen more. My act was booked to run twelve minutes, in One, but I was determined there should be encores, and I wanted to have songs for them.

Perhaps I should explain. "One" in the language of show business refers to the first division of the stage nearest the footlights. The stage is divided into One, Two, and Three. Stage directions always specify in which of these an act is to be played. Of course there is also "Full Stage." Drops are let down to form a background for One, Two, and Three, thus allowing the stage crew to set the next scene. In vaudeville, traditionally, behind One is always a park drop, a street drop, or drapes. Knowing this, and knowing in advance that she is booked to do her act "in One," a performer can plan her costume with some sense of security.

At Tony Pastor's the matinee opened at one-thirty. The first hour was always taken up with what we called "fill-in acts"—singers, acrobats, freaks. At two-thirty the main show with the standard acts and headliners came on. I knew I, as a newcomer, would be billed in the first show. But I had no way of knowing what number I would be on that bill.

After a look at my two shabby velvets I decided a new outfit was a must. At a secondhand costumer's I found a dress of dull gold mesh lace with ruffles and long sleeves. The sleeves bothered me; how was I going to pull my final stunt with the glove to show the audience I was a white girl?

"Why not take your wig off?" suggested Mrs. Simon, who ran the place. "You're so blonde it will give the audience a shock to see your own hair."

Here was a new idea. I would do it. The dress with new accessories (no cotton stockings or gloves on Tony Pastor's stage, silk ones), my wig cleaned and dressed, and a red flower for my hair set me in debt fifty dollars. The magic words "I'm playing Tony Pastor's" made Mrs. Simon trust me. In my state of mind I could probably have persuaded J. P. Morgan to advance me half a million.

The few days until Monday's opening were the longest I ever lived through. I never closed my eyes that Sunday night. At eight the next morning I was at the theater for the nine-thirty rehearsal. The doorman gave me the key to my dressing room and my rehearsal check—number One.

At nine-thirty Burt Green (later the husband of Irene Franklin) sat down at the piano. I went over and handed him my check.

"The big show is rehearsing first," he told me. "You'll have to wait."

All the while I watched the headliners rehearse their acts I marveled at the way Burt Green played for them. That boy was some pianist. Every act he played for a hit. Gosh, I thought, what I won't do with him at the piano!

When the last of the big acts had rehearsed I bounced up to Burt Green, ready to do my turn. But he was getting up from the piano.

"Mr. Brody will rehearse you," he said. "I only play for the big show."

Mr. Brody was an older man; he had been with Tony Pastor for years. He played a nice, straight piano. But after listening to a master such as Burt Green for two and a half hours Mr. Brody seemed like an amateur. All at once I began to get panicky. The songs didn't sound right. They didn't sound like anything. I kept trying to show him what I wanted, but all my playing was done with one finger and I couldn't read a note of music. (I can't to this day.)

There wasn't a thing I could do about it. I couldn't complain to the stage manager or to Tony Pastor. They would throw me out. Who was I to complain? Above all, I must not offend Mr. Brody or get myself worked into a lather. I'd seen other acts do this at times, and I'd seen how it injured their work. What I had to do was to get it out of my mind that things were going wrong.

A brisk walk up to and around Gramercy Park, a bite to eat, and I was back in my dressing room getting ready. Now I had other worries on my mind. There was the overture. The callboy came up to tell each act in turn to be down in the greenroom one act in advance of his own.

I was all ready; might as well go down. I overheard one of the boys on the stage say, "Nobody in the house yet."

"What's the matter?" I asked.

"Nothing. It's always like this. The regular patrons all know the big show doesn't start till two-thirty. They don't start coming in till after two-fifteen."

Where did that leave me? I studied the time sheet on the wall. I was next to the last on the bill before the big show. My time was two-fifteen. Did that mean I would have to play to rows of empty seats? Then reason came to dissolve those fears. *Somebody* must be in the house now. *Somebody* must come to see the small-timers, or else how did any of them get to be hits and get a chance on big-time as I had always heard could happen at Tony Pastor's? And if some of them were hits, got encores, stopped the show, then that would take up time and bring my act on later than the time sheet called for.

Standing there, with my eyes glued to the clock, I prayed the act then playing would be a big hit. And it was. I heard calls for encores. The act that followed went over big too. Two-fifteen . . . two-twenty . . . two twenty-five. . . . It was two twenty-eight when the boy put up my card:

SOPHIE TUCKER
COON SHOUTER

Then came the introduction to my first song.

I am out on the stage now. I feel that I look nice, gold lace dress, red flower in my black wig, the perfect black make-up George Le Maire showed me how to put on. I smile at Mr. Brody and he smiles back. Nothing wrong there. All set? I start the song. . . .

But I might as well have tried to sing against the racket of the Third Avenue El as against that tramp of feet coming down the aisles, the click and rattle of seats being let down, the careless laughter and calls of an audience who came only for the headliners and didn't give a hoot about the rest of us on the bill.

I shut my mouth like a clam. The tinkle of Mr. Brody's piano died away uncertainly. Then the boom of my own voice, unaccompanied and so spontaneous it scared me out of my shoes, shot across the footlights like a cannon ball, "What for you-all so late gettin' in hyar? Hyar I am, all dressed up and with some most special songs you-all ain't never heard yet. Don't you-all know you're keepin' the show waitin'? Mr. Pastor's gwine raise hell with me, I reckon, holdin' up the rest of the bill."

It got a big laugh. Where did I get the nerve to holler out like that to a New York audience? Out in the sticks kidding with the audience was one thing; this was New York's top-notch house. Now I had to sing my head off to make up for that amount of nerve.

Maybe it stirred up something in Mr. Brody too. Together we sailed into my program. One . . . two . . . three songs. The house was giving me all the encouragement in the world. Why, it was a wonderful audience. A fourth song . . . then a fifth. . . . The applause seemed to fill that big house right up to the roof.

"Go on," they cried from the gallery, "sing us some more."

Out of the tail of my eye I saw the stagehands fussing. They had the regular bill ready to start. I was holding up the show.

"Listen, you-all," I said to the audience, "that's all the songs I rehearsed. I ain't got no more."

"Sing 'em over again," came back from the gallery.

In the wings the stage manager shook his head at me warningly.

"I cain't do that," I told the house. "But you-all come back tonight and I'll have some more new songs for you."

In the midst of laughter and applause I was off. My first big-time New York showing was over. I was a hit. I'd stopped the show at Tony Pastor's cold.

In the greenroom Mr. Brody came up and congratulated me. He was so generous about it and so kind it gave me courage to say, "If Burt Green would play for me I would do even better."

"Wait and see," Mr. Brody advised. "Mr. Pastor always watches the Monday matinee, and then he changes the bill around for the night show. I wouldn't be surprised if you didn't get moved into the big show tonight and have Burt Green to play for you."

Which is what happened. When the new time sheet went up I found I was down for Number Two in the big show. Tony Pastor himself sent for me to come down to the greenroom and told me. Burt Green was there, too, ready to take my songs.

"You've got something, young lady," said Tony Pastor. "You're going places. You've got personality."

(So he thought that too. First, the music teacher, then Mr. Charles L. Ames, the school principal, then the Howard Brothers. And now Tony Pastor, the master showman.)

"You're changed to the Number Two spot on the regular bill, and Burt Green is going to play for you. Good luck, and God bless you."

He saw me coming at him and ducked behind Burt.

"For the love of God, *don't kiss me.*"

Through the rest of the week I missed the chance for a laugh I'd had at the first matinee. Still, the act went over at each show. Sime Silverman gave me a swell paragraph in *Variety;* and the *Clipper,* reporting that I had stopped the show cold, called me "an attractive-looking wench."

Fine, said I to myself, but where are the offers from managers and booking agents? Where is next week's board money coming from? You didn't have to be a whiz at arithmetic to figure that forty dollars wouldn't pay off a fifty-dollar debt and leave much over to carry on with until another job happened along. By Friday, with no bids in, I was as mournful as a torch song. What was I, even if I had held up the first show? Nothing but a fair-to-middling Number Two act. I compared myself with some of the bill's headliners. How smooth and finished their work was! How perfectly timed! Beside their performance my own was as crude as a first rehearsal.

All the bounce was out of me by now. I shivered when I remembered how I'd thrown the bull around Tin Pan Alley because I was booked for Tony Pastor's.

Saturday, and my heart felt as if it was lying in a morgue. Two Sunday shows, and then what? In words of one syllable, you are up against it, Sophie.

I was changing after the night show when the callboy came to my dressing room to say that a gentleman in the greenroom wanted to see me. "Name of Mr. Gus Hill."

"Tell him I'm changing. I'll be down in ten minutes."

The name didn't mean a thing to me; but suddenly, as soon as the boy had clattered down the stairs, I thought: what if this Gus Hill is a manager, or somebody important? I wasn't taking any chances leaving him loose around the greenroom for some other act to snap up while I dug black grease paint out of my ears. I gripped my kimono around me and tore down to the greenroom at the boy's heels.

No, Gus Hill hadn't vanished. He came right up to me very businesslike.

"I'm Gus Hill, of Manchester and Hill's burlesque wheel," he announced. "I've seen your act and I've got a place for you in one of our shows. It's on the road now. Plays Pittsburgh next week. You'll have to leave right after the show Sunday night, get to Pittsburgh at eight Monday morning, go right to the Gaiety Theatre to rehearse your songs and one or two bits to go on for the Monday matinee. Can you do it?"

A job. But—burlesque! Was that all that being a hit at Tony Pastor's had done for me?

But a job was a job. And when you didn't have one, or the money for next week's room rent, you thought twice before turning down any offer— even one that might entail letting the comedian in a false nose swat you on the face with a custard pie.

"I never played a part," I stammered to Gus Hill, "or spoke lines. I don't know as I could."

"Oh, Mr. Emerson'll teach you all that," he said, easy as anything. "He's the star. Harry Emerson and His Gay Masqueraders. He's been on the burlesque wheel for years. Knows all the ropes. A great dialect comedian Harry Emerson is."

Suddenly a conversation overheard in the greenroom that week came back to me. Someone had sneered at burlesque. And another of the acts, one of the headliners, had picked it up. "Don't sneer at burlesque. That's the greatest training in the world. That's the place to learn, to get your schooling in show business. And the managers know it. They all watch the burlesque shows. That's where they pick up talent that has had enough training to have the rough edges rubbed off. . . ."

Gus Hill was going right on: "We will want you to do your present blackface act in the olio. We'll make you the headliner of it. You'll have to supply your costumes for the blackface act, but we'll provide the costumes you will wear in the show. Mr. Emerson will decide when he sees you how he wants to use you. We pay all railroad fares. You will have to agree to stay with the show to the end of the season. That's the end of June. The salary is fifty a week."

Fifty a week, and steady work for eight months. Why, that would put me on Easy Street. No railroad fares to pay. I'd save money. Mrs. Simon would be paid off for the rented clothes and I could send Mama money regularly.

Like a conjurer, Gus Hill whipped a folded paper out of his pocket and produced a fountain pen as from thin air. "You can sign the contract right now."

I signed. For fifty a week, guaranteed for eight months, I'd have signed on to do a grass-skirt act in a honky-tonk. Though I did ask Gus Hill feebly, "You haven't any idea what sort of part I'll be required to play?"

"Oh, we'll leave that up to Harry Emerson." He patted my shoulder. "So long. Remember, you're due at the Gaiety Theatre in Pittsburgh at nine o'clock Monday morning."

"I'll be there," I promised.

It didn't seem likely, after he'd seen the one hundred and sixty-five pounds of me, that Harry Emerson would cast me for pink tights and a spangled G string. Still, if he did, and would pay me fifty bucks a week . . .

Oh, to hell with Hartford!

CHAPTER 7: *On the Burlesque Wheel*

IT WASN'T PINK TIGHTS and a G string. It was a prim dress, a gray wig, and a make-up of cleverly simulated wrinkles that turned me into a crabbed, fault-finding woman of sixty.

When the wardrobe woman presented me for Mr. Emerson's inspection he beamed approvingly. "Great! She stays just like that. No change." And to me: "Like that you'll play the part of my wife. And all the time I'm putting things over on you with the girls, see? You'll get the hang of it in a day or so. Meanwhile, learn the lines and be ready to rehearse tomorrow morning. I want you to play the part on Saturday at both shows."

I took the part he handed me, changed, and went back to my boarding place in a daze. I had done my blackface act in the olio at the afternoon show. It had gone over big with the audience, and the Gay Masqueraders' Company had gathered in the wings to watch me. They gave me a big hand. Playing in the olio—which was originally the variety show put on by members of the company between the two acts of the old minstrel shows, and which burlesque adopted—was no different from playing on a bill in any small-time vaudeville house. But playing a part in the show, making up and pretending to be a character, that was a horse of a different color. I wasn't at all sure I was going to be able to do it. And with only four days to rehearse.

Some of the chorus girls from our company were living at the same boardinghouse. They encouraged me. "You'll be great in that part, kid. Gee, what a break! To play opposite the lead! If you make good, why you can play the burlesque wheel forty-five weeks out of every year, steady. That's something, ain't it?"

Forty-five weeks, steady, was something, I had to admit. Forty-five weeks of two shows a day, seven days a week, in states that permitted Sunday shows. And if you made good you stayed on the wheel, show after show, until you were too old and shaky to play any part at all. And by that time, if you'd lived sensibly, you had a nice little savings-bank account to carry you to the end of your days. Oh, "legit" and musical comedy and vaudeville could say what they liked about burlesque. Burlesque was safe, because the people liked it and supported it. Folks weren't so highbrow they cried for Ibsen and Shakespeare the way babies cried for Castoria in the ads. Folks wanted a belly laugh every so often. They wanted to let down their hair and unbutton their vests and be natural. They wanted to laugh at sex. Sex was funny, not necessarily intense and tragic the way the playwrights such as Ibsen made it out to be. Why, weren't the best jokes in the world the ones that played on sex? And suppose burlesque was "vulgar," the way vaudeville said it was. Hell! folks were vulgar. Otherwise burlesque wouldn't be the good business it was, playing to full houses forty-five weeks of the year.

I listened to the chorus girls talking this way, sprawled out on the thin, lumpy mattresses of the boardinghouse beds, or taking turns with the landlady's flatiron, ironing out our white shirtwaists to wear with our street clothes. And I learned a lot about burlesque. We were lucky, they agreed, to be in a company built around a man star. The women stars were bitches. They expected you to fetch and carry for them, do their errands . . .

And if the audience liked you, and gave you a hand, the star would be furious. She'd take it out on you for weeks. Mr. Emerson was different, though. He gave everyone in the company a chance. Everyone wanted to get into his shows. Why, there were actors playing with him that had been with him for years. That was what was so good about burlesque. Once you got the hang of it, it was easy.

"Oh, you'll like it, Tuck," the girls assured me. "You'll get along just fine, starting out with a real part in the show besides headlining the olio."

I only wished I had their confidence in my ability. I had memorized my part, about four sides of dialogue, sitting up all that first Monday night to have it down by heart for the Tuesday-morning rehearsal. I was always a quick study. I could always learn a song or lines overnight and be ready to rehearse in the morning. But the rehearsal was a flop. I knew the lines but I couldn't put life into them. Mr. Emerson worked with me patiently.

"Remember, you're not singing a song, young lady. You're speaking. And not to the house. To me. Speak to me. When you come on and say, 'Henry!' your voice ought to hit the back wall of the house like a cannon ball. Remember, everybody's got to know you're a domineering woman. Everybody's got to laugh at you, and get a kick every time I put something over on you. You've got to let them know what kind of person you are. And right off, the minute you come on. Make your first word count."

I tried it again. And again. Ten, twenty, forty times. I couldn't seem to get it. Even my voice wouldn't obey me. I had no confidence in my ability, and that lack of confidence gave me a stage fright that began in my vocal cords and ended in my feet.

That week I lived in hell. Day and night, when I wasn't on the stage for my blackface act in the olio, I had my part in my hand, studying it, trying to get the intonation Mr. Emerson wanted. Every day he and the stage manager rehearsed me. There was no getting round it, I was terrible.

The others in the company did their best to buck me up. "What do you care, Tuck? Nobody's ever any good at rehearsal. Wait till you go on, you'll knock the audience dead."

If I don't drop dead first from stage fright, I thought.

At rehearsal after the late show on Friday I overheard Mr. Emerson say to the stage manager, "There's no use working with her any more. We'll try her out tomorrow. If she's rotten, we'll put the character woman back in the part. She can do her act in the olio until Gus Hill finds a spot for her in one of his other shows."

Going home that night, clutching my part, I felt as though the bottom had dropped out of everything for me. Here was I, thinking I was going to go places in show business and I couldn't hold my own in burlesque. Now I knew why burlesque was a great school. I began to have a respect for actors who could read lines and make a character come to life on the stage.

All that night I sat up in bed with a petticoat pinned around my shoulders to keep off the draft and studied my lines. Softly, under my breath, so as not to wake the girls in the next room, I tried reading them. With eyes tight shut I tried to feel myself a nagging wife with a gay cheater for a husband. By morning I was worn out and a wreck.

A cup of regular boardinghouse coffee didn't make me feel any better. There was no rehearsal for me that morning. Mr. Emerson had thrown up his hands after the one the night before. However, I decided to go down to the theater and try out my lines alone. Maybe, I thought, if I go over them all alone, in the empty theater, I can get the intonation right.

It was early in the morning, before nine o'clock. The theater was shut tight and apparently deserted. I remember I walked round the block and discovered an alley leading to the back of the building. I banged on several metal doors before I roused a grumpy janitor, who looked as though he had been sleeping in the ashcan.

He didn't want to let me in, being suspicious of anyone who wanted to rehearse all by herself. But I insisted. Finally he opened the door wide enough to let me squeeze past him, jerked a thumb in the direction I was to go to find the stage, and went back, I guessed, to his bed by the furnace.

I stumbled and felt my way along a passage until I came to the wings. The stage was dark and the house pitch black except for little streaks of light that outlined the exit doors in the gallery. I stood a moment in the wings, remembering what Mr. Emerson had said about making my first word count. Then I took a deep breath and walked onto the stage.

"Henry!" I shouted.

My voice hit the back wall of the house like a blitz. The rafters shook. From somewhere in the dark there came a yell, a clatter, and the slamming of doors. The lights flashed on. In ran the janitor, a couple of scrub women, and a policeman.

"My God, what's happened? You scared the hell out of us."

I laughed till my knees shook. I told them I was rehearsing. "If I can just do it that way this afternoon."

That afternoon, at the matinee, I did it just that way. "Henry!" It scared Mr. Emerson so he jumped. And it rocked the house. They howled so loud and so long I began to get hysterical. I shook all over. Mr. Emerson came over to me, put his arm around me, made believe he was making up to me, while all the time he was whispering, "Steady. Keep steady. You're fine. Get a grip on yourself and you'll be all right."

"All right," I whispered back, "but I can't remember another darned line." Mr. Emerson prompted me, also the stage manager from the wings. My nerves quieted, and the lines came back to me. I went through the show from that point without any trouble.

"You see," said the girls at the boardinghouse. "You were fine. Keep at it and who knows? You may get to be a queen of burlesque like Lizzie Freligh and Mollie Williams."

For six months the Gay Masqueraders toured the Midwest. Behind us, coming into each theater as we moved out, was another burlesque show, one of Hurtig and Seamon's. Occasionally, when we were playing a territory which did not permit Sunday shows, the two companies would be in town together for a day.

The dancer in the Hurtig and Seamon show was a tall, lanky, funny-faced kid with rubber legs. Yes, meet Fanny Brice. She didn't have the Jewish accent then. Fanny didn't know a word of Yiddish until years later, when she learned the dialect from Harry Delf, a grand Jewish comedian who used to play the joints in Brooklyn and Coney Island.

Our friendship dates from that season. We were two kids brimming over with ambition, with ideas, schemes, and plans for what we would do when we got into the big-money brackets. Neither of us had any doubt but that we would get there someday. Our first appearance on a bill together was one Sunday in New York at the Murray Hill Theatre. They played burlesque there through the week. Burlesque was banned in New York on Sunday. On that day they ran vaudeville bills. Our companies were playing the Pennsylvania territory (Pennsylvania banned Sunday shows), and so Fanny and I were both free to take a date in New York and pick up an extra ten dollars apiece. After the show, I remember, Fanny took me to a hotel on 125th Street to meet the star of her company, the burlesque "queen," Lizzie Freligh. She was a tiny, dainty creature, adored by the galleries for her roguish smile and her gift for being naughty in a nice way. Fanny thought the world of her and ran her errands with the devotion of a schoolgirl for an older girl crush.

Whenever our two shows played simultaneously in New York, Fanny and I palled up. Later on, however, we never seemed to meet in New York, where Fanny was first a Ziegfeld and later a Shubert star for so many years. But I have never come into Chicago to play in vaudeville or in the cafés that I haven't found Fanny was playing there too. Then what times we have had together, catching up on the news, swapping experiences, laughing over old times, exchanging confidences. Stretched out on a couch, with our corsets off and our hair down, with no one around to horn in, we've spent hours telling each other what we would have done if only life had been different. Meaning, as women do, if the men in our lives had been different.

My friendship with Fanny Brice, ripening through more than thirty years, is one of the good things I got out of my season on the burlesque wheel.

Another good that season brought me was the training in making friends with the people I met in the theater. Playing in a company did a lot for me. There were none of the achingly lonesome days I had gone through when I played the small-time vaudeville circuits. The Gay Masqueraders traveled together; we were like a big, noisy, intimate family. Oh, there was plenty of doubling up. That goes on everywhere in show business. Some of the girls wondered why I didn't. I hated it as much as I ever did. Besides, I wasn't the type of girl the boys liked to play around with on tour. But they liked me as a pal, a good egg: good for laughs, good to know if they were broke or in some trouble. I could josh with them, listen to their troubles, pan them for getting tight or mixed up with some girl. We were friends. They knew they could always borrow a few dollars from me. But I was right there when the salaries were paid on Sunday, to get my money back. The money order went regularly every week to Mama, and another to Brother Moe, who had started to Yale that winter.

In every town we played I would hunt up the local entertainment bureau to see if I could pick up any extra jobs singing at stags or smokers or banquets. In that way I could earn many an extra five or ten dollars which gave the budget a boost. And that kind of work made friends for me in the towns. I figured it would help to build up an audience for me when I came back to that town again.

I've said there were no lonesome times. But sometimes I used to stare at the four walls of my boardinghouse bedroom and wonder if I had really ever had any other home. Whitewashed walls, or walls papered in nightmarish designs. The bed, the dresser with its mirror that made you wonder why they ever let anyone who looked the way you looked get on a stage, the straight chair, the rocker, the one window with white cotton lace curtains, the washstand with pitcher and bowl, the little rug beside the bed, the one electric light above it and the white china night pot beneath it. From Worcester, Massachusetts, to Kansas City, Missouri, from Dallas to Duluth, the pattern of those rooms remained the same.

But the photographs of my three dear ones were on the dresser to welcome me when I came home after the night show and to greet me when I opened my eyes in the morning.

"Yes, Mama, Papa, Son. I'm doing fine. Have faith in me. Just wait till I get on top. It won't be long now. I'll be seeing you some of these days."

Those words which were destined to play such a large part in my life seem to have been the theme song of my early letters home.

Wherever the show took me I was constantly on the lookout for new songs to use in my blackface act in the olio, visiting the offices of the big music publishers in all the key cities. I knew I mustn't get stale, or caught in a rut. When we played a week in Chicago at the Trocadero Theatre on State Street I haunted the offices of all the music publishers in that city. It was in one of them that I met Bernie Adler and heard him play a smooth new rag that I felt sure was destined to be a smash hit. "The Lovin' Rag," he called it. I asked him to keep it for me and I would introduce it in my act when the show came back into Chicago to another burlesque theater after a few weeks.

For all the years I have been in show business, to singers who have asked my advice I have said: "Get new songs. Pay a writer to write them for you. Get songs that you can make your own. Don't copy other singers. Don't sing their songs. Don't do their stunts. Don't make your act a carbon copy of someone else's. Not if you want to succeed. And not if you want to stay in show business more than a season or two. Put off buying that mink coat or the diamond bracelet and buy songs instead. They'll pay you dividends and cost nothing for insurance or storage."

I began doing that early in my career, and I've never stopped doing it. I know it pays.

In March we played a week in Holyoke, Massachusetts. It seemed ages ago that Louis and I had gone there to get married. Only an hour or so from home, but I hadn't yet made good on my promise to be a headliner. I couldn't run in on the folks. Not until I was really among the topnotchers.

I only hoped there were none of the old gossips from Front Street snooping around Holyoke to see the bills plastered outside the theater and carry back the news that Sophie had gone from bad to burlesque.

Our first matinee in Holyoke was marked by a tremendous tension backstage. The rumor had gone round that no less a person than Mr. Marc Klaw, of Klaw and Erlanger, had come on from New York to look us over. He was scouting for talent for the second Ziegfeld *Follies*. Everyone, from Corinne de Forrest, the soubrette, to the rawest chorus girl, was jittery. Opportunity, in the shape of Mr. Marc Klaw, was sitting somewhere in the darkened house, with a Broadway contract for one of us if she made good. The whole show was suddenly pepped up; the performance came alive. The atmosphere backstage tingled with the electricity of suspense.

I played my part that afternoon with a prayer in my heart that Mr. Klaw's sharp eyes would be able to pierce the old-woman make-up I wore and discover *me* underneath it. When the time came for the olio I made up for my blackface act with careful regard for all I had learned since George Le Maire gave me lessons in putting on a blackface. How carefully I selected the songs I would sing that day. Only the best. "Rosie," that had been a hit at Tony Pastor's, and "That Lovin' Rag," which I felt sure Mr. Klaw had never heard, and the others that audiences always went for. I knew my act was better now than when I had played at Tony Pastor's in the fall. I'd learned a lot that year. I had burlesque to thank for it.

And yet, standing in the wings, waiting for the first bar of my first song, determined to do my best to win that opportunity on Broadway if I possibly could, a deep resentment welled up in me. Why did I have to appear in blackface? Why couldn't I have my chance as myself, as the other girls in the company had theirs?

"Too big and too ugly"—Chris Brown's words came back to me tauntingly.

Hadn't I overcome those obstacles yet? I'd worked so hard. My hands were smooth and white now. No one would suspect them of long association with the dishpan and scrub pail. My own hair under the wig was a mass of burnished gold curls. Nature and my Crimean ancestors had done that for me. They had given me, too, my smooth, fine skin, that was pleasingly white now, since I had learned how to care for it.

Why couldn't I show these to Mr. Klaw instead of a countenance painstakingly smeared with black grease paint, a black horsehair wig, and a pair of black suède gloves?

"Tum . . . tum . . . tum, tum, tumpty tum tum . . ."

My song. I'm on. Keep your eye peeled, Mr. Klaw.

Well, this time real life behaved just like the movies. I got the job. I couldn't believe it myself. Standing there in the greenroom after the show, hearing Mr. Klaw say things like "a spot for you in the *Follies* . . ." "Opening in Atlantic City in June, then playing the New York Roof . . ." "One hundred dollars a week . . ." I kept thinking: this isn't really happening. It's that cheesecake you ate last night. You'll wake up in a minute and find yourself in the same old, lumpy bed with the sagging wire spring that has felt the weight of a thousand troupers before you. Things like this don't happen.

But they do happen. Mr. Klaw stayed real and substantial even after I'd given myself a pinch in the thigh warranted to put an end to any dream.

"We'll want six minutes of your act. In One, so we can set the big finale scene," he was saying.

The pinch had brought me back to life.

"Let me work in whiteface," I suggested. "Really, I'm not bad looking. And I'm only twenty-one. Honest, Mr. Klaw. If you'd just give me a tryout."

He shook his head. "No. Blackface is what we want. You'll be notified when to come for rehearsals."

And that was that.

During the next week Harry Emerson was taken seriously ill. The show had to close. Gus Hill came on from New York to wind things up for us and to place members of the company in other shows on the wheel to finish out the balance of the season.

To me he said, "You can go on to Boston and do your act in the olio of the show playing the Howard Atheneum Theatre. It needs bolstering up. Then I'll find a place for you in one of our other shows."

I told him about the contract I had signed with Mr. Klaw for the *Follies*. The rehearsals would start before the end of the burlesque season.

"You can't do that," Gus Hill said sharply. "What about that contract you signed with me? You'd better read it through. We have an option on you for another season."

I had forgotten the contract. I had never read it, being too busy from the first learning a part and getting up my songs for the olio. And if I had read it, the word "option" would have meant nothing to me.

"Oh, but, Mr. Hill, this is the *Follies*. It's a chance on Broadway . . ."

"Well, this is your chance on the burlesque wheel. We're featuring you now in the olio. We'll give you lots of advertising when you go on to Boston. We've built you up with our audiences and we aren't going to lose you now."

Here was my precious contract with the *Follies* threatening to take wings and fly away. I pleaded with Gus Hill. I begged. It was stupid of me, of course, not to have told him when Mr. Klaw made me the offer. But since the theater manager knew of it I took it for granted everyone else did, too, and that it was all right for me to accept.

"One hundred dollars a week, Mr. Hill. Think what that means. Think what I can do with that money. Not just for myself, for my folks."

He listened, and he gave in.

"All right. It isn't legal, but I'll do it. You can't ever say Gus Hill stood between you and Broadway."

"I'll say he helped me get there," I promised.

I've kept that promise and I'm keeping it now.

There were big billposters plastered on the Howard Atheneum Theatre and on billboards all over Boston:

SOPHIE TUCKER
WORLD-RENOWNED COON SHOUTER

They looked good to me. I stood there, gripping my music case (I never trusted that out of my hands when I traveled), and read it over and over. Maybe that was how they would bill me in the *Follies*. Maybe the news that the *Follies* was taking me had gone round and the Boston papers would play me up as somebody to pay attention to in show business, not overlooking the fact that I was a Boston girl. Maybe they would give me glowing write-ups and Mr. Klaw and Mr. Ziegfeld would read them and would give me more than just the one spot in the show. Maybe . . .

After the rehearsal I looked around for my trunk which I had checked. No trunk. I went down to the railroad station. The baggageman took my check, rooted around in a pile of luggage, and came back with the news that my trunk had gotten in with a lot of other theatrical trunks and had been sent on to Lowell, Massachusetts, by mistake.

"It'll come back all right, miss," he said comfortingly.

"When?"

"Sometime this afternoon. We'll get it right over to the theater soon as it comes in. You'll have it in time to dress up pretty for the show tonight."

"Tonight!" I blared at him. "Hell! it's today's matinee I've got to think about. I'm a blackface comedienne and all my stuff is in that trunk."

"Well, it ain't my funeral," said the baggageman, and turned away.

No, I thought, it's mine. And what am I going to do?

I hurried back to the theater and saw the manager. He took it as calmly us the baggageman. "Oh, that sort of thing happens all the time. Trunks are always getting lost. The audience is used to that."

"But what will I do?"

"Go on in your street clothes, the way you are. A good-looking, hefty squaw like you don't need black make-up."

I stared at him. He'd called me "a good-looking, hefty squaw," which was quite another bill of goods than Chris Brown's description of me. He said I didn't need black make-up. Wasn't that just what I'd tried to make Mr. Klaw believe? Well, here was my chance. If I could prove it. If I could put my act across without the coon shouter's make-up maybe the word of it would get to the great Ziegfeld. Maybe I would be through with blackface forever.

Now here's something funny. Remember, though, that I had never yet walked out on the stage without some sort of disguise. It was the hardest thing in the world for me to step out of the wings in my tailored suit, white linen shirtwaist hastily pressed in the dressing room, with no covering on my blonde hair, and no make-up except lipstick, a dab of rouge, and a dusting of white powder. In tights and a G string I wouldn't have felt more stripped.

The leader and the boys in the pit gaped at me. They expected blackface So, of course, did the audience. I could see them consulting their programs. I'd have to explain. Somehow, telling them about the trunk that had gone on to Lowell by mistake started me getting even more confidential.

"You-all can see I'm a white girl. Well, I'll tell you something more: I'm not Southern. I grew up right here in Boston, at 22 Salem Street. I'm a Jewish girl, and I just learned this Southern accent doing a blackface act for two years. And now, Mr. Leader, please play my song."

"That Lovin' Rag" got them started. They were right with me. All the time I was singing five numbers, six, seven, then an eighth, inwardly I was exulting: "I don't need blackface. I can hold an audience without it. I've got them eating right out of my hand. I'm through with blackface. I'll never black up again. And I wouldn't have known I could do it if that damn trunk hadn't got lost. God bless that dumb baggageman. He's done me the best turn I've had in many a day."

Afterward, up in my dressing room, peeling off my wet clothes (believe me, it's no joke singing in a heavy tailored suit), reaching for the alcohol bottle (I mustn't catch cold), I was jabbering out loud to myself: "What will I do tonight? I can't repeat that about my trunk being lost. I'll have to think of something else to start off with. It's my chance to show 'em I can make good in whiteface. I'll get myself a swell evening gown. The stores aren't shut yet. But I haven't got the money. I'll make the manager advance me my week's salary. I'll dress up grand. I'll look important. Like a head-liner. I'll ask the girls to show me how to put on eyelashes and a real make-up. . . ."

Outside the dressing room the property man shouted, "Miss, your trunk's here."

Before I could answer came the manager's voice, "Throw out that trunk. The kid doesn't need blackface. Miss Travers"—Josephine Travers was the star of the show. She was reputed to have the finest wardrobe on the wheel—"give the kid one of your gowns. Put a make-up on her. We're going to do great business this week. The men all went for her in a big way."

That's how it happened that I went on that night in a tightly laced black velvet princess gown. It made me feel like a boloney in mourning. I didn't know whether I could draw breath to sing. But Miss Travers, who dressed me herself and made me up and showed me how to swish my train of red chiffon ruffles to give point to my songs, said, "Now you look like a head-liner."

When I filled up my lungs I was in a panic for fear the seams of the dress would split, and the train, the first one I'd ever worn, had me nervous as a cat, but a good look in the mirror told me Miss Travers was right. I did look like an important act.

Oi, Chris Brown, you should see me now.

I had a wonderful reception. The relatives had turned out loyally. I had taken pains to send them cards to say I would be at the Howard Atheneum that week. Already I was using that address book of mine.

No apologizing now for not being in blackface. I was living up to my grand gown, swishing my tail around like a tomcat, copycatting the head-liners I had watched at Tony Pastor's.

The act went perfectly. Then came the moment to bow gracefully and run off stage. I backed up a step, felt the red ruffles catch my feet, and stopped. The audience was calling for more songs. But I'd already sung all I had rehearsed and had run over my time. A glance into the wings showed me the stage manager beckoning.

"Don't milk the audience," I heard him call. "Come off."

I tried to kick the ruffles away from my feet. My heel caught in them. I hopped back, trying to loosen it, and kerplunk, down I went on my fanny like a ton of bricks.

There was a howl of laughter: "Funny act." "Very funny girl." In the wings the cast were shrieking.

"What are you laughing at?" I shouted, crying. The fall hurt, and the shock of it set my nerves on edge. My feet, too, were all snarled up in those damn ruffles, and the dress was so tight I couldn't move myself to get free. "It isn't funny at all," I bellowed. "I never wore a dress with a train in my life before. I don't know what to do with the damn thing."

Still the house went on laughing, applauding while I did the only thing I could do, slide off stage on my backside. And that was the climax of my elegant performance.

The manager clapped me on the shoulder. "Kid, you're a knockout. Immense. Don't tell the audience about your train. That's a great piece of business. Keep it in your act. You're a real comedienne."

Yeah, I thought, feeling myself gingerly. If I have to do that two shows a day, seven days a week, I'll never last to make the *Follies*. Right now I must be getting a nice blue stripe to run alongside that red one across my rear. It took Boston to paint Old Glory on Sophie Tucker's backside.

CHAPTER 8: *In—and Out of—the* Follies

THE first of the Ziegfeld *Follies* rang up the curtain on a new era in show business. It marked the beginning of the super-shows, elaborately staged, costumed, and lighted—spectacles whose production costs ran into hundreds of thousands of dollars.

The *Follies* were "Class." They offered Americans something Americans used to think they could get only in Paris, and at prices that lifted this form of variety way out of the vaudeville class. The suggestion of French naughtiness was implied in the name of the special theater, the Jardin de Paris, built on top of the New York Theatre in Times Square and dedicated to Ziegfeld's venture. People simply couldn't get over the first *Follies* in which Nora Bayes had starred. You would think, to hear the talk, that Ziggy had manufactured those long-legged, beauteous show girls.

And now a second *Follies* was being advertised, bigger, more glittering, more marvelous, and even more expensive than the first. What, everybody in show business was asking, can they find to put into it? How are they going to make the *Follies of 1909* live up to, let alone surpass, the first *Follies of 1908?* In mid-April, just when the theatrical season was folding up, show business was all a-tiptoe with curiosity about the new show on the New York Roof, rehearsals for which had just been called.

Never in my whole life have I seen so many beautiful girls. Their assembled good looks seemed to fill the Jardin de Paris to the exclusion of every-

thing else. Moving across the stage at Mr. Ziegfeld's orders, their perfect figures left you breathless.

If that was what just watching a rehearsal did to me, I could imagine what
these same beauties, made up and gorgeously costumed, would do to the
audience when the show opened.

The queen of the Venuses was Lillian Lorraine; petite and exquisite with
her auburn hair, perfect complexion, and enormous brown eyes. A girl with
looks of that order didn't have to do anything in order to get the center of
the stage in any show. An eyeful of her knocked you cold. Next to her, to
my eyes, came tall, statuesque, queenly Annabelle Whitford, known as the
"Nell Brinkley Girl of 1909." As though these weren't enough, we had Mae
Murray, destined for Hollywood stardom, Vera Maxwell and Florence
Walton, who later joined up with Maurice to form the internationally famous dance team.

The *Follies* dancers were Bessie Clayton, the world's greatest toe dancer,
and two swell modern dancers, Gertrude Vanderbilt and Rosie Green, the
mother of Mitzi Green. For comedians we had Harry Kelly and the team of
Bickle and Watson; like me, they had come to the *Follies* by way of
burlesque.

But all these and the ponies were only the backdrop, you might say, for
the stars of the show, Nora Bayes and her partner and husband Jack Norworth. Nora was then at the peak of her career.

Also, of course, there was Sophie Tucker. Though no one at that first
rehearsal seemed even aware of her existence.

After waiting an hour or so, when no one questioned me or showed any
interest in my being there, I presented myself, contract in hand, to Mr. Ziegfeld, who was watching a scene being rehearsed.

"Glad to meet you, Miss Tucker," he said with that pleasant manner for
which he was famous. He gave me a quick looking-over. "You sing, don't
you?"

"Yes," I said. I was just opening my mouth to explain that though my
contract called for a blackface act I had turned myself into a whiteface
singer, when he added in a tone that dismissed me completely:

"Sit down somewhere. We'll call you when we're ready for you."

That, incredible as it seems, was the extent of my contact with Mr. Ziegfeld until the *Follies* first night. Through the eight weeks of daily rehearsals
I sat obediently "somewhere," waiting for a call. Mr. Ziegfeld gave no sign
that he knew I existed. Mr. Klaw never stuck his head inside the theater the
whole time. Julian Mitchell, the director, deaf and over his ears in the job

of staging a Ziegfeld show, took no more notice of me than if I had been a shadow. One hundred and sixty pounds of Sophie Tucker sitting impatiently on the edge of an orchestra seat, gripping her contract and trying to figure out whether she was in the *Follies* or not.

There was plenty to watch. I had never seen a show put together before, and watching Julian Mitchell and Mr. Ziegfeld mold and weld all those diverse elements into a whole fascinated me as nothing I had ever seen in my life before. Here was magic, the power to create something vivid and alive which would appeal to all the senses. I watched the ponies rehearse dance steps, the show girls practice their distinctive parades and poses. I watched Harry Kelly, that grand comedian, work over his business dozens of times, with a painstaking care for detail and timing that I realized amounted to genius. A year before, without my experience in burlesque, I might not have appreciated all that I saw during those eight weeks of daily rehearsals. I might have thought they were fussing over trifles. But a season on the burlesque wheel had opened my eyes to the fact that in show business there are no trifles. Everything is important. Your way of walking on the stage, your manner, how you hold your hands, turn your head, bow— all these are a part of your act, and as important in their way as the song you sing or the lines you read. Watching that great showman, Florenz Ziegfeld, rehearse his *Follies* cast, and listening to his directions were an education which I was only too eager to accept.

We were starting on the seventh week of rehearsals. One week more and the show would open in Atlantic City on June 17. Still I hadn't the faintest idea of what would be expected of me, or where my spot would be in the show. My hands gripping the pocketbook with my contract in it were often cold and clammy with fear. In my mind the worries chased themselves around like rats in a trap. Suppose I never was called? Suppose Mr. Ziegfeld persisted in ignoring me till the opening day? What would become of the one hundred dollars' salary on the promise of which I had rented a tiny apartment in New York and arranged for Brother Moe to live with me there while he finished his law course at New York University? Visions of being dispossessed for non-payment of rent, of being haled into court, disgraced forever, filled my mind while I sat there watching the rehearsals go endlessly on.

For days the papers had been full of stories of Teddy Roosevelt's return from his African hunting expedition. The cartoonists' pencils had been working overtime on pictures of Roosevelt grinning at lions and lions grinning the familiar Roosevelt grin at the G.O.P. elephant. One cartoon, by

Davenport, widely circulated, showed all the animals of the jungle climbing to the top of the tallest tree because they heard that Teddy was coming.

From my seat in the theater I heard Mr. Ziegfeld arguing with the writers and producers.

"We ought to have a jungle number. It's topical. Timely."

"But we're opening in a week," someone reminded him. "There's no time to add anything more to the show now."

"Time"—Mr. Ziegfeld brushed this away as of no consequence—"there's plenty of time. You boys get busy and write a jungle number."

"Who's going to sing it?" another voice objected. "Everyone has all she can do right now."

"Damn it," Mr. Ziegfeld exploded, "here's a singer. Miss Tucker. Go on, boys, get busy. Write the song. Teach it to her. Mitchell will stage it."

And he turned back to the rehearsal.

The next day the boys brought in the song, "It's Moving Day Way Down in Jungle Town," which Davenport's cartoon had inspired. They rehearsed me. I memorized the song overnight. Once again I thanked God for that quick, accurate memory of mine. Now I had something to do, a spot in the show. I sang, dressing to go to the theater for rehearsal. Now I would have a chance to show Mr. Ziegfeld and the others that I could sing.

But, funny as it sounds, I never had that chance. I sat on the side waiting to be called while Mr. Mitchell instructed the wardrobe mistress about costumes. For me a leopard skin, with the animal's head for a cap, brown sandals, bare legs. For the chorus, costumes representing other jungle animals. As he staged the number I was to lead the chorus, who were to do a dance also. He rehearsed the chorus that day and the next and the day after that, still without calling me to sing the number. Not until the fourth day did I hear:

"All right, Miss Tucker, we're ready for you."

And then I had to reply that I had caught cold and couldn't sing a note.

"Never mind," said Mr. Mitchell. "It's okay, anyway. Just walk through the number; save your voice. That's it. Fine! All set now. The number is finished." He beamed at me. "Miss Tucker, you will do the jungle song. And six minutes, in One, before the finale number of the first act. Get three songs ready. You will rehearse them and the jungle song with the orchestra in Atlantic City. The wardrobe mistress will get a dress for your six-minute specialty. You're all set for the jungle costume. We don't need you for rehearsals any more. Thank you."

And that, believe it or not, was all the preparation I had for my first appearance in the *Follies*.

I know it sounds incredible, none the less it's true. Through eight weeks of rehearsals not one member of the *Follies'* management or cast ever heard me sing a note. Even after I got to Atlantic City for those three hectic days before the opening, though I rehearsed several times with the orchestra, it so happened that neither Mr. Ziegfeld nor Mr. Mitchell nor Mr. Erlanger was ever in the theater at the time. I had been engaged to do a six-minute specialty, but apparently no one was in the least interested in what I sang or what I did.

I couldn't understand it.

I looked at the dress the wardrobe mistress had had made for me, a gorgeous gold lamé gown. I thought of the three songs Irving Berlin had selected for my act: two of his, "The Right Church but the Wrong Pew" and "The Yiddisha Rag," and "The Cubanola Glide" by Harry Von Tilzer. The boys in Tin Pan Alley had coached me in them well. I *knew* those songs were smash hits. I *knew* I could sing them. I *knew* when I tried on the gold gown that I looked stunning. All right, I'd show Mr. Ziegfeld, Mr. Mitchell, Mr. Erlanger, the stars, and everybody else in the *Follies* that I could do things.

"I'll tie the show up in a knot," I promised myself. "Suppose that big finale number did cost forty thousand dollars to produce and all they want me for is to fill in time while they get it set. They're going to see something tonight. I'll hold up that forty thousand dollars' worth of finale or my name isn't Sophie Tucker."

When I went to my dressing room to hang up my things I found I was dressing with Annabelle Whitford, the "Nell Brinkley Girl." Next door to us was Lillian Lorraine with her colored maid. Annabelle and Lillian were great friends apparently.

"What do you do in the show?" they asked me curiously.

"I sing."

"That's funny. We never saw you rehearse."

"Hope you're a big hit," Annabelle said kindly.

Presently she and Lillian left the theater. I was alone. Everyone, it seemed, but me, had friends waiting to take them to dinner, to ride in the chairs on the Boardwalk, to go swimming. I had looked forward to this, my first trip to Atlantic City, and to having fun there. Now that hope was dashed. I could feel rising now the cold wave of loneliness that used to sweep over me back in the days when I was on the small-time circuit. It threatened to engulf me.

I knew I mustn't let it do that. I knew I must keep calm and secure inside if I was going to make good on the promise I had made to myself to stop the show cold. I knew I mustn't let myself feel lonely and out of things. That sort of thinking killed your work. If only there was somebody, anybody, I could talk to.

In the next dressing room I heard somebody moving about, singing softly to herself. I knew Lillian Lorraine had gone out. This must be the maid I had seen with her—a handsome, light-colored woman. I'll go in there, I thought. Black or white, what does it matter? It's somebody to talk to.

I pushed open the door of the other dressing room. The maid had her back to me, hanging Lillian's exquisite costumes behind a dust sheet.

"May I come in and sit down here with you for a while?" I asked. It surprised me to find my voice shook. "I'm so blue."

The maid turned halfway round and gave me a glance over her shoulder. Then she smiled. That smile, wise and kind and tolerant, said more to me than all the fine words in the dictionary. I flopped down on the chair in front of the dressing table. Before I knew it I was pouring out all my worries, chief of which was the fact that Mr. Ziegfeld didn't seem the least bit interested in me or in my work in the show.

"Well, you got to take that," she said. "This show business is funny sometimes."

"You know a lot about show business?" I asked.

"I ought to." Again she smiled. "One way or another I've been in it most of my life." She went on to explain that she had been one of the beauties in the Williams and Walker colored show that ran on Broadway a couple of seasons before. Her name, she added, was Mollie Elkins.

"And did you ever know of anything like this happening to a singer in a show before now?" I persisted.

"Listen, honey"—she might have been instructing a child—"every show I've been in, every show I ever heard of, there was always one kid who was the goat, the 'patsy,' that nobody paid no mind to. But always that patsy was the one that ran off with being the hit of the show. Why can't it be you?"

"It's just that I'm scared."

"Huh! What you scared about?"

"Scared I won't make good, I guess. I *must* make good. Everything depends on it now." Briefly I sketched my plans for the family: two years in law school for Moe—"He started in the morning I left to come down here to Atlantic City"; a home of her own for Mama, no more hard work in the restaurant. "And I've got a son, Mollie. The cutest little fellow you ever saw. I want him to have an education, advantages, a break. What's going to happen to all of them if I'm a flop tonight? If Mr. Ziegfeld doesn't think I'm any good he'll fire me. And he can't think much of me because he's never once asked me to sing for him."

"Mr. Ziegfeld must think you're some good, or he wouldn't have you in the show at all," Mollie retorted.

"But Mr. Ziegfeld didn't hire me. Mr. Klaw did. And I've never set eyes on him since. And none of them have heard me sing, only the song writers, the pianist, and the orchestra."

"Well then"—Mollie shook out a skirt briskly before hanging it—"don't you suppose these people have told Mr. Ziegfeld you were good or bad by now? Come on, Patsy, keep your chin up. Go on out on the Boardwalk in the sunshine. Don't hang round the theater. That kind of moping never did nobody no good. Remember, I promise I'll be rooting for you tonight. Run along now, child. I've got to tend to Miss Lorraine's things."

That friendly, wholesome talk, that promise to root for me, the feeling that there was now at least one person in the theater to whom Sophie Tucker was something more than just a name on the program, sent my blues flying. I came out of it with a snap. Hell! Of course I could put across those three grand songs of mine as well as the jungle number. Just let me once get out in front of the audience and I'd show the *Follies* what I was made of.

God bless you, Mollie Elkins, you bucked me up just when I needed it most.

An Elks' convention wouldn't have drawn a bigger crowd to Atlantic City than the *Follies* opening brought there. That first-night audience was of a kind to start you shivering with stage fright or inspire you way beyond anything you ever thought you could do, depending on the way your nerves behaved. Every New York paper had sent its dramatic critic to report the opening. Most of the big music publishers came down to hear the songs. Everybody in show business, and a lot of those who played around the edges of it, managed to run down to the Jersey resort to take in Ziegfeld's new show.

The only ones from New York whom I knew were Irving Berlin, Harry Von Tilzer, and Henry Watterson—all music publishers. Naturally, they were interested, as I was singing their songs.

They pointed out Diamond Jim Brady, Lillian Russell, so gorgeous looking that even the *Follies* girls paled beside her, Fay Templeton, Weber and

Fields, George M. Cohan, Sam Harris, C. B. Dillingham, and a lot more celebrities.

"You've got your chance tonight, Sophie," Irving said to me just before the show was on. "If you carry this crowd, nobody can stop you from now on."

"Watch me," I replied.

Take it from me, a first-night audience of New Yorkers or Londoners is the toughest audience in the world to play to. A first night in Chicago is pie; the audience is right with you from the start to the end of the show. They *want* the show to go over, and they let you feel it. But New York first-nighters—and that was what our first audience at Atlantic City was made up of—make you quiver and shake. Oh, they're polite. They never fail to give each performer a reception when she comes on. But the next minute they freeze up and lean back in their seats and defy you to get them. That's what makes them so tough.

I had my first taste of them that night in Atlantic City. I had stage fright, as who wouldn't at her first big show, and playing to the most critical audience in the world? It was the first time I'd ever played to an audience all in evening dress. I can't explain why the clothes seemed to make such a difference, but they did. But I quickly discovered that my fright was shared by every member of the company, even by Harry Kelly and Bessie Clayton and others who were veteran performers.

Of course that kind of audience puts you on your mettle. It challenges you to do your best. It's as stimulating as a new love affair. What receptions they gave the stars that night! The house buzzed with enthusiasm when Lillian Lorraine made her entrance, coming from the flies in a rose-covered swing— a beautiful number, and her beauty dominated the whole stage. A skit followed this; then came my jungle song.

Everybody laughed at our animal costumes, got the idea, enjoyed the timeliness of it. It was a good number, but that was all. No sensation. I had the feeling that it followed too close on Lillian Lorraine's appearance. It would have gone better later in the show. As for me, all the audience saw in me was a big gal with a big voice. I was miles away from making any impression.

I dressed for my specialty: cloth-of-gold gown, gold slippers, my hair brushed till it shone like the same golden metal. The callboy knocked on the dressing-room door.

"Fifteen minutes, Miss Tucker," he warned me.

I would have liked to stand in the wings to watch the show but I was told I was in the way. My eye fell on a ladder leading to the flies. I mounted it a few steps, so I had a clear view of the stage. Nora Bayes and Jack Norworth were on singing "Shine on, Harvest Moon." She was dressed exquisitely. What an artist! They took six or seven encores. Bessie Clayton followed them. Her dancing brought the audience to its feet, cheering her. Then came the first bars of my music.

I had brought along a cup of water and I set it on a ledge of the switch-board where I could reach it quickly when I came off to the wings. A man was sitting on a high stool beside the switchboard, watching the show and making notes. He spoke to me.

"It's a big scene we're staging behind you, Miss Tucker. Give us time to set it."

This, I knew, was the costliest number in the show, the big battleship finale in which each girl represented a country and wore a ship headdress. That one number cost forty thousand dollars to produce.

"I have rehearsed only three songs," I told the man on the stool. "But there are more in my book if you want me to kill time."

I missed his reply because just then came the bar on which I made my entrance.

Funny, isn't it, how a person will remember some things in her life so vividly that every little detail stands out? And other things, that may be a lot more important, are just a blur. Even the time it took for those things to happen shortens up, like a concertina when you squeeze the wind out of its folds. That's the way it is with my appearance in the *Follies*. I know I sang my three songs. I know that critical, hard-to-please audience ate them up and yelled for more. I know I sang three additional songs and still the applause kept up, demanding more. I know instead of playing six minutes— just long enough to give the crew time to set the big battleship number— I did twelve minutes and held up the scene that cost forty thousand dollars and which Mr. Ziegfeld considered the smash hit of the show. I know that I, the "patsy," stopped the *Follies* cold.

The man on the stool was Mr. Abe Erlanger. Not that I knew it, or cared, when I ran off to the wings, frantic with the excitement of my success.

"Where the hell is my glass of water?" I shouted at him.

"Who do you think you're talking to?" he snapped back.

"What do I care? Quick, give it to me. My throat is dry." I took a good swallow from the cup I found off in a corner. "I tied the damn show up in a knot," I crowed at him. "Listen to them out there. They want more."

They did too. There was no getting round it. Those hard-boiled first nighters liked Sophie Tucker and wanted more of her. I could have gone on singing for another twelve minutes but I was up against the hard-and-fast rule of show business.

"Out of the way, please, Miss Tucker," Mr. Erlanger ordered sharply, "The show must go on."

What did I care about the rest of the show? Mollie's arms were around me. She was hugging me while I laughed and cried all together. "I did it, Mollie. I did it, didn't I?"

"You were great!" Mollie was nearly as excited as I was. "From now on you're going places, Patsy."

"Yes, and when I do, you're going with me. You'll be my maid, Mollie. We'll go all over the world, you and I."

The battleship number was on now, but for all the attention the audience paid the marvelous set and costumes or the singing, the stage might have been dark. Oh, they applauded. But it wasn't the forty-thousand-dollar scene they were applauding. It was me—Sophie Tucker. All through the number the house kept on applauding and calling for me to come back. The battleship finale fell flatter than a pancake.

Of course after what had happened there was bound to be an upset of some sort. You simply couldn't pass it off. Even the evasive Mr. Ziegfeld couldn't go on ignoring Sophie Tucker.

What's next? I asked myself, changing in my dressing room during the intermission. Already I heard rumblings downstairs where the stars had their dressing rooms.

Ordinarily I would have left the theater then, since my part in the show was over. But I decided to hang around and see what was going to happen. What was Mr. Ziegfeld going to say to me?

Nothing happened right away. The second act began; the show went on. Number after number played to a hit, though none had the success that had been mine. Then came the final curtain and applause and curtain calls. There was no doubt of it, the *Follies of 1909* was a success. We would move into New York in a few days to find the town ready to storm the New York Roof.

Gradually I became aware of something going on downstairs that I knew must have to do with me. Angry voices. Nora Bayes's, quick and sharp. Mad. "I won't have her in the show with me. I'm the star. I'm the singer of this show. No other singer, I tell you. Either she goes out, or I go."

Bang! A door slammed violently.

I stood petrified, my heart bursting, all my jubilation exploded like a balloon. There was no mistaking who it was Nora Bayes objected to. And if she objected, if the star threatened to quit, why, my own common sense told me that Mr. Ziegfeld would send me packing before he risked upsetting her. I peeked over the railing. Mr. Ziegfeld, Mr. Erlanger, and Julian Mitchell were huddled together in a knot outside Miss Bayes's door. I sneaked back and waited until I heard the stars leave the theater. Everyone else had gone, too, to supper parties and fun. Only the maids were left, hanging up costumes, packing up. I stole into Lillian Lorraine's dressing room to find Mollie.

"Mollie, you heard what happened? What will I do? Why should Nora Bayes do that to me? I didn't interfere with her. It isn't fair she should take my chance away."

"Now, Patsy"—Mollie's face was grave—"you've got to remember this is show business. Even a star like Miss Bayes has got to protect herself. Remember, no one must interfere with her success."

"But what will become of me? If Mr. Ziegfeld puts me out like she told him to . . ."

"Go on home," Mollie advised. "Go to bed and get some sleep. Rehearsal is called for ten tomorrow morning. Maybe everything will be fixed up by then."

Out on the Boardwalk I found Irving Berlin waiting for me. I poured out the story to him: "Nora Bayes told Mr. Ziegfeld he'd have to put me out of the show. They can't do that to me just when I'm getting a start."

"Listen, kid"—Irving repeated Mollie's words—"this is show business. You know what you did tonight, don't you? After this there's no stopping you. You're going places, young lady. Only yours will be the hard way. And remember, the hard way is the best way. I've got to go back to New York tonight. Keep in touch with me. Let me know what happens." And he was gone.

Tossing on my boardinghouse bed I thought of a thousand things. To lose my place in the *Follies* was bad enough. To lose the salary attached to it was calamitous. Every dollar of that hundred a week was already laid out according to carefully considered plans. If Nora Bayes won out and I received my notice, then all those plans would fail. As the first streaks of dawn glimmered in the dark square of my window I considered taking Mr. Ziegfeld into my confidence, begging him to keep me on for just a few weeks until I could get a chance to go back into vaudeville. Of course it was midsummer. It would be hard to get bookings now, still I could try. The milkman was rattling bottles along the street as I finally dozed off.

I was prompt for the morning rehearsal. From my seat in the last row

I watched the company come in—all but Nora Bayes. Mr. Ziegfeld announced several changes in the running order of the show.

"Miss Tucker," he said, and my heart bobbed up into my throat, "you will do only the jungle song."

The stillness that filled the theater spoke louder than any words what everybody was thinking. Every member of the company knew by now what had happened. Probably they all had been waiting to see what Mr. Ziegfeld would do. They began to crowd round me.

"Sorry, Miss Tucker."

"Rotten luck, Miss Tucker."

"Better luck next time, kid."

It was good to feel their understanding. They meant to be kind. But they couldn't know the relief I was feeling. True, I had lost my chance on Broadway. But I wasn't fired. So long as they kept me in the cast, even just to sing the jungle song, I could draw that hundred dollars a week. Moses's law course was safe. Mama could go ahead and pick out the house she wanted. Son could go away to a good boarding school. Anna could have new, pretty clothes—a good time. Somehow or other I would pull out. I kept hearing Mollie's words of advice:

"There's other shows. Do your one song great, Patsy, and when the season's over you'll get a chance in another show. You'll see. It'll turn out all right. If you've got the goods, and you have, there's nobody can take your chance away from you."

What a wise Mollie! And what a lot I owe to her. She kept me from feeling resentful and bitter. She made me see that this was just one of the tough breaks that show business is full of. You have to learn to take them without flinching, without letting them turn you sour or making you want to get even, either with the person who does you the injustice, or with others who might seem to be in your way.

The summer of 1909 is a long time past. Today I know that my experience with Nora Bayes in the *Follies* taught me more than anything else that ever happened to me in show business. It taught me that show business *is* a business, and a hard-boiled one. If you are in it, it's up to you to protect yourself. No one else is going to do it for you. And there's no room in show business for hurt feelings, resentments, or self-pity.

I learned that lesson early in my career, and I have never forgotten it. You might say that my whole career has been built on it. Certainly, I can truthfully say that a very large part of what success I have had I owe to Nora Bayes, who taught me, even in a backhanded way, how to win that success. It is what I learned from her more than any other one thing that made me what I am today. In all the eight weeks of rehearsals, and afterward until she left the show, Nora Bayes never spoke one word to me or gave a sign that she knew I existed. Naturally, I couldn't speak to her. She was the star. That experience in itself is something I can never forget. In every show I have been in, as the star, or headlining the bill, I have known every single person in the cast. I've made it like one big family.

Nearly ten years after that experience in the *Follies* I was formally introduced to Nora Bayes at a luncheon party. She was immediately cordial. Neither I nor she ever said a word to reveal that I was the girl she ordered out of the *Follies*. I was always one of her admirers and always went to see her work whenever I could. As years went on we became close friends. I think I was one of the last to be entertained at her home before she went to the hospital to have the operation from which she never recovered. But the *Follies of 1909* was something neither of us ever mentioned.

Knowing Nora taught me another lesson: to live modestly. Nora was extravagant in all that she did. She loved life and living. She traveled with a staff of secretaries, servants, pianists, and manager. She adopted three lovely children and added them and a governess to her train. And she was always surrounded by hangers-on. Her party filled several suites in the hotels.

When I would meet Nora in some city she would always fuss with me:

"Sophie, you *must* take a suite. You must live well. It helps your prestige. People take notice of you. It makes you important."

"I can't afford to do those things," I would answer.

"Nonsense. You're in the big brackets."

"Just the same, I can't spend money just on myself. It's enough I spend lavishly on my clothes and on my acts. I have my family, remember. I must save a few dollars too. I can't sing forever. What if I lose my voice? Who is going to take care of me, or them, then?"

But Nora wouldn't listen. She earned a lot and she lived the way she wanted to. I would have liked to live extravagantly, too, as she did. But I couldn't, not when I knew that money would buy things for other people that they wouldn't have otherwise. Yes, I learned a lot from Nora Bayes.

We came to New York and opened at the New York Roof on the twenty-second of June. Nora Bayes had had her way with Mr. Ziegfeld, still she was not happy. There was constant friction which was felt by the entire cast. Then we heard that she was leaving the show. Eva Tanguay was coming to take her place.

For a day I had a wild hope that now Mr. Ziegfeld would let me do my specialty again. No such luck, however.

Tanguay came. She heard the jungle song and asked to rehearse it. The next day there was a notice in my box telling me that my services were no longer required.

CHAPTER 9: *Mollie & Co.*

NEW YORK may have had hotter summers than that one of 1909, but I don't remember them. Through those late July and early August days the city sweltered under a burning blanket. No air-conditioned restaurants and theaters then to give you a breathing spell when you felt you couldn't live in that furnace another minute.

In our apartment the temperature hung persistently around one hundred. Moe and I pushed our cots as close as possible to the fire escape and tried to pretend we got more air that way.

We did a lot of pretending. We pretended we weren't afraid of being alone in New York and stony broke. I pretended I didn't feel like something stepped on and squashed flat by being let out of the *Follies* after only four weeks' work. Moe pretended he didn't mind hunting for a job to work at after law school which would help to pay some of his expenses at least. And I did my best to pretend I wasn't scared blue because something terrible had happened to my throat which tied my singing pipes up into a knot and wouldn't let me do more than croak like a frog.

To be out of a job was bad enough, especially in late summer when it was next to impossible to pick up any bookings in vaudeville. To lose your voice, and not to know whether it would ever come back, made you know what it is like to live and sleep and wake again with terror for a companion.

But we had one bright star on our horizon—Mollie. She had taken me under her wing that night of the *Follies* opening and she never let me forget that she was my friend whose faith in my ability to get somewhere, someday, never wavered. On those nerve-racking, sultry afternoons, when the heat and the city's noise seemed to fill our little apartment so full that you couldn't draw a breath, she would come in, fresh and beaming, on her way over to the theater to work for Lillian Lorraine.

"You've got to rest up," she advised. "It's all that upset about losing your job in the *Follies* that's got into your throat and tightened it up. The doctor told you that."

It was Mollie who had insisted on my going to a doctor and who was paying for the visits and the medicine he prescribed. He, too, had ordered rest and freedom from worry. "Give your voice and your nerves a complete rest," he said. An easy prescription to take when you have no money and no job, when the landlord will be looking for his rent on the first of the month, and the grocery stores don't give credit. Confronted by these problems I couldn't help thinking bitterly, why did Nora Bayes have to do that to me? And why did Eva Tanguay have to take away my one song in the show and with it my salary? With one hundred dollars a week Moe and I would be sitting pretty. And I would be able to help Mama and keep Son, and save too.

"You can't afford to let yourself get bitter," Mollie said, again and again. "Getting bitter never did nobody no good. It docs harm. A lot more harm than just losing a job. You do what the doctor says: rest, don't worry. Bill and I'll see you through. (Bill was her husband.) We'll look out for you till you get your voice back again and get into another show."

"Mollie, I can't take your money. All my life I've earned for myself."

"Sure, and you'll do it again," she replied confidently. "You ain't finished, Patsy. You've got what it takes to go places."

I looked around our sparsely furnished flat, at the bare kitchen, the empty icebox. "This doesn't look like it," I said grimly.

"You didn't see yet what I brought you." Mollie spoke as soothingly as though I were a sick child. "Lamb stew. That Bill Elkins just gets to hankering after a lamb stew every so often; seems like nothing else just hits the right spot with him. I cooked enough for all of us. For you and Brother Moe when he gets home. And coming down I stopped at the grocery and fetched along some eggs and milk and things. You eat a good supper now, Patsy, and see what it does for those pipes of yours."

"I can't let you spend your and Bill's money on me," I objected, but faintly. The stew, as Mollie unwrapped the package, smelled wonderful. You can't live on a cup of coffee a day and not get hungry.

"You don't need to worry about this money," said Mollie, and gave me a wink.

"You made it on the horses?"

"That's right. So long as the luck stays with me and I've got two bucks to bet 'em on the nose, you ain't going hungry, Patsy."

Then while I ate the stew she entertained me with backstage gossip from the *Follies* and a couple of stories that made me laugh for the first time in days. It wasn't till after she had gone and I was washing up that I found the dollar bill she had dropped into a cup on the kitchen shelf.

Mollie played the horses—a two-dollar bet was her limit—and the luck stayed with her. Out of her winnings she kept Moe and me. We might have been her children the way she mothered us. She shared with us her money, her food, and, what was even more valuable, her philosophy. Hers was a philosophy which would admit neither defeat, resentment, nor despair. She radiated a goodness that was invincible. In later years I was to meet a fair number of men and women the world considers great. For true greatness of spirit I have never met anyone who outmatched Mollie.

She was determined that I should not let my experience in the *Follies* build up a resentment against either of the stars who had refused to let me shine near them. I have already told of my friendship in later years with Nora Bayes. I have always been glad that Mollie herself was a witness to my meeting with Eva Tanguay.

It happened some fifteen years later, when I was headlining the Majestic Theatre in Milwaukee. I opened that Monday afternoon with a very bad cold. Eva Tanguay had been the headliner the previous week. She was the biggest attraction in vaudeville, barring none; the most publicized and highest-paid performer. Her salary at the time was five thousand a week. She was laying off in Milwaukee, spending a few days with friends, and she came to see my opening matinee. The manager brought her backstage to meet me.

I'll never forget that meeting. I was sitting in a light-weight kimono over silk underwear when Eva came in. She took one good look at me and then started in to give me hell. No wonder I had a cold. "You don't dress properly. . . . In the winter . . . A girl with your voice . . . You should take better care of yourself. . . . Wait a minute, I'll be right back. . . ." Out she dashed to the nearest department store and to a drugstore, and back she came with a lovely set of silk-and-wool underwear and a bottle of cough medicine. She, herself, insisted on getting me into the one and dosing me with the other, scolding me the whole time. The minute I was fixed up to her liking off went the dynamo. Neither of us said one word about the *Follies of 1909.* In fact, I am sure Eva Tanguay never associated me with the girl who had sung the jungle number and whose job she had taken away. She didn't know who I was any more than a rabbit.

Mollie, pushed into a corner by Eva, was taking it all in with a big grin on her face.

"Well, Mollie, are you proud of me?"

"Yes, Patsy, you've learned all right not to carry any bitterness in your heart. I'm going to live to see you getting five thousand a week, same as Miss Tanguay."

Eva Tanguay was famous not only for the sums she made, but for those she spent. Every gown she wore cost from five hundred to fifteen hundred dollars. Her bill for gloves and hose alone was one thousand dollars a month. She dressed and lived in the grand manner, giving away her money freely. She was a tradition in show business. Several years after our meeting in Milwaukee, Eva Tanguay was in Chicago, at the Hotel Sherman, her life savings, furs, jewels all gone. Her eyes had started to go bad with cataracts and she suffered from arthritis.

It was a tribute, I think, to Mollie's philosophy that it should be I to whom Eva Tanguay turned for help in those dark days. I was able to raise the money immediately among the members of our profession so she could have the needed operation on her eyes. While she is still alive and bedridden her stanch friends such as Joe Schenck, Eddie Cantor, Irene Castle, as well as many others in and out of the profession who answered my call for help for one of the great stars of American vaudeville, are standing by.

It was about this time, 1929, that I had my first meeting with Florenz Ziegfeld since I was in and out of his *Follies of 1909*. He was then producing Noel Coward's *Bittersweet* at the Ziegfeld Theatre, Fifty-fourth Street and Sixth Avenue, in New York, starring Evelyn Laye.

I had met Noel and Evelyn in London. On their arrival in New York they phoned me to lunch with them and to watch a rehearsal. Evelyn, Noel, and I were walking arm in arm toward the theater when whom should we bump into but Mr. Ziegfeld—the same charming Mr. Ziegfeld I remembered from those weeks of rehearsals twenty years before. He was full of praises for my work.

"But, Mr. Ziegfeld"—I couldn't resist putting it up to him—"why haven't you played me in any of your shows all these years?"

"You made too much money in cafés and vaudeville," he replied. "I should have placed you under a personal contract when I saw you tie up the show in Atlantic City in 1909. But I had so many worries, so much to think about, I let you get away from me. Much to my regret."

I waited nearly twenty years for that bouquet.

After the third or fourth week of rest I found my voice coming back. Immediately up went my spirits. One day I went down to Tin Pan Alley to the office of Watterson, Berlin, and Snyder to have a talk with Irving Berlin. He knew about the bad break I had had in the *Follies*. So did all the boys at the music publishers'. They were all sorry for me. More than once they'd slipped me a buck or two to help out through those idle weeks. But now I didn't want sympathy or a loan. It was songs I was after.

Several days later I was rehearsing in one of the music rooms when the door suddenly flew open. A man's voice shouted: "Who's the colored gal? What a pair of pipes." Then, catching sight of me, "I beg your pardon. A white girl. My God! you're Abuza's daughter from the restaurant in Hartford. Do you remember me?"

"Of course I remember you," I sang out. "You're Harry Cooper, of the Empire City Quartette."

"That's right. Many a time I ate in your father's restaurant and you sang for me."

"Funny I never bumped into you since I've been knocking around," I said. "I've been in New York nearly three years now."

He wanted to know right away where I was working. I said nothing about the *Follies,* only that I had been having a bad time with my throat and was hoping to get started again.

"Listen," he said. "On Sunday night I'm playing a benefit at the hotel down at Arverne, Long Island. You come down too. I'll make a place for you on the bill. There's no money in it, but there'll be a big crowd, and there are sure to be some booking agents or theater managers on hand to look the acts over. Do you know who William Morris is?"

"No."

Harry Cooper proceeded to explain that William Morris was then opening his own circuit of vaudeville houses, the American Music Halls.

"Music hall is what the English call a vaudeville theater. Morris is one swell guy. If he thinks you're good he'll give you every break. If you make good in one of his houses he'll play you in them all. I'll have a talk with Ed Bloom. He's Mr. Morris's manager. He'll be over at Arverne Sunday night. Remember if he likes you you're all set. And listen, kid, with pipes like yours you can't miss."

That's how it happened that on a Sunday morning in late August Mollie and I took the train out to Arverne. I had Mollie's suitcase (mine was pawned long since) and in it a dress which Mollie had worn for years, her purple slippers, her silk hose. Even her make-up kit, plus a new box of white powder.

My first impulse on getting a chance to perform again had been to go to Mrs. Simon and rent a dress. But Mollie had put her foot down.

"You can't afford it. Take my yellow lace. I'll refit it for you. It'll be lucky. I've seen you through so far. I'm going the limit now!"

"If you could only go with me," I sighed.

"I am going. I'll go down and dress you. It'll make you look important. Your personal maid. After all we've been through, Patsy, do you think I'd miss seeing you tie this show up in a knot?"

We started early, as I had to be there to rehearse with the orchestra. I carried the suitcase. Mollie had the luncheon box she had packed with fried chicken, tomatoes, bread and butter. Mollie was very light-colored. She could have passed anywhere as white. We might have been any two girls off for a day at the beach, instead of two adventurers with wildly beating hearts and hopes too big and glittering to put into words.

I rehearsed three songs: "The Lovin' Rag," which always went well with audiences and which no one in the East was singing; a dramatic Southern song, "My Southern Rose"; and Irving Berlin's new "Wild Cherry Rag." Thank God my voice sounded all right.

After the rehearsal Mollie and I found a quiet spot on the beach where we could eat our lunch. "We've got to save some for supper," Mollie said prudently. Even though Harry Cooper was going to give me a big build-up with Ed Bloom, there wasn't any money for me in this benefit performance.

The sun was still hot on the beach when we started back to the hotel to get ready. Mollie dressed me, even to the gold rose she had bought for my hair.

"You strut like a peacock," she said, proud of her work.

I still didn't know what spot I'd be on the big bill of so many acts. Suddenly I was scared. The chicken was talking to me. Suppose my voice failed suddenly.

"Mollie, I'm frightened. Suppose they put me on one before closing."

Before she could reply came a voice: "Miss Tucker. Mr. Cooper wants to see you."

"Go on, Patsy." Mollie gave me a little push. "Pick up your train. Here" —she held out something—"it's my diamond ring. Put it on. Put on this gold bracelet. The horses ran right for me yesterday and I got my jewelry out of pawn. Wear them for luck. Go on now, strut your stuff."

I found Harry Cooper ready to go on the stage.

"Stand by in the wings," he told me. "You follow our act as soon as we finish. I will introduce you."

"But, Harry," I protested, "I'm a singer too. It's no good. You'll take the edge off my work. I can't follow a singing act."

"We're four men," he reminded me. "There hasn't been a single woman on the second half of the bill. I heard you rehearse this morning. Your songs are different from ours. Pull yourself together, kid. I'm going to give you a big build-up. You can't miss."

He was on, and I was standing in the wings watching him, with Mollie standing alongside me.

The Empire City Quartette was the greatest comedy and singing act of the day. Harry had a marvelous baritone voice. The other boys were Harry Mayo, the tenor; Harry Tally, bass; and Harry's brother, Irving Cooper, the soprano. That night the house gave them a terrific reception, as always when they appeared anywhere.

I clutched Mollie's arm. "I'll never make it after this," I whispered to her. "My legs are wobbling under me."

"Come on, Patsy," she steadied me. "You've been waiting for this chance for weeks. God gave you back your voice. He gave it to you for a purpose. Use it. Don't forget those promises you made to me. Don't let me down. And don't disappoint Mr. Cooper."

I heard Harry Cooper talking to the audience: "Ladies and gentlemen, I was up at the music publishers' a few weeks ago and I heard a singer rehearsing. I thought it was a colored girl at first, until I walked into the room, and there was a kid rehearsing coon songs—a kid who used to wait on me in her father's restaurant back in Hartford, Connecticut. I want you to hear her. If my judgment is wrong, and if she doesn't do to you what she did to me—I mean *thrill you*—with as big a pair of pipes as you've ever heard, then blame it on me. Introducing to you Miss Sophie Tucker. . . ."

"Go on, Patsy," I heard Mollie whisper, and felt her gentle shove.

I was out on the makeshift stage. The ballroom was packed. I could hear the women buzzing. They thought I looked nice. I had my hair up on top of my head in a million curls. My gown was long, with a train of ruffles. I looked twenty-five years old. I caught the voices: "What a kid!" "A husky kid."

The audience was warmed up now. Harry had disarmed them completely. The build-up he had promised me was marvelous. I gave them the first song, my old stand-by, "The Lovin' Rag," and I felt the audience swaying with me, tapping their fingers on their programs, beating time. They liked the song. Then the second number, "My Southern Rose." Suddenly I remembered I'd forgotten to ask whoever was taking charge of the props to have a chair ready for me so I could lean on it while I sang this number. That was how I had rehearsed it.

"Oh, Mollie," I called. "A chair, please, for this number."

Out came Mollie, toddling as only colored people with their inborn sense of rhythm can. Toddling to her own humming, and grinning broadly, she brought out the chair. The audience began to laugh.

"Here's yo' chair, honey chile," and off she toddled, to a roar of delighted laughter. I was laughing too.

The orchestra was now beginning to play the music for "My Southern Rose." Suddenly I remembered I needed a prop red rose to hold in my hand while singing. I had forgotten to buy one that afternoon. But there was the flower in my hair. That would have to do. It seemed as though a million hairpins got in my way; as though all my fingers were thumbs. But I had the gold rose.

The stage was all blacked out. I was in a white spotlight, leaning over the back of the chair, the gold rose in my hand. I forgot all about the audience, everything, everybody. I had to make believe I had a real red rose in my hand, singing a dramatic song of the South. I had laughed so hard at Mollie the tears were in my eyes. Never mind, the tears will help put the song across. If I cry, the audience will cry too.

All through the darkness of the ballroom I could see hankies coming out. Good! It worked. A new trick. I'll keep those in the act: the business with Mollie over the chair, the rose. They're good stuff; make my act different from just standing in the center of the stage singing one song after another.

All this I thought to myself as I was singing. To this very day, when anything strikes me, when I get a new idea or if some accident happens on the stage that I can turn to advantage, I always try to elaborate on it and keep it in my act.

I had saved "Wild Cherry Rag" for my last song. It was a novelty song, with a very catchy melody. In my excitement at the rehearsals I'd omitted to show the orchestra leader where the musical breaks in this particular number came in. When it came to the part for the orchestra to play them, the musicians didn't know what to do, so I whistled them. My intention was just to show the orchestra what I meant for the first strain, thinking they would catch on for the balance. But my whistling a rhythm break was more of a novelty than for the orchestra to play it. The audience picked it up so quickly that when I came to the second break the whole house whistled it. And the song, just by this accident, was a riot. Had I rehearsed it properly, the song possibly would never have meant a thing. So in one performance I discovered two new tricks, *my own tricks,* to make my singing of songs different.

The audience wanted more. But three songs were all I had rehearsed. I felt I was a big hit. Better not spoil it, singing without a rehearsal. Besides, the Empire City Quartette had sung for over thirty minutes. I mustn't overdo it. But Mollie must take a bow. She had made a hit, toddling on with the chair. She must get credit for helping put my act over.

"Come on, Mollie, and take a bow," I yelled off stage. "You're part of my act now."

There was terrific applause as Mollie toddled on again.

Harry Cooper was standing in the entrance. I walked over, took his hand, and drew him on the stage with me. "Harry, I hope I didn't disappoint you. You made this tryout possible for me and I'm grateful to you."

Harry put it up to the audience. "Are you satisfied with my judgment that this kid can sing?"

The applause said that they were.

Well, it wasn't just my imagination that the audience liked me. Ed Bloom came back after the show and booked me for the following week at Mr. Morris's ace house, the American Music Hall at Forty-second Street and Eighth Avenue in New York. Salary, forty dollars.

"We're starting to climb," said Mollie, packing up the yellow lace dress. "I'll just run out and give that box of chicken to the first hungry-looking man I see. After that, Patsy, you and me'll celebrate on a beefsteak!"

CHAPTER 10: *Vaudeville, Big-Time*

No WONDER that day at Arverne stands out in my mind after all these years as clearly as if it was only yesterday. I turned a corner that day, perhaps one of the most important corners in my life.

I didn't know it at the time. I don't suppose we ever do realize when we make the fatal swing out of one road into another. It isn't till afterward, when we have climbed a hill and caught our breath, that we can look back over the way we've come and see where the important turns were and where, only for a friend's helping hand and what seemed an accident at the time, we got started on the right road. At the time I was chiefly excited about getting a job that would give me some money and a chance to get bookings in vaudeville. Now I know that infinitely more valuable than the job itself and the chance it offered to get out of debt was the connection it gave me with that great man in show business, William Morris.

A finer man and a more lovable character never lived. For twenty-eight years, except for the interval after the failure of the American Music Hall and Mr. Morris's stay up at Saranac to get back his health, he was my "Boss." The agency he founded still handles me. I'm their oldest client; not in years but in terms of paying my weekly commissions. "Junior," whom I remember in short pants, inherited me along with the firm. Back in the early days there was an office boy named Abe who used to usher me in to see the Boss. He was Abe Lastfogel, who is now an equal partner in the agency and continues the tradition the Boss trained us both in.

William Morris had been a booking agent on his own and then for a combine of Klaw and Erlanger that invaded the vaudeville field. The competition between this company and the United Booking Office formed by the Keith-Albee interests was so keen, each side bidding against the other for popular acts, sending up the salaries of performers, that finally United paid Klaw and Erlanger $150,000 to get out of vaudeville and stay out for ten years. Promptly, and determined to stay in vaudeville, William Morris started his own circuit of American Music Halls. This was just a few months before he signed me on.

He was a man of imagination, terrific foresight, and big ideas. And he had the daring to follow them through. He believed ardently in vaudeville as the greatest popular entertainment. And he believed the American people appreciated great performers. But what endeared William Morris to everyone and especially to the performers he booked was his personal interest in *them*. That was the grandest thing in our show business. If he watched you work, he would come around backstage and give you the best creative criticism a performer could possibly get. "I'd tone it down just a little bit if I were you," he might say. "I wouldn't play it quite so fast. Slow it down a trifle," or, "You weren't right on your timing tonight, dear. It didn't get across the way it should. Watch that." "Always play to your audience," was one bit of advice he gave you again and again.

What that kind of criticism does for a performer! It gives you a feeling of security, of knowing there's somebody who wants you to do your work well and who is standing by to see that you do. In the case of foreign actors it makes all the difference between their being a success with American audiences and a flop. Harry Lauder knew this. That was why he stuck to William Morris without there ever being a contract between them for all the seasons he played this country. In all the years I have been with the Morris Agency there has never been a piece of paper between us.

That interest in the actor was backed up by big salaries. William Morris's circuit was the beginning of big money paid to vaudeville performers. In his houses the bills ran from twenty to twenty-two acts, as compared to the eight or ten acts on the Keith bills. Continuing the tradition of Tony Pastor, Mr. Morris brought over every British music-hall star he could find—Sir

Harry Lauder, Marie Lloyd, Alice Lloyd, Lily Lena, Arthur Prince, Vesta Victoria, Charlie Chaplin in "A Night in an English Music Hall," George Lockwood, and many others. He paid these British stars three and four times more than they got in England.

To the American performers playing his circuit he was just as generous. Nowadays, a lot of people seem to think that big money for actors didn't start until Hollywood became the capital of show business. As a matter of fact, way back in 1909 and 1910 William Morris was paying such weekly salaries as:

Julian Eltinge, Female Impersonator	$3,500
Pauline, the Hypnotist	$4,000
Montgomery and Moore	$2,500
Empire City Quartette	$2,500
Jim Jeffries, Prize Fighter	$5,000
Grace La Rue	$2,500
Consul the Monk	$2,500
Elizabeth Murray	$1,500
Juliet	$1,500

Besides these, I, engaged to play my first week at the American Music Hall at Forty-second Street and Eighth Avenue, New York City, at forty dollars, was an also-ran. But the act went over, and I was held over for a second week. Immediately Mr. Morris raised me to seventy-five dollars, making it possible for me to buy another dress to have a change. When I started on the road my salary was raised again to one hundred dollars.

At last I was on "big-time." Two shows a day instead of three. Top prices, one dollar and a half. And every bill with two or three—occasionally four—headliners.

With such salaries as I have cited paid to headliners and standard acts it is easy to figure that the salaries for a week's bill on "big-time" would run easily to twenty thousand or twenty-five thousand dollars. In the small-time houses the salaries for a show usually ran weekly from five thousand to seven thousand dollars.

Mollie couldn't go with me, of course. Even on a one-hundred-dollar-a-week salary I couldn't afford a personal maid. Besides, Mollie still had her job with Lillian Lorraine, who was making a big hit in the *Follies,* and there was Bill and her home to be looked after. Whenever I played any house in Greater New York, Mollie would manage to be with me.

"Someday I'll be making enough so I can afford to take you with me everywhere I go," I promised, hugging her.

"Remember, Patsy, I'm always rooting for you," was her final farewell to me.

For the first time since I started in show business I knew what it was not to be worried about money. With the responsibilities I was carrying I couldn't be wasteful or extravagant, but every Sunday night my pay envelope was there for me and enough in it to take care of me and the folks back home. Every Monday morning I would be the first one at the post office to buy the three money orders I sent every week, regular as clockwork: one to Mama, one to Moe who was now able to give all his time and attention to his law course at New York University, and my commission to the "boss."

The sense of security that I got out of that pay envelope along with the greenbacks did a lot for my work. I know I worked harder to make my act a success and sang better because I was free from the kind of anxiety that had caused me to lose my voice after my experience in the *Follies*. William Morris was wise enough to know that by paying performers good salaries he got better work from them.

He never let one performer on a bill interfere with another. Everyone had an equal chance. Though his bills ran to twenty and even twenty-two acts, he was careful to have only one singer, one mimic, one wire walker or trapeze performer on each bill. Every act had its chance, and every act was expected to prove its value in the only way that this ever can be done—by box-office receipts.

The system of the New York office was to send out weekly, to every house on the circuit, a list of the performers on that week's bill, starting with the headliner and running down to the opening act. The headliner was always put on one or two before the end of the show. The value of each act on the bill was indicated by the size of type used for the name. After each name came a line telling what the act was—toe dancer, ventriloquist, comedian, et cetera.

From this list the theater manager knew how to arrange his bill. The local publicity man knew who to feature in the newspapers that week and what each performer's specialty was. Billing—that, as every theater manager would tell you, was their grief. It seemed as if the headliners—who got all the space in the press, anyway—were never satisfied. I have known them to walk out of a show simply because their names didn't appear in type as big as they thought they were entitled to. Or, if there were two headliners, and their names appeared side by side, the one who drew the left-hand side of the bill would be jealous and ready to bite the manager's head off.

Jack Lait, *Mirror* editor, was then William Morris's publicity man in

Chicago when I arrived there to play my first week at the American Music Hall at Peck Court and Wabash Avenue. I found myself Number Four on an eighteen-act bill. Pauline, the Hypnotist, and Julian Eltinge, Female Impersonator, were the two top headliners that week. Jack Lait, following orders, had spread big stories about them both in all the Chicago papers. I didn't get a line. Even on the program there was nothing after my name to tell the audience what I did to entertain. For some reason or other the New York office had failed to send Jack Lait any information about me. He didn't know whether I was a singer, a juggler, or a leopard tamer.

That house was very much like Hammerstein's in New York, with a bar on the mezzanine floor. A long, narrow theater, very intimate, and a very warm house. The audience at the Monday matinee was wonderful. I found that in Chicago, as in New York, the same people came to every Monday matinee, week after week, fifty-two weeks a year. They knew every performer on big-time and they welcomed their favorites with a grand reception. I had had absolutely no build-up, but they liked my songs, and they kept me there on the stage, calling for more and more, refusing to let the next act go on until I told them I had no more songs to sing. I sang for a half-hour.

The minute the act was over Jack Lait dashed to his typewriter and tore off a piece for the evening editions, telling Chicago to come to the American Music Hall and hear "The Mary Garden of Ragtime." That title was a burst of inspiration, not only for Chicagoans who worshiped their gorgeous-looking prima donna, but for American audiences everywhere. I carried that line for many years as my billing. It was Jack Lait, too, who spread the word to Ashton Stevens, Amy Leslie, Percy Hammond, and Charlie Collins, the dramatic critics of the Chicago press: "Go to the Music Hall and see and hear a great gal with a pair of pipes, that the audience made their own headliner at the opening matinee today from a twenty-act bill."

Seeing my name played up in the papers for the first time was a thrill. Now to repeat the hit at the night show when, so Jack Lait said, the critics would be there. I went on with my heart in my mouth. The green chiffon hanky in my hand shook like a lettuce leaf with the jitters. But the reception the audience gave me cured my stage fright immediately. That reception could only mean that the people who had liked me that afternoon had already told their friends about me. What a friendly gang to do a thing like that! Chicagoans are wonderful that way. If they like you they let you know it, and no halfway about it, either. They had made me their headliner and their headliner I've stayed up to this very day. Jack Lait grinned when he showed me the report he was wiring in to the New York office. It read: *"Sophie Tucker the hit of the show."*

The critics came across as gracefully as it is possible for professional highbrows to bow to the public's choice. They all took a whack at my size and the size of my voice and my brand of coon songs which, according to Charlie Collins, "were not for parlor use, but were certainly a success with the audience." Amy Leslie, of the Chicago *Daily News,* qualified her calling my songs "near to shocking" by adding: "But Miss Tucker's fairness, her calm amiability, ready smile, and emphatic gestures carry her through, even without a bump."

Ashton Stevens's piece in the Chicago *Examiner* still gives me so much pleasure I can't resist giving it in full:

. . . And speaking of elephants and ladies, there is Sophie Tucker. If life were as large as Sophie Tucker there would be room for all of us. I don't mind saying at once that Sophie Tucker is my headliner, even if the American management does employ other type and position for her.

She has a voice—well, if Julian Eltinge's singing voice was as virile as Miss Tucker's, he would be executing a long overdue male impersonation. Miss Tucker could have sung right through the matinee and into the evening performance, so far as the audience was concerned. Actually, she had to chase herself away from us with a stupid song. You may recall that Lucy Weston used to do that when the motorcar was honking at the stage door. And Miss Tucker reminds, heavily, of Miss Weston. Some of her songs are red, white, and blue, and some of them omit the red and white. But they are never quite dark navy blue. Rather they are inclined to be evil only to the fellow that brings evil with him.

If your heart is pure and your mind like the beautiful snow, you will have a lovely time while Miss Tucker is singing "But He Only Stays Till Sunday" and "I Just Couldn't Make Ma Feelin's Behave." Even less secular is the New York rag "Carrie," which becomes a syncopated hara-kiri before Miss Tucker has finished you with it.

Miss Tucker can move an audience or a piano with equal address. Don't miss any of her. . . .

I don't know whether it surprised any of the critics to receive a note from me in the next morning's mail, thanking them for their criticism and promising to benefit by it. I sent off the notes right after the second night's show. I do know that we became good friends in the years when I played Chicago so often and for such long engagements that that city became my theatrical home. I lost a good friend in Percy Hammond, and when Amy Leslie died in 1939 a light went out of my life.

For years Amy Leslie was one of Chicago's "characters." No first night in Chicago could begin until Amy, dressed in very gay colors, fluttering shawls and scarves and fur pieces—more of them than any other woman could wear at one time—carrying a staff, not a cane, came down the aisle to take her seat. She was a short woman, on the plumpish side, with bright red, frizzly hair that rose defiantly above her rainbow of colors. When I met her she was already in the fifties. Her penetrating mind and her fearless and witty pen made her one of the powers in the world of show business. Producers, managers, and performers paid court to Amy. Her rooms at the Parkway Hotel, where I knew her for more than twenty-five years, were crowded with rare and beautiful things given her by the show people whose success she helped to make. She had a collection of clocks, I remember, of every sort and description. She adored big, stunning-looking handbags, and her assortment of these was greater than that of any of the performers whose photographs literally covered the walls of her rooms. Amy's bags were given to her and replenished regularly by her friends—David Belasco, Florenz Ziegfeld, A. H. Woods, the Frohmans, C. B. Dillingham, Sam Harris, and others.

One night while I was playing a return engagement in Chicago I was having supper at the Hotel Sherman with Jack Lait. He pointed out Amy Leslie.

"I'd like to meet her," I said impulsively. It wasn't just because she was Chicago's most important dramatic critic. There was something about the little woman with her flaming topknot and her shouting gay colors and glittering jewels that made me love her. There was pity mixed up with the love. For all her gaiety, her importance, her popularity, Amy Leslie impressed me as a very lonely woman.

"Come on, then." Jack Lait jumped up and motioned me to come with him. He took me across the crowded room to Amy's table. From that minute we were friends.

I was right: Amy was lonely. The bright colors were her defense against an enemy I could understand. We never talked about it, but she knew I knew. Then came her marriage to Frank Buck, of "Bring 'Em Back Alive" fame. Frank was twenty years her junior. She was bursting with pride of him. Meanwhile her colors grew gayer, her jewels bigger and more gorgeous, her smile a beam of content. At this time, I remember, her red hair got to misbehaving so she had it all shaved off and wore a lovely red wig until her own hair came in silvery white. In a white, mannish bob Amy looked much more distinguished than she ever had before.

Then her marriage went on the rocks, at about the same time my marriage to Frank Westphal (I'm coming to that part of the story soon) sprang a leak and had to be towed into court. I hadn't seen or heard from Amy in some time when I arrived to play Chicago and phoned her. As usual she came over to the Hotel Sherman and lived with me while I was in town. I knew whatever hurt she had suffered hadn't killed her sense of humor when she greeted me.

"Well, beloved, we *will* have our Franks."

And that one line is all Amy ever said to me about her married life.

She had a terrific sense of humor, and she loved telling stories on herself. I remember her coming in one day grinning over an encounter with the policeman at Clark and Randolph streets, Chicago's busiest corner. Amy was up in years and afraid to cross the traffic alone. She called to the mounted cop:

"Hey, Paul Revere! Help me across the street, please."

"Sure, lady," he beamed down at her, "I'm glad to. Only you've got my name wrong. 'Tis Paul McCafferty, it is."

George Ade, the humorist, was Amy's best friend. On one of her visits to New York with me, George was in town. Knowing what a terrific appetite Amy had, he sent her a big Virginia ham. As ham was taboo in my house, Amy had to take her ham around to George's hotel for her breakfast. How Amy loved to eat! "Remember, food is not to be wasted," she'd say, and finish everyone's plate.

As the years went by and Amy drew near eighty it was pitiful to see that bright mind grow confused, her letters rambling. The *News* pensioned her. She retired into her rooms at the Parkway, hung with relics of the days when she was sought after and courted. Sad to see how few of those who used to wait on Amy Leslie's favor remembered her when her mind and her eyesight were fading and when she could no longer be of use to them. Texas Guinan was the only one I know of who visited Amy in those last dark years. But Amy went to the end undaunted. As she said to me:

"Beloved, my eyes are only tired. They need a rest. Soon I will see you and the sunshine."

And how she loved the sunshine! She made several trips with me to California. While we were there she ordered a copy of the Chicago *News* to be delivered to her. Amy couldn't begin her day without it. The paper came before we were up and was thrown over on the lawn. The neighbor's little six-year-old boy always got it and took care of it till he saw Amy come out on the porch. One morning, as he handed her the paper, she asked him if he would like to marry her. The youngster hesitated a moment. "I don't know if I can marry you," he said, "but I wouldn't mind being your sweetheart." Quoting Amy: "That's Hollywood, true to form."

From the start, when I got my first vaudeville engagement, I had kept all my press notices and letters, even post cards, pasting them into ledgers I bought at the Five-and-Ten. While in Chicago I invested half a dollar in a regular scrapbook. Now that I was on big-time, I was determined to be strictly businesslike about my career and keep a perfect file of everything connected with it. I've kept that self-made promise all these years. There are now five big trunks filled with scrapbooks—the day-to-day records of more than thirty years' work.

As a result of that first big day at the Music Hall in Chicago Jack Lait telegraphed the Boss, advising that I be held over for a second week. I nearly lost my voice from the excitement. I had had no billing for my first week, but for the second week Jack Lait billed me as "The Extra Added Attraction" and "The Mary Garden of Ragtime." I simply *had* to live up to a line like that. Out I dashed to the music publishers' on a hunt for new songs, and stayed up nights learning them. A holdover like that cost money. It meant a new dress for one thing. The audience mustn't hear the same songs or see the same gown a second time.

One of the new songs I found that week was called "There's Company in the Parlor, Girls, Come on Down." It was a *double-entendre* song, and the first one of the sort I ever used in my act. Way back in the days when I was singing at the German Village, Fred Fisher, who wrote a lot of swell songs, used to tell me that that was the kind of song I could and should sing. His argument was that because I was big and gawky, and entirely lacking in what the fashion writers nowadays call "allure," I made a song such as that funny but not salacious.

"Why is it that jokes on sex always get the biggest laughs?" Fred would say. "Because they're about something everybody knows about and thinks about. They're jokes about life—and about a side of life most people don't dare mention above a whisper in the dark. Give an audience a chance to laugh at sex, instead of feeling afraid and ashamed of it, and God, how they love it! They get a feeling of relief right away.

"Of course not everybody can handle a comedy song about sex. You have to walk a hairline. Take a pretty, sexy-looking girl and let her pull something of the sort and it's offensive right away. It's smutty without being funny. There are damn few singers who have what it takes to put a *double-*

entendre song over. But, Soph, you've got it. And if you don't make use of it, cash in on it, you're losing a bet that's worth thousands of smackers to you."

When I heard "There's Company in the Parlor, Girls," those words of Fred's came back to me. It was the kind of song that if you were a prim little teacher from Squedunk you would think mildly amusing, but it would have a very different meaning for the wise guys in the audience. The innocents couldn't find a thing in it to object to, and the others would find a belly laugh in every line. The song, as I figured, was sure to go over big with a Chicago audience because of the famous Everleigh Club in that city which was so popular with all the Chicago playboys. At the same time, every city across the country had a club, patterned more or less after the one owned by the Everleigh sisters. Yes, that song would panic the wise guys in every audience in every town where I might be billed.

I introduced "There's Company in the Parlor, Girls," in my second week at the Music Hall. I was right about it: it brought down the house. After the Monday matinee Jack Lait came back to tell me that all the girls from the Everleigh Club were there to hear me sing the song. The girls became my biggest boosters.

After that week I made it a rule always to have a *double-entendre* song in my act. I would start off with a lively rag, then would come a ballad followed by a comedy song and a novelty number. And finally the hot song. In this way I left the stage with the audience laughing their heads off. For encores I always had popular songs, new ones. I very seldom sang numbers for the audience to sing with me. A lot of performers did that. I was determined to be different.

Occasionally theater managers would ask me to cut out the hot numbers. They were afraid of offending the prissy patrons. But I always came back: "The audience likes them. Listen to them laugh. So long as folks like those songs they stay in my act. My job is to entertain." And the box office continued to show how right I was about this.

Often I am asked: "Why do you sing hot songs?" And I can answer truthfully: "I've never sung a single song in my whole life on purpose to shock anyone. I sing to entertain. My 'hot numbers' (and especially the songs Jack Yellen has been writing for me for the past twenty years) are all, if you will notice, written around something that is real in the lives of millions of people. They are songs that mean something to everybody who hears them." One of the most popular songs I ever used was Jack Yellen's "Life Begins at Forty!" It's a hot song, and, I insist, it's not dirty. It expresses what everybody who shivers at the word "middle-aged" feels; that is, the longing to make life over, to live it more fully and freely. To have more love and a lot more laughs.

Another thing about my "hot numbers," they are all moral. They have to do with sex, but *not* with vice. That, I believe, is one secret of their unfailing popularity with American audiences.

The other secret that makes for their success is the fact that they are all written in the first person. When I'm singing them I am talking about myself. This makes me do them better than I could do a song about some indefinite third person. And the audience likes them better that way. Right at the outset of my career in vaudeville—that afternoon in Boston when I fell on my backside and the audience laughed and applauded, and thought it the best thing in my whole act—I got something out of that black-and-blue mark that has put thousands of dollars in my pocket. It was the discovery that the audience found my distress funny. All right, I thought, I'll capitalize on that. And I have, consistently. I've found that audiences always enjoy it when I make fun of myself in my songs. They laugh at me, at whatever predicament I find myself in, just as they laughed when I fell down. And at the same time their laughter is tinged with the knowledge that the same thing could happen to them.

If I should sing the songs in such a way as to point them at *them,* not at me, they would feel too self-conscious to enjoy them. Making it a song about myself leaves them free to apply it to themselves.

And they do.

Jack Lait made it possible for me to play return dates at all the houses on Mr. Morris's circuit. New York called me back to play. So did Brooklyn. Each time I had new songs and new gowns. I had a lovely wardrobe now, and the Boss raised my salary to one hundred and seventy-five dollars a week. I was getting to be the most booked act on the whole circuit. No other performer played Chicago as often as I did.

At this time C. B. Zittell was playing up the American Music Hall and William Morris's performers in a column in the New York *Journal* called "The Vaudeville Chart." Zit was a warm friend to newcomers in show business. He had an unquenchable admiration for talent. It was he who built up Eva Tanguay to the point where she was the highest-salaried performer in vaudeville.

What a thrill I got when I saw his charts build me up from fourth and fifth position to third, then to second place, and then to the headline spot.

The ladder of vaudeville fame is indeed a hard one to climb, and the public never knows the obstacles strewn in artists' paths. On this week's program there appears a name—Sophie Tucker. The electric sign does not bear her name as she passes in front of the theater. Her name is not even in large letters on the three sheets. . . . But what a wonderful strike it was for Sophie Tucker at the American track this week. Appearing in a study of black velvet, Miss Tucker sang six riotous songs to such applause that the statue of Purity fairly shook in Times Square. Miss Tucker is fortunate in having an act that is somewhat out of the ordinary. Her selections of songs are perfect. Her renditions of them are exquisite. From Miss Tucker's success last night her path in the future cannot help being one golden line. The electric signs will come, so will the large type on the three sheets, and she will be able to dictate her own spot on the bill before many moons go by.

So wrote Zit after I played my second return date at the New York Music Hall. Just five weeks after that I rang him up from Atlantic City to tell him that my name was up in electric lights at the Criterion Theatre there.

"I'm coming down to see it for myself," he said. And he did, over that week end. I remember him doubled up with laughter when he caught me standing outside the theater trying to take a snapshot of the electric sign with my Brownie and dripping tears of excitement.

"Big crybaby," said Zit.

He couldn't possibly know what those bulbs flashing SOPHIE TUCKER over the Boardwalk meant to me. It was just a little more than a year since the first night of the *Follies of 1909* and the disappointment and heartache that began for me that night. And right there in Atlantic City too. All that came over me when I first saw my name up in lights. Even before I telephoned Zit I sent off a hasty note to Mollie with a ten-dollar bill tucked into it to give her the news and to tell her to come right down and see for herself that her prophecy had come true. I was a headliner, not a "patsy" any more.

She came. A broken leg wouldn't have kept her away. She and I stood hand in hand outside the theater staring at those lights like two kids at a circus. And after the night show we squeezed into a double chair and rode up and down the Boardwalk, enjoying the crowds and the noise and the fun, talking our heads off.

CHAPTER 11: *High, Wide, and Handsome*

THERE'S NO GETTING ROUND IT, success does things to you. Makes you feel different, act different. I was strutting now.

"Don't let it go to your head, Patsy," Mollie would warn me whenever we were together, and in every letter she wrote me when I was on the road.

"Not me," I'd reply. I meant it too. But Lord! I could no more keep the success feeling from getting me than I could keep from catching measles in a room full of them. Not after the lean, hard years I'd come through. Just you try walking out into the blazing sunshine after spending three years in a dark room and see if you don't blink and stagger and get a bit dizzy in the head.

For the first time since I was a kid I was enjoying life; finding in it something more than just hard work and the worry about getting ahead.

There was still plenty of work. In Chicago, in the residential districts of the suburbs, theaters were springing up everywhere—the President, the Wilson, the Kedzie, the Willard, the Circle, and many more. As soon as an act was a hit at the American Music Hall it would be engaged for these out-lying ten-cent houses. I found myself the headliner in all these theaters. Whenever I played Chicago this meant I would play there eight to ten weeks at a stretch, and when I could manage it, I lived close to the theater. Then I would hop out of bed, in pajamas, just half an hour before I had to go on for the first show around noon. With a coat over the pajamas I was round the corner, into the stage door, and in my dressing room ready to make up. From then on I stayed in the theater until I finished my act in the night show, around eleven. Then out for some supper and perhaps a poker game. And back to bed by three o'clock.

Playing two months or more in one city meant new songs all the time. I couldn't afford to go stale. If people paid their dimes to see and hear Sophie Tucker they didn't want to hear the same songs over and over or see the same clothes. If something happened so that one or a couple of the other acts on the bill fell flat I had to work like hell to make it up to the audience, give them something extra, so they would go home feeling satisfied. I was finding out that topping a bill means responsibility. But working that way I was able to run my salary up to two hundred and two hundred and fifty dollars a week in those ten-cent houses. The Boss was pleased with me. Whenever I played a return date at the Music Hall he would raise my salary twenty-five to fifty dollars.

The Circle Theatre, on Chicago's West Side, was the first of the now famous Balaban and Katz circuit of houses. I played there when Barney Balaban, president of Paramount Pictures, was in the box office selling tickets. In those days Ida Balaban, the first Mrs. Sam Katz, played the piano, and her brother, A. J., used to sing with the illustrated slides. The Balabans revolutionized show business. They started the new era of big movie houses in Chicago. A. J. was the first to put on presentation shows in all the picture houses. It was he who brought out the first big bands. His houses with their huge orchestras, stage show, and pictures, all for less than a dollar admission, killed vaudeville.

A. J. had a positive genius for knowing what the public would go for. And if he felt any doubts about his own ideas he would go to William Morris for advice.

All of us knew that the Boss knew best.

While I was in New York playing one of my return dates I made up my mind to follow a hunch I had. I'd heard that the Edison Recording Company was paying a thousand dollars for ten records by singers who already had a popular following. What, I asked myself, was to prevent me making ten records and chipping off the thousand dollars to make a down payment on a new house for Ma and Pa?

I went up to the Recording Company's office, saw the manager, and got him to come to the Music Hall to hear me. He offered me the contract, and it was arranged that I should make one record (two songs) the following week. I would be paid one hundred dollars for these, and would be paid in the same way for the other nine records as I made them during the year.

This arrangement didn't suit my plans at all. I tried to get the manager to let me draw the thousand dollars in advance, after the first two songs had been recorded, but he said it could not be done.

I made the songs "The Lovin' Rag" and "That Lovin' Two-Step Man." I worked a whole morning on them. When I heard the playback I turned to the boys and let out a yell: "My God, I sound like a foghorn!"

I was terrible.

However, the manager seemed satisfied with the recordings, and when I read the advertising the company put out about them I said to myself: the Edison Company must know what they're doing. They can't think I'm as bad as I think I am. They even wanted me to make a second record before I left New York. So I cheered up a little and right away my business instincts went to work. Those two records *had* to sell.

I got out my address book and sent off post cards to everyone I knew, all over the country, telling them about the records and urging them to buy them. I felt I must prove my worth to the Recording Company. I had the two hundred dollars for the first two records safely put into a postal money order and I was holding on to this like grim death until I could collect the eight hundred dollars balance. Like everybody in show business in those days who wanted to save any money, I went out and bought a post-office money order made out to myself. This could be cashed anywhere you happened to be. All of us who were constantly on the road used to do that. We let Uncle Sam keep our savings for us.

While I was still in New York that time Mama came down and brought Son to spend a day with me. Every time I got to New York I would let them know at home and send the railroad fares so Mama or Pa or Anna could come down on an excursion ticket and bring Son along. He was growing up fast, going to kindergarten at the Brown School where I had gone; not a baby any more. Pa just worshiped him. He wouldn't let Anna take Son to school on his first day there. He insisted on doing it himself so he could tell the teacher how smart his grandson was.

Every time I saw my boy I felt I must work harder, get ahead quicker, make more money so I could do more for him. I wanted to send him away to a good boarding school, a military school where he wouldn't be spoiled the way poor Pa spoiled him at home. And every time I saw Mama, getting old and bent, still working hard to make the restaurant pay and to catch up on what Pa lost in those pinochle and poker games, I felt I couldn't wait another week to get her out of that life and into a home of her own where there would be no restaurant business for her any more.

But to do that would take a good lump sum to start off with besides what I could send her regularly every week out of my salary.

After I put her and Son on the train at Grand Central to go back to Hartford I hurried back to the theater to get ready for the night show. My mind was in a whirl. Somehow or other I *had* to get the money to buy Mama a home of her own. I had two hundred dollars toward it, but I needed one thousand dollars. There was a house on Maple Avenue she said she liked. I had asked her some questions about it, not letting on, though, that I was figuring on a way to buy it for her. Then back in the theater, putting on my make-up, I got my big idea.

I'll write to Mr. Edison himself, I said. No, I'll go to see him. I'll tell him right out why I want the thousand dollars, and I'll promise to make the other eight records any time he wants them if only he'll pay me for them in advance. Then, still smearing on the cream, I let my imagination run on, planning how I'd dash up to Hartford before I started out on the road again, and how I'd pull the grand out of my pocket the way a magician takes rabbits out of a silk hat, and say to Mama: "There's your home. Now let's go right out and buy it."

The next morning saw me over in Orange, New Jersey. I couldn't see Mr. Edison, but I did see his secretary. I explained the matter to him, and he promised to take it up with Mr. Edison. He said I could expect a letter in a few days' time.

So I didn't go to Hartford after all. I didn't have any wonderful good news to take me there. Instead I left for Indianapolis to play a week's engagement. I'd given the secretary my address, and every day the first thing I did on coming into the theater was to look in the mailbox for the promised letter.

On Wednesday, I remember, I got to the theater early for the matinee. Maybe I had another hunch that I would hear that day. Anyway, there was the letter. And in it a check for eight hundred dollars.

I didn't waste a minute getting down to the post office and buying another money order for eight hundred dollars payable to Brother Phil. And right after the matinee I got the letter off to him enclosing the order and telling him to buy Mama the house on Maple Avenue she wanted and to move the family into it right away. Now that I was working steadily I would send money regularly every week to keep up the payments and to take care of Ma and Pa. No more restaurant. That was done with forever.

In the same mail went a heartfelt note of thanks to Mr. Edison, who had made all this possible. Enclosed in this was a signed agreement to make the remaining eight records when I came back to New York.

I had heard a lot about the Pantages time and the Sullivan-Considine time, a circuit of independent theaters west of Chicago to California. These were small-time houses running in opposition to the Orpheum Circuit. I made contact with the Pantages Circuit and booked my first trip to the West Coast at two hundred and fifty dollars and railroad fares. There were houses in Vancouver, Winnipeg, Calgary, Tacoma, Portland, Seattle, Sacramento, Oakland, San Francisco, Los Angeles, Salt Lake City, and Denver, besides other theaters in the smaller towns where we had to take a cut in salary. I was headlined now and carried Jack Lait's billing—"The Mary Garden of Ragtime."

What a thrill to see my own U. S. A.; picturesque and historic spots I had read about; towns I had heard other performers talk about!

I was determined to prove my value. I had great songs with me, and a lovely wardrobe. To see my name up in electric lights in every city made me work all the harder. In every town I played I tried to make friends, and when I came back to that town to play a return engagement I would let those friends know in advance that I was coming and counted on seeing them again. My address book was filling up fast.

I have always believed (I still do) that an entertainer who builds up for herself a friendly audience has the most valuable asset in the whole show business. There's a wonderful stimulation in playing to people who know you. You can feel the warm wave of friendly interest come across the footlights the minute you step onto the stage. It eases some of the terrible tension which every performer, no matter how long she has been in the game, feels at the start of her act. And then it acts like a powerful stimulant. You *can't* let your friends down.

Looking back over that first trip to the West Coast is like the series of quick flashes the movie directors use to give you the feeling that a lot of events are happening very fast.

Seattle means a tangle of queer-looking ships in the harbor and a supper of crawfish so good I ate too many and lost two shows being sick as a poisoned pup. It was in Seattle I first met Texas Guinan. She was doing a Western act on the Sullivan-Considine time in opposition to the Pantages houses I was playing. Tex couldn't sing or dance, but she had a line of chatter that went over big with the audience. And her personality was terrific. She was then the same Texas Guinan who was so beloved later on in New York's night clubs where she reigned as the queen of good fellows. She had something that made everyone feel instantly at ease and ready for a good time. And she had a heart as big as her native state.

In Seattle, at Pantages Theatre, I saw the funniest thing I have ever seen in any theater. A man was sitting in the upper right-hand box. During my act he leaned over, laughing so hard his false teeth fell out onto the stage at my feet. I picked them up and tried to hand them back to him, but he was so embarrassed he ran out of the house and sent a messenger boy back to claim his ivories.

In Denver, on that trip, I made one of the best friends I have to this day— Reverend Garrett J. Burke. I had plenty of work cut out for me to do in Denver in connection with the tubercular colony there. For years Mama and her buddies back in Hartford had been raising money for a cottage to which tubercular cases could be sent and where they would be with others from their own home town. I had strict orders from home to visit the Hartford cottage and see what I could do for the patients. After that first visit whenever I have played Denver I have entertained the tubercular colony and have made a host of friends through that work. Father Burke has long been resident in the East, but he knows I'm as interested in his work wherever that happens to take him as when he ministered to the white-plague victims out in the Rockies. What a grand sense of humor that man has! And what spiritual power! When he comes to see me, and he does whenever I am playing any city near enough for him to spend an afternoon with me, we have a grand laugh. Then, before he goes, I kneel down and he blesses me.

My first engagement on the Pantages Circuit was at the Chutes in San Francisco. Art Hickman, who brought the first California band to the Ziegfeld Roof in New York, was employed there then. It was there, too, I got to know Bob Fitzsimmons and his tiny, delicate wife, who had come West with him in a new act. Bob was passionately fond of music. He was as crazy for new songs as any vaudeville performer.

We had a lot of fun seeing the sights of Frisco, especially the Barbary Coast. In those days it was full of spots such as Purcell's, the hot colored joint, and the Cave, which San Franciscans boasted was the toughest place in the world. I was keen to see and hear the entertainers there so we made up a party to go one night after the show. We had a guide because we had been told it wasn't safe to "do" the Barbary Coast without one.

I was taking it all in—the singers, the dancers, the girls hustling, just as they used to at the German Village—and asking the guide a hundred questions, when all of a sudden one of the hustlers let out a yell like an Indian: "What the hell are you doing with my man?" and made a grab for my hair.

I ducked. Somebody upset the table. There was an uproar, and all the lights went out. Our party managed to get outside unhurt.

The others were all for going on to another joint, but I'd had all the Barbary Coast I could take at one dose. I went home, escorted by the policeman on duty in that section. Dan O'Brien was his name. We became good friends, Dan and his family and I, for I played a great many return dates at the Chutes. How proud Dan was when his son George O'Brien made his first success in the movies. I still have the little gold cross which Dan gave me as a good-luck piece, and I know he kept and treasured to the end of his days the little gold *mogandovid* (the five-pointed star of David) which I gave him. He used to show it to me every time I was in Frisco.

San Francisco in those days had a lot of great entertainers. Al Jolson was playing there. Mary Lewis was singing at "Tait's." Others I remember were Lee Lloyd, Baby Ruth, the Three White Kuhns, and that swell song, dance, and comedy team Blyler and Brown. Jimmy Blyler and Fred Brown were doing their act in Nome, during the Klondike Rush, when Rex Beach saw them. He brought them to Frisco, where they were a terrific hit. They were the first to sing "Turkey in the Straw."

Playing a return engagement in Portland, Oregon, on that trip I ran into trouble. I had a song called "The Angle-worm Wiggle." The song itself had nothing to it (it was a gospel hymn compared to some of the numbers you hear today), but I got a jeweler to make me four rings of bright green stones which I could wear on the second and fourth fingers of both hands to glitter as I used my hands snakily up and down my body as I sang, producing, as I hoped, a naughty effect to put the song across.

Of course I had no way of knowing that a Mrs. Baldwin who then headed Portland's Department of Safety for Women was having a political row with the chief of police, or that the lady would seize on me and my "Angle-worm Wiggle" to make trouble for the chief. After the first matinee Mrs. Baldwin swore out a warrant for my arrest on the grounds that my act was "immoral and indecent." I believe I was represented as a muscle dancer from the Barbary Coast. Of course the papers ate it up.

The chief of police came to see the show and declared that my act was all right. He gave it as his opinion that "The Angle-worm Wiggle" was less indecent than some of the other acts on the bill which apparently hadn't brought a single blush to Mrs. Baldwin's cheeks. This made the lady furious. She took the matter to the mayor. She also swore out another warrant against me on the grounds that I had ridiculed her from the stage by ad-libbing as I wiggled my fingers up and down my torso, "very immoral."

I had opened on Monday. On Friday, after the press had been full of the case all week, I was taken off the stage. My friends in Portland, Mr. and Mrs. Percy Egbert, got me a lawyer. I put up fifty dollars bail and offered to sing any song the mayor, the chief of police, and Mrs. Baldwin should select to prove that my act was neither indecent nor immoral. When this offer was refused, my friends took me to the district attorney. I made the demand of him that he give me a jury trial at which I would sing "The Angle-worm Wiggle" for the jury.

The D. A. read the lyrics and then threw out the case. He bawled out the mayor and Mrs. Baldwin and the whole kaboodle. I was left sitting on top of the world with pages and pages of publicity and a line at the box office three blocks long. The theater held me over for two more weeks, and I had to promise to play a return engagement before I went back East.

Rigo, the gypsy violinist, was playing at the Multnomah Hotel in Portland and was all the rage there. His wife, Kathryn, was a gorgeous big blonde and a very shrewd businesswoman. She was Rigo's manager. But the fiery, dark little man was temperamental, like so many real artists, and that clever, stunning-looking woman waited on him like a spoiled child.

They invited me to have supper in their rooms with them after the show one night. That was the first time I ever saw a real suite of rooms in a hotel, a retinue of servants, and a background of luxury. My eyes nearly popped out of my head. Kathryn swept about in a regal-looking tea gown worthy of a headliner. I remember she cooked something spicy and hot in a chafing dish. It was the first time I'd ever seen anyone do that, either.

Kathryn's bedroom gave me another jolt, with its draperies of real lace, the flock of tiny lace pillows on the bed, the flowers, the big signed photographs of celebrities in silver frames. She pulled open the drawers of a dressing table and showed me her jewels—boxes and boxes of them. She threw wide a wardrobe and showed me the gowns made for her in Paris. She opened a closet that held a fortune in furs.

When Kathryn saw my eyes get bigger and bigger she began taking one fur coat after another off their hangers and trying them on for me to get the effect. They were superb. There was a sable coat, a mink coat, a sealskin coat, an ermine wrap, a chinchilla wrap, and I don't know what more besides. But what caught my eye and held it (I didn't know sable from mink or chinchilla from gray squirrel in those days) was a leopard-skin coat. Right then and there I made up my mind to have a leopard-skin coat if I never had another thing. Kathryn's was a short sports model. But mine, I promised myself, should be down to the ground, with a border of sealskin and collar and cuffs of seal.

I got the coat and a sealskin muff. And a hat of sealskin with a big leopard-skin bow! I went in hock to get them. I wore them proudly when I came back to Portland to play a return engagement. I sure was a loud baby. I advertised to the whole world that I was a performer. You could see me coming five blocks off.

Gradually I began to notice something queer. Whenever I sported my fur coat the others on the bill were never anxious to go anywhere with me, for a walk or to dinner. If I didn't wear the leopard-skin outfit, the gang was always around. When I wore it, it seemed as if I was alone a lot. After a few seasons I got wise. No more loud, showy clothes. Ultimately I had the fur coat cut down to a sports model. But that style wasn't becoming to a woman as big as I, so I turned in the leopard skin and two hundred dollars to boot and got a plain sealskin coat. When I wore it you would never have known I was in show business.

Never after that did I go in for showy coats. But I developed a love of fine furs and began to buy them to wear on the stage—an ermine wrap in which to make my entrance. The press began to comment on how well I dressed. Nothing shoddy. I never kept my fine clothes to wear in New York and the big cities and used second bests or soiled or out-of-date gowns in the smaller places as many performers did. The folks in Calgary and in Indianapolis and Nashville got the best I had. That didn't escape the press, either.

Does anyone think I am talking too much about clothes? The reason is not because I am a woman, or vain, but because I am in show business. In show business clothes matter. This was proved to me at the first matinee I went to at Hammerstein's in New York when I heard the women seated near me commenting more on what the performers wore than on what they did. Vaudeville, playing daily matinees, depended on women. You had to please the women patrons to be and stay a headliner.

Thinking over some of my costumes and the publicity they got for me makes me remember my sheath skirt. This was very tight and had a slit up the right side so that when I walked you saw my leg to the knee. Very, very daring in those days. I had the dress made for the stage and I copied it for wear on the street for publicity stunts.

I was playing the small-time houses in the Midwest that summer. The sheath skirt was a big publicity getter in Canton and Youngstown and other towns. I would wear it to take a stroll down Main Street and the crowd would follow me right back to the theater.

When I got to Dayton to open at the Monday matinee I decided to go out after rehearsal and parade down the main stem and drum up business. I found the streets crowded. Was there going to be a parade? If so, I had some idea of joining in the line of march.

I asked several people where the parade was to start from.

"What parade?" they said, and looked surprised.

Funny, I thought. This town is jammed with people, and I'm walking around in my sheath skirt and nobody follows me. Nobody even notices me. Finally I went up to a traffic policeman and asked him when the parade would start.

"Parade? Hell!" said he. "Look up there in the sky. See that airplane? It was made right here in Dayton, and it's going to revolutionize the world. There's two people in it: the man who built it and his mechanic. They are testing it to see how long they can stay up there. Didn't you read about it in the papers?"

My leg didn't have a thing on the Wright brothers' airplane. The matinee was a flop. Everybody was too busy staring up at that speck in the sky that was "going to revolutionize the world." But the next day, and for the rest of the week, Dayton's main stem saw my sheath skirt. I wore it when the theater manager took all the performers out to the factory to see the first airplane. I'll never forget the Wright brothers, how they laughed when I told them they were too tough competition for me that Monday morning. Me with my sheath skirt and leg and they with their airplane.

I got back to Chicago from my first Western tour in April 1911. I was playing at the Wilson Avenue Theatre when Earl Lindsay came to see me. He was putting on a musical show, *Merry Mary,* at the Whitney Opera House, and made me a flattering offer to be featured in it at two hundred and fifty dollars a week.

I had run my salary in vaudeville up to five hundred dollars a week, but there was something more to be considered than just the salary.

My mind started to work fast. A show, if it is good, gets great publicity. If it is a hit, it boosts your prestige and consequently your salary. The way I saw it, I would be a fool to let a chance like that get away from me.

I was green as to knowing whether the part was a good one for me. And I hadn't the Boss to go to for advice. He was up in the Adirondacks getting his health back after the closing of his Music Halls. All I could think of was that if the show was a hit I would be made. If it was a flop, I could always go back to vaudeville. So I signed up.

Rehearsals started. Costumes were made to order and I saw my whole salary being invested in clothes. However, a show is a show. And I guess some of the gambling instinct I inherited from Pa was coming out in me. I was playing *Merry Mary* to the limit.

Playing in a show with several quick costume changes to make I needed a maid. Besides, a personal maid made a performer important. Here was a chance to make good my promise to Mollie; a chance to have her with me. With her there to rely on, to love me, to inspire me with her philosophy that "what happens, happens for the best," I felt confident of new and greater success.

Well, *Merry Mary* opened, and flopped. The press gave us the cold shoulder. The critics didn't like the show, and they didn't like me in it. The general comment was that I could sing, but I needed a lot more experience in acting before I tried to carry a part. And they were right. I know now that I was pretty terrible.

However, there was one person in Chicago who didn't think so. It was during *Merry Mary's* brief three weeks of life that I had my first experience with a stage-door Johnny. Night after night I had seen the same man sitting in the same front-row seat. It never dawned on me that I was the attraction.

Then one matinee flowers and a jeweler's box were brought to my dressing room. Mollie's face was one broad grin as she handed me the box.

"Well, Patsy, guess you got yourself a man now."

I opened the box and a pair of diamond earrings sparkled at me. I was no glamor girl, and a gift like this, while it thrilled me, made me feel there must be some mistake. I sent for the gentleman whose card was in the box.

"You must take the earrings back," I said to him. "It was nice of you to send them, but surely the flowers were enough to tell me that you enjoy my work."

"You must take them, Miss Tucker," he insisted. And he went on about how much pleasure I had given him, and how much he admired me, until I began to feel as though I were running up on Lillian Russell.

So I kept the diamonds and wore them every night and as often in the daytime as I could find an excuse for doing so. Those earrings marked me. They started me itching for diamonds, just the way the sight of Kathryn Rigo's furs put me in hock to the Connecticut Fur Company for years. I wanted diamond rings, a diamond bracelet, a diamond necklace. A performer, I told myself, strutting before the mirror admiring the sparklers in my ears, has to have diamonds. They make you important.

Mollie and I were living at the Hotel Sherman, and Frank Behring, then the manager, was a good friend of mine. He recommended me to a jeweler from whom I bought my first diamond ring. We made an arrangement that I was to pay twenty-five dollars a week. As soon as the ring was paid for I bought a bracelet, then a brooch, and so on.

"It's the diamonds or the poker games, Sophie," Frank Behring said shrewdly. "You can't have both. You'll have to choose between them."

"Then poker is out," I told him. "Anyway until I get my fill of diamonds."

"Maybe that's the only way you'll save any money. You people in show business—and I've seen a lot of you—when you get into the big brackets you throw money around like nobody's business. You go haywire."

"Listen. Not me. I don't forget the responsibilities I've got back in Hartford. And I'm not likely to. Only, when you work hard the way we show people do, you've got to have a little fun once in a while."

"Sure. Don't I know? You and Fanny Brice and Jack Lait and the Dolly Sisters and a lot more of you playing poker till dawn."

"I told you. I'm through with gambling. I'm buying diamonds now."

"Okay. See that you pay for them. I swore to Thompson that you were straight."

"He won't lose any money on me," I promised.

Merry Mary folded. As soon as the notice was put up a week before clos-ing I went out and got busy for bookings in vaudeville. Then I started on a circuit in the Midwest. Mollie went with me. Every week, no matter where I was playing, I sent off my sheaf of money orders: to the folks in Hartford, to the Connecticut Fur Company for my fur coats, to the jeweler for the diamonds I was sporting.

My first stage show may have been a flop, but I wasn't giving up.

"There'll be more shows," Mollie said wisely.

And again she was right. Harry Askin was producing *Louisiana Lou,* starring Alexander Carr, at the La Salle Theatre in Chicago. He engaged me for the show to be featured with Bernard Granville.

CHAPTER 12: *"Hartford's Own"*

MERRY MARY had taught me more about show business. I knew now that I must have a good part and good songs. The manager must be reliable and prominent or I would have another flop. Two failures in six months would make the comeback as hard as roller skating uphill.

Louisiana Lou, however, was a very different kind of show from *Merry Mary.* It was a book show by Addison Burkhart and Fred Donaghy; music by Ben Jerome. I had two swell songs: "Now Am de Time" and "The Puritan Prance." The last was a burlesque of the bunny hug and grizzly bear which everybody was dancing that season. The plot was built around two families, one Irish, the other Jewish, living across the street. And this, years before *Abie's Irish Rose.* My part was Jenny Wimp, the servant in the Irish family. When I read the part I said to Mr. Askin, owner and producer of the show, that I didn't see why they wanted me at three hundred and fifty dollars a week for a role that any fifty-to-seventy-five-a-week actress could play.

"Young lady," said Mr. Askin, "if you can make a small part stand out in a show you will be more valuable than the star."

"All right," I said. "I'll give it the best I've got."

I spoke right from the heart. My pride had suffered a lot in the *Merry Mary* flop, especially as this happened in Chicago, where I had been so suc-cessful in vaudeville and where I had so many friends. I was determined to show Chicago audiences and the Chicago critics that I could handle a part.

I was bad at rehearsals. When it came to reading lines from the script as the others did, I was flat. I just couldn't do my stuff on an empty stage. I could memorize my part overnight—cues, positions, everything—but at rehearsals, though I was all right with the songs, I couldn't give satisfaction with the lines. I could see that Mr. Askin and Frank Smithson, who directed the show, were very much annoyed with me.

I kept remembering my experience in burlesque, how hopeless I had been at the rehearsals, and yet when I opened how I panicked the audience. I kept telling Mr. Askin that when the show started he would find I would be all right.

"I'm just rotten at rehearsing. Once I'm in front of an audience I'll deliver. See if I don't."

"H'm!" he said doubtfully.

At the next rehearsal I saw another woman sitting on the stage, and I knew that she had been engaged to play my part. It damn near killed me. I ran over to Mr. Askin and the director and begged them not to give my part to anyone else.

"I'll make a bargain with you," I said. "Keep me on and let me open with the show in Milwaukee. I'll play the opening week for nothing. You won't have to pay me one cent. If I'm no good, no hit, then no salary. And you can let me out. Only give me the chance to show you what I know I can do."

They talked it over and finally agreed to my proposal. Just the same, the other woman had to go along to Milwaukee with us in case I fell down on the job, and so she would be ready to step in for the Chicago opening.

"I've just *got* to make good," I said to Mollie desperately.

"Keep your shirt on, Patsy. Take it in your stride and you'll come through all right."

"If I don't," I snapped, "I suppose you'll say, the way you always do, 'Whatever happens, happens for the best.' "

"Seems like that tumble you took onto your rear end when you was playing Boston that time kind of set a pattern you've been following ever since. Something happens and you come down with a bump, and boy if you don't land with your nose in the butter! That's the way it's been so far, ain't it?" she came back, cool as a cucumber.

And of course when I stopped to think over the years I had to admit that Mollie was right.

However, this philosophy didn't help me much on the night we were to open at the Davidson Theatre in Milwaukee when eight o'clock came and my wardrobe had not yet arrived from the costumers in Chicago. I was in a panic. Here everything depended on my showing Mr. Askin I could be a hit, and no costumes.

Eight-ten, eight-fifteen. . . . The curtain was at eight-thirty. Mollie was trying to improvise something I could go on in. I was dancing up and down with impatience and rage. With fear too. I couldn't keep my mind off that other woman who would be standing in the wings ready to smile slyly at my failure, which would mean a chance for her.

Eight-twenty, and the messenger boy rushed in with my things. I jerked out the tissue paper and hurried into the green chiffon harem pants with a little lace apron effect in front, which was the costume for my entrance. The callboy was calling me to go on stage. My fingers were all thumbs. Mollie was kneeling on one side of me fastening the pants when I heard my cue. I nearly knocked her over in my rush to get on the stage for my opening line.

Suddenly the audience began to scream with laughter. I asked myself: Why? I haven't said anything so terribly funny. I don't look funny in the pants; it's a smart outfit. What's got into them? Every time I moved, or spoke a line, the shrieks began again.

A horrible thought hit me. Suppose Mr. Askin thinks I've bought tickets and padded the house to put myself over. Nothing else would explain that hysterical laughter.

Then I happened to lift my lace apron and saw, to my horror, that I had omitted to button up the whole front of the pants.

"Well, I'll be damned," I said. I couldn't help it.

At this the house went into an uproar while I fumbled and tried to fasten the pants while going on with my song. They wouldn't let me forget it, either. Every time I came on they started to laugh and kid me.

"Once is enough," I had to kid them back.

I kept the job. The other woman disappeared. I opened with the show in Chicago, where we played nine months and were the season's greatest success. But I've never been able to convince some people I didn't pull that stunt with the harem pants on purpose.

Louisiana Lou was a hit with the Chicago press from the start. Alexander Carr was magnificent. Very temperamental, but a superb actor. Later on he and Barney Bernard made nation-wide fame for themselves as Potash and Perlmutter. When *Louisiana Lou* went on the road after the Chicago run, Alexander Carr left the comedy and Barney Bernard took his place.

Bernard Granville, whose dancing was a constant delight to me, made his first hit in *Louisiana Lou*. Later he was a star in Florenz Ziegfeld's New York shows. Bernard's daughter, Bonita Granville, is carrying on for him now.

Mary Quivé, sister of the opera star Grace Van Studdiford, played an important part in the show. One of my show girls, "Brownie," is now the wife of Jorges Sanchez, the Cuban sugar millionaire.

I was making a lot of money now, playing club dates and at private parties. I had fun too. Mollie and I were living at the Hotel Sherman and my suite was a gathering place for a jolly crowd nights after the show. It was a fast crowd too. The poker games began again, in spite of Mollie's frowns and her warnings to me. When spring came and we were due to go on the road I realized that though my earnings had been up to a thousand dollars a week many times that winter, I was in debt to the Hotel Sherman for two thousand.

I couldn't alibi myself out of it. Poker had cleaned me out just the way it cleaned poor Pa time and time again. Here I had been making big money for nine months, and though I had taken care of my responsibilities back home and had bought myself some gorgeous diamonds, that was as much as I had to show for the season's hard work.

I had to make a clean breast of it to Frank Behring. He gave me hell. For gambling and for backing shows (which I'd been doing too). He had the goods on me, for he had seen me take a thousand dollars out of the hotel safe to help finance Ed Bloom's *Hanky Panky* starring Montgomery and Moore. I kissed my grand good-by, as the show closed after a few weeks in New York.

I asked Frank to trust me for the bill I owed, and he said he would if I would promise him to stop gambling.

"Tucker will never be a sucker again," I vowed.

"Okay," said Frank, and we shook on it.

I went on the road, and for the eight months we played out to California and back as far east as Philadelphia I forgot gambling and the fast crowd. I paid up my debts·and saved money.

We never came into New York. At that time New York had the reputation of not liking Chicago-made shows. Why, I never could understand. It has always seemed to me that a good show is a good show no matter what town it hails from.

We closed around Christmas, and I ran on to Hartford to see the family. It was my first visit home since that bitter one early in my days in vaudeville. And what a difference! Neighbors, friends crowding the house. Mama and Papa proud, not ashamed of me now. Son, home for the holidays from military school at Peekskill, and looking so cute, buttoned up tight in his little uniform. Anna so pretty, and making good in her job. Moe in the office of the criminal attorney Moses A. Sachs in New York, and Phil married to my old school chum Leah Zwillinger.

Those few days were wonderful after the months on the road. The Hartford papers were full of the news that Sophie Tucker, the star of *Louisiana Lou*, was visiting her folks. Papa boasted about me to his cronies, and Mama dug a good big contribution out of me for her pet charities. I went down to visit my teachers at the Brown School and my principal, Mr. Charles L. Ames. They were all proud of me as a home-town girl who had made good.

We sat up late the night before I left for New York, Mama, Sis, and I, talking over my plans. I was going back into vaudeville, I told them. Before too long I would be playing Poli's Theatre in Hartford as the headliner. I had my heart set on that.

How I needed the Boss! He would have known just what I should do next. After two years in a show I felt out of touch with vaudeville. What I needed was a booking agent—the right one.

I had heard a lot about Max Hart and that he had a hundred-per-cent entrée with the Keith Circuit officials. The Orpheum Circuit was booked out of the Keith office. This circuit started from Chicago and went to Winnipeg, Calgary, St. Paul, Vancouver, Seattle, Spokane, Portland, Tacoma, Sacramento, Oakland, San Francisco, Los Angeles, Denver, Salt Lake City, Omaha, Kansas City, St. Louis, and back to Chicago. I had already played those towns, but in the cheaper vaudeville houses, and again in *Louisiana Lou*. I had every confidence in my being a big box-office attraction this time.

Max Hart's office was in the Palace Theatre building in New York. I went up there, cocky as hell. I thought: I won't have any trouble now getting bookings. Everybody knows me after two years in a big show.

I sat in the outer office over an hour while a dozen acts of first-rate importance that I had seen or read about came in and out. Finally, I got in to see Max Hart. I told him that I was Sophie Tucker.

"Is that so?" said he, looking me over and not a bit impressed by what he saw. "I never heard of you and never saw you. Just what do you do?"

Well sir, the floor just came up and hit me. I was stumped for an answer. Max Hart was a very rough, aggressive, crude man, but as I found out afterward, after you knew him and his ways, when you worked for him, he was okay.

That day I told him if he would book me in some small theater for a try-out, I'd like him to handle me.

He shook his head. He let me know that he was only booking the cream acts of vaudeville and couldn't be bothered with me.

"You'll be glad to book me some of these days," I said to myself as I went out the door.

I soon found another booker, Max Hayes, and got started. I had some swell songs, new ones that the boys in Tin Pan Alley coached me in. And one song that I got in Chicago and introduced there at White City Park before I went into *Louisiana Lou*. It was a wonder song that never failed to make a hit wherever and whenever I sang it—"Some of These Days."

"Some of These Days" is one thing more I owe in a way to Mollie. I was riding high in Chicago, palling around with a fast crowd, too full of myself to pay attention to a lot that was happening around me. Many song writers used to bring me their work, beg me to try the songs in my act and plug them. Every performer is besieged with that sort of thing. At first you hear them all, consider them all, you're so fearful of missing a good thing. But after a few years of it you get careless. I guess it was that way with me.

One day Mollie came and stood in front of me, hands on hips, and a look in her eye that I knew meant she had her mad up.

"See here, young lady," said she, "since when are you so important you can't hear a song by a colored writer? Here's this boy Shelton Brooks hanging around, waiting, like a dog with his tongue hanging out, for you to hear his song. And you running around, flapping your wings like a chicken with its head chopped off. That's no way for you to be going on, giving a nice boy like that the run-around."

"All right. I'll hear his song," I promised. "You tell him."

"You can tell him yourself," said Mollie. And she brought him in.

The minute I heard "Some of These Days" I could have kicked myself for almost losing it. A song like that. It had everything. Hasn't it proved it? I've been singing it for thirty years, made it my theme song. I've turned it inside out, singing it every way imaginable, as a dramatic song, as a novelty number, as a sentimental ballad, and always audiences have loved it and asked for it. "Some of These Days" is one of the great songs that will be remembered and sung for years and years to come, like some of Stephen Foster's.

Later Shelton Brooks wrote "Darktown Strutters' Ball," which I sang too. But nothing else he ever did touched "Some of These Days."

For five months or so I worked around the Middle West as Max Hayes booked me. Everywhere I went I kept my eyes open—and my ears—for new ideas, stunts I could work into my act. I remember at Rock Island, Illinois, I got a laugh unexpectedly. I used to ask the audience to call for any song they wanted to hear. A fellow called out for me to sing "If I Had One at Home Like You," to which I fired back: "What would you do with her?" There, I thought, that's a trick I can use. I went to work, and soon I had an answer for all song titles, and it gave me a start for a lot of comedy in the act.

I hadn't given up hopes of getting Max Hart to book me. I wanted to get on the Orpheum Circuit and everybody said he was the man who could put me there. I asked a lot of questions about him and who his friends were. Whenever I played New York I managed to get around with the crowd he played with. I became friends with his wife, Madge. She was very quick at picking talent too. She knew show business. One night when I was with them Max suddenly asked me where I was playing.

I told him Max Hayes had booked my next date at Proctor's Fifth Avenue Theatre, which was at Twenty-eighth Street and Broadway. I was opening there on Monday.

"Then I'll see you," said Max Hart. "I've booked the greatest comedian of all times to break in there before he opens at Hammerstein's. Frank Tinney."

This was an important date for me, especially if I could get Max Hart interested. I got a new gown and I chose my songs carefully: "I Sent My Husband to the Thousand Isles," "Where Was Rip Van Winkle When His Wife Went Away?" "Waiting for the Robert E. Lee," and of course "Some of These Days." I was on the first half of the bill, Frank Tinney on the second half, but I phoned Max Hart, and he promised to be in the house in time to hear me.

I went over big. Even I was satisfied. I went back to my dressing room and waited for Max Hart. No sign of him. Finally, the second half of the show was on. I went out to watch Frank Tinney. What a comedian! For some time Frank had been a big hit in the vaudeville houses in Texas, but he had never played New York. Someone told Max Hart about him and Max went to Texas to look him over. He came back boasting he had discovered the greatest comedian of all time. This tryout at Proctor's looked as if Max knew what he was about all right. I never heard an audience roar so loud with laughter. Frank's repartee with the orchestra leader (this was the first time a performer did his whole act with a leader) was excruciating. I laughed myself sick, standing in the wings, watching.

The show was over, I was back in my dressing room ready to leave, when there was a knock on the door. Max Hart.

"I caught you," he said. "You're all right. A little rough, and your routine is rotten. I suggest you switch your songs." He gave me a few orders. Then: "I'll see you at my office tomorrow at eleven. 'By."

That is how I became one of Max Hart's acts. I got a release from Max Hayes, and Max Hart promised to book me at the Colonial Theatre on Sixty-first Street and Broadway.

"It's a tough house," he told me. "They let you know at once if they like you. They've got a gallery there with a claque, so watch yourself. If they don't like you, they throw pennies at you."

I was to get three hundred and fifty dollars for the week, with the promise of five hundred for the next date if I went over well at the Colonial.

Mollie was helping me in the act again. With new songs I had new tricks and different props. I looked over my wardrobe and decided the date at the Colonial was worth a new dress. I had heard of Madame Francis, who dressed the topnotchers on Broadway, a great friend of the performers. I went up to see her. I told her I was going to be up against a tough house and I wanted to make a grand impression.

"If they see me dressed nice they'll respect me. I'm sure I won't have any trouble with them."

Madame Francis studied me for a minute or two. She said: "I would like to see you make an entrance in a lovely white beaded gown and a gorgeous royal-blue velvet wrap. You should have a headdress to go with the gown. That will make you look very important."

"How much?" I asked her, point-blank.

"The cheapest gown I make is two hundred and fifty dollars. The cheapest I can make this ensemble is six hundred dollars."

I had the Colonial contract in my purse. I took it out and showed it to Madame Francis. "I'm starting at three hundred and fifty dollars. If I make good at the Colonial my agent says he will get me five hundred dollars in all the other theaters. Can I give you a two-hundred-dollar I O U against my salary now, and pay you two hundred dollars a week for the next two weeks if I get the bookings? If anything happens that I don't get them, I can always get a salary of three hundred and fifty a week. And in that case I'll pay you fifty a week until I'm paid off."

I guess Madame Francis had had a lot of performers who made promises like that and failed to keep them. She said "no." But I phoned Max Hart, got him to okay me to her, and she agreed to make the dress and wrap on the terms I offered.

Meanwhile I gave a lot of thought to that claque at the Colonial. A claque always has a leader. If I could find him, win him, I would be all right. After the rehearsals on Monday I went out to the gallery entrance where a few customers were already standing in line. Pretty soon I heard a boy yell: "Hey, Mike, what's the routine?"

Mike was a heavy-set, foreign-looking fellow. I watched him. When another boy called: "Hey, Mike, what do we do?" I knew I had my man.

I eased up to him. He didn't know me or recognize me from the pictures which showed me in evening clothes. "Let's walk down to the corner, Mike," I said.

He looked me over, sensed I wasn't one of the gang.

"What do you want, sis?"

By that time we were out of the line and the crowd, and I told him: "I'm opening this afternoon. I heard there's a fine bunch of boys and girls who go to the Colonial gallery and are very kind to newcomers. Will you please help me? This is my first appearance in this house, and I've got to be a hit. I'm sure you'll like my act. Please help me."

He must have liked me for being so frank and for singling him out as the leader. He gave me a pat on the back. "Sure, kid, we'll put you over. Just be good." And away he went.

The matinee was on. It was a very good bill. Most of the acts were a hit. Then came a monologuist. The gallery went after him. Pennies rained down on the stage. The poor man tried to argue with the gallery gods, but they wouldn't listen. He got sore, and the gallery booed him off the stage.

I came next. I was shaking from head to foot. I'd told Mollie about my talk with Mike, but suppose he didn't keep his word? Suppose the gallery started to razz me?

"Go on, Patsy," Mollie whispered. "When they see how nice you look that will put you over. And when you start to sing you'll have them in the bag. Go on, honey. You always use your head when you're in a tight spot."

Now I was on the stage. If I say so myself, I did look nice. No single woman playing these theaters went to the expense I did. Madame Francis told me I was the first vaudevillian she dressed. My knees were knocking against each other, but I looked up at the gallery and smiled. They began applauding.

"Thanks," I said. "I'm happy you like my outfit. I hope you like my act as well."

From that minute I played my whole act to Mike and his gang. I had to please them first; the orchestra and balcony customers were at their mercy. I could see the lower part of the house enjoyed my songs. I watched their faces, could see them applaud. But Mike and his gang gave me a great hand.

Max Hart caught the matinee and came back to tell me he was pleased. He booked me in all the houses, and I played return dates at the Colonial for a long stretch. I paid off Madame Francis because I got the promised raise, and she and I became friends. She took a great interest in dressing me until she left business to marry Nate Spingold, who is associated with the Columbia Picture Company in Hollywood.

As for Mike, he and his gang adopted me. For a long time they followed me around and put me over in all the houses in New York where I played. In return, whenever "The Gang" had an entertainment—a dance or a smoker —if I was in town I would go to sing for them. It wasn't that I was building up a claque for myself. The claque already existed. Every performer was up against "The Gang" at the Colonial until the police broke it up. I couldn't break it up, so it seemed to me the thing to do was to get it on my side and keep it there. A lot of performers don't bother about things like that. I always have. Maybe I've a knack for doing it. Maybe it's foresight. I only know it has always paid in the long run.

I suppose everybody has one week in her life that stands out as the climax —seven days that more than make up for all the effort and disappointment and sorrow that have gone over the dam. My week is the one in October 1913, when I headlined the bill at Poli's Theatre in Hartford.

From the farthest back that I can remember this theater stood first in my affections. It was where Dora Diwinski and I used to go and pay down our dimes to see shows. How many times I've had my bottom spanked for hanging around Poli's instead of coming right home from school. How often I've stood in the alley beside the stage door waiting for the actors to come out so I could tell them about our restaurant. How often I've comforted myself when I was lonely or downhearted or sad, off somewhere on the road, planning how I would go back to Hartford some of these days and be a headliner at Poli's.

And now this is coming true.

Never was there such a slow train as the express that took me from New York to Hartford. I thought over the preparations I'd made for the week— the new clothes, my fine jewels and furs, even a new trunk (my first wardrobe trunk) with SOPHIE TUCKER painted across it in big white letters. I was sure of myself. I'd been playing big-time houses under Max Hart's booking for over a year. Now I was going to headline the ace house in my own home town.

Now we're getting into Hartford. The sun shines on the capitol's big gold dome. There's Bushnell Park with the trees all red and gold. We're pulling into the station. There's Mama and Papa. And Son, God bless him, home from school for the week. And Anna and Moe and Brother Phil and his wife. And a big crowd, and every reporter in town.

Up on the boardings, and plastered all over the city, are posters:

SOPHIE TUCKER
THE PRIDE OF HARTFORD

HARTFORD'S OWN SOPHIE TUCKER

Think that didn't make me feel good?

When the hugs and kisses and some of the tears were over, the theater manager, Mr. Lou Kilby, came up. "Come on, Sophie. Your suite at the Heublein is ready for you."

I caught a glimpse of Mama's and Papa's faces. The smiles were wiped off. "Sorry," I said to him. "No hotels for me. I'm going home with my family." And we went.

I'd forgotten for a moment that the family had moved from Maple Avenue to 160 Barker Street. It was a two-family house, and Mama rented the downstairs apartment, which paid the taxes and gave them a little revenue. Upstairs were a living room, dining room, a bedroom for Mama and Papa, and another for Anna. Up in the attic were two more bedrooms, one for Moe whenever he came home and the other for any relative who came to visit. Anna moved up into this and gave me her room.

Mama was so proud of her house, her little nest. So proud of her comfortable beds with their big down pillows and feather-filled comforters. And all so snowy white. The whole house was spick-and-span; you could eat off the floor. Mama wouldn't have anyone in to help her with the housework. "What's the use? I have to go over everything they do. They're only in my way."

She kept taking me round and round, calling on me to admire everything: her front porch, her little garden. Everywhere, on every wall, were photographs of me. Some of the first ones I had sent home Mama had had enlarged, framed, and hung in places of honor. To her they ranked as works of art beside the portrait painted by Jean Negulesco. I'll never forget, in later years, Carl McCullough who started at the American Music Hall in Boston with me, played Hartford, and went to Mama's for dinner. He said to her: "Mrs. Abuza, your home is lovely. Your food is delicious. You and Papa are wonderful people. The only criticism I have to make is, what a pity you haven't got a picture of Sophie in the house."

Mama didn't get his ribbing at first. But she, too, had a grand sense of humor. She told him: "Be sure when you leave here you buy yourself a good pair of glasses. You certainly need them."

In one corner of the little dining room stood Papa's samovar steaming away all day and all through the evening, just as I remembered it. Ten to twelve glasses of tea a day were Papa's routine—a habit he had brought with him from Russia and which he never changed. Another habit of his, which none of us liked but which not one of us would have dared find fault with, was to sit sidewise at the table with his spittoon beside his chair, which he used continuously throughout the meal. Even as little girls, Anna and I used to wish he wouldn't. But what could you do about it? We might feel ashamed, but ours was an Orthodox home, and not one word of criticism could be spoken against the head of the house.

There was the spittoon, just as usual. I might be the headliner at Poli's that week, and "Hartford's Own Sophie Tucker," but at 160 Barker Street I was just a daughter and had to keep my mouth shut.

But not Son, fresh from boarding school and what he had learned there. He piped up: "Grandpa, it isn't proper and it's very bad taste to sit like that and spit during meals."

Will I ever forget Papa's face? If the ceiling had dropped on him he couldn't have been more surprised. Mama and the four of us let out a whoop of laughter.

"It isn't funny, Mother, to correct anyone," said Son, very solemn. "It's important."

Papa was in convulsions, his mouth full of food. The spittoon was handy, but obeying his grandson he got up and went into the bathroom. The next day all the neighbors heard him tell how his grandson was making a dude out of him. Sophie, for all she was a headliner, was just folks. But not Son, after a year away at military school. "Oi, oi, the chickens have more sense than the hens."

It was proof of Papa's love for the boy that he changed his table manners from that day. I think my son meant more to Pa than all his own children. I don't think he ever got over the separation from Son, after the boy went away to school. He missed their walks together, going downtown every day hand in hand. Poor Pa, with no restaurant to keep him busy and make him feel important. No people coming and going. No card games upstairs. His gambling was confined to the old neighborhood and the back room of the saloon there. This meant a streetcar ride there and back. The cars on that line stopped at midnight, and Mama was severe about late hours. The idleness and the loneliness made Pa an old man before his time. He would perk up whenever he came to spend a day or two with me in New York or some other town. His step would get brisk, his air jaunty. Even the way he wore his hat was different from when he was in Hartford. He was seeing Life, and believe me he didn't miss a single thing. And the tall tales he told Mama and Anna when he got back to them! He would get them sitting around the kitchen table, wide-eyed, not knowing how much to believe and how much was *chutsba.*

I remember when I played Poli's Theatre in New Haven—the very same house where I had gone so fearfully to ask Willie and Eugene Howard to make a place for me in their act—Pa came down and spent the week with me at the Taft Hotel. It was brand-new then, and the Connecticut papers had been full of stories about how grand it was. That was Pa's first experience of staying in a real hotel. What impressed him most were the push buttons. He spent hours every day pushing them, curious and eager as a child to see what would happen. I know when he went home and Mama wanted to know: "How is Sophie?" Pa brushed the question aside. All he could talk about was how wonderful it was to live in a hotel and push a little button and have a waiter or a chambermaid appear and ask you what you wanted.

"Is that all you have to do, push a button?" Mama wanted to know.

"That's all."

"I don't believe it," Mama said flatly.

"But I tell you it is true. Just push a little button and there is the prettiest young girl ready to do whatever you want."

"And I tell you I don't believe it. It can't be like that. Not even in America. Not even in a hotel."

"But, mein Dolly, it is."

"It can't be."

And they had it back and forth till Anna put her hands over her ears and ran out of the kitchen.

Mama never did believe him, not until several years later when she came and stayed with me in New York and experimented with a few push buttons for herself. Then she broke down and cried. Poor Papa was dead then, and she remembered she had called him a boaster and a liar. And all the time he had been right. And now there was nothing she could do about it.

All that week when I played Hartford you couldn't keep Pa away from the theater. It was he who came running to me with the news that the manager had had my contract framed and hung in the theater lobby so everybody in town could see that they were paying me five hundred dollars for the week. Nothing would do but I must go with him and see it too. We were looking at it when Lou Kilby, the manager, came along and told me:

"You know, Sophie, the mayor called me up and wanted to know if it is true we are paying you five hundred or if it's a publicity stunt."

"Tell him to be over here Saturday night when you pay off and he can count it," I replied.

The big blowup pictures of me in the lobby thrilled me as much as they did Pa. And the banner stretched across the street, "HARTFORD'S OWN SOPHIE TUCKER—THE PRIDE OF HARTFORD." Those words put up for everyone to see wiped out a lot of the bitterness and the struggle and the heartache of the years since I had left Hartford with the words "bad woman" stinging my ear.

I thought, I've got to be good now. I guess I didn't appreciate all it meant when other performers said to me: "Wait till you play your own home town. That's where you'll find out how good you are. It's only in your home town you can lay eggs and big ones too."

I opened that Monday matinee to a house jammed to capacity. I wore my loveliest Madame Francis outfit: a perfectly plain, clinging gown of white satin with a dashing big black bow across the front; a black lace skull-cap with a big black bow to give me height, and all my diamonds, of course. How I wished Mollie could have been there too. But, knowing there wouldn't be room for her at Mama's, I had left her in New York. Mollie would have loved the excitement, the reception they gave me—fully five minutes I stood there, bowing, smiling, but with tears in my eyes.

There in the stage box was my family, all of them, looking so proud, and loving too. In the next box was my old principal, Mr. Charles L. Ames, and the teachers I had had at the Brown School. In the stage box on my right was the mayor of Hartford and his family. Looking up at me from the front row were the faces of all my old school chums. The second row was taken up with Mama's buddies, most of whom couldn't speak a word of English or understand it. But they had heard so much about "Mein Sophie" that they had to come to see for themselves.

Maybe you think I was proud? I wasn't. I believe I felt humbler at that moment than I've ever felt before or since. "O God," I prayed, holding tight to my big chiffon hanky so nobody could see how my hands were trembling, "please don't let me lay an egg today, and I'll die happy."

Maybe that prayer was heard. All I know is I damn near broke a blood vessel that week, I worked so hard. But Hartford was satisfied, I guess. We played to capacity all week. Papa would nip out in front and count up the house every show. He'd come backstage rubbing his hands, grinning from ear to ear, proud as a peacock because I was doing good business.

"Lots of customers tonight," he would say. "And I've been talking to some of the boys around town. They say you're all right. *Oi,* Sophie, I guess Sylvester Poli will clear expenses this week. *Nicht?"*

Best of all was coming home each night after the show to supper in the kitchen, the table loaded with special dishes Mama had made for me because I liked them. All of us gathered round the table, with the samovar bubbling away in its corner and Papa keeping us convulsed with all he had to say about show business as he saw it. He was full of curiosity about everything and everyone he saw backstage. The little soubrette in her short skirts, showing legs he said were too crooked and hairy for his taste. The Musical Family of Five, with two or three little tots that were in and out of the dressing rooms all day and half the night. Papa was worried about them until I explained that our kids of the theater are often better behaved than the children the audience have left at home. Backstage everyone learns self-control and discipline. You have to learn how to take it on the chin, and to smile while taking it. You learn never to be late. Never to be caught unprepared. Above all, never to think you are the whole show.

"Those kids you think are running wild with nobody to teach them anything are learning how to be good troupers," I finished.

He professed to be scandalized by some of the loose ways and frank talk he observed among a lot of show people. Papa pulling the Puritan on us!

"Listen," I protested. "In our profession we call a spade a spade. We make no bones about life. But take it from me, those very same performers you think must be evil-minded and evildoers, are honest, hard-working guys sending money home to their families every week and always ready to put their hands in their pants' pockets to help some other trouper who gets caught in a jam. There aren't any people in the world so kindhearted and generous as show people. If a few of the self-righteous hypocrites who are so ready to sling mud at us had half as much real goodness of heart . . ."

"Sophie," said Mama, looking at me hard over one side of her spectacles. That look took me down a peg just the way it used to when I was eleven and would fling out about having to stay home and help in the restaurant when I was itching to go somewhere with the rest of the kids in the block. My ears were all ready for what Mama was going to call me: A *zovarecha,* a wild animal, which was what she used to say I was when I would hustle through the housework and be out the door, banging it after me.

Mama was always a stickler for the respect she considered due your elders. And she hadn't changed any as I found out one night that week when Phil

and I got into an argument about some people I didn't like. I lost my temper.
"What the hell do you know about anything?" I snapped.

Smack! Mama's hand caught me flat across the face.

"Don't forget, young lady, you may be a headliner, and you may be the
breadwinner of this family, but just the same this is my house. And in my
house you'll show respect for your elders at all times."

I wasn't likely to forget, not with that stinging mark on my cheek. Believe
me, I watched my P's and Q's from then on. Mama never had occasion to
smack me again until just a few years before she passed on in 1924. Then she
heard me let out at Phil again for not doing something I had asked him
to have done in the house. I was smacked right down, and I was in the
two-thousand-dollar brackets then too. Not that that made any difference
to Mama.

But one thing Phil did get out of me that week was a promise to send him
every dollar I could save from my salary for him to invest and look after, so
I would be sure to have a few dollars for a rainy day. He knew I took after
Pa in loving to gamble. Living the kind of life I lived, here, there, and
everywhere, with always the temptation to get into poker games or to play
the horses, I would have been in the same spot that a lot of performers I've
known, and ones who made big money, but for Phil keeping me to that
promise all through these years. Oh, I've broken it time and time again.
And I've always been sorry. I've been furious at Phil for budgeting me and
keeping me to that budget, but even when my temper was hottest I've
known deep down inside myself that he was right, and that I was a fool
for not paying attention to what he said.

Saturday. My closing day. I'm leaving for New York right after the night
show, as I am booked for a Sunday concert. Directly after the matinee I
must go home and pack and take everything to the theater to be ready to run
for the train.

The house when I come in is full of women: all Mama's friends—Mrs.
Katzman, Mrs. Koppleman, Mrs. Susman, Mrs. Laschever, Mrs. Gaberman,
Mrs. Diwinski (Dora's mother), and Mrs. Greenberg—Ettie, who is Mama's
oldest friend.

"It's my committee," Mama explains importantly. "We're planning how
to raise the money to build the Jewish Home for the Aged."

I knew what that meant: going from door to door, collecting pennies,
nickels, dimes, quarters, whatever they could get. They were all women past
middle age, with grown sons and daughters—women who had been born

in Russia and Poland and Hungary, who had come to this country with no
more than they could carry in their linen-wrapped bundles—the way Mama
had come. All of them had had to work hard helping their men support
and bring up their families. And now that those families were grown, and
were looking out for them, they were concerned for other old people, the
ones of their faith who didn't have children or grandchildren to care for
them.

They had all been to Poli's that week to see my act. And now all of them
more or less complimented me. Not too extravagantly—it's the Jewish way to
be cautious about compliments—but enough to seem polite to Mama.

I am sitting at the table, having my early dinner, when Ettie, Mrs. Greenberg, comes over to sit beside me. This is the conversation. All in Jewish, of
course:

SOPHIE: "Well, Ettie, did you go to Poli's this week?"

ETTIE: "Yes, I had to go and see what everybody was talking about."

SOPHIE: "I hope you enjoyed my act."

ETTIE: "You yell just as loud in the theater as you did in the restaurant.
I see no difference."

SOPHIE: "What did you expect me to do? I am a singer."

ETTIE: "Why can't you dance?"

SOPHIE: "I don't know how."

ETTIE: "Why can't you tumble like the other acrobats?"

SOPHIE: "I don't know how."

ETTIE: "Why can't you play the piano? Your mother spent plenty money
for your lessons."

SOPHIE: "But I'm a singer of songs. That's my specialty."

ETTIE: "Well, I can't speak English. I don't understand English. How do
you expect me to enjoy your act?"

SOPHIE: "Surely there was something you enjoyed?"

ETTIE: "Yes, I liked the dancers. And the musical act. And the acrobats."

SOPHIE: "But didn't you think I looked nice? I wore some very lovely
gowns and diamonds."

ETTIE: "The night I saw you you wore a white *schmatie* (a rag) with a
black bow. I saw bows like that at the Five-and-Ten. And your diamonds
can't be anything but chips. They were so small. From the back of the
theater where I sat they looked like nothing. They didn't shine at all. Tell
me the truth now: are they paying you five hundred dollars?"

SOPHIE: "If you'll come with me to the theater tonight I'll let you see the
treasurer pay me my salary. And if they don't pay me five hundred dollars,

I'll give you one hundred dollars toward the home. If they do pay me five hundred dollars, I'll give you fifty dollars. Is it a go?"

And that, believe it or not, was the windup of the most wonderful week in my life. I was in no danger of getting a swelled head as long as I stayed in my own home town.

CHAPTER 13: *"I've Got a Man"*

WHEN I was playing in George Jessel's *High Kickers* I had a song with that title and that refrain. It was my hit of the show. Why? Not for the sophisticated lines. Not for the innuendo. But for the idea on which the song was built—that, come hell or high water, hard luck, middle age, world wars and five-per-cent income taxes, you can take whatever life deals you and smile *if you've got a man.*

There isn't a woman in the world who doesn't feel like that, no matter what she tells her hairdresser. And there isn't a man who doesn't secretly want his woman to feel that way about him. I don't need any psychologist to tell me this. I know it, because that's the way I'm made, myself.

Coming back to *High Kickers,* every night it came time for me to take that number I'd start thinking: "Why the hell couldn't it have been that way with *me?* What's the matter with life, or with Sophie Tucker, that I've never had a man in my life to stand up to me and give me as good as I could give him?"

There was Louis Tuck, the boy I married when I was just a kid myself, the father of my son. I've told you about him. Louis was never unkind to me. He never gave me a cross word. But he wouldn't put his shoulder under the responsibility of marriage. And I had seen Mama work too hard through too many years to be willing to start that way myself. So I pulled out and set my mind and my heart on making a career for myself that would make me independent. Maybe that was my big mistake. Not leaving Louis, but turning myself into the family breadwinner. Something happens to a woman when she does that. She may kid herself that it's just temporary, only until the right man turns up, and then she'll throw her arms around his neck and be a clinging vine all the rest of her life. It doesn't work that way. Once you start on the independent circuit, you're committed for life. There's no backing out or breaking that contract. Once you start carrying your own suitcase, paying your own bills, running your own show, you've done something to yourself that makes you one of those women men may like and call "a pal" and "a good sport," the kind of woman they tell their troubles to. But you've cut yourself off from the orchids and the diamond bracelets, except those you buy yourself.

Naturally, I didn't know this when I turned my back on Hartford and my face toward New York and a start in show business. Even after I started on the road in vaudeville I used to dream that someday, maybe in the next town I played, there would be a man whose eye, when it fell on me, would light up with that unmistakable look that tells you you've gone over big with him, and when you come out the stage door after the show, hungry as a horse at the end of a hard day's work, and ready for some fun, and a little loving, he'll be there waiting for you. One of those strong, masterful men, who know their own minds, who never say: "I'll take vanilla too." A man who thinks a woman is somebody to be looked out for, and not somebody to borrow money from.

I looked for him, and I went on looking. For years. If he exists, all I can say is that he and I never hit the same town together. We're on different circuits.

There have been a couple of times when I thought I had him spotted.

Back in September 1909, when I was playing my first date at the American Music Hall on Forty-second Street and Eighth Avenue, I used to walk from the Times Square subway station down Forty-first Street to the stage door. On the corner where the Hotel Hermitage now stands was a very popular bar. I mean a corner saloon, the kind we had in those days, with the street door opening into a back room with tables for ladies. Then, if you wanted your husband, you went to the back room and asked if he was at the bar. Today a husband can find his wife and children in any bar.

Going back and forth I noticed a fine-looking man, around thirty, who evidently owned the place, standing at the door. He would smile and nod at me. And I would nod and smile back, "Hello, there," and go on to work.

About the third day this happened Mrs. Bernstein, my first friend in New York, was with me. "Who is he?" she wanted to know. "You know as much as I do," I told her, adding that we had been nodding and smiling for several days.

I had dinner with the Bernsteins, I remember, and they both walked me back to work. There was my friend again. The Bernsteins laughed and teased me about it. "It looks like he's on the make for you. He's a fine-looking fellow too."

After the show that night I hesitated. Should I walk up Forty-first Street again, or take the next block and put an end to this nonsense? I remembered the Bernsteins' comments. I thought: I've always said I didn't want a man in show business, and this man is not an actor. Four years, always alone, is a long time. Well, anyway, I walked up Forty-first Street that night and into my first romance since I eloped to Holyoke with Louis.

His name was—— I'll call him Joe. I don't want to hurt anyone's feelings. I didn't have to tell him my name. When I started to, "I know who you are," he cut in. "I saw you at your opening matinee. You're grand."

That went over like a bang with me.

When I told Mollie about him she grinned. "Good for you, Patsy. Just what you need, someone to be interested in you. You mustn't give your whole life to your family and your career. It ain't natural. Get some fun out of life too."

All that year I was in and out of New York, working hard all the time. But wasn't it a grand feeling to come back to somebody who cared? All through those months I was on the West Coast I looked forward to playing New York again with Joe there to welcome me and make me feel, what every woman wants to feel, *wanted*. It wasn't as if we could be married. I wasn't divorced. And being constantly on the road, as I was, I knew if I were tied up I would start to worry and fret. Best to leave well enough alone.

So for a while I was happy. I had a man.

Then, gradually, things began to change. First, the Hotel Hermitage was rebuilt, and Joe's place had to come down. When I came back to town I found he was in a new business—horse racing. Right away when I heard that my heart gave a big flop and dropped twenty degrees. I knew what a gambler's life was. I thought of Pa and of others I'd known. But Joe was so hopeful, so sure he was going to be in the money.

"The next time you hit this town, honey, we'll be sitting pretty."

You can see, can't you, how things were shaping? Me working, pushing my salary up as I have told. The house for the family to be paid for. Brother Moe finishing law school. Son growing and needing things. And now feeding the horses. It just didn't work out.

When I was in Chicago, rehearsing for *Louisiana Lou,* I made myself think hard. If the show was a hit, it would mean a long run. I couldn't get back to New York for months. It was no way to go on, Joe in New York playing the ponies and me footing the bills for the ones that ran wild. I wrote Joe: "Best to call everything off. It doesn't work."

He took it hard. Joe cared for me a lot. And I cared for him. He came on to Chicago, thinking there was some other man in the picture, but there wasn't, and I made him see the real reason for my decision. I might play poker myself. Or the horses. As I did. But that was *my* money I was gambling with—money I earned. I couldn't carry him too. And I wouldn't.

I missed him dreadfully, but I knew I was doing right. And Mollie helped me. I had her wisdom, her philosophy to lean on when I felt my own knees wobble and my courage begin to slide.

"The trouble with you, Patsy, is you're a one-man woman," Mollie would say.

"I know. But where in hell is that one man for me?"

In Chicago, a retired businessman made quite a fuss over me. He was great fun, and I liked him. Then one night I saw him in the theater where I was playing with a very lovely-looking woman. When he told me she was his wife, I called a halt immediately. I knew there would be no luck for me, no successful career if I hurt anybody. I was never one to go out after the other woman's man, and I wasn't starting now. So that romance had a quick curtain.

People used to kid me because I was always alone. No man of my own. I'll never forget August (Gary) Hermann, the president of the Cincinnati Reds and the Exalted Ruler of the Elks, one of the best friends I ever had, teasing me: "Come on, Sophie. What's wrong with you? I never see you with any men."

"Not a thing, Gary. Only I guess the men are hep to me that I wear tin drawers."

That crack was our standing joke for years.

One season when I played Cincinnati, Gary threw a big party for me at the Sinton Hotel. The mayor was there, and all of Gary's brother Elks— two hundred people seated in the ballroom. After the banquet, speeches, all in my honor. Finally up got Gary. "I have here a little token which I hope Sophie will always cherish and appreciate from her friends in Cincinnati." He handed me a jeweler's box tied with blue ribbon.

"Open it, Sophie," everyone yelled.

Inside was a tiny pair of drawers made of tin with ruffles and a huge safety pin.

How we laughed! Especially Jeweler Sol Gilsey, who had made this work of art for the occasion. After the laughs, Gary presented me with a lovely gold wrist watch. Often, when I looked at it, I thought: "What right have you got to feel lonely and sorry for yourself when you have such swell friends? You're doing what you want to do, and doing it successfully. You've got a family you love, and who love you. You have friends in every town, in every state. Good friends. You haven't an ache or a pain, or a real worry. What more do you want?"

But all the time I knew what I wanted: a man.

A short time before I played that week at Poli's in Hartford I met Frank Westphal. He was on the same bill with me, booked as a piano act. A very funny entrance he used to make, coming off the street with topcoat, hat, and rubbers. He would take these off one by one, then go into his piano act. Frank could play a mean piano.

Many times we had lots of fun on these vaudeville bills, butting in and clowning on one another's act. The audience loved it because they never knew what to expect. That was how the famous "after-piece stunt" we did on the big-time at the close of the regular vaudeville bill got started. It became quite a fad, and a great drawing card for the box office. As for the butting into one another's acts, you had to be on your toes the whole time. You never knew when one of the other performers would suddenly come on and start to stooge for you. One day, I remember, Frank Westphal suddenly pushed his piano out on the stage during my act. The house shrieked with laughter when he said: "Excuse me, Miss Tucker, I forgot to play a song in my act. I know you won't mind if I do it now."

"Of course not. Go right ahead," I replied.

I walked toward the piano, and as Frank played a popular song I started to sing it. Before we knew it, we were a riot, ad-libbing back and forth. The audience wanted more, but we had nothing more to offer. It was just a gag— a laugh to break up my act. But it had something.

In the next town we played we did it again. Pretty soon the managers began to report to the main office that these two performers had a good stunt. As we played through the Midwest, Frank and I were booked together, and we went on improving the stunt, building it up. I started to write to the New York booking offices that Frank and I had a great double act.

After I finished playing the Midwest I went East and opened at Hammerstein's in New York, first time with Westphal. This was my first appearance in New York in over two years. I had a lot of new songs: "Floating Down the River," "Somebody's Coming to My House," "Swing, Swing, Swing," and others.

It was quite a feat to come into New York in July and do a big business. I was getting a thousand dollars a week now, and earning every cent of it by hard work. I was working steadily, off on the road playing the Keith theaters (I started to play them in 1913), back in New York for return dates at Hammerstein's and at the Alhambra and the Royal. The vaudeville bills were getting bigger every season: Louis Mann (he would condense one of his legitimate shows for a vaudeville act), Gene Green, Chic Yorke and King, Emma Carus, Nat Wills, Evelyn Nesbit, Frank Joyce and Dorothy

West, dancers (Frank was Alice Joyce's brother), the Dolly Sisters, Lew Lockett and Jack Waldron, the Three Keatons (including Buster)—all the big B. O. acts of those days.

"The first time I played the Palace . . ." How many times I've heard performers start off a story like that. And immediately all listeners sighed with envy. To play the Palace was to American performers what a command performance is to a British actor. Something to live for. Something to boast about all the rest of your days.

The Palace was New York's top-notch vaudeville house through so many years it became a tradition. To go on there was what "going on at Tony Pastor's" was in the Gay Nineties.

The first week of August 1914 goes down in history for events of world-wide importance. Even in the midst of the most startling headlines our generation had seen I could still feel a thrill that I was "playing the Palace." Chic Sale was on the bill with me, I remember. I had some swell new songs: "There's a Girl in the Heart of Maryland," Irving Berlin's "International Rag," "Papa and Mama Left Me All Alone," and for my risqué number, "Who Paid the Rent for Mrs. Rip Van Winkle?" Frank Westphal was billed with me, and together we put those songs across with a wallop, if I do say so. The press said it first. The boys handed me the biggest bouquet of my life in vaudeville:

. . . she just walked out and owned the place, putting over eight songs so quick and great that at five o'clock she stopped the show dead still, until she made a speech. She has a chap, Frank Westphal, at the piano who is some accompanist, and with some songs she had a walkaway. Sophie made the biggest hit ever made in this house by a single woman. . . .

I nearly wore the paper out reading those lines over and over. It seemed as if, now, I hadn't anything left to wish for.

Frank and I were getting along together very comfortably. He had a sense of humor and our act was a big success. We might have gone on the way we were indefinitely, but after we had been out on the road a while I could see it was a case of splitting up or getting married. I gave a lot of thought to it because Frank was younger than I, about seven years. True, I had always said nothing on earth would induce me to marry an actor. But this, I told myself, was different. (I suppose every woman says that to herself some time or other, and thinks it's true.) Still, as I say, we hit it off well. Louis Tuck had passed away by this time, so there was no barrier to my marrying again.

Of course Frank was not of my faith. I didn't know how Mama would take that, so I decided not to say a word to the family until after we were married. As it turned out, Mama made no objections. "It is your happiness that matters most," she wrote me afterward.

Frank and I were playing Chicago and were billed to go West from there on the Orpheum Circuit. My old friend Frank Behring made the marriage arrangements for us. Gary Hermann was in Chicago that week, and gave us a wedding supper at the Café Royale, at Clark and Munroe streets. Who should be dining there that same night but the great Paderewski? He congratulated us and joined our party and the fun. With a wave of those famous hands he sent the pianist away from the piano, sat down, and played the Lohengrin Wedding March in our honor.

I was thinking: this is some step up for Sophie Abuza, to have Paderewski play for her wedding. Frank squeezed my hand under the table. "I couldn't play it much better myself," he said with a straight face.

It was Frank's sense of humor, as much as anything else, that kept us together so long. Life on the road, from one hotel and one theater to the next, gets pretty tough. It isn't the audiences that take it out of an entertainer; it's the train trips, the everlasting packing and unpacking, the hotel bedrooms all so much alike, the drafty, often dirty backstage and dressing rooms, the tempers and jealousies of the other performers on the bill. Most of all, it's the theater managers, each with his own pet notions about how an act should be put across. Each with his own pet hates and prejudices.

You've got to have a sense of humor to be able to stand it. God help you if you haven't.

Naturally, I'd heard a lot of talk from other performers all along the line about whether a husband and wife can play together and at the same time keep their marriage from going on the rocks. There were lots who said it couldn't be done. They said the only way to stay happily married and in show business was to work separately, and not worry about who was two-timing who through the season. Then to go down to Freeport, Long Island, together and enjoy a summer honeymoon. A lot of them did that.

That kind of married life never appealed to me, which was one reason I always said I'd never marry an actor. Just the same, as I pretty soon found out, there's an awful strain in working constantly with the person you're married to. What with two shows a day, six—sometimes seven—days a week, and continually rehearsing new songs and new business, neither husband nor wife ever gets any time off.

I'm honest. I admit there were plenty of days when I wanted to throw my cold-cream jar at Frank's head and burst into a fit of hysterics to raise the roof. Mollie kept me from doing it. She had not favored my marriage except, as she said, "Go on and do it if it makes you happy." Likewise, there were times when Frank probably felt he'd like to wring my neck. Those were the times when his sense of humor and mine (which were pretty much alike) saved the day and our act. Something ridiculous would happen, and both of us would have to laugh. Or out of our mad one or the other of us would get an idea to put into the act. We'd go to work on it and forget whatever it was started us calling names.

We were always looking for something new. Once, when we were playing a return date at the Palace Theatre in Chicago, Frank and I had a row. He flung himself out of the theater, and I went into my dressing room and slammed the door so hard it sounded like a bomb. Show time came, and no Frank. The curtain went up. Still no Frank. I got madder and madder. Maybe, too, I was a little scared. Coming up the hard way, as I have, has given me a respect for the law of show business, which is that a performer shall be there and ready when his call comes. Two minutes to go, and along came Frank. With him was the crumbiest-looking bum you ever laid eyes on.

I was ready to let all the fireworks loose, but Frank shushed me: "Hold everything, Soph. The bum goes on in the act with us."

He went. And what a riot! The bum had a mouth organ, and could he play it? He accompanied Frank and me as if we'd rehearsed the act a hundred times. Frank had found him in a saloon, entertaining customers for the price of a drink. Frank's "find" later went with the Gallagher and Shean act. If only he hadn't been so fond of the bottle he might have had a career in show business.

It was Frank who sold me on the idea that I should buy a car. I'd never owned one, but Frank knew cars: at one time he used to race them. Soon our family had an addition: a big maroon, underslung Mercer, with SOPHIE TUCKER painted in big letters on the doors. We used the car to drive from date to date, instead of crowding into Pullmans any more. It was fun, and plenty of publicity. There never was any doubt when Sophie Tucker hit town.

Whenever we played New York I'd send for Son. He would come down from the Peekskill Military Academy and stay with me. It was fun showing him the town. I remember taking him to Churchill's to dinner when that place was in its heyday. Son was cute in his uniform with his solemn little face. I got a great kick out of the other diners turning to look at us, saying, "Why, that's Sophie Tucker. That must be her little boy."

Never will I forget; we had oysters—big ones. I had to gulp to get mine down. Son tried to do it, failed, and had to pull the oyster out of his throat with his fingers. Maybe he felt everybody was watching him. Anyway, he flopped the oyster down on his plate, took a knife, and cut it in two and ate the pieces with a fork, while the customers laughed.

Whenever I could, I'd run up to Hartford for a few hours with Ma and Pa. I always tried to be with them for our High Holidays, knowing how much it meant to them to have all their family with them at these solemn times. I knew Ma would boast to her buddies about "mein Sophie" that was a headliner and made so much money coming home. And Pa would be doing the same to the pinochle players in the back room of the saloon down in our old neighborhood he used to go to every day.

Sure, I felt puffed up and pleased with myself and my fine clothes and diamonds and willow plumes going home, a success. I got a big kick out of taking presents to all the family. Giving Ma the diamond earrings that that stage-door Johnny in Chicago had given me years ago. I had much bigger ones now that I was buying on time. Ma wore hers proudly till one day, riding in the streetcar, she fell sucker to a couple of con men who offered to exchange her diamonds for a pair of much bigger blue stones. She thought she was getting a bargain until her friend, the jeweler on the corner, told her the big blue stones were glass.

But no matter how set up I was with myself, the minute I set foot in Ma's house I had to fall in line with the rules of an old-fashioned, religious household. I had to stop being a headliner and the boss, and remember I was just a daughter, who had to sit back and let the men of the family take the lead. Even Son, the eldest grandson, ranked ahead of me when it came to our religious ceremonies.

I nearly choked with pride and tears one time when I was able at the last minute to run home for *Pasach,* and I heard Son ask Pa the four *kashas.* These are the ritual questions which must always be asked by the youngest male at the feast.

We were all there: Pa at the head of the table in the king's chair, banked up in pillows, and Son at his right hand; Ma at the other end of the table as "queen," and close to the kitchen door so she could slip in and prepare each dish as Pa read the ritual—and bring them in at the right moment; Phil and Leah, Moe, Annie, Frank, and I on the other side of Son. And always guests, according to the ancient custom of our people. How sweet it was! How homey! How solemn! How far away from show business with all its ambitions, struggles, disappointments, and heartaches.

"O God," I prayed, looking at all those dear faces in the candlelight, "please let us stay like this, together, for a long, long time."

CHAPTER 14: *Five Kings to a Queen of Jazz*

MAX HART had done well by me. It had helped my prestige a lot to be known as one of the acts he handled. Just the same, for me there never was, never could be, but one "Boss." So when William Morris, Sr., came back from his stay at Saranac, cured, and opened up the William Morris Agency, I couldn't wait to get a release from Max Hart and go back to work for the man who first put me on big-time.

Abe Lastfogel and I have gone along working together all these years. In Abe we have the Boss again, not only in his ways of handling people, working with them and for them, but also in his foresight and understanding of the amusement world. To this day, when you take a difficult problem to Abe he thinks it over and usually says: "If the Boss was here I'm sure he would suggest such and such."

Then there is young Bill Morris. As a kid in short pants he used to come into the office and sit at his tiny desk. The Boss adored him, and made him his confidant. You could see his eagerness to have Junior learn the business and follow in his footsteps, as he has done so successfully.

The Boss and I had many a good talk. It was wonderful how he had his finger on the pulse of show business. He could see changes coming long before other people knew a change was possible. There was one thing, though, he kept telling me never changed. That was the customers' response to an entertainer who met them at their own level; who was one of them. "It isn't that the public doesn't like success. It does. But if the performer's success, and what she does with it, separates her from the life of the folks who plunk down their dollar bills to see her and hear her, something happens to her that kills her work."

I listened, and I thought a lot about what the Boss said. On the road—the office booked Frank Westphal's act and mine together, although we were billed individually—I used to watch the box office all the time. I would go out in front of the house to hear what the customers said when they bought their tickets. After the show I would go out into the lobby to catch the comments. When I heard them say: "Sophie Tucker with the man who pushes his piano out on the stage while she's singing is awfully funny," I knew we were all right. We hadn't lost touch, as the Boss called it. Of course we had to keep the act alive with new ideas, new tricks all the time. You can't let yourself get stale in this business. And each new piece of business we added had to be put to the same test—did it have human appeal? Was it the kind of thing everybody was going to laugh at?

"What gives an act its great entertainment value," the Boss used to say, "is its spontaneity. It's the way an actor seizes on something that happens unexpectedly and turns it into a laugh. The public loves that."

How right he was; just as right today as twenty-five years ago.

Frank and I worked together on big-time through several seasons. I was gradually changing my style of singing, getting away from the coon shouting. I was more subdued, smoother. The press noticed it approvingly. Meanwhile, as the war in Europe went on and everyone realized that America would inevitably be drawn into it, you began to notice a difference in the audiences. Everywhere we played you felt an emotional tensity. Folks were keyed up; on edge. They were quick to respond to songs of emotional appeal.

At the Royal Theatre in the Bronx I introduced the ballad "M-O-T-H-E-R, the Word That Means the World to Me." You couldn't possibly go wrong with a song like that. It was sure-fire.

There were a lot of clever young performers breaking into show business in those years. Fred and Adele Astaire were one team that was getting a lot of notice. Gus Edwards, who deserved the title of star maker if anyone ever did, was playing his famous school act. And what kids he had with him! Eddie Cantor, George Jessel, Georgie Price, Lila Lee, Walter Winchell.

The first time I played a bill with them was in Harrisburg, Pennsylvania. The kids put on a great show, and the customers loved it. They were fun around the theater too, always in some deviltry, playing tricks on one another. It was that season when I played a week in Knoxville I came down with a bad cold and laryngitis. I went to a doctor, who gave me a lecture on the way I was ruining my voice coon shouting. I finished the week, then took the M. D.'s advice—canceled my next date and went home to rest.

That week the Edwards act played Knoxville, Tennessee, and Eddie Cantor caught cold. He went to the same doctor, who told him he had a patient named Sophie Tucker who abused her throat so much she couldn't possibly last long. He warned Eddie against following my bad example.

Well, the good doctor has passed on, but Eddie and I seem to be still in business.

Gradually, as Frank and I worked along together, my eyes opened to something I should have been on to long before. This was the bad effect on my husband of my making more money than he made. Frank was developing what in those days was called a steady grouch. Now we call it an inferiority complex; but it all comes to the same thing in the end. On paydays he would cringe and slink off. I wouldn't see him again till show time. And it would take a couple of days to get him back into the state of mind he needed to be in to put our act across.

I didn't know what the hell to do about it. I talked it over with Mollie, who could see what was happening. She made me see it was my fault. And yet I didn't see how I could be or do any different. Maybe I was bossy and domineering. If I was, it was the good of our act I was thinking of. I wasn't out to ride my husband because I was pulling down seven hundred and fifty or a thousand dollars a week. I swear I wasn't. Just the same, it was my success that brought about the failure of my marriage. Since I've been in show business I have been married twice. Both marriages were failures, due—as I can honestly say—to my earning capacity. As Mollie said, no red-blooded man can stand that situation.

I worried a lot about Frank. I could see that his act alone would never be in the big money. Meanwhile, this double act of ours, with me earning more than twice what he could earn, was the worst thing in the world for him and for our married life. Frank needed a business of his own—something unrelated to show business.

Before he went on the stage he had fooled around with automobile racing in Chicago. He knew a car from A to Z. That gave me an idea. The next time we played East I talked it over with my brother Phil, who was investing my money for me. He approved the idea of a garage for Frank. No more show business.

Frank fell for the idea. I guess he was sick and tired of being "Mr. Sophie Tucker." A place was found out in Baldwin, Long Island, on the Merrick Road. We called it, in big, block letters you could read as far as you could see the place, THE SOPHIE TUCKER GARAGE.

Another mistake, of course, as I can see now. Then, all I thought of was the publicity: for the garage and for me. I never thought what that name was

going to do to Frank. Just dumb. I know I'm not dumb when it's a matter
of show business, but in my love life I've certainly laid plenty of eggs. My
experience with Frank was the beginning. And what it has cost me in hard
money! Not long before Ben Bernie died he said to me: "Sophie, how much
do you figure your love life has cost you? A couple of hundred thousand?"

"A couple of hundred thousand nothing," I fired back, thinking of Frank
and then of my third husband Al Lackey. "It's set me back a million if it has
a cent. And what have I got for it? Not a damn thing but experience!"

With Frank started in the automobile business I was up against it for a
new act. I couldn't go back to do a single again—it wouldn't mean a thing.
What could be different about a single woman on a bill singing songs when
so many were doing that?

I talked it over with the Boss to get his advice. He agreed with me that
I should have something entirely new. He made me feel good when he said
that I had developed a grand sense of comedy, and that I could no longer do
my best stuff as a single. "Loaf for a while," he advised. "You haven't done
that for a long time. It will do you good. Get out and see what's around
town. You'll get an idea."

Frank and I started out to go cabareting. New York had a lot of places
to see. There was Shanley's, the Everglades, Pabst's on Columbus Circle,
Rector's, and a lot more. Rector's drew the Broadway crowd as it featured
the best dance orchestras in town. Those were the days of the famous ballroom dance teams—the Castles, Maurice and Walton, Joan Sawyer. Nobody
yet had heard of torch singers, and jazz was just coming in.

We had no master of ceremonies in those days. At all the hot spots the
proprietor kept things going. Usually whenever any professional entertainers
came in he recognized them and would call on them to come out on the
floor and entertain the crowd. It was free entertainment, impromptu, and
it created a feeling of real camaraderie. It wasn't often that the vaudevillians
went to such places. For one thing, most of us couldn't afford it; for another,
we preferred to get together in one of the crowd's hotel room for supper and
poker where we entertained ourselves.

Going around to all the smart places in New York, which were new to me,
I thought I might see something different that would give me an idea for an
act. But I didn't. After one of those evenings when I was about ready to
give up and go home somebody said: "Come on, let's go over to the Tokio."

The Tokio was one of Broadway's hot spots. Henry Fink ran it. He was
there at the door with a big "Hello" to everybody. The place was packed,
and it seemed as if everybody was having a grand time. In a few minutes

I heard him sing out: "And now, ladies and gentlemen, another great comedy and singing act—Sophie Tucker and Frank Westphal."

There was nothing for us to do but get out on the floor. It was the first time I'd ever worked on a floor in New York, and if you are used to working on a stage it comes hard at first to sing to people who are so close to you and on the same level, and who are sitting at tables eating and drinking, instead of sitting quiet in rows facing you. A lot of performers can't work on a floor at all. They can't stand the nearness or having the customers see their make-up. Some get a complex about it. I'm one of the lucky ones who can feel as easy on a floor as on the stage.

Frank went to the piano. As I started to sing, I heard the band that played the dance music join in with the piano. That band did something to me; I sang so different. I looked behind and saw five boys, none of them over eighteen or nineteen years old. Fine-looking kids, smiling, peppy, and hot. I sang for an hour. I guess I enjoyed the band playing for me more than the audience enjoyed my singing. I whispered to Frank: "This is it. A band like this. I've got my new act."

That was the start of Sophie Tucker's Five Kings of Syncopation. The Boss liked the idea. "Okay, dear. Get your boys. How long will it take you to get the act set?"

"Give me a couple of weeks."

He could see how enthusiastic I was to get going. It seemed as if I couldn't wait for Frank to find five boys and sign them up so we could start rehearsing. My mind was working a mile a minute thinking of things to try out with the band. When we started the rehearsals, I worked the boys to a frazzle. I was a regular Simon Legree. If a boy showed he could sing a note, or play a solo, or dance a step, we made a place for it in the act. I was hell-bent on getting the utmost entertainment value out of the "Five Kings of Syncopation" as we decided to call them. Instead of "The Mary Garden of Ragtime," I became "The Queen of Jazz." That change in my billing marks the end of one era and the opening of another. I've lived through coon shouting, ragtime, jazz, swing, the hep-cat, jitterbug, and zoot-suit eras.

I knew there wasn't an act on the road anything at all like what I had in mind. I was determined to make mine so good that the press would hail it as something new, "different," and all the customers who had been coming regularly to see me would say this new act was the best I'd ever given them. It was some work I was laying out for myself.

We opened at the Greenpoint Theatre in Brooklyn for a break-in. The building was once a church that was renovated to be a theater. Those walls never echoed to anything like what the boys and I gave them that afternoon. The boys were on their toes, eager to make good. So was I. I must have been, for I was able to sing ten songs in twenty-five minutes. Not only that, but I made a change of costume during the act, coming on in semi-formal and changing to full evening dress with all my diamonds. I still kept in mind that the women in the audience like to see stunning clothes.

The Boss came over to see the act. He said it was still rough and needed lots of work, but he liked it. He booked us for several weeks at the Islesworth Gardens in Atlantic City, and then on the Orpheum Circuit. It would be my fourth trip to the Coast.

Mollie went with me, as usual. I needed her as I never needed her before. I had my hands full managing the boys, keeping the act up, trying out new stunts to introduce as we went along. I was using props in the act for the first time: gorgeous Spanish shawls to fling over the piano, a grass skirt for a "hula" song, a big Mexican sombrero for a song about the Rio Grande. Up to this time the only prop I ever used, since that rose I used to take out of my hair and sing to, was a big chiffon hanky. The big hanky, which I believe I introduced, was something more than a bit of colorful decoration. It was a prop in every sense of the word.

When I started singing, I was terribly clumsy with my hands. I didn't know what to do with them, and I was conscious of their size long after I had eliminated the red dishwashing look. I used to stand in front of the mirror every day and make gestures, learning how to use my hands gracefully. Today, when I see a singer standing in front of a "mike" hanging on to it for dear life while she sings into it, instead of to the audience, I feel like yelling at her: "Let go, sister. If you only knew how terrible you look like that, you'd lower the mike and stand clear of it and use your hands as a part of your act, the way an entertainer should."

At the beginning the handkerchief gave me something to pull on if I got nervous. It helped me, and as it became identified with me (here's Sophie and her hanky) I always carried one. I do to this day. One night, not long ago, a taxi driver driving me home after work in Chicago turned round in the seat and said: "Say, ain't you Sophie Tucker?"

I admitted it.

"I seen you a long time ago, in vaudeville. Say, do you still use one of them big handkerchiefs?"

It's funny what folks remember.

At the break-in with the Five Kings my salary was six hundred and fifty dollars. Out of this I had to pay each of the boys fifty dollars and traveling expenses. I wouldn't be in pocket nearly so much as when Frank and I did our act together. But I figured I was doing the right thing: branching out into something bigger and more important. It was just as it had been when I realized it was to my advantage to give up work and good pay at the German Village to get into vaudeville, even at twenty-five dollars a week. It was stepping out in the right direction. If the customers liked my new act, then I could soon raise my price for it. First, though, I had to sell it to the public.

Out came the good old address book. Off went hundreds, thousands of post cards as we traveled the circuit. I wrote everybody I knew everywhere along the line: *"Look out for me. I'm coming your way with a brand-new show. New songs. New clothes. Don't miss it!"*

My hopes were high, for the press in New York when we opened there had been terrific. The critics praised the new act: said it was something entirely new, and prophesied it would go over big. *Variety* said: "Sophie Tucker is back. In all, a fine combination. Back with the best act she has ever been identified with."

God bless Sime Silverman for what those words meant to me.

We played in luck for the whole tour to the West Coast. The press stayed enthusiastic and the customers showed they approved of the new act. It was up to the minute. Peppy.

The original Five Kings who went on the first tour with me were Slim Pressler, pianist; Sam Green, violinist; Ralph Herz, drummer; Phil Saxe, saxophonist; and Peter Quinn, cellist and clarinetist. Now and then I'd have trouble with one or another of them. They would get out of hand and have to be smacked down. Rehearsals were very trying at times. How often I regretted not having kept on with my twenty-five-cent piano lessons when I was a kid. To this day I can't read a note of music and I know nothing about a piano keyboard. But when I hear a tune my ear is quick to detect in it what will suit me and what has to be changed for me.

Many times the boys and I lived at the same hotels on the road, and many a night after the show we six would get together and play poker. No high stakes (I usually got trimmed anyway). One thing I made clear to them right from the start—no drinking. If a boy started that, his contract was canceled at once and he left the band. But the boys were all nice kids and hard workers who wanted to get ahead. Lord knows I lectured them enough about that. Save your money; send home your money order every payday; take out insurance and annuities. Remember there's many a rainy day in show business.

When we left California, heading for Salt Lake City and Denver, I was given a chance to satisfy any latent mother hunger I had in me.

Mollie and I were sitting in my drawing room when a little girl came by and peeked in the door at us. "Come on in," I said.

She was a friendly little thing, very talkative; she told us her name, June Campbell, and that her mother was in the Pullman coach ahead. She added importantly: "She's an actress too." (I found she had been traveling with an illusion set, handling the props.) A little later the youngster came out with: "We're going home so my mother can have a baby."

After dinner I walked through the Pullmans to see whether I knew Mrs. Campbell or if there were other show people aboard. I asked the porter about the child and her mother and was told they had retired. I spent some time in the observation car, then Mollie came to tell me our drawing room was made up and I should get to bed.

Going back through the Pullmans something—one of my hunches, I guess—told me to hunt for that porter again and ask him what berth Mrs. Campbell and her little girl were in. He told me the number, and I went down the aisle to it. I touched the green curtains.

"Mrs. Campbell," I said, "it's me, Sophie Tucker. Your little girl told me . . ."

I heard a low moan.

I put my head through the curtains. "Your kid told me about you. Can I help you?"

The poor woman was in agony. She had her face buried in the pillow to stifle her groans while her hands reached up to the upper berth to hang onto something.

I got the conductor and a couple of porters. We managed to carry Mrs. Campbell into my drawing room while the conductor wired ahead for a doctor to board the train at the next place we came to. Mollie and I held the fort till the doctor came aboard. A couple of hours later, while we were racing over the great salt desert, the cutest little trick was born in my drawing room. At Jericho, Utah, the doctor took mother, baby, and the sleepy little girl off the train to the local hospital. A few days later I got a wire:

HEARTFELT THANKS FOR YOUR KINDNESS AND HELP. SOPHIE TUCKER CAMPBELL AND I ARE WELL AND WE SEND YOU OUR LOVE.

MRS. ELRI CAMPBELL

Little Sophie is married now, and has a small son. There's always a welcome for me at her home in Detroit.

CHAPTER 15: *Trouping*

As we swung round the Orpheum Circuit playing to big houses everywhere I always looked forward to playing Chicago; always wondering how my good friends there were going to like the Five Kings.

We came into the old Palace Theatre with a great bill: Herb Williams, the comedian, and Hilda Wolfus; Laura Nelson Hall in a sketch; Frank Orth; Tom Dugan and Babe Raymond; Bensee and Baird; Bert Kalmer and Jessie Brown, dancers. Later Bert Kalmer turned song writer and wrote *High Kickers,* in which I played with George Jessel. I was headlining the bill.

The act had a wonderful reception at the Monday matinee. This was always a great day for the regular customers, especially women. Many of them never missed a Monday matinee at the Palace from one year's end to the next. They knew all the performers and had their favorites. They didn't miss a single trick of what you wore and what you did. Besides these at the opening matinee you had the press, with their notebooks and pencils; and this was the show all the performers who happened to be laying off in Chicago always came to. Turning over my book of clippings I find that the critics noticed a number of members of the profession in the house that afternoon. Al Jolson was there; Ann Pennington, and Emma Haig, two wonderful dancers from the Ziegfeld *Follies* then playing Chicago; William Hodge from the legitimate stage, and many others.

I didn't know they were there. I had other things on my mind. I'd played Chicago so often, more than any other city in the country, by this time I thought I knew pretty well what the Chicago customers wanted. Were they going to like my new act which was so different from anything I had given them before?

I need not have worried. The press gave me the best notices I had ever had in Chicago—a city that has always been wonderful to me. Dear Amy Leslie beamed and crowed over my success. Praise from her, from Charlie Collins, "Doc" Hall, and Ashton Stevens meant a lot to me. Speaking of Ashton Stevens, when I opened in Chicago in November 1942 he wrote in his column that he had been reviewing me steadily for twenty-five years— "After a quarter of a century, Sophie is an institution."

We did great business in Chicago. I doubled at the Marigold Gardens, which was the smart place on the North Side where Ruth Etting was wardrobe mistress of the line of girls, and where she skyrocketed to fame as a singer, helped by her husband, Moe Snyder (Colonel Gimp).

The boys were getting better all the time. I felt confident of a great response as we swung round the last of the circuit, playing Detroit, Buffalo, Rochester, and Montreal where Mike Shea, when I told him how much the act was setting me back, fixed things with the head office so I got more money after playing his theaters. Then back to several dates in New York.

And was the Boss pleased! As I always did every week I was on the road, I wrote him telling him how I was doing; what the box office was like. Those weekly reports were strictly on the level; no kidding. I was like a salesman on the road sending in weekly reports to the head of the firm. I had seen other performers come into his office and start to tell him how marvelous they were. Many a time I'd seen the Boss get up from his desk, button up his coat, and say so gently, but with so much meaning, "Let *me* tell *you* how good you are."

We were playing a return date at the Palace in Chicago. I remember I was very restless and jumpy all that day. Every little thing annoyed me. It seemed as if I sensed something was wrong: not with the act, but at home. Sister Annie always wrote me several times a week—wherever I was playing—but I hadn't heard from her for several days.

The show was on and I was in my dressing room. At the Palace the headliner's dressing room was right by the stage door. My door was open; that was how I saw a messenger boy come in and heard him say to the doorman: "Telegram for Miss Tucker."

One of the rules that governed life backstage was that a telegram was never given to a performer before he went on for a show. It was always kept till after his act was over, then put into his mailbox, or handed to him. The managers weren't taking any chances of a bit of bad news queering an act at the last minute.

Ordinarily, I wouldn't have had this telegram until after the show, but I'd caught sight of the boy and heard my name. I sent Mollie to get it from the boy before the doorman could even sign the book. When she handed me the yellow envelope, I didn't need the three stars in the corner to tell me it held bad news.

"You open it," I said. "Something is wrong back home, I know. I can feel it."

She read me the message: *Come home at once. Pa very low. Annie.* Mollie's arms went round me tight. "Now, Patsy, keep a stiff upper lip. We've got to think fast what to do."

There was only one thing to do: send for the manager, tell him I would have to leave after the matinee to catch the first train I could get to Hartford. No planes then, and very few fast Limiteds. Meanwhile, I'd have to go on, give the customers the best I had. I couldn't let the show down.

While Jack Lait, who was then with the Hearst newspapers in Chicago, got busy for me about tickets and reservations, the theater manager found that Blossom Seeley and Benny Fields, always big favorites at the Palace, were laying over in Chicago that week. They agreed to pinch-hit for me. I've never ceased being grateful to them for that.

By the time I got to Hartford poor Pa was gone. I was too late to see him alive. If only I'd had Sis's wire a couple of hours earlier, I could have caught the Century and been there in time. After he had the fatal stroke, and couldn't speak or move, they told him they had sent for me. I was always his favorite. He kept watching the door for me to come until he finally closed his eyes.

I found a host of friends there at the house when I reached home. The Boss, and Zit, and dear Emma Carus with her strong arm around Ma, as well as Carl McCullough and Harry Cooper and the whole bill that was showing at Poli's that week. Everyone was so kind, so loving, I thought: yes, this is show business. We may squabble and feel jealous of each other, but when any sorrow touches one of us, all the others are quick to show their sympathy and to lend a hand, and money if it is needed.

I couldn't help wishing poor Pa could have seen them and heard the nice things they said about him. He always loved performers.

I felt his death keenly, all the more because I knew he had been lonely in the last few years with Son away at military school and living in a new neighborhood, too far for him to join his old pinochle-playing crowd as often as he used to. He loved visiting with me whenever I played a theater where he could come and spend the week with me; but I had been West for a good many months, and he had missed this pleasure for a long time.

His death affected my work. Even though I sang comedy songs, I didn't feel funny. That made me turn to ballads, "tear-jerkers," and I found myself singing them more and more. Because I felt them, I was able to make the audience feel them, too, and I would see the handkerchiefs come out and hear the sniffs as people tried to keep from crying. Then the managers started complaining. Where's the comedy? I had to shake myself out of it. In show business you can't let your personal feelings get you off on the wrong track with the customers. I went back to the comedy songs, but meanwhile I had learned something: that I could sing a ballad effectively. I had always loved the cello and violin in a song; that combination brought out all the drama I had in me.

Thinking over how some of the audiences had responded to the ballads sung to violin and cello started me on something I'd never done before: dramatizing songs with the help of the band. I remember one song called "I'm Waiting for Ships That Never Come In." When I found it, I sent for the writer and asked him to write me a recitation as a preface to the song. He brought it to me, a recitation that began: "Life's a game of poker . . ." That reminded me of the poker games the boys and I often had, and I got the idea: how about opening the act like that? The stage set like a living room. The boys dropping in, the way they would in their own home, somebody suggesting a game of poker; all of us playing, then an argument. One by one the boys leaving the table to go to their instruments, the stage blacking out—just the light from under the glass top of the table playing on me; and I would start the recitation: "Life's just a game of poker . . ." leading into the song with the band: "I'm Waiting for Ships That Never Come In."

When I started dramatizing songs like this, it was an experiment; I was feeling my way. What made me know I was on the track of something good as entertainment were the letters I began to get from the customers. You could see what they liked were songs that were built around something that might have—sometimes had—happened to them. For instance, I never sang a song called "You're Cheating on Me," which I dramatized, that I didn't receive letters from women in the audience who wrote me that I was singing their own experience with their men, and that the philosophy underlying the song seemed directed especially at them. They thanked me for singing it.

As we went along I changed the setup of the band several times. In the second set were: Al Siegel, the brilliant pianist who later married Bea Palmer, that gorgeous-looking singer of hot numbers. In later years, Al introduced Ethel Merman with a new style of singing a song, by which she skyrocketed to fame. And Richard Himber, violinist, now maestro of his own famous band. Dick was about fourteen when he came to me looking for a job; a fat, stubby, round and rosy-faced kid, fresh as paint. I wish I had a dollar for every time I put him across my knee. Others of the second set were: Manny Klein, cornettist; Julius Berken, cellist; and Dan Alvin, drummer, who could do a mean shimmy and still beat his drum. He could throw the sticks up in the air and catch them without losing a beat. As the boys changed, their salaries varied; some were paid more than others. All of them were getting more than I paid when the act started. There was a lot of responsibility and expense carting seven people around the country, what with railroad fares, sleeper jumps, excess baggage, and so on. The boys' clothes cost me money, as I had to get tuxedos, patent-leather shoes, et cetera, for all of them. I was determined to dress the act smartly to make it stand out.

My dressing room was my home. I carried two trunks—one for the theater and one for the hotel. In the theater trunk, besides my gowns and accessories, were cretonne hangings, wall sheets, chair and table covers, and a cheap, homemade rug for the cold cement floor. What a blessing those furnishings were as I look back at some of the theaters we played—drafty old firetraps, no toilets, filthy dirty cracked walls that let in the wind and the rain, old broken floors . . . One hard jump and down into the cellar you went. Never enough heat. I would come into one of these places, take a look around, and then roll up my sleeves. I would borrow a hammer and nails, get a heavy cardboard to cover up the ratholes in the wall and ceiling of my dressing room. I would go out and rent a heater—gas, oil, or electric, whatever I could get.

Those were the "good old days" of trouping. But today these conditions aren't any better, if you are touring one-night or two-night stands, playing in any theaters the motion pictures haven't gobbled up. Just as bad in their way are the civic auditoriums and Shriners' temples (seldom completed). These places have gorgeous auditoriums. Hundreds of thousands of dollars have been spent on the front of the house, on the lobby, theater, stage, and lighting equipment. But it seems as if the architects who designed them never gave a thought to the comfort of the performers. Trouping is tough. Curtain down at eleven-fifteen . . . a bite to eat . . . bed . . . train call at seven-fifteen, which means up at 6 A.M. Breakfast before you get on the train. You have to be in the next town by noon so as to hang the show and get it set for that night's performance. And there you walk into your dressing room to find it filthy dirty, cold, eight or ten people huddled in one dressing room, no sink, no toilet. . . .

It's not quite so bad for the stars, who don't have to leave with the company. They can make a later train, or take a plane. But for the rest . . . Take it from me, trouping today is just as bad as it was twenty-five years ago. I know what I'm telling you. In 1940 Billy Gaxton, Victor Moore, and I did four months' hard labor with *Leave It to Me* on tour, and I couldn't see any improvement over the "good old days" of before World War I.

There were many theaters that I liked to play. First the Palace Theatre, in Chicago (now Erlanger). I always went to Chicago first with everything new I had to offer. If they okayed the act, I had greater confidence in it everywhere else. Second, Keith's Theatre, Philadelphia. Harry Jordan, the manager, was always on the stage on a Monday morning to greet the actors with a smile and a kind word to those of us who had a rotten jump into Philadelphia. Harry Jordan made you forget how tired you were. He treated you like a human being. If the orchestra didn't play the rehearsal music just right, he was there to see that they did. At his theater, if you had been a hit at the Monday matinee, you could go to him and tell him how much the act was costing you and ask for more money. And if you were a hit, Harry Jordan would go to the front for you and get you a raise. He helped all the acts this way and, because he did, he always got the best out of them. His house had the best shows not only in Philadelphia, but on the whole Keith Circuit.

Mike Shea, Harry Jordan, and Fred Schanberg of the Maryland Theatre, Baltimore, were all like that. The Maryland was a smaller house and a cut week. Still, it always had a great audience and we all liked to play there. The Temple Theatre, in Detroit, was another grand house. Manager Williams would sit in his comfortable chair in the first entrance watching every act, making notes, cutting out this or that. He never was seen to smile, but you could tell by the way he shook his head whether you were going over okay with him.

The Keith theaters boasted a number of managers who were very self-important. They made things tough for the performers. Take the Davis Theatre in Pittsburgh, Keith's in Boston, and the Hippodrome Theatre in Cleveland.

It's not going too far to say that the Davis Theatre was hated by every performer in the business. Lots of them refused to play it, knowing that a date there let you in for a hell of a time. The manager of the Davis was very strict, and he had his own ideas which he insisted on the performers carrying out. During the Monday matinee we all knew he was watching and making notes; not on what the audience liked or didn't, but on what he liked or—more frequently—disliked. Between the matinee and the night show the blue envelopes began to appear in the performers' mailboxes backstage. You came back from getting a bite of dinner to find one of them in your box. Inside would be a curt order to cut out a blue line of a song, or a piece of business. Sometimes there was a suggestion of something you could substitute for the material the manager ordered out.

Poor Eugene Connolly, who was publicity man for the Davis Theatre, used to have to invent these substitutions at the manager's command. And all changes had to be made in the Monday-night show.

Is it any wonder we used to hit the ceiling? Me especially, being one of the worst offenders in the manager's eyes. What went on backstage every Monday between the matinee and the night show was enough to crack the walls. I've heard more violent and fluent cursing backstage at the Davis than in all the other houses I've played in put together.

As a result, the Monday-night shows were always terrible. Everybody was too mad, too upset, too nervous, to do good work. Come to the Monday matinee if you want to see a good show, or later in the week. Only, for God's sake, don't come on Monday night, for it's sure to be terrible, we all said.

But—and this tells better than anything else what show business really is— no matter how rough the Monday-night show was, with all the cuts, every performer was ready on Tuesday with a smooth performance. In that short time they would have rewritten their acts—using Eugene Connolly's suggestions or working up something new of their own. The customers who came then, or later in the week—unless they had caught the Monday matinee— never knew anything had been cut or changed.

There was no arguing about the orders in the blue envelopes. They were final. You obeyed them or quit. And if you quit, you got a black mark against your name in the head office and you just didn't work on the Keith Circuit any more. During my early years on the Keith Circuit I took my orders from my blue envelope and—no matter what I said or did backstage (and it was plenty)—when I went on for the Monday-night show, I was careful to keep within bounds.

It used to make me furious because the lines the manager ordered cut out of my songs were always the ones that got laughs from the customers. What he was doing was ruining my act; not to please the audience, but to satisfy his own self-importance. Like the rest, I had to obey his orders, but I used to boil. I would tell myself: "When I'm a headliner, I'll tell that such-and-such I'll play my act my way, and so long as the customers like it, there'll be no changes."

I'd been promising myself that for several seasons. When I played the Davis Theatre with the band, headlining the bill, I made the promise good.

During the Monday matinee, which went over great, I knew the manager was there at the back of the house scowling and sharpening his pencil. When I came back to the theater after dinner, to dress for the night show, there in my mailbox was the blue envelope.

I took it out, and without reading the note inside, I tore it up and dropped the bits in the scrap basket in my dressing room.

"Huh!" said Mollie, her eyes very big. "Ain't you going to pay attention to what he tells you?"

"I am not!"

"But, Patsy, you know what that man is like."

"He's going to find out what I'm like, and about time!"

The boys were hanging around, waiting for orders what to cut and what to change. They nearly popped out of their collars when I told them: "No changes, boys. We play the act just the way we played it this afternoon."

And we did.

When we came off, there was the manager waiting for me. He wanted to know if I hadn't got my orders from him.

"I got them," I said. And I pointed to the scrap basket.

He blew up. The show he put on there in my dressing room was better than anything on the stage of his theater. The boys gathered around the door, looking scared, and behind them all the others on the bill stood where they could hear and see. They heard and saw plenty.

"Okay," I yelled in the midst of the row, "I'm through right here and now. Mollie, start packing. We'll get out of this town tonight!"

He began to argue with me that I couldn't do that.

"Can't I?" I yelled. "Get going, Mollie. Either I sing the songs I want and the way I want to sing them, or I leave. As long as the customers like my songs—and they do—no manager on earth is going to tell me to rewrite them."

Mollie was throwing things in the trunks and cleaning up the dressing room as though the train left in five minutes. I started to pull off my clothes to change. "One of you boys run down to the station and get the reservations," I hollered. "We've no time to waste around here!"

It wasn't bluff. I meant it. I never was more serious in my life. The manager realized it. By the time Mollie had one trunk locked and called the porter to take it, the manager came round to see things my way. He agreed, if I would finish out the week, to let me sing the songs I wanted to sing in my own way.

The manager of the Davis Theatre let me alone after that one experience. I had similar trouble once at the Hippodrome Theatre in Cleveland. That time I packed up, left the theater, and was in the station just about to get aboard the train before the manager came after me to ask me to go back.

In New York, the Riverside, the Alhambra, and the Royal were great houses, always with fine bills. But *the* house in New York, of course, was the Palace. I suppose more careers were made and more hearts broken in that one theater than in all the other houses of the entire Orpheum and Keith circuits.

I'll never forget the week Rosa and Carmela Ponselle opened their first vaudeville date at the Palace as a sister act. Two big, husky, fine-looking girls. They stopped the show cold. And then a few years later Rosa was singing at the Metropolitan with Caruso. Marilyn Miller appeared at the Palace with her father, mother, and sisters in an act called the "Five Columbians," and was promptly discovered and started for stardom.

Your success in show business depended on how you went over at the Palace. At a Monday matinee there were more upset stomachs backstage than at a Metropolitan opening. Would the czar of vaudeville, Mr. E. F. Albee, see your act and would he like it? Would Mr. J. J. Murdock okay the price you asked for it after the matinee? Every booker in New York, and many from London, would be standing in the back of the theater at a Monday matinee. So were all the "legitimate" managers and producers, scouting for talent. The Palace was like an auction block. Knowing this, many performers would go on at the Palace for less money than they got elsewhere. No actor can truthfully say he ever walked on the stage of the Palace calm, cool, and collected, and with an "I-don't-care-how-I-go-over" manner.

I never remember playing the Palace in all the years, from a small act to the headliner, that I ever walked on the stage without new songs, new gowns. Later, when I went to Europe, I always brought back handsome props and clothes for my engagement at the Palace. I would spend as high as two thousand dollars on the act before the Monday matinee.

The actors had two great friends in the Keith booking office: Harry Jordan and Eddie Darling. Eddie's layout of a Palace bill was second only to that of William Morris. He always gave a great show, even though there were plenty of headaches for Eddie every Monday. If you were a hit at the Palace, you got a week each at three Brooklyn houses—the Flatbush, the Orpheum, and the Bushwick—which Eddie Darling booked. This meant you played ten to twelve weeks in and around New York.

The Palace was the rendezvous of all the legitimate actors in town. Alfred Lunt and Lynn Fontanne never missed a Monday matinee when they were in New York. The Lunts were great vaudeville fans, though they had never played in vaudeville themselves. I met Alfred first at a party at Noel Coward's. Several years later I had a note from him asking if he could come and see me on very important business. He came and brought Lynn along. I didn't have any idea what the business was until Alfred got up and went over to the mantelpiece and draped himself against it—preparatory to telling me he was going to play the part of a vaudevillian in *Idiot's Delight.* "And I've come for help to the greatest vaudevillian of them all."

I coached him there in my sitting room. My son, who is a dancer, taught Alfred a few steps. I added what I could to give his acting the genuine vaudeville flavor. What an actor he is! And how he worked over every little detail to keep it all in character. And what a performance he gave! And how the critics praised him and marveled at a legitimate actor out-vaudevilling vaudeville.

I was making more and more friends in the profession. As I toured the country with the band, we would meet on the road and have a good time during the week we played the same town. One of my good friends of those days was Trixie Friganza. I first met Trixie when J. J. Shubert wired me to pinch-hit for her in his *Town Topics,* then on tour. Trixie had opened with the show at the Winter Garden in New York, but fell ill while on tour. I took her place for eight weeks. Later, when she played in vaudeville we were sometimes on the same bill and often playing in the same city Trixie—her baptismal name was Delia O'Callahan—was a devout Roman Catholic. She was Irish, but as thrifty in her way as German-born Emma Carus. I believe Trixie and I were the first vaudeville performers to buy annuities. Trixie managed her career as a business. She invested money in exclusive songs that made her act a tremendous success and always individual. She was very lovable and lots of fun to be with. I remember she used to say that she wasn't going to be like a lot of performers, afraid to quit while she was still a headliner. Trixie did just that. She left the stage and went into a Sacred Heart Convent in the Midwest. I hear from her frequently, and always her letters bring back the days of twenty-five years ago, when we were troupers together.

Lots of times performers would ask my advice, knowing that I had come up the hard way and knew some things by experience that you can't learn in any other school. One of these was Belle Baker. She was then married to Lou Leslie and was just starting out on the British stage after playing in the Jewish theaters on New York's East Side. I remember I was riding home in the subway, one night after the show, and she came and sat down beside me. She told me some of her personal troubles. She went home with me that night and we talked for hours.

It was while I was playing a long run in Chicago that I got to know the Four Marx Brothers and their redheaded driver of a mother, Minnie Palmer Everybody called her Minnie. She was hell-bent her boys should be a su cess. She put on their act and rehearsed them; one minute she was out in front of the house, watching, the next she was backstage ready to wallop the kids for doing something wrong; arguing with them, protesting that if only they would listen to her they could be headliners. When the kids did well, Minnie would laugh louder than even Milton Berle's mother laughed at his act. The few times the boys played on the same bill with me I would sit out in front with Minnie and she'd ask me to watch them so she could go back and remind them of something they missed doing. After a show I would listen to what the audience said about the boys and report it to Minnie: "Can Harpo talk at all?" "Is he really dumb?" "Chico, he's an Italian." "Groucho, what is he supposed to be?" "Zeppo, that's the baby." "They can't be brothers; they all look different." She would think over such comments as these and sometimes get ideas from them. Minnie lived to enjoy the boys' success for a long time, and nobody enjoyed it more than she, who had put her whole heart and soul into creating it. They were four wonderful boys to her, and four grand friends to me to this very day.

Often a vaudeville act would be a great hit in the out-of-town theaters from coast to coast and yet couldn't get booking in the New York houses. One of these was a comedy talking act, Whipple and Huston. They played with me a number of times and I used to rave about the act to every agent and booker in the Keith office that I bumped into. Finally, the act played the Palace in New York.

Unfortunately it got a bad spot on the bill and was not noticed. That often happened. You might get the spot on the bill just after the intermission, before the house was in. If you did, it was almost impossible to make a hit. Or you might be billed too early in the show. Those were the chances and the heartaches of vaudeville.

I lost track of Whipple and Huston for several years. Then one week, when I was laying off in New York, I decided to see a show which people were raving about. I didn't know who was in it. I was late getting to the theater, too late to read the bills outside or even look at my program. So I got one of the surprises of my life when on came Walter Huston of the old vaudeville team, Whipple and Huston.

Walter is one of the friends I made twenty-five years ago who is still the same today. When I was in London, he was having a great success there in *Dodsworth,* and I used to swell with pride when I heard the British people rave about him.

When I first went out on the road with the band there were two boys who had a musical act who sometimes turned up on the same bill with me.

They were Ben Bernie and Phil Baker. Back in the days when I was an entertainer at the German Village, Ben Bernie, then playing the piano at the smart Haymarket Café down the street, sometimes came up to the Village to look over our show. However, it was in Montreal, back in 1918, that Benny and I really became friends. The way he used to tell it:

It was as freezing cold as it can be in Montreal, and then some. A blizzard had hit town just ahead of us, and the snow was piled up in the streets to the level of the street lamps. (Yowser! it gets like that in Montreal.)

Everybody on the bill was out of sorts from the cold and being delayed on the trains getting in. It didn't seem likely we'd do much business that week. According to Benny, he and Phil Baker got bluer and chillier as they heard me—the headliner—rehearse. My Five Kings and I were using two or three numbers Phil and Benny had counted on using in their act—all their best numbers.

They got into a huddle to see what they could do. As the headliner, I had first right to the numbers. It was up to them to rearrange their act not to conflict with mine. But there was no time to learn and rehearse new numbers. The show was due to start in another hour. It looked as though their act would just have to fold up for the first show anyway.

Then Benny paid me a real, straight-from-the-heart compliment:

"Sophie's a good *schnuck*," he told Phil. "Let's put it up to her."

They did. Sure, I knew my rights as the headliner. But I also could remember a few experiences of my own a few years back, and what it meant to have other performers come out with songs you had been counting on using yourself. That had happened to me once, playing a date in San Antonio, Texas. Five of the six songs in my act were rehearsed by other singers. I went to the manager about it, but there wasn't a thing to be done, and I had no time to work up a new set of songs before the Monday matinee. I had had to go on and apologize to the audience for giving them songs they had just heard, and then do my best to make my singing of the songs so different that the customers would find them interesting. That was an awful experience, and I've never forgotten it.

I called the boys in the band and rearranged our act to use different numbers so that Benny and Phil would not lose their week's work.

Benny always insisted that from that minute I took him and Phil Baker over—not as part of my act, but to play poker with me after the late show every night. They were rooming in a five-dollar-a-week actors' boarding-house a long way from the Hotel Windsor. They say I kept them playing till three and four every morning, and then they had to stagger back to their rooming house through the drifts—"breaking a trail for the milkman."

One night, they say, I dragged them and a lot of others on the bill to a house down the line to entertain the girls. The Madame had come backstage to call on me. She invited all of us to the house for supper. After supper we put on a show for the girls who weren't doing any business that evening in our honor. It was a swell show, I remember, and as chaste as a Sunday-school picnic. Afterward, the boys say, I lectured them all the way home on how they ought to be glad to do a good deed like that once in a while.

They got their revenge on me that week, though. I love to play poker, but I inherited poor Pa's bad luck with the cards. Those two kids took enough money off me in that one week in Montreal to buy each of them a fur-lined coat to finish the tour in.

CHAPTER 16: *Reisenweber's*

WHEN the Boss first wrote me that he had sold me and the band to Reisenweber's for a four weeks' contract, I let out a groan. I'd been headlining in big-time vaudeville, rolling up successes from coast to coast, and now here was the Boss putting me right back into the restaurant business that I had worked so hard to get away from. I had a long talk with him the minute I hit New York.

"What," I objected, "is the use of going back if I don't have to?" All my life it seemed as if I had been trying to get out of working in restaurants and to establish myself in show business.

The Boss let me register all my objections, then he explained, and what he had to say about the restaurant business and vaudeville I've never forgotten. The way he explained it, vaudeville really began in eating places. Once upon a time, it seems, there was a miller somewhere in France who had the bright idea of setting out some tables and benches under the trees by his mill and selling the farmers red wine and homemade bread and cheese while they waited for their grain to be ground. This mill was just one of many in the valley of the Vire River. Competition was pretty keen, and this particular miller counted on his restaurant to draw trade to his mill. It drew something else as well—the show people who traveled along the highroad through that valley up to Paris. There were jugglers and acrobats and singers of songs and men with dancing bears and trained monkeys. When these saw the crowd gathered by the mill, eating and drinking, they would stop in the road and put on a show for the customers and then pass the hat. That gave the miller an idea. He offered them a free meal and a night's lodging to stop at his mill and put on regular shows for his customers. I don't know what became of the miller; probably he ended up a millionaire. Anyway, other restaurant proprietors got the idea that most folks like entertainment as they eat and started to offer their customers shows. That, the Boss told me, is how vaudeville began. Even its name is derived from Vaux de Vire (valley of the Vire). And wasn't one of the great cabarets in Paris the Moulin Rouge (Red Mill)?

The Boss assured me that I wouldn't lose prestige by going on as a cabaret entertainer. Cabaret was the new name then just coming into use for restaurants such as Reisenweber's, Bustanoby's, Maxime's, Jack's, Café de Paree, Moulin Rouge, and a lot more springing up all over New York. The competition among all these places was cutthroat. Each had to offer some extra attraction besides good food and wines to draw the crowd. Up to the time the Boss took his idea to Mr. Reisenweber and his son-in-law, Louis Fischer, and John Wagener, most of the attractions consisted of ballroom dance teams. The dancing craze was still running strong.

The Boss sold them the idea of giving the customers something different in entertainment—a vaudeville headliner, a woman who could sing and with her own band. It was a new idea, but it worked. Once again it proved how well the Boss understood the entertainment world. Following his advice, Reisenweber's started the Jazz Era and changed New York night life completely. We opened two days before Christmas, 1916. We entertained during the dinner hour and put on a late show. My band played for the dancing during dinner and again during the supper hour. Another band relieved them until the supper crowd came in.

Reisenweber's was on Eighth Avenue, near Columbus Circle. The building had four floors. On the first floor was the main restaurant. The third floor was above the swank Paradise Room. Above this was the Hawaiian Room, where Doraldina became famous for her Hawaiian dances. Just above the main restaurant was the room called the 400-Club Room where I went on. It didn't keep that name long. The customers started calling it the Sophie Tucker Room, and so it became and remained all through my first engagement there, which ran on into eight months—instead of the four weeks originally contracted for. Not only did I play there steadily all those months, but I played return engagements at Reisenweber's regularly for the next five years. What began as an experiment grew into an institution. I became as closely associated with Reisenweber's as John Wagener, the manager of the place, or John Steinberg or Christo. Steinberg later went with Paul Salvin and Jimmy Thompson and ran Rector's, the Palais Royale, and the Plantation for them.

Steinberg brought Paul Whiteman from the West Coast and featured him. He introduced Abe Lyman and Guy Lombardo to New York. Out at his Pavillon Royal at Valley Stream, Long Island, which was one of the first big high-powered and high-priced roadhouses of the Prohibition Era, Steinberg put on shows, copying those I originated at my Bohemian Nights at Reisenweber's. I entertained there several times. So did Eddie Cantor, Al Jolson, Ruby Keeler, Ray Bolger, Ethel Merman, and a lot more. What I started at Reisenweber's soon was spreading all over the country.

A big revue featuring Ruby Norton and Midgie Miller and a capable cast of twelve was playing at Reisenweber's when I came in. I had worked up a stunt for our opening, with Dick Himber sitting up in a tree built to a column and heckling me. It was a stunt that went over big with the customers. I sang about twenty songs a night. I changed the bill every Sunday. This meant a lot of rehearsing and kept me on a constant lookout for new material. I made it a rule to introduce new songs all the time. But all that paid dividends. My original contract was for seven hundred and fifty dollars a week, but I was soon making a lot more than that, just as the Boss had prophesied. His foresight was terrific.

Reisenweber's was a place where the same people came night after night. We had no cover charge except on Saturday and Sunday nights. The food was marvelous; and, if I do say it, the entertainment was the best the town had to offer. One proof of this is that all the other places started to copy what we were doing at Reisenweber's. People began to demand jazz bands and something more than ballroom dance teams and a line of girls. Over at the Palais Royale they started to feature Ted Lewis and his band. I remember going over there to see what Ted was doing and how he worked, in case I wasn't up to the minute with my own boys. Ted and his wonderful wife, Adah, have been friends of mine for years. Ted is the personality the public knows, but Adah is the power behind the scenes, the one who manages everything and who is largely responsible for her husband's long, successful career in show business. Of the many bandleaders who came to fame during the Jazz Era, Ted Lewis is the only one who has lasted and who is still drawing big money—up to sixty-five hundred dollars a week. And for a season of fifty-two weeks a year! Ted's outstanding success is due to his being a stylist in his way. Like all stylists, he has created his theme song which is identified with him everywhere. "When My Baby Smiles at Me" means Ted

Lewis to the customers just as "Some of These Days" means Sophie Tucker. But Ted has never let himself get into a rut. He has watched the trend of the times and gone on developing and changing his act to keep pace with them. He has always surrounded himself with grand performers and has staged his act magnificently. His career is another proof of my contention that success in show business doesn't come from luck or favoritism. It grows out of intelligence and hard work.

Joe Frisco, Eddie Cox, Loretta McDermott, Bea Palmer all entertained at various times, and when they were a success with the customers at Reisenweber's, the theater managers engaged them. Even Willie Moore, Dinty Moore's son, who wanted to be a dancer, got his chance one Sunday night. But George Raft outclassed Willie, who went back to the restaurant business.

It wasn't only performers who were publicized on our Bohemian Nights. I would look over the room and see who I recognized—it might be a fighter, a beauty-parlor specialist, a song writer, the owner of a new dress shop. Whoever they were, I would introduce them to the crowd and call on them to stand up and take a bow. A lot of new songs were tried out at Reisenweber's. If the song went over there, we knew we had a hit on our hands. Inside of a week it was being sung all over America. Remember, all this before radio!

I had heard of a team of singers, May Gray and Mildred Vernon, and a wonderful dancer, Chic Barrymore. Someone came in from Chicago raving about them. Just about that time Frank Westphal had to go to Chicago on a trip and I asked him to see the girls, and if he thought they were as good as the reporters made them out to be, to get them to come on to New York for a tryout at Reisenweber's on one of our Bohemian Nights. They came during July 1919, right after the wartime prohibition measure had been put into effect, and everybody was wondering what was going to happen to cabaret life. I remember Chic was sitting at a table with Ford Sterling, one of the first comedians of the silent pictures; Joe Pincus, now of Twentieth-Century Fox; Jimmy Hussey, an Irish lad and one of the funniest Jewish-dialect comedians we had in show business; and several others, including Harry Cohen, then a song plugger for one of the music publishing houses and today president of Columbia Pictures in Hollywood. They coaxed Chic to get up on the floor and dance for the crowd. She was a riot. Marlene Dietrich never had legs like Chic's.

The following Sunday night I put her in my act at the Winter Garden Sunday-night concert, in which I was then doubling. Later she was engaged by J. J. Shubert for *Hello, Alexander,* starring McIntyre and Heath, in which I played too.

Of the team Gray and Vernon, Mildred had a glorious voice, but she knew she didn't have the sex appeal to make a success in show business. So she gave it up and went back to Chicago and married. May Gray, however, quickly became the sensation of Broadway. May was a little Polack, with frizzy blonde hair, skin like a baby, a body as agile as a snake's, an infectious smile; and a toughie. When she came on from Chicago, she was poorly dressed, and had no idea how to groom herself. When she came out she looked like a million dollars. The night I introduced her to the gang at Reisenweber's she wore a silver lamé gown, very tight fitting, with a big bustle bow at the back. Her hit number was the "St. Louis Blues," in which she did the shimmy. She brought the word "shimmy" from Chicago, and New York picked it up. It made her famous overnight. She became the talk of Broadway and everybody rushed to see her. She panicked the Winter Garden audience the first Sunday night I introduced her there, and I had to keep her in every show after that.

But, you say, that was Gilda Gray. Sure! But she never heard of the name Gilda until I gave it to her. I was going up to Hartford to visit the family and in the Grand Central I bought a ten-cent magazine of short stories to kill the two-and-a-half-hour train ride. The first story I turned to started off: "Gilda Gray was a fascinating blonde." The minute I got back to New York from Hartford on the milk train, which got in at 4 A.M., I rushed up to May's room, on the floor above mine at the Circle Hotel, next door to Reisenweber's.

May was sound asleep. "Wake up!" I yelled. "I've got a new moniker for you—Gilda Gray! You'll never make a cent with a name like May Gray. It sounds just as tough as you are. But Gilda is class!"

Gilda was with me a lot and I grew very fond of her. She had a terrific sense of humor. She was crazy about my son, Bert, and would fool with him and go around town with him whenever he came down from military school. I didn't know until later that Gilda had a boy of her own whom she had left out in Milwaukee. Gilda was my first protégée, and she was a sensation. After her first showing at the Winter Garden, J. J. Shubert sent for me and signed her up for five years on a sliding scale of one hundred and fifty to five hundred dollars a week, starting her off in the show starring Ed Wynn. Gilda was going to the top fast, and deservedly so, because she was a hard worker. Then she fell in love with Gil Boag, a publicity man. I could see what I was up against when J. J. Shubert called me to his office to tell me Gilda would not go on tour with the Ed Wynn show which was due to open in Philadelphia, and what could I do about it. The answer was, nothing. I tried to tell Gilda that a contract is a contract and she owed it to J. J. Shubert to go out with the show. Moreover, she owed it to me to live up to the agreement which I had gotten for her. I never had Gilda under contract. I never made one cent out of all her engagements. Whatever money I got for her, she got it in full. I wasn't Gilda's agent, or anybody's agent, but I tried to be her friend and adviser. After we had that showdown about the Shubert contract, I didn't see Gilda again for a great many years, not until she played the old Club Richman on West Fifty-sixth Street, New York. During that time she had made a name for herself in pictures, made big money, and was the toast of show business. She had married Gil Boag, who acted as her publicity agent.

I have spoken of Sunday-night concerts at the Winter Garden. The Winter Garden, which was organized and owned by J. J. and Lee Shubert, was famous as the theater where Al Jolson played. His shows were very popular. They never ran less than a year. The show did not play Sunday nights, so J. J. Shubert got the idea of staging a series of Sunday-night concerts. Actually, he was putting on a high-class vaudeville bill in competition with my Bohemian Nights at Reisenweber's and the big vaudeville houses in town. J. J. had to pick his talent for these shows from the small houses and cabarets for the reason that the Keith Circuit would not let their stars double in other shows. Naturally, this made it hard for him to get big names that would draw the crowd. When Jolson went on the road with his show, J. J. Shubert sent for me to be the headliner at his Sunday-night concerts. I was cashing in on my success at Reisenweber's, but I can tell you it took some hustling to do it. I would go on at Reisenweber's for the dinner show, jump into a taxi, and race over to the Winter Garden to change my dress and close the bill of the Sunday-night concerts; then back to Reisenweber's and another change of costume for the late supper show. I knew I was on probation, and I was determined to make good and draw the crowds as well as Jolson did—some job. But I did it. These concerts—later called the Sophie Tucker Sunday-Night Concerts—were the feature of the 1919 theatrical season. They were really top-notch vaudeville, and they gave New York the entertainment it loved.

Oh, but New York was gay in that year right after the war. The town was full of men just home from France and hungry for fun, laughs, gay songs, pretty girls. Cabarets—how the word had taken hold!—were springing up all over town and doing big business, though everybody was wondering what Prohibition was going to do to them and to the whole entertainment world. I don't think anyone guessed what we really were in for—that is, the

Speak-easy Era. But everybody in the café business felt jittery, and wondered what would happen after the Volstead Act went into effect.

I was working as I had never worked before at Reisenweber's, doubling at the Winter Garden and then in *Hello, Alexander,* which opened in New York in October 1919. I was booked in the show as a specialty.

We broke the show in at Wilmington, Delaware, where I had my first piece of bad luck, losing one of my diamond earrings. I must have shaken it off as I sang. It fell either on the stage or in the orchestra pit, and it disappeared so completely and so quickly it wasn't funny. I offered one thousand dollars reward for it. There was a sentimental value attached to the stones. Three of the six diamonds I bought on time, paying off twenty-five dollars a week for them. They were the first of my jewels. I couldn't help thinking a lot of my luck was invested in those stones, and I hated losing them. But no one turned the earring in, and the police could do nothing about it. I left Wilmington for New York, feeling pretty rotten. And with reason, as far as *Hello, Alexander* was concerned. McIntyre and Heath were very funny, but the rest of the show was only fair as the New York press immediately pointed out. The press didn't care much about me, either. However, the show ran in New York several weeks, and I had my first opportunity to see my name up in electric lights on Broadway.

Frank Westphal had a small part in the show and he was also appearing at the Winter Garden with me, which was like old times. I guess show business is like any bug, once it bites you you've got it in your blood forever after. Frank was like that. Even though he had a chance to make more money in the garage business he couldn't get over wanting to get back behind the footlights again.

Meanwhile, I was constantly buying and rehearsing new songs for Reisenweber's, working up new bits of business with the boys of the band, disciplining them when they got to thinking they were the whole show, getting new clothes, new accessories, to keep the customers pleased. In that season of 1918-19 it seemed like the whole A.E.F. passed through Reisenweber's on its way home from France. I remember meeting William Gaxton there for the first time—then Sailor William Gaxton. It was just before he married Madeline Cameron, of the famous dancing team, the Cameron Sisters. In 1939-40 Billy and his side-kick, Victor Moore, and I played together in *Leave It to Me,* Vinton Freedley's smash hit.

Yes, everybody ultimately turned up at Reisenweber's, including the boys of the underworld. They were all great spenders and a wonderful audience to work for. I remember one night, just before the show started, I came into the room to look around to see who were there that night. My room had settees built around the wall. I stopped off at several tables to say "hello" to the customers and to shake hands.

That's something I've always done and always will do as long as I play in cafés. It's something I think the performer owes to the customers. I know it's good business. I've proved it so all during the years. Bill Jones who comes to town on business likes to be able to go back home and tell the boys of the local Lion's Club he shook hands with Sophie Tucker. The next time he comes to town, or I play his town, he turns up again, because he feels he's a friend of mine. Other performers sometimes josh me about doing this. "Soph, you're always the Madame of every joint you play in," Ben Bernie used to say. "Oh, what the hell, Benny," I fired back. "What is this but a saloon business, anyway? We're all of us bartenders!"

Well, to get back to my story, as I was going around the room a man reached out and grabbed me by the arm. Very quietly in my ear he whispered, "You're a swell broad. I'd go to hell for you. I had some of your matzoths you sent to Dannemora. I just got back from a stretch up there."

I thanked him. I said something about hoping he'd never go back there. "The world is too beautiful to be buried behind prison walls. It's tough enough to be buried under ground when your time comes."

I left his table and went on up to my room to change and put on the show. I had just started to sing when I heard a commotion in the rear of the room. I saw it came from the table and the chap who had whispered to me. The audience were getting to their feet and craning their necks to see what was going on, but I beat everyone to it and got to his table first. There was my friend from Dannemora standing up with a gat in his hand, pointing at a woman a few tables away. I grabbed him by the arm. "Listen," I said, "you just told me you'd go to hell for me. What do you want to do? Ruin my business by shooting up the joint?"

That got him. "Get that broad out of here, Sophie," he muttered, "and nothing will happen. Just get her out."

I went over to John Wagener, our manager, to see that the woman and her party were asked to leave the room immediately. Then I went on with the show. After the show was over, the gunman came back to my dressing room to apologize for starting a rumpus. The woman had been his moll before he was sent up.

"I saw red when I saw my old girl with another guy on my first night out. I'm sorry, Soph, it had to be where you were working."

Later, in Chicago, where I played twelve consecutive weeks doubling in vaudeville and at the Marigold and the Edelweiss Gardens, I met more of the underworld. I knew the boys by their first names and nicknames only. They were great fans of mine and had a lot of respect for me as I have reason to know. I was sporting gorgeous diamonds, furs, and clothes. I was living at the Hotel Sherman, just a block away from the Palace Theatre. One night a phone call came through, just as I was leaving the hotel to go to the show. An unknown voice said, "Don't wear your diamonds any more."

I hung up, with no idea who it was, but I paid attention to the warning. I went to work that night very nervous. After the show I met some of the boys and told them about the call, and asked them to find out what it was all about. A few hours later a message came back to me. A cokey in a small cigar store on the North Side had made a crack to his pal, "Let's go after Tucker's diamonds tonight." It was the pal who had called me not to wear them, after he had beaten up the cokey and told him to lay off a regular fellow.

A few years later, when I was playing out at the South Side Theatre in Chicago, I was just about to go on the stage when a phone call came through, "Don't go home tonight on the outer driveway." I didn't recognize the voice, and I got panicky, especially as I knew that just the week before Paul Whiteman had been relieved of his salary on pay night when he played the same house.

What I did was to ring up Mayor Thompson, whose apartment was on the floor above mine at the Sherman Hotel, and tell him about my mysterious phone call.

"Don't worry," he said, "I'll have somebody take you home okay when the show is over."

When I got out to the front of the theater, there was an armored car with half a dozen police and detectives waiting to escort me home. What a ride that was! A crowd gathered in front of the hotel, and what a roar went up when they saw me get out of the car. I learned from these two warnings never to carry large sums of money or wear valuable jewelry any more. The only times I sported my jewels was at an important occasion.

Like lots of performers in those days, I had been in the habit of going about the streets wearing as much of my jewelry at a time as I could, telling the world I was in show business. But I learned better. One morning I was walking down Broadway, all aglitter, when I heard a woman remark, "What a load of ice that gal wears in the daytime!" It was her tone as much as the words that taught me how vulgar it was to wear so much jewelry in the daytime. I never did it again.

I feel I must speak about that twelve weeks' run in Chicago because it really was phenomenal. I opened at the Palace Theatre and at the end of the week was held over to play *three weeks more*. It was the first time this had ever happened at the Palace, and since then only one headliner was ever held over and then for only one more week. While playing the Palace I doubled at the Marigold Garden on the North Side. Then I went on at a theater on the West Side; played there four weeks, doubling at the Edelweiss Gardens on the South Side. Then I came back to the Palace for another four weeks' engagement, doubling again at the Marigold Gardens. Chicago went wild about my Five Kings of Syncopation and the songs we were giving.

And speaking of songs brings me to the big event that occurred while I was playing Chicago. This was my first meeting with Jack Yellen.

At that time Jack was just another young song plugger selling his wares. He had written "Down by the O-H-I-O," which was a hit. His songs had something—something that seemed especially right for me. He brought me "Dapper Dan" and "Hard-Hearted Hannah," two swell numbers which went over big with the audience when I used them.

There was no doubt that this fellow had something on the ball and was going places as a song writer. What he had was a new type of song. It was something I could dramatize and something I could identify with myself, which I always wanted to do. Another thing Jack would do was to write a special chorus or a recitation—something that made the song part of Sophie Tucker. Jack has been writing songs for me for more than twenty years. In all that time we have never had a contract. We have never needed one. We have an understanding that when Jack writes a song for me, that song is mine. It is never published. You never hear another singer sing it. If you want to hear "If He Is Good Enough to Fight for His Country, He Shouldn't Have to Fight for His Love," or "When They Start to Ration My Passion, It's Gonna Be Tough on Me," you've got to go where Sophie Tucker is singing them, or buy a Sophie Tucker record.

Jack Yellen's songs have a lot more to them than their news value. Every one of them is packed with sound psychology. They bring the laughs, and the reason the customers laugh is not because the songs are funny or risqué, it's because they express some truths which all of us know, deep down in our hearts, and which a lot of us are afraid to mention above a whisper even to ourselves. Take that song of his, "You Can't Serve Love in Dishes, and You Can't Sew a Button on a Heart." What is it, except good, straight-from-the-shoulder advice to women on how to keep their men? Isn't that what most women want to know?

It is hard for me to write about Jack simply because I've known him so long and so well—and I'm so fond of him. After William Morris, Jack Yellen is the best friend I ever had. His friendship, his "Well done, Sophie!" his advice mean a hell of a lot to me. This book is dedicated to him with reason, because after the Boss he has done more for me than any other human being. Jack is a wonderful person, as a lot of people will agree. The world knows him as a song writer—one of the most successful in the country. Remember "I Wonder What's Become of Sally"? Remember "Happy Days Are Here Again"? These are two of Jack's and Milton Agar's songs. "Happy Days" was a hit. It was made the theme song of the second Roosevelt presidential campaign, and swept the country all over again. But Jack is a lot more than a successful song writer. He's a great reader, a student, especially of the history of our Jewish people, and he is one of the most devoutly religious persons I have ever known.

All his success has never gone to his head. He still gets a kick out of finding that the public likes his songs. I know, for when I'm off on the road, every so often I get a wire or a penciled scrawl from him demanding: "You tightwad, why don't you wire me how my songs are going?"

One time I landed in London to play in *Follow a Star* at the Winter Garden Theatre. Jack went along, as he had been engaged to write the lyrics for the show. As soon as I was settled in my rooms at the Savoy, he turned up, and we rolled up our sleeves and went to work. It was spring, and the windows were open and the noise of London—so different from the voice of New York or Paris or any other big city—and the peculiar damp, sooty smell of London came into the room. Presently something else came through the window too—the sound of a barrel organ being played just outside. The tune? "Happy Days Are Here Again!"

Jack's thin, sensitive face broke into a schoolboy grin. I really think hearing his song played like that in London made him happier than all the attention he was getting from important show people in Britain.

CHAPTER 17: *"Personal"*

PLAYING LONG ENGAGEMENTS at Reisenweber's and at the Brighton Beach Hotel, which Mr. Reisenweber also owned, gave me the feeling of being settled in New York as I had not felt since the days when Brother Moe and I had our little apartment. When summer came round, I followed the lead of other vaudevillians and rented a house at Freeport, Long Island. It was handy for Frank, who was supposed to be running the Sophie Tucker Garage on the Merrick Road, and it was handy for me. Frank would come in and meet me after the late show and drive me home. In a way, I was having my first experience of normal married life in a home, in a community, and with a circle of friends.

Freeport was always the place for vaudevillians to summer in. Our colony that year included the Frank Tinneys, my old friends Max and Madge Hart, Jimmy and Myrtle Conin, Mr. and Mrs. Victor Moore, the Four Mortons, Gracie and Eddie Carr, Nellie Nichols, and a lot more show people I had been meeting on bills for years.

Week ends were gay, as we always had a house full of guests. The whole crowd would gather at the Lights Club and put on impromptu shows—not for the public, just for the "pros" and their friends.

Inevitably there was a lot of drinking. Not because it was a crowd of show people; the same was true of most groups in the country at that time. Americans were thumbing their noses at Prohibition. I had had my lesson that gin and I didn't get along together, and this cut me out of some of the parties. I was working too hard and too steadily to take any chance with liquor. I managed to enjoy my holidays without the stuff. One thing I couldn't get used to, though, was the gossiping that went on all the time. Everybody knew too much about everybody else, or *thought* they did; and everybody told what he did know, and then plenty more. Drinking parties and gossip have broken up a lot of homes. They broke up mine too.

Frank was having too good a time to pay attention to the garage, as he should have done. The expenses there grew bigger every month while the profits fell off. I was going out on the road with the band until I was due to come back for a second engagement at Reisenweber's, so I wrote Brother Phil to go down to Freeport and check up on the garage and find out where the leak was. Phil wrote me after a couple of weeks: "Frank is not a businessman. He is a good mechanic, knows a car backward and forward. Pull your reins in, Sophie, and do something before you get in too deep with your hard-earned money."

When I got back to New York, I had a talk with Frank. As tactfully as I could I tried to show him the necessity for having a businessman run that end of the garage, leaving him on the mechanical end. As Brother Phil was not doing anything at the time, why not have him take over? With the two of them at it, the Sophie Tucker Garage was sure to be a success.

Frank never gave me the feeling that he resented Phil's going into the business. He and Phil always got along. However, though there were no more demands for more money to be invested in it, business didn't seem to pick up. Letters I had from Phil, while I was out on the road, hinted that Frank wasn't very active around the garage any more. Phil didn't know a bolt from a screw; he wrote he'd had to hire a mechanic. I figured something was wrong, and I knew I would have to check up on things when I got back to New York again.

I was booked to play at the Palace. When I got in town, Frank wasn't at the station to meet me. I figured he'd be at the theater, to drive me home after the night show. The matinee and night show over, still no Frank. I wasn't too worried. It was raining cats and dogs, and I said to myself, Frank couldn't make it in the storm. He figured I'd probably stay at a hotel in town. However, several acts on the bill with me lived out at Freeport, and I had an offer to drive home after the show, so I went.

Never will I forget that night! The storm was raging as if D. W. Griffiths were directing the show. The lightning snapped, the thunder crackled, and the rain pounded on the roof and sides of the car. When we drew up in front of my house, it was pitch dark, no light anywhere. I tried the door. It was open. Inside the dark hall I switched on the lights and started calling, but there was no answer. The house, I discovered, was completely empty. Where was Frank? Where was the cook? There was no getting anybody by telephone in that storm—wires were down all over the island. I locked up and went to bed, and, ultimately, to sleep.

It was after ten when I woke and found that I was still alone in the house. Then I got busy on the phone. Nobody I called could, or would, tell me anything. Around noon, when I was getting ready to go back to New York for the matinee, Frank strolled in, unshaven—not the Frank I knew. When I asked about the cook, he said she had left. When I asked if drinking parties had been going on, "So what?" he demanded.

It took me several days to get all the facts. I went over to the garage. Phil was glad to see me. I knew if I questioned him about Frank he wouldn't say anything. No need to put him on the spot, so I quietly snooped around, put some questions to the mechanic, and began to find out things. At the homes of some of our friends I picked up some more. And in a week or so I had enough to make the story complete. There was nothing new about it. A wife away on the road, a good-looking young husband left in Freeport who soon found someone who could make him happy—and not boss him.

Well, I took it. You have to take things like that when they happen to you, even if they do hurt your pride and your affection and your trust. There was nobody to blame but myself. Frank wasn't any different from most men who can't stand having a wife more successful and making more money than they do. Oh, I did my share of crying, but not in public. As I had been doing for over ten years, I turned to Mollie for comfort.

"Well, Mollie, I guess you nicknamed me Patsy for some good reason. I never have any luck with my men."

"It's like I told you years ago, Patsy, you're one of the ones that has to learn the hard way. Just the same, you'll get over this one and likely enough you'll get into other mistakes. (How well she knew me!)

"What you've got to do now is stiffen up your backbone, don't tell yourself any lies, and carry on."

When I played the twelve weeks' run in Chicago, I applied for a divorce in that city where Frank and I had been married. The divorce was granted— not without some unpleasant newspaper publicity—but I was free.

I did a lot of thinking about my experience with Frank. When I married him, I had gone against my better judgment, which always was not to marry anyone in show business. Well, I had done it, and it hadn't worked out. I couldn't blame anyone but myself. I still hoped that somewhere in the world there was a man for me, someone I could be happy with through the years, and who would give me companionship and love, not only when I was in the big money, but through years to come. That desire is in every woman's heart. I knew I would never be completely content while that desire was unsatisfied. But I'd learned quite a bit from my two mistakes in matrimony— enough to know that the greatest obstacle to my happiness as a woman is my success as an entertainer. I said to myself: "If I ever marry again, it will be a man who has his own business and is successful in it, so I needn't be afraid he will resent my success in my profession."

Maybe I enjoyed playing Chicago all the more because of my unhappy experiences at Freeport. The Edelweiss Gardens was my favorite spot. Frank Libuse, the Mad Waiter, was making his debut there and was a riot. Benny Davis came to the Edelweiss and introduced his song hit, "Margie." I wanted to sing the number for him, to plug it, so I had a pair of rompers made of large checkered pink-and-white gingham, with a big white muslin sash. I wore socks, low-heeled shoes, my hair down in curls with a big bow, and sang it for the customers.

It was during this long run in Chicago that I palled up with the Three Musketeers—Alderman Dorsey Crowe, Alderman Joe Kostner, and Alderman George Maypole. William Hale Thompson was then mayor of Chicago and living at the Hotel Sherman. Many nights after the show we all got together for laughs and a late snack. Then Alderman Anton Cermak wanted to join our gang. I remember he sent his card up—a gallon of red Bohemian wine. He was a grand person and a good friend to remember.

I don't mind telling, though the laugh is on me, that I fell for Dorsey Crowe. He looked pretty good to me, and I couldn't help hoping he felt that way about me. He asked me out to his house to meet the family—and that was where the romance did a nose dive. Not that they didn't like me, but they started calling me "Mom," and Dorsey took it up, and that was the end of the romance.

In those months after Prohibition came in—you can't say it ever was enforced—night life rapidly began to change. In competition with the big cabarets, thousands of speak-easies opened up for business. These places offered nothing in the way of entertainment. They were dark, gloomy rat-holes—stables and cellars—that people crept into to drink bootlegged liquor. Prohibition did terrible things to our country; even the theaters were different to work in in that era. All the gaiety was gone. The homes I used to visit were troubled. Entertainment was reduced to a bottle on the hip—a bottle that was emptied before the night was out. Trying to compete with that bottle was hell.

But there was a boomerang for me in the stand I had taken on drinking with Frank and the crowd at Freeport. I was playing at the Café de Paris at Atlantic City in the summer of 1920, doing good business and seeing a lot of my friends. One day Prohibition agents staged a raid on my apartment and went away with the few bottles I had there and which really belonged to the Boss, who came down occasionally to see how the act was going. My stock turned up in the headlines as nine cases of champagne and twenty-five gallons of scotch! The public whistled, and my friends, who knew me, called it the best joke of the Prohibition Era.

I used to run up to Hartford for a few days with the family whenever I could. Ma had kept up wonderfully after poor Pa's death. From that time on she gave herself, heart and soul, to the poor. Every afternoon about half past one she would go to the corner and wait for the streetcar to take her downtown for her charity work. The four of us—Phil, Moe, Sis, and I—all gave her a weekly allowance, but at the end of every week she was broke. She'd given it all away.

One day the streetcar conductor came over to her and said: "Mrs. Abuza, excuse me for asking you a personal question, but you've been riding my car for over twenty years, every day—rain or shine, snow, all kinds of weather —always the same time, always getting off at the same place. You're not a young woman. Please tell me, where do you go? What do you do every day?"

Ma looked around, to make sure nobody was listening. In a very low voice she said: "If you promise not to tell anybody, I'll tell you."

"No," he said, "I won't tell a soul." He bent his ear down, and Ma whispered: "I'm taking piano lessons."

She told us about it when she came home, very indignant because the conductor was so nosey. "So I told him, and I gave it to him good!"

She was still the queen of her own home, and demanded the respect and obedience of her children as if we were still kids. For years after I started smoking I was afraid of Ma catching me with a cigarette. Whenever I went home for a visit, I would snatch a smoke in the bathroom, or the cellar, or after she had gone to bed. Then one night when I was there, and very much worried about some changes I was making in the act, it seemed to me I'd die if I didn't have a cigarette. We were having dinner—just Ma, Sis, and I—in the kitchen. Sis knew how I felt. When she saw me reach for my bag which had the cigarettes in it, she said: "Don't be surprised at anything Sophie does today, Ma. She's nervous."

"Yes," I added, lighting up. "I've gone to the dogs, Ma. I smoke, and don't you invite your cronies up here to the house to catch me at it."

I watched her face out of the corner of my eye, expecting a scolding. But she didn't say a word. Nor did she mention it during the rest of my visit, though, after that, I smoked frequently in her presence. Sis told me later that after I had left she had said to Ma: "What do you think of Sophie smoking?"

Ma gave her one of her looks. "Who is she fooling? I knew it all the time!"

Occasionally Ma came to New York to visit me when I was playing a long engagement there. She never would come unless she had a new dress. She was so pretty with her lovely baby complexion, in which there wasn't a wrinkle, and her plump, dimpled little hands, which she had always washed with naphtha soap. She loved pretty clothes, and all her early life she had been poor and had to do without them. Now her little vanities all came to the top. She wouldn't admit it was vanity, though. "It isn't fitting for Sophie Tucker's mother to be seen in the same dress twice," was how she used to put it.

Never will I forget her joy in her first mink coat, which I sent up to Hartford to her. And her diamond earrings. She loved it when my friends complimented her on her fine clothes. One trouble about her coming to New York was she didn't want to miss anything that my crowd was doing. After the show, when a bunch would gather in my apartment for a poker game and play till four or five in the morning, Ma would sit up to the very end. "Why don't you go to bed, Mama?" the boys would say to her; "it's getting very late."

"No one has to rock me to sleep," she would retort.

One night I took her to a cabaret. Not to just one. That night we made quite a few spots and it was around 4 A.M. when we finished up for a bite to eat at the Moulin Rouge. Ma wouldn't eat anything in any of the places, as she was strictly Orthodox. Finally, we insisted that she order a box of sardines and a pot of tea. In fact, there were six of us and all of us ordered tea. Twelve little silver pots, all on the table at once. Ma had never seen so many at one time.

Later, when we got back to the hotel, and I was helping her undress, she pulled something from the pocket of her mink coat. "What have you got there?" I asked her.

"There were so many little teapots on the table the boss will never miss one," she said. "And I remember Leah said she needed a little pot for Phil's tea."

I laughed till I cried. She went off to bed clutching her souvenir. The next day I called up the manager of the Moulin Rouge to tell him what Ma had done. I asked him to rib her over the phone, and tell her if she didn't return the pot he would send the police for it. Half an hour or so later, when Ma was in the room with me, he did phone to ask, very severely, if we had a teapot from his place. Ma turned white as a sheet.

"Quick, quick!" she said, "give it back and put me on a train for home before they arrest me! It will be a scandal if the papers say Sophie Tucker's mother stole a teapot!" It took the rest of the day to convince her that it was all a joke and that the boss had given her the teapot for a souvenir.

Even more than fine clothes Ma loved dressy hats. And I mean dressy! She was never satisfied with those Sis or I would pick out for her. She thought them much too plain. Her idea was that if you paid ten to twenty dollars for a hat it should have plenty of trimming on it! Consequently, it was Moe who bought her hats, because he would buy the kind she liked—dripping with willow plumes, birds of paradise, flowers, jeweled buckles, and Lord knows what else!

For years she had heard me talk about Chicago, my second home, and about my friends there. One day she asked me if she couldn't visit me in Chicago. It was arranged that Brother Phil would bring her out to meet me in Milwaukee the week I was playing there, and then she and I would go on to Chicago. The trip out West was wonderful to her. It was the first time she

had ever slept on a train or seen a Pullman drawing room. Phil told us how
he tucked her up for the night in the lower berth and told her if she felt
cold and didn't want to wake him in the upper, all she had to do was to push
the button and the colored porter would attend to anything she needed. It
was bitter cold that winter, and when Phil waked in the morning and looked
down to see if Ma was all right, there she was asleep with her shoes on and
her fur coat over her for an extra blanket.

"Why didn't you push the button, Ma?" Phil asked her.

"I was afraid," she said. "I didn't want to have a black man get into bed
with me."

Our week together in Milwaukee was lots of fun. Then we came into
Chicago to play Christmas week at the Palace. Who should be playing on the
same bill but Jack Rose, one of the greatest comedians we ever had. A riot
on every bill, and the grandest, sweetest, craziest soul in show business. One
of Jack's stunts was to wear funny-looking hats and smash them during his
act. The first thing he did, when he hit a town, was to make the tour of all
the secondhand shops and buy up all the old hats available. Sometimes he
would break fifteen to twenty hats during a performance.

On our opening night at the Palace Ma sat in the front box. The house was
packed and every box jammed to capacity. Ma was sitting there among
strangers, never cracking to them that I was her daughter, just listening and
taking in everything the folks around her had to say about me. I had tipped
Jack Rose off not to say anything to the audience about Ma being there. I
wanted to spring a surprise on them. For years Chicagoans had thought I
was born and brought up in their city, that I came from Halsted Street. I
never denied it, or confirmed it.

The whole show that night was a riot of fun. My act went over bigger
than ever. Flowers were coming over the footlights and I was getting a great
kick out of having Ma there to see the way Chicago welcomed me. After the
act I was center stage with my arms full of flowers and baskets of flowers
banked around me. I started to make a speech of thanks. Out of the corner
of my eye I could see Ma, wiping her glasses, blowing her nose, straighten-
ing her hair, primping up.

"Ladies and gentlemen," I said, "ever since 1909, when I first played the
William Morris American Music Hall and you made me a headliner, you
and the press have publicized me as Chicago's Favorite. Tonight, after eleven
years of your hospitality and accepting me as a Chicago girl, may I introduce
to you a little lady who has just made her first trip to Chicago from Hartford, Connecticut. May I introduce to you my mother."

I could see the handkerchiefs coming out in the first fifteen to twenty rows in the house and every man in that theater stood up. The spotlight played directly on Ma. I had a moment of terror, not knowing how she would take this, but I might have known Ma would be ready for it. She stood up in the box, straight as a tree, smiling, bowing, and throwing kisses to everyone. And was she a riot! Jack Rose jumped into the box, hugged and kissed her. That scared her.

"You crazy man!" she cried in Jewish, "get away from me!" How the audience laughed. Afterward, back at the hotel, where we had a big Christmas party, I asked her if she was nervous when I called on her to take a bow.

"Why should I be nervous? In my mink coat and the spotlight on my plumes! I was thinking, now I get my money's worth out of my expensive hat. And isn't it nice all Chicago can see me dressed so nice!"

During the four years I played with the Five Kings there were frequent changes. Al Siegel left to play for Bea Palmer, and I engaged Jules Buffano as pianist in his place. Other boys came and went.

Meanwhile, I worked my salary for the act up into the big brackets—twelve hundred to fifteen hundred dollars a week. The boys were getting top money, but not all at the same salary. I paid them according to their value to the act. Then toward the end of 1921 I began to have serious trouble with the boys. Rehearsals were more trying than ever; the act was sagging. The boys weren't cheerful and peppy any more. They were quarreling among themselves about their pay. I wired the Boss to book me into New York, that I would have to change the men in the band. He got me dates at the Flatbush Theatre in Brooklyn, with the Palace in New York to follow.

When the Monday matinee in Brooklyn was over, I felt something was very wrong. I said to myself there was no use putting off the showdown any longer, so I sent word up to the boys that none of them should leave the theater, that I wanted all of them to come to my dressing room. When they were all there, I put it to them straight: "What the hell is the matter with you fellars!"

There was a shuffling of feet on the floor, but no answer. "Come on," I said, "out with it!"

There was a lot of hemming and hawing. Finally, one boy said: "We feel that the five of us should be getting more money, and that all of us should be paid alike."

"Yeah!" I said, "and what brought this on?"

His reply was: "We feel we are too valuable to the act not to get more money."

"You mean you feel you mean more to the act than I do?"

No answer, but you could see that that was the way they felt.

"Well," I said, "what about next week? We are booked to play the Palace."

They gave me their ultimatum. They wanted more money or they wouldn't open at the Palace. I thought fast. The act was a big success; the theaters all over the country wanted it. The Palace was an important date. Just the same I saw no reason to let five smart alecks tear down something I had spent years to build up. I gave them *my* ultimatum:

"Okay, fellows. The act closes here at the Flatbush Sunday night. No more Sophie Tucker and her Five Kings of Syncopation!"

After they'd gone, I called up Eddie Darling. "I'm closing the act with the band on Sunday night. I'm through with that headache. I'll work out something else. If you'll put the Palace date off for a few weeks, I'll be ready to open with a brand-new act." Eddie okayed it, and that was that.

The rest of that week at the Flatbush was sad. I guess the boys never thought I'd let them go. They soon realized they'd made a mistake, and they tried to talk me out of closing. But I knew better than to change my decision. I knew once there was dissension among them, once they got the idea they were the whole act and could run me, or that I couldn't play without them, I'd never be able to handle them. We closed on Sunday night, and that was the end of the Five Kings of Syncopation.

In the meantime, I was scheming what to do next. I'd heard that Al Siegel, who had been my pianist, was not working, so I got hold of him. Jack Yellen, Jack Lait, who had come on to New York for the Hearst papers, Al Siegel, and I built up a new act. We got entirely away from the jazz idea. We had Siegel at the piano, Morris Blumenthal, violinist, and Ida Forsyne, the colored dancer, who doubled as maid. I had nine new songs, all different from the type of song I had been singing with the Five Kings.

We had a break-in at Hartford, and tried it out in a couple of other places before we opened at the Palace. I was jittery about the press; the act was so far away from what the public expected of me. But my luck held. As one reviewer put it:

. . . Sophie Tucker's act without the aid of a jazz band was thought to be something like *Hamlet,* with Hamlet left out. But the comedienne came along yesterday minus a jazz band and showed that, as far as she was concerned, syncopating songs had lost none of their fascination to the ear when she was the singer. Her art is mightier than the jazz band, so to speak.

The Boss booked us on the road, and we played around for several months, coming back into Reisenweber's this time for a short engagement.

It was while we were there that Al Siegel left me. I phoned round to the music publishers' asking for a piano player. One of the publishers sent over a tall, thin kid in horn-rimmed glasses, solemn as an owl. Ted Shapiro was his name. He had a record in show business as having been Eva Tanguay's accompanist and also with the Wellington and Cross dance team. The boys at the music publishers' said I wouldn't go wrong if I took him on.

I had to have someone at once, so right after the performance—about 3 A.M.—I took the kid over to my suite at the Hotel Claridge and rehearsed twenty-six numbers with him. I pushed the lead sheets into his hands and told him to be on hand next day for rehearsal.

The rehearsal was terrible. The kid wasn't good at transposing, which was very important for me, as I didn't sing the songs in the keys in which they were written. I had no set routine, which made it difficult for my piano player. I had a habit of fitting the songs to the audience. He had no way of knowing which number would follow which; and as I always sang from the center of the floor or room, and the piano was always set up on a platform and behind the orchestra, he could hardly see me and couldn't possibly catch a signal from me which song to strike into.

I was desperate, not knowing what to do. I was ready to let the kid go, but he asked could he take the songs home with him. I let him. I figured he would work on the songs by himself, which meant he was a good, hardworking kid who wanted to make good on the job. The next night was Sunday, and Celebrity Night. I had a lot of acts to go on for me, and I asked Ted to play for them. He had no time for rehearsal. He pushed the piano out on the floor, and all the acts that night went over so big I began to feel maybe the kid was going to shape up into something, after all.

From then on I kept easing him into my act on the off nights at Reisenweber's, and he kept getting better and better. I thought he was working on the songs at home. It was years before I tumbled to the fact that his taking them home was just a stall. Something to impress me. What Ted did was to memorize the songs as I sang them. His memory was so accurate he could trust it completely.

He had his first stage appearances with me at the Jefferson Theatre and at the Academy of Music in Fourteenth Street, New York, just before I was due to sail for London. He asked me then if I was satisfied with his piano playing. I was in a big rush.

"I'll let you know later," I said.

Well, that's over twenty years ago, and I still haven't told him whether I'm satisfied.

I guess it's characteristic of Ted that in all the years we have been working together, and with everybody from newsboys, bellhops, and bus boys up to three-star generals and royal princes calling me "Sophie," he still calls me "Miss Tucker," or sometimes "Boss."

It was at the Academy Theatre that I played the first time with Jack Benny, then just a fresh kid from Waukegan. He did a single act. On opening day he came into the theater just in time to go on. He worked in his street clothes, carrying his violin. Jack walked out on the stage and said his opening line to the audience: "Oh, hello." Somebody in the gallery gave him the good old "bird." Jack said "Good-by," and walked off the stage without playing a note. And he never came back.

Meanwhile, I got to thinking, the way I generally do: "What next?" I'd been playing Reisenweber's for five years and headlining in the big-time houses all over the country between engagements. I could do that for some time, provided I kept on changing and improving my act. But I wanted something different. One day I went downtown to see the Boss.

Abe Lastfogel was sitting in the outer office when I breezed in. He gave me a sharp look. "What's eating you?" he wanted to know.

"Wait till I try it on the Boss," I answered.

As soon as I was in Mr. Morris's office I brought out my idea. "Boss," I said, "how about me going over to London and trying my luck over there?"

The Boss leaned back in his chair and thought it over. I was watching his face for the little gleam in the corner of his eye that always told you before he spoke if he thought your idea was good. I went on: "I've been with Reisenweber's so many years. I've played the Palace over and over again. I've got to open a new field, a new home. If I could do that in London, it would mean great prestige for me when I came back here."

Then I saw the gleam.

"Good idea!" said the Boss. "We'll try it. I'll get busy with bookings. Have you any idea what you're going to do for an act?"

I told him I would take Ted along to play for me. And an extra piano player, in case anything happened to Ted. I wouldn't risk being stranded and having to break in a British piano player who might not be up on American jazz rhythms. I would show the folks over there what American jazz was like.

"Good," said the Boss. And I went out, walking on air.

A few weeks later he phoned me that he had booked me for four weeks, to open early in April at the Finsbury Park Empire Theatre in London at a salary of two hundred pounds. A big price for England, I was told.

As soon as I knew I was booked, I began to get the jitters. What did I know about British audiences and how to entertain them? London was a hell of a long way from Times Square. "If only you were going to be there," I wailed to the Boss, "then I'd feel I was playing safe."

Back came his voice over the wire, the sweetest words I could hear: "I shall be there. I am taking the family over and I'll meet you when you land. There's nothing to worry about."

"Not now there isn't!" I sang out.

So long as the Boss was on hand I knew I wouldn't lay any eggs.

CHAPTER 18: *My Battle of Britain*

WE SAILED on the *Homeric,* on Sis's birthday, March 25, 1922. Getting away was exciting and lots of work. The family came down from Hartford to see us off, for Sis was going along. There would be Sis and me, and the two boys, Ted Shapiro and Jack Carroll. I decided not to take Mollie.

A few nights before we sailed the boys at Reisenweber's gave me a farewell party. Everybody who was there that night joined in. There were quite a lot of stage and screen stars on hand—Conway Tearle, Bert Lytell, Viola Dana, and a lot more—and they all helped to keep the fun going. Nobody got more fun out of that night than Ma. She got up and danced and was the hit of the evening. And with another new dress, of course.

Everything about the trip across was wonderful to me. Not the least wonderful was the thought, how different this trip was from my first one coming to America in the steerage. Thinking about that, I could realize something of the meaning of America, the only country on earth where the sort of thing that had happened in my life could happen. America had given me the opportunity to make good. I owed it everything I had. Now I was going back to Europe in a way to represent America to audiences. It was going to be up to me to show the British what America can do for an immigrant girl.

On the way over there was a ship's concert, of course, at which I was asked to sing. That wouldn't have been important except for something that happened which gave me an idea on which I later built my act. The lounge on the *Homeric* was so big and the piano was screwed down to the floor some distance from the platform. All right if you were going to sing with an orchestra, but the ship's orchestra wasn't up to playing my American jazz. I needed the piano near me. What we did was to move in another piano onto the stage and the two boys, Ted Shapiro and Jack Carroll, played the two pianos for me. Right away I saw that this was a good stunt, and decided to work it up when we got to London and try it on my first theater audience. At that time no singer had used a two-piano team.

England was different. You felt that the minute you landed at Southampton. What impressed me, I guess, is what impresses most Americans the first time they go to England—the smallness of everything. And the neatness. No kids playing in the streets. Rows of little red brick houses, every window with the whitest of white old-fashioned lace curtains. The pubs. The chemists' shops, so different from American drugstores. No ice-cream sodas, no hot dogs, no hamburger White Castles, no big advertising signs. So few telephones. Going up to London in the train, I read a newspaper story of a girl suing a man for a large sum of money for throwing her over. The judge asked the girl why she thought the man could pay such a sum, and she replied she was sure he must be rich because *he had a telephone in his flat.*

The Boss and Mrs. Morris, with Junior, George Foster, and his son Harry, the London correspondent of the William Morris office, were at Waterloo Station to meet us and drive us to the Piccadilly Hotel, where the Morrises were staying.

Before the Boss had left for England he and I had had a long talk. We decided that no advance publicity was to be used before I opened in London. No blasting in the press about Sophie Tucker, singer of hot songs, or what I had done at Reisenweber's, or the big money I was making. I was to go over quietly and sneak up on the British, unannounced. If I made good over there, then so much the better for the surprise element. If I didn't, then I could always fall back on the old gag—"there's a boat leaving every Wednesday and Saturday."

Right away I saw I had a lot to learn about British ways of doing things. The Boss suggested we take in a music hall (British for vaudeville) to give me an idea of what goes over with a British audience. We went to the Coliseum, which was then the ace variety house. It compared with the Palace in New York. It was a huge place, and packed. Everybody smoking. Those British pipes damn near killed me. There was a bar at the back of the house, as in every theater I saw over there. There were a lot of other differences I noticed at once: the billing out in front of the theater was different from our way. The first and second headliners were printed in top boxes, with the smaller acts, in smaller boxes, down the sheet. Inside the house the fire curtain was kept up until the orchestra came into the pit. Seats in the pit—·

meaning the first two or three rows in the orchestra—were cheaper than the other rows. If a show was a success, you would always find a queue waiting for the pit seats, the same as they queue up for the gallery. It's wonderful how patient the Britishers are about standing in line for something they want. They bring along campstools and shawls and make themselves comfortable while they wait all night for the box office to open. Hawkers go along the line selling sandwiches and hot tea, and sometimes street musicians, singers, and conjurers entertain the queue and then pass round the hat. I used to love seeing that. It was all a part of show business and made me think of the Boss's story about how vaudeville began.

I'll say one thing for the inside of British theaters: every seat is big and comfortable and has an ash tray. At that time the lighting systems were superior to ours. Not one spotlight from a booth, but three played on every act, besides the stage lighting. In this country, even in the finest theaters on all the circuits, we wouldn't have more than one lousy spot. The drops and curtains at the Coliseum were lovely and richly colored. Quite a change from the standard drop or park scene that was used, week in and week out, for generations in every American vaudeville house I played in. Over here, every sketch had to use the same old library scene that you saw in every town from Boston to Seattle.

But what struck me funny at the Coliseum was the show. Though the stage drops and curtains were fresh and beautiful, not a single act that came out on that stage dressed smart or looked up to date. Most of them wore comic clothes. None of the men wore tuxedos or tails, or even well-tailored street clothes. And the gowns of the women performers looked like something out of the old-clothes shops in Petticoat Lane. I couldn't get over it. I said to the Boss: "Hell, I've got one thing that'll put me over here—some clothes that are worth looking at!"

The show at the Coliseum was very much like our bills, with the acrobats to open, the neat dancing girl, the street comedians, the jugglers, the monologuist, the women singers, the comedienne, the ballroom dancers, the pair of hoofers, the comedy sketch, the dramatic sketch, then the headliner, and the standard acts. But there the likeness ended. Men predominated on every bill. The songs were drawn out from eight to ten minutes. While performers made changes there were many stage waits. It all seemed slow and draggy to me.

But there was no doubt that the audience liked it. There was a lot of laughter and plenty of applause and cries of "Core! Core!" Later I found out this meant "Encore." All the time I sat there cold as a dead fish. And it wasn't just the lack of steam heat in the theater, though the house was so chilly everybody kept their coats and hats on. I didn't understand one word that was said on the stage. I didn't get the point of a single joke or gag. I couldn't make head or tail out of the songs.

My teeth began to chatter. "Boss," I said, and grabbed his arm, "let's get out of here, quick. I'm sick. You've got to get me home."

Outside, he looked at me, worried. "What's the matter, darling?"

"Get a taxi," I said. "Let's get back to the hotel."

In the taxi I told him: "I've made a terrible mistake coming over here. I'll never be able to entertain these Britishers. If I can't understand them, how the hell are they going to understand *me?* They speak a different language from me. I'll flop over here, sure as hell."

He tried to buck me up. He said it was just an attack of nerves. (As though I ever had the damn things.) But I knew better. I knew I was up against the toughest proposition I'd run into since my early days. "Listen," I told him, "you've got to cancel that Finsbury Park date. I won't open Monday. (This was on a Wednesday night.) Put it off for a week and give me time to get around and find out some things about these folks over here. Give me time to learn their tricks. If you make me open on Monday, I'll lay an egg!"

The Boss tried to calm me the way he always did when one of his acts got the jitters. I can still hear his beautiful voice saying: "Now, now, everything will be all right. Leave it to me. If you want time to change your material, I'll call Foster and Gillespie tomorrow and fix it with them."

He was as good as his word, and Harry Foster and Mr. R. H. Gillespie, who was general manager for the Moss Empires, Ltd., agreed that I was right.

I found out later that they had had plenty of trouble with many American performers whose acts didn't go over with the British. The same was true of lots of British performers who came to America. The Boss was always trying to make them see the importance of adapting their acts to American tastes. Those, like Sir Harry Lauder, who listened to the Boss and took his advice, made fortunes in America. The ones who didn't, found out the meaning of a Bronx cheer.

They had grand beds at the Piccadilly Hotel, but I didn't get any good out of mine that night. I tossed and turned. I lay staring into the dark, worrying as I hadn't worried in years; not since I started on the burlesque wheel and found I was up against a kind of entertainment I didn't understand. How,

I asked myself, was I going to get a line on these British folks? And how in hell was I going to make the British understand Sophie Tucker?

When the Boss and I got together the next day, we mapped out a campaign. First, to see all the successful shows in London. We began with the revue at the Hippodrome, *Round in Fifty,* in which George Robey was starring. The idea was a trip around the world in fifty days. (Funny, to think of that now, when we make it in a week.)

Robey was a scream. I gathered that he was considered off color, but funny, so I watched him carefully. I had to find out where the British drew the line. How we howled at the scene where he got to Chicago and all the men wore cowboy pants and ten-gallon hats. But the California scene was even funnier. There were orange trees hung with oranges stuffed with cotton. The backdrop was painted with the Rocky Mountains, the Grand Canyon, the Alleghenies, the Catskills, and the Mississippi River. At a cue a Mississippi River stern-wheeler came up the river, all lighted up and crowded with coon shouters. Our party laughed so loud an usher came down the aisle and asked us to be quiet, as we were disturbing the people around us.

Well, London producers sure didn't know much about the U. S. A., and the British audiences didn't know any different either. They took it as "a bit of all right, what?"

The next night we took in *Welcome Stranger,* in which Harry Green was making a big hit. At that time not many American acts had made a success in London. Nora Bayes had. And Ethel Levey, who was George M. Cohan's first wife. I found out that her great song over there was my "Some of These Days." The song was identified with her. This meant I couldn't include it in my act, as according to custom when a British music publisher brought out an American song and gave it to a performer no one else sang it until it was published for the general public. The Trix Sisters were playing to a hit in *A to Z,* and Yvette Rugel's golden voice was making her a lot of friends around town and in the provinces.

The more I saw of London's music halls, the surer I was that I would have to have my songs rewritten. I suggested to the Boss that he invite a few British people up to his suite and let me try my stuff out on them. The next day he had a dozen people up for the tryout. There was only one piano in the room so I couldn't give them the two-piano-act stunt. I sang "I Know It," "I'm Nobody's Fool," "When They Get Too Wild for Everyone Else, They're Perfect for Me," "Bluebird, Where Are You?" "Dapper Dan," "There's More Music in a Grand Baby Than There Is in a Baby Grand," "The Broadway Blues." and others.

While Ted played for me, Jack and Sis were over in one corner dancing. I remember the crowd thought that the dance was part of the act. They liked it better than they liked my songs. Oh, they were polite. Said they liked my rhythm, and that I had great vitality and a wonderful personality. But no laughs! At that moment I would have sold my chances of being a success in London for a wooden nickel.

After that tryout the Boss got hold of the best song writer in London— Eric Valentine—and we went into a huddle. Again I went over every one of my songs. All the all-American words we changed to British equivalents. Gas became petrol, nickel and dimes, bobs and tuppences. Meanwhile, Ted and Jack and I went to work on slowing up all the songs. I've always been proud of my timing; it's something I've worked at ever since I've been in show business. I know it's good (it ought to be after years of work at it). My figure may bulge, but my act is streamlined.

The boys and I sweat blood that week. We had two pianos in the hotel ballroom and rehearsed there while Sis went sightseeing and brought me back news of London.

Harry Foster had booked me at the Stratford Empire Theatre for one show only on the next Monday night for the break-in. In London, variety shows played twice nightly, at six-thirty and at eight-thirty. We couldn't get two pianos for the opening, which, maybe, was just as well. I was saving that for my date at the Finsbury Park Empire. London had never seen a two-piano act up to that time. Ted was to play for me at the Stratford, with Jack standing by.

The Boss, Mrs. Morris, Junior, Mr. Gillespie, Harry Foster, Sis, the boys, and I filled three taxis, and drove out to the Stratford—a long ride. The theater was on a par with the old Jefferson Theatre on Fourteenth Street, New York, before it became a Keith house. I had played there to an audience of foreigners, workingmen with no collars and ties. A great audience if they liked you and if you had something to give them. But impossible to fool. The crowd at the Stratford Empire made me think of them: British workingmen with their wives and sweethearts. They were going to be hard nuts to crack. If I could put my act across to that crowd, I felt I'd be safe with the audiences at the Finsbury Park. If I didn't make good at the Stratford, I knew I'd get the razzberry. And no mistake! I'd already learned in the week I went around to shows that British audiences give it very quickly.

We sat in a box to watch the show. I sat at the back so none in the house would see me. Act after act came on—the comics, comedienne, dancers, singers—and not one woman or man on that bill wore dress clothes. I was wearing a very lovely white fringed dress, an ermine wrap, and gorgeous jewels. My hair was dressed in the height of fashion, like shining spun gold. I felt I didn't fit into that bill.

"Why did you book me in here," I whispered to Harry Foster, "and why didn't you tell me what the place was like so I would have dressed simply?" I was still spluttering about it when the manager came to tell us the act was going on that I was to follow.

Backstage, and waiting. Then the piano was pushed onto the stage and the manager beckoned to Ted. He came over to me. "Very good, Miss Tucker. We're ready. You can go on."

"Wait a minute," I said. "How about introducing me?"

"Oh, we don't do that over here," he told me. He waved his hand, and a boy went out in front of the drop with a sign which he held up for everyone to read. I craned my neck and saw that the sign held just one word:

DEPUTY

There was nothing to tell the audience my name, what I was going to do, or anything about me. I might have been a performing horse, for all they knew.

"Go right ahead," said the manager.

Ted went to the piano and I walked onto a stage that sloped so steeply down to the footlights that I nearly fell on my face. Later, I found that all British stages are built that way. Between my terror of my first British audience and that ski slope I was expected to perform upon, all I could do was to sidle over to the piano and hang onto it for dear life. It felt as if my knees were shaking the fringe of my dress like a hula dancer's skirt. The hanky I was carrying was torn to shreds before I even knew what I was doing to it.

I looked out at the house. Were they going to be friendly? From here and there I caught sounds of tittering. So that was what they thought of my fine clothes!

As my eyes became accustomed to the darkness out front, I could see no faces. Only hundreds of backs. The audience was moving out on me. For a second I stood there paralyzed. Then I thought fast: they're going back to the bar. I've got to stop them. I've got to make them forget they want a beer, and make them want Sophie Tucker instead.

I've heard other performers tell of similar experiences and how upset they were—too upset to be able to handle the situation. But they hadn't been schooled in the Ten-Twent'-Thirt's as I was. Everything I'd learned from handling the gallery gangs in some of the tough houses in New York and

Chicago came back to me that night in London. I knew I mustn't give those guys a chance to get to the bar. I'd have to catch them midway. I whispered to Ted to change the opening number and struck right into "Dapper Dan."

That song had a great syncopated melody. It was catchy. You couldn't pass it up. Those British workingmen didn't know where Alabam' was, or care a damn. That didn't matter. What caught them and stopped them in their tracks was the American rhythm and all the power in my pipes.

As I sang, I could see I'd turned the tide. They were forgetting about wanting a beer. They were moving back to their seats. I could see faces now. A lot of them were smiling.

"I've got 'em," I said to Ted. And without a break we swung into a comedy number: "When They Get Too Wild for Everyone Else, They're Perfect for Me."

That number brought the laughs. The crowd loved the blue lines Eric Valentine had written into it especially for them. They never missed a point. I slowed down my usual tempo, feeding it to them as they could take it.

It paid. At the end of the number there were cheers and cries of "Core! Core!" I'd shown them I could sing to them in their own language, whoever I might be.

I had planned to do a ballad next, but I threw it out of the routine. Now I'd found their level, I didn't dare risk losing it. Better stick to rhythm and comedy songs. I finished with "There's More Music in a Grand Baby Than There Is in a Baby Grand," with the British blue lines. They simply ate it up and yelled for more.

My throat was drying up. I left the stage while the house was still shouting. The manager stood in the wings with his arms out, barring my way. "Go back," he said. "They want more!"

I grabbed a glass of water and swallowed it. I was wringing wet and my nerves were shot to pieces. In the fifteen minutes I'd been on that stage I had worked harder to win that British crowd than I had ever worked for the customers at Reisenweber's or at the Palace in New York.

The manager insisted I go back.

So I gave them three more songs—all off-color ones, since those were what they liked. I was to find out that British audiences love a good bawdy joke. They take their meat rare and they like their humor on the raw side too. That goes for all classes and both ends of London. Most of their own performers who have made themselves tremendously popular with the crowds have been off color in their work. Look at George Robey. And Gracie Fields. And Marie Lloyd. In Britain there are some things you can't say in a song without giving offense, such as mentioning a member of the royal family. (As I was to find out later on.) But sex they don't mind. Quite different from the U. S. A., where an entertainer can take all the cracks he wants at the President and other national figures, but brings the wrath of the censor down on him if he mentions some of the well-known facts of life.

The audience was still applauding when the Boss and Harry Foster and Mr. Gillespie came backstage, grinning from ear to ear. They said they were sure now that I would go down with the British audiences from the way I had handled this tough assignment. It had gone far better than they hoped.

As for me, I was a wreck. There wasn't a thing in the world I wanted but a steak—and then bed.

When I was back in my hotel room, undressing, I got the scare of my life. My diamond bracelets were missing. I knew I'd worn them to the theater, but where or how I lost them I had no idea.

"Get into bed," Sis ordered. "Try to go to sleep. Teddy and I'll do the hunting."

So at 3 A.M. Sis and Ted got a taxi and went back to the Stratford Empire. It was locked tight, and they couldn't raise the night watchman. So they hung around, waiting for dawn and the arrival of the charwomen to clean the theater. When the chars came with their mops and pails, Sis and Ted went in with them. Luck was with them, and with me, for they found the bracelets on the floor of the box where we sat to watch the first part of the show.

The Boss okayed an opening date for me at the Finsbury Park Empire on the following Monday. I was all set to go. Meanwhile, I suggested to him that he get me a chance to make one appearance at a fashionable night club before my opening. I wanted to test myself and my songs on a smart, sophisticated audience.

That season the Metropole Hotel was London's swank place for supper. Paul Murray was putting on a revue there called the *Midnight Follies*. I had met Paul in Chicago a season back when I was there with my Five Kings. Then he had offered me a spot in his London show, but the salary he held out was too small to make it an inducement. Besides, at that time I didn't see that I would get enough out of a London engagement to make it worth the trip across.

The Boss liked the idea, and he and Harry Foster arranged for me to sing at the Metropole on Wednesday night. This was always a gala night there. Wednesday and Friday were "extension nights," which meant that you could drink until 2 A.M. On all other nights all drinks had to be off the supper tables at twelve-thirty. The British Blue Laws also prohibited performers from sitting around a café after they had entertained. You had to leave the premises.

When we got to the Metropole, the room was packed. Such handsome-looking people—all in evening dress. The men very distinguished in "tails." Whenever you saw a black tie, you could be sure there was an American behind it. The women, though they appeared to better advantage in their evening gowns than in street clothes, still didn't have the style of our American women. What struck me at once about the London cabaret crowds was the predominance of elderly people. One of the results of the war.

The smartest people in London society flocked to the Metropole for late supper. Prices were high: admission one guinea for men, ten shillings for ladies. Champagne sold for one guinea per bottle; cocktails at two shillings. This was the other side of the London I had seen at the Stratford Empire Theatre.

But another thing I noticed about the crowd at the Metropole was its easy friendliness. All those who came there seemed to know each other very well and to be ready to be amused and have a good time. It was like Reisenweber's.

We had a table at the back of the big room. We could watch the people at the other tables as well as the dance floor and the big staircase, which the revue came down. It was a fine show. The stars were one of our best American dance teams—Dorothy Dickson and Carl Hyson.

We watched the show, me sitting on pins and needles wondering when Paul Murray would call on me. As time went on, and the show, and Paul never came near us, or made an announcement about me, my heart began to sink. I did want a crack at the smart people of London.

Then I spotted Carl Hyson sitting at one of the tables. At the same minute he caught sight of our party and came over.

"I didn't know you were in London, Sophie," he said. "I dare you to sing for us here tonight."

"Go ahead, Carl. Introduce me." I was thinking, to hell with Paul Murray. Why should I sit around and wait for him to make up his mind?

Carl left us and went backstage. Now, I thought, we'll see what happens.

The comic of the revue was Fred Duprez. Fred was an American who had made good in England and remained over there. We had worked together in vaudeville years before and he knew me well. It was he who introduced me that night at the close of the revue:

"Ladies and gentlemen, a great American star, a singer of songs, is here tonight. With a little coaxing I think we can get her out on the floor to sing for us."

I didn't need any coaxing. That was my cue. It didn't matter that Fred hadn't mentioned my name. Sophie Tucker didn't mean a thing to that London audience. Fred could have said "Tillie Klutz" and they would have given Tillie the same warm reception. As I made my way through the tables to the dance floor, the folks all smiled and were so friendly. I gave a big "hello" to everybody, the way I did at Reisenweber's. "Happy to sing for you," I said to them all, pulled off my ostrich-feather hat and put it down on the piano as Ted took his seat there. In that moment I certainly congratulated myself that we both looked nice and that I had taken Teddy and Jack to a good tailor and ordered "tails" for them as soon as I saw what was what in London. I went into hock fifty apiece for their suits, but it was worth it.

Maybe thinking about our appearance threw me out, because, for the life of me, I couldn't hear the piano. Ted looked over at me, and his eyebrows went up. I could see his hands moving over the keys, but I had no idea what song he was playing.

"That's funny," I said to the audience. "Here I'm dying to sing for you, and I'm so damn nervous I've forgotten the words." It was a natural. They howled. Probably they thought it was a gag. It wasn't, though; it was the honest truth.

"Give me a minute," I said. "I'll be okay."

They laughed again. "Okay" was new to them. I could hear them repeating it to each other, trying out this new sample of American slang.

They were so friendly that my stage fright left me as fast as it had come on. Suddenly I could hear the piano, and the words of the song came back to me. I opened my mouth and sang. One song after another. I guess I was on the floor a full half-hour; the crowd wouldn't let me go. It was Reisenweber's again in London; and was I happy? Not just because I was a success with that smart crowd but because I felt now that I was on the right track with British audiences. After this experience I wouldn't be afraid of playing their theaters anywhere.

Still, thinking it over the next day, I felt there was one more thing I ought to do before my opening at the Finsbury, and, when I put it to the Boss, he agreed with me.

"Maybe it's superstition," I said to him, "but I have a hunch if I were to sing once for my own people—the Jews in London—and if they accept me, nothing will stop me over here."

The Boss never laughed at my hunches; he always treated them with respect. He said he would find out what Jewish benefit was scheduled for that Sunday, and would get to the head of the committee and see that I appeared on the bill. It turned out there was to be one at the Palladium Theatre for the Lying-in Hospital.

I went into a huddle with the Boss as to what songs I would do. We decided on a jazz song first, then a comedy song, and a ballad for the third number. I wore a handsome white satin gown studded with brilliants, my ermine wrap, and gorgeous diamonds. I knew the audience would admire the outfit, and it's just as important to look well at a benefit as in a theater or a café. Even if you aren't making money out of the performance, you are building popularity and prestige, and making friends, all of which are tremendously important in show business.

The Boss was able to have two pianos on the stage for me at the Palladium. This was important because Ted, Jack, and I needed a tryout together before we opened the next day. We needed to get at least one showing under our belt to know how the act shaped up. The pianos were set in front of a black-velvet drop and the stage manager went out in front and introduced "Miss Sophie Tucker, an American singer, who has asked to appear at this benefit."

I had forgotten to tell him to announce that I had a two-piano act, so when the curtain parted, showing Ted and Jack seated at the pianos, there was a rumble of wonder and applause for them. When I parted the black-velvet backdrop and made my entrance between the two pianos, I was conscious of the nice picture we three made—black and white.

The sloping stage bothered me again, but now I was getting onto British ways. The confidence I had won at the Metropole stayed by me. The boys didn't take it as easily, though. As they played the introduction to "Dapper Dan" I couldn't hear the melody. It was just a jumble in my ears. After all, we had never tried out the two pianos on a stage before. I had to stop them.

"For goodness' sake, boys, there's nothing to be nervous about. We are among our own *Yiddisher kinder.*"

I heard the audience gasp. They didn't know whether I was a Jewess, or whether I just learned to say those words for the occasion. Then they laughed. I kept on with the asides in Jewish till the boys got their bearings and I got mine. Then we swung into the first song.

The audience liked the jazz and they liked the comedy song with its blue lyrics. It brought a lot of laughs. I had told the Boss about the ballad. "This will be the number that will put me over with our people in London." When

I was ready to give it to them, I announced: "My next song is a very simple one. I shall sing it first as it is written, 'Bluebird, Where Are You?'"

I sang the first verse and the chorus. It is a very beautiful, light ballad, and I could feel the audience liked it.

"Now," I announced, "I will sing the song like a *chazin* (a cantor)."

The effect of that real Jewish word, pronounced correctly as it is done only by Orthodox Jews, electrified the audience. They sat spellbound while I sang the verse and chorus. Then came thunderous applause, cheers, "Bravo!" and that London cry of "Core! Core!" When I went back to thank them, I tried to tell them what their acceptance of me meant. I said: "My work in England will be easy now."

And I didn't overlook putting in the plugeroo:

"Don't forget, I open tomorrow night—Monday—at the Finsbury Park Empire Theatre. Be sure to come and see me."

CHAPTER 19: *The British Are Regulars Too*

MY OPENING at the Finsbury Park Empire went without a hitch. I had a few minutes of worry because the orchestra wasn't up to handling the orchestrations and arrangements for my songs. Those arrangements had cost me a lot of money, but I figured it was better to drop them over the side rather than worry myself sick getting a British orchestra to play them my way. We arranged it so that the two pianos did all the work, and the orchestra came in at the finish of the numbers. This had the advantage of making the boys stand out in importance, and it put my songs over better than if I had depended on an inadequate orchestra. What's more, I didn't have to appear before British theater managers as a temperamental American dame.

Again, I found I had to slow down my tempo on all the songs to make sure the audience would understand every word. And again at the Finsbury Empire and in the theaters I played in Glasgow, Edinburgh, Nottingham, Cardiff, and Manchester, it was the off-color "point" songs that the audience liked best. The British are just folks, same as those in the U. S. A.

Every day the boys and I were at work, throwing out songs that didn't seem to mean much to the British audiences and substituting others. Fortunately, we had brought plenty. Everywhere I played I found the second show, at eight-thirty, easier to play to than the first one. That was the same as at home. In every theater in the United States the "supper shows" were the toughest. But aside from the rehearsals and playing every night, I had time to go sightseeing in London and to make friends too.

One of those friends was Hanan Swaffer, the dramatic critic. The first I heard of him was when Harry Foster rang me up about noon the day after I had appeared at the Metropole.

"Did you see Hanan Swaffer's article about you?"

In my excitement I didn't ask who Hanan Swaffer was or what paper he wrote for. At the hotel newsstand I asked for a copy of Hanan Swaffer's paper.

"Sorry, Miss, we have the *Daily Express,* the *Daily Telegram,* the *Sketch,* the *Star* . . ."

"But I want Hanan Swaffer's paper!"

The man thought I was crazy. Finally he called the manager, who told me: "Mr. Swaffer writes for the *Daily Express.*"

I hunted through the pages until I found his column and read:

A big, fat blonde genius, with a dynamic personality and amazing vitality, an American singer of songs, took the Metropole audience by storm last night. Her name is Sophie Tucker.

Naturally, after that I wanted to meet Hanan Swaffer. Harry Foster said he would arrange it, but as it happened he didn't have to. The next day the Boss took us all over to the Savoy for lunch. At a near-by table I noticed a party of four—two little stout ladies, who looked like sisters, and two men, one tall, thin, with scanty gray hair, dark clothes, a black tie askew and poking up from his collar, a cigarette hanging from his mouth, and ashes all over his coat. The ladies kept smiling and nodding at me as though they knew me, but not the man I've described. The Boss said he didn't know who he was, but we agreed he looked like someone of literary importance. I made up my mind to find out. When I saw the ladies from the other party go to the ladies' room, I followed, and there I met Madeline and Ida Cohen, two of the four daughters of Mr. Edgar Cohen, director of Harrod's, London's great store. They took me back to their table and introduced the literary-looking man—who was none other than Hanan Swaffer!

My friendship with the Cohens, begun that day at the Savoy, has flourished through the years. Their home at No. 4 Hall Road was open to me from the first Sunday I spent in London. What a family! The Governor, as they called their father, four daughters, Ida, Madeline, Connie, and Hilda, and the son, Stanley. Every Sunday at the Cohens' was open house. People from all walks of life came there—theatricals, newspapermen and -women, authors, politicians, and titled patrons of the arts. I met my first lord and lady there that afternoon—Sir Alfred and Lady Butt. At the Cohens', too, I met our American Fannie Hurst and Dame Sybil Thorndike, Leslie Henson, the great comedian, and a lot of other show people. Jack and Teddy went there with Sis and me and shared the fun. We entertained for the crowd, and I tried out some of my songs and stunts to get the British reaction.

Then, and later—all during my time in London—Hanan Swaffer's advice about my routine was a tremendous help. I'll never forget the panning he gave me after a show in which I sang a ballad called "Dear Old Lady." I had engaged a sweet-looking elderly woman to sit in a chair, dressed in a lovely black taffeta dress I bought her. I paid her five pounds a week for appearing on the stage with me. The Cohens were horrified. They said I would ruin all the help in London. Swaffer caught the show in which I did it, and back in my dressing room he laced hell out of me for doing a sob song that meant nothing, when I had grand songs, such as he had heard me sing at the Metropole and at the Cohens' home. I paid attention to his criticism and cut the song out of my act at once. When I paid the old lady off for the week, she was terribly mad at Swaffer and me for killing her career in show business. She even dropped a few tears. "I've never had so much loving before in my life," she sniffed.

The Boss had booked me for the provinces, which gave me a chance to see more of England and Scotland, to find out more about British audiences. Playing the provinces was like trouping in America, only more so. Most of England we saw through the rain. I had to go out and buy high boots and rubbers. I never was warm once. Nothing in the hotels had been changed since Queen Victoria was crowned. Private baths were practically unheard of. No central heating. And fifty-five cents for a bucket of coal to keep up a pretense of a fire in your bedroom! But there were great houses to play to in all the towns, the press was enthusiastic, and, when I wasn't shivering and worrying about getting pneumonia, Sis, the boys, and I had a swell time.

Manchester was different. No trouble there about getting rooms with baths. And the best food since we left London! I liked the Manchester people too. They were like Americans, in a way. Not easy to fool and generously appreciative of what they liked. Manchester had two variety theaters. I was booked at the Empire for a week. The Four Marx Brothers were booked at the other house that same week; so was Yvette Rugel. We were all at the Midland Hotel. Every night after the show we had supper together and a barrel of fun. One night we decided to have a get-together party—all the American performers in town. There were about twenty of us at the table. As we sat down Harpo Marx was on one side of me and Groucho on the other. It was an eight-course supper and, as usual in England, the table was loaded down with silverware. This gave Harpo and Groucho a chance for a stunt. They mixed up all the knives and forks on a big tray and Harpo tied a napkin over his eyes and picked out a tool for each of us to eat with.

I was beginning to wonder—what next? I had no wish to play around the British provinces indefinitely. If there was nothing more exciting to do than that, better go home. Then came a wire from the Boss saying he had booked me to play with George Robey in the revue, *Round in Fifty* at the Hippodrome Theatre—just to sing a few songs. After the show I was to double in the *Midnight Follies* at the Metropole.

Back in London we went to live at the Hotel Metropole, which would make it more convenient for me working in the club. The first thing to do, of course, was to report at the Hippodrome Theatre to get a line on what I was to do in the show. That first day I met all the cast, including the principals—Alec Haloway, Helen Gilliland, Barry Lupino. All except George Robey, the star. I never saw him the week rehearsals were called. The rest of the cast were friendly, though, and didn't make me feel strange a bit.

After a bit I asked Frank Boor about it. Frank was the manager of the Hippodrome—a new type to me with his corset, his tails, his monocle. Such an ardent worshiper of all London—its towers, abbeys, old streets, and, above all, its ladies.

I asked Frank why Robey wouldn't meet me. What was eating him? Frank hemmed and hawed, then showed me an article in some paper which read:

Sophie Tucker says she will show George Robey a thing or two when she joins *Round in Fifty*.

"Well!" I said to Frank, "that just goes to show how the newspaper boys and girls over here are like some of those back home. They don't give a damn what they write in their columns—whether it's true or not—so long as it fills up space. Wouldn't I be a fool to say a thing like that and stir up trouble for myself over here before I had a chance to get started? What's more, anybody who knows me knows I never boast ahead of time. Maybe I'm superstitious; maybe I'm scared. I've been in show business too many years to make a break like that! And I wish you'd tell George Robey so for me, if he's too dumb to think of it himself."

Frank said he would, and I had to leave it at that.

It got around to the night I was to open—Wednesday, May 17. All the members of the company sent me wires. All the members of the chorus knocked on my dressing-room door, wishing me luck. Everybody connected with the theater, it seemed, from the stage manager down to the stagehands, was friendly and encouraging. All but George Robey! I didn't like the feeling it gave me. I felt I couldn't walk out on that stage with him sore at me, especially over something I hadn't done.

I dressed on one side of the stage. Robey's dressing room was at the head of the stairs as you came in off the street. I put on a robe, went over to his room, and knocked on the door.

"It's me, Mr. Robey, Miss Tucker. Please, may I come in?"

"Yes, come in."

I opened the door. "Mr. Robey, I'm awfully sorry about that article in the paper, but I swear to you I never made, nor did I ever give, such a statement to the press. In my country, I'm known as a hell of a good scout. And once you get to know me, you will say so too. I'm opening tonight, and I just can't go out on that stage with you sore at me."

By this time I'm crying like a baby; so I shut the door, go back to my dressing room, and finish getting dressed. I kept waiting for a knock, for Robey to come in and wish me luck, but he didn't come. The show was on. Soon it was time for me to go down to the stage. I was standing in the entrance, waiting for my music to strike up, nervous as a pup, even though I know I looked well in my stunning outfit of light blue crepe, with ostrich sleeves, made for me by Madame Isobel on Regent Street. (Forty quid it set me back!) I kept hoping Robey would come by and say a friendly word. I don't think I'm any more superstitious than most performers, but my mind kept going back to the opening of the *Follies of 1909* and what had happened to me because of Nora Bayes's jealousy. There's no getting around it, it's unlucky to open in a show with the star down on you.

I was taking my last look off stage, and suddenly there was George Robey dashing toward me. "Good luck, young lady. Kill 'em out there! Sorry I'm late, but I was making quick changes throughout the show, or else I would have seen you sooner. Go ahead, you bloody bitch, and God bless you!"

There was just time to say, "Thanks, Mr. Robey. I'm so happy." Then my music began. I went out on the stage feeling fine. When Robey called me a bitch I knew he liked me; wasn't mad. I tried to make myself believe I was standing on the Palace stage in New York, entertaining the audience there, and I guess it worked because that London audience acted just the way the crowd at the Palace used to act. The songs went over with a bang. It was a glorious night. What touched me most deeply was to see George Robey, Barry Lupino, Helen Gilliland, and the rest of the cast standing in the wings applauding and glad I was a hit. We had a jubilee in my room after

the show for the entire company and all the Americans who could crowd in.
We put away thirteen quarts of champagne and twelve bottles of scotch.
Teddy and Jack were at the two pianos, playing American jazz, and every-
body was dancing. What a night!

The next night when I drove up to the Hippodrome there was my name
in big electric lights on the sign in front of the theater. The bobbies on that
beat got used to me standing across the street, staring at it from every angle
and taking snapshots. Me, Sophie Tucker, blazing away like that in the
West End. Even in the wildest dreams I'd dreamed back in the days after
I was let out of the *Follies,* my imagination never reached to this. This was
something I owed to the Boss, and to his faith in me and his constant encouragement.

As I went along with the show *Round in Fifty,* I got to know Robey better,
and I guess he found out that I was a right gal because he was always very
friendly and nice to me. Robey, with his funny blackened heavy eyebrows,
his naughty vocabulary, and his heart of gold. One time when the London
fog and smoke were playing the devil with my throat, Robey insisted on
taking me to his Dr. Lloyd. "Take care of this gal. We need her in London,"
he said.

I played nearly three months in *Round in Fifty.* Meanwhile the British
reviewers started to go American in writing about my act. Some of their
attempts at Broadway slang gave us a lot of laughs. It flattered me when they
said I reminded them of their own Marie Lloyd. I had met Marie Lloyd in
New York, where we became friends. What a trouper she was! And what a
marvelous entertainer. To have the British critics link my name with hers
set me up no end. If they could go American, I could go British!

I loved J. J. Shubert's comment after he saw me in *Round in Fifty*
"Sophie, how lovely and quiet you are, working over here."

Hell! I had to soften down after my first performance at the Finsbury
Empire. In the front row sat two elderly ladies, with their hands up to their
ears for fear I would burst their eardrums. Right away I knew I would have
to tone down. And I did.

When my time in *Round in Fifty* was up, at the end of my act on the closing night, George Robey brought me down to the footlights and presented
me with a huge gold jewel box engraved with the name of everyone in the
company. I didn't know then, what I learned later, that it was unheard of in
London at that time to stop the show to make a presentation of this sort to
one of the performers. I was too touched by Robey's little speech. "Sophie,
after we have played together three months it is with a great deal of pleasure

that I am privileged to present this token of affection from the entire company to a hell of a good scout."

London had its autograph hunters, as I soon found out. One night, as I was coming out of the stage door of the Hippodrome, a little girl came up and spoke to me. She had been waiting there in the rain for me to come out, to get my autograph and to tell me she had a brother in California whom she had not seen in many years. She told me his name, Maurice Gebber, and it turned out that I knew him. I had bought a fur coat from him on one of my trips to Los Angeles. I'll never forget the child's face when I told her I knew Maurice Gebber. She asked if she could bring her mother to see me. That Sunday, and every Sunday thereafter, while I was in London, Betty and her mother used to come to see me and bring me Jewish delicatessen. Years later, when I was playing in Los Angeles, a card was sent backstage to me: "Mr. and Mrs. Jack Leibo," and penciled underneath it, "The little girl who used to bring you the delicatessen in London."

Working at the theater and doubling at the Metropole was tough, but I loved it. I loved meeting the British people at the café. The same ones came again and again. The British never seem to get too much of what they like. Everybody was very kind to the boys and to me, and made us feel at home. At the Metropole I got to meet members of the nobility, important business people, producers, and artists. Ethel Levey and her husband Grahame-White, the celebrated aviator, were my big boosters in London. They gave a lot of theater and supper parties, and brought their friends to see me. I noticed, though, that very few British artists patronized the cafés. They all had their lovely homes—mostly out of London. Our first invitation to an actor's home came from Barry Lupino and his wife Gertrude to spend a Sunday with them at their country house near Maidenhead on the Thames.

Several times I went to Fannie Ward's house in London. I met Eddie Darling there. He was scouting for acts for the Palace. Heather Thatcher, the English actress, was there that day. She couldn't get over my handbag, kept exclaiming over its size. "Oh, I always carry an extra pair of drawers," I told her airily. She never cracked a smile.

Some of the houses we were invited to were something to see. I remember going to an "At-home" with Eddie Darling. At the door of the drawing room he grabbed my arm, stopping me to take it all in—the velvet hangings, the dark, carved furniture, the bronze and marble statues, the paintings in heavy gold frames.

"What a swell whore-house set!" he exclaimed.

One night at the Metropole I suddenly decided to give the customers a typical Bohemian night, as we used to at Reisenweber's. John Charles Thomas was there, so I introduced him to the customers, and what a sensation he was when he sang. Others I called on were Sam Bernard, Harry Green, who starred in *The Cherry Tree,* Anatole Friedland, our fine song writer and producer of great acts, and Ella Retford, an English variety artist who had never been on a floor before. All entertained that night. The Metropole crowd loved it; especially the impromptu feel of it.

One night there was great excitement backstage at the Metropole. The whisper ran through the dressing rooms: "Yes, he's here! Give a good show." The stage manager came back to caution us all. "Remember, this is his first visit here."

"Who's here?" I piped up.

"His Highness, Prince Henry." (Now the Duke of Gloucester.)

"Listen," I told the boys, "we're entertaining royalty at last." My music was playing, and I was making my entrance down the staircase, meanwhile trying to spot His Royal Highness in the crowd at the tables. I should have watched the steps. I missed one of them and damn near rolled down the balance, only I caught the balustrade and just saved myself from going on my fanny on the floor.

"It's your fault, Prince; I was looking for you," I said, and shook my finger at him.

There was a dead stillness as the whole room waited to see how he was going to take it. When he let out a yell, the rest joined in. Later, when I was presented to him and tried to apologize for doing something that isn't done in England, he wouldn't let me.

At the Metropole lords and ladies flowed in and out till I found myself able to use their titles as nonchalantly as we use nicknames on Broadway. What I couldn't get over was that none of them were stiff or hard to entertain. They all seemed crazy about everything American and eager to take up American jazz, American dance steps, American slang, and American mannerisms. One thing I had to learn was that though you could sing "point" songs to a gathering of these swells, you couldn't sing one, even an innocent one, in which royalty was mentioned. I had a song in which I referred to the Prince of Wales. I sang it just once, then the censor asked me to substitute another name for that of the prince in singing that particular song. I wrote in Sir Thomas Lipton, who got a great kick out of the joke.

A lot of the same people came again and again to the Metropole: Sir Francis and Lady Towle, Lord Cowley, Lord Napier Allington and his mother Lady Allington, and Lord Ned Lakam. Lady Allington asked me to help her with the benefits she held at the Palace Theatre for the waifs of London. The Princess Royal, King George V's eldest sister, was the patroness. (The kick I got when I heard a woman comment: "Look, she's wearing her last year's hat!") The minute I heard that I switched all my songs. No off-color lyrics for that audience!

After the benefit I enjoyed seeing everybody curtsey to the members of the royal family. Everybody but me. Just the same I was thrilled when Her Royal Highness gave me a real American handshake and said, "I'm delighted to know you, Miss Tucker, and my sincere thanks for your wonderful help." Gosh, I thought, I wonder what she'd have said to me if I hadn't switched those songs!

London was very gay because it was the season and there were a lot of benefits for every sort of charity. I averaged three to four a week; some of them tough, such as Lady Maud Tree's at Wyndham Theatre. A small house and nearly all women in the audience, with the Countess of Athlone sitting in the royal box. I sang my first song, and I could see they didn't know just how to take me. I guess I was like a gust of wind and hit them in the nose. During the second I could see them look at their programs, asking each other, "Who is she?" During the next song they wanted to laugh, but were too full of British reserve. With my last number I got a few laughs and I could hear the kid gloves applaud. But the ice sure was thick that day.

Mr. and Mrs. Benjamin Guinness gave a party in a converted mews back of their big house. It was a very intimate, jolly party, with a buffet supper served on the piano. There I met His Royal Highness Duke of Connaught and Princess Victoria.

One of the parties I was asked to sing at was given by Lord Beaverbrook. His house and the treasures in it were so wonderful I nearly forgot my songs. Lord Beaverbrook was so friendly, and insisted on introducing me to everybody. To this day I carry with great pride an onyx cigarette case, the gift of Lord Beaverbrook.

The Duncan Sisters were very popular in London at this time. They introduced me to Lady Michelham—"Cupie," as she was nicknamed by her large circle of intimate friends. She was then a little over forty-five—dark, not too short, and on the plumpish side—a widow with two sons. We had been told of her great wealth, her host of friends, and her beautiful homes in Paris and in London. She invited me to a luncheon she gave for Madame Cecile Sorel, who came to London. Lord Allington and Harry Melville picked me up to take me to the luncheon.

On the way the men kept raving about "Cissie" Sorel who, they said, had more lovers than any other woman in the world, besides being the idol of the Paris stage. Well sir, I took one look at Sorel and it fairly staggered me. She was a middle-aged woman, very homely, gaudily dressed, but wearing jewels worth a king's ransom. I sat and stared at her. I could have murdered Hanan Swaffer for saying I was ugly. What chances that guy spoiled for me! But I quickly found Sorel a most talented woman and a great artist. Even if both of us were not in the "good-looks" department, we each had something else worth having.

When Cupie invited the boys, Sis, and me to dinner, we drove up to 20 Arlington Place and saw a house which seemed all boarded up. I thought at first there was some mistake, but when the boys rang the bell, the footman ushered us into an enormous hall covered with rich red carpet so thick our feet sank into it. All around were marble statues and paintings, as in a museum. The footman announced, "Miss Sophie Tucker and party," and we were ushered into an enormous drawing room—more paintings, more statues, exquisite laces, brocade hangings, furniture you were afraid to sit in. There must have been thirty people there and almost as many servants handing around cocktails. Our eyes nearly popped out. I couldn't talk intelligently to Lady Michelham as I was trying to take everything in. The Duncan Sisters and our party were the only Americans there. Most of the guests had come only for cocktails. They left, and a small party went into the dining room for dinner. When I saw the solid-gold service on the table, my heart just about stopped. Sis gave me a look and I gave one back to her. We sure were up against it, with all that elaborate table service. I whispered to Sis, in Yiddish, to watch Lady Michelham, and do what she did.

At my right sat Lord Ned Lakam, a handsome young man, a writer, who was crazy about professional people. I had seen him at the Metropole and at the theater too. He had a grand sense of humor and was a fine storyteller. Between listening to him and trying to wangle my way through the ten courses—most of it food I had never tasted, seen, or even heard of before—I got more and more excited. "My God, Lady Michelham, what's this? What's that?" I kept asking.

The table was in an uproar. By the time we got to dessert, Ned was telling me a very funny story. The butler was serving peach ice cream in glass plates, finger bowls, fruit knives and forks, and what not. I hunted around for a teaspoon, but took my cue from Lady Michelham, who picked up what looked to be a small soup spoon and a fork. I followed suit, and was getting along all right with the dessert when I put down my fork and spoon to lean toward Ned to catch the finish of his story. Immediately the butler removed my plate. I'll never know what prompted me to sing out: "Hey, there! Bring back that dessert!"

Right away I knew I'd put my foot in it, and I'd have to think fast. I figured, I'll have to turn this into a laugh to save my ignorant hide. I turned to Cupie. "Now, look, Lady Michelham, when I sat down I told you that never in my life had I seen such elegance as at this table. I asked you a lot of questions as we went along, and I watched every move you made with your knives and forks and spoons. Everything you did, I did, and I didn't make a single mistake. But I haven't finished with my dessert and I want it back."

The table was in an uproar with laughter; Cupie was hysterical. The butler came back with my dessert, his face twitching, trying not to grin. Lady Michelham said: "Sophie dear, you failed to watch how to place your fork and spoon when you have finished eating. You placed them parallel on your plate which over here means you want the plate removed. You should have crossed them." She showed me how it was done, and I told her she was the best teacher I had in London.

The next day I read in the society columns:

You must invite Sophie Tucker to your home. She is great fun. The questions she will ask . . . Her frankness about everything is priceless.

Cupie and I became friends—a friendship which increased with the years until her passing. Every time I went over, her home in London and her home in Paris were open to me.

Cupie fell in love with and married Fred Almy, who had the American Rodeo in London. How upset and unhappy she was because her two sons, Lord Michelham and young Jack Stern, were displeased over her marriage. Cupie came to America several times and we were together frequently during those visits. I lost a grand friend when she passed away. It meant a great deal to me when her son Jack sent me a miniature of his mother, which hangs near my bed. I was proud, too, when I read in the London papers about the auction at 20 Arlington Place, and the reporters mentioned "on the mantelpiece in Lady Michelham's bedroom were only two large photographs, handsomely framed—His late Majesty, King George V, and Sophie Tucker."

One night after the show at the Metropole Lord Napier Allington came to my dressing room to take me to a party at the house of his cousin, Mrs.

Belleville, in Grosvenor Square. He said the Prince of Wales was to be there.

"Look, you're not kidding me?" I said.

"No." He shook his head. "His Royal Highness is there. I was asked to bring you over to entertain for him."

As we were starting, who should we bump into but Bill Gaxton and Madeleine coming to ask me to have supper with them. I told them I couldn't, as I was on my way to meet the Prince of Wales.

"You big liar," they said, and began to razz me for trying to high-hat my old friends.

"Naps" had hurried me away from the café so, as soon as we got to Mrs. Belleville's, I asked to be excused to fix my hair and my make-up. The room the maid took me to was at the top of the house. When I came downstairs, I couldn't find Naps. On every landing of the staircase were people laughing, eating, drinking, having fun. I looked into one or two rooms, but found nobody I knew. Standing in a doorway of a large drawing room on the second floor, I said to myself: "This is probably the room where I will sing." As I stood there a young man came through the room and smiled at me. "Good evening," he said. "I am so glad you're going to sing for us."

"Yes, brother, and I'm raring to go," I said.

With that I suddenly sensed a lot of eyes were focused on both of us, and my teeth started chattering. If this was the prince, I sure had let myself in for something. The way he smiled, I realized it was. Fortunately, Lord Allington and Mrs. Belleville arrived in time to stop me from making another wisecrack.

The prince escorted me to the piano, and then he and all the others, following his lead, took sofa pillows and sat down on the floor around me. That got into the papers too. To quote the press:

Sophie has them sitting on the floor around her, like children listening to fairy tales.

I sang and sang, the prince and all the others laughing, swaying with the music, and enjoying every song. I guess I didn't know when to stop. Teddy and Jack both played solos to give me a breathing space. The crowd that night went wild about the boys and danced to their music. London society sure was going crazy about American jazz. My night was perfect when the prince danced with me. What a fine dancer he was, and how apt when I showed him the fox trot we were doing back home.

The Duke of Manchester—"Kim," as he was called by his friends—loved professional people, and he asked Mel Gideon and Con Conrad to bring me out to his house at Battlemead-on-the-Thames one Sunday. His daughter, Lady Mary, was there too. Con Conrad was one of our ace song writers, who later married Francine Larrimore. He wrote a great song which I sang for him, "The Continental." Mel Gideon was an American song writer and a fine artist. He was in the *Co-optimists* show which was then running in London. He and his wife, Mabel Bunyea, made a big success in England and never went back home.

Another Sunday we went down to Brighton to play a concert on the pier. Brighton is the Atlantic City of England, with a side dish of Coney Island. On the train going down were Leslie Henson and the American performers, the Trix Sisters, Mel Gideon, and Roy Royston, so we had a jolly trip. I'll never forget the thrill I got when we saw our American flag waving on the pier. I hadn't seen it since we left home. Sis and I wanted to stand under it for just a moment. Imagine how we felt when we got out to the end of the pier and found the Stars and Stripes flying on top of a public toilet. We were plenty mad, but there wasn't a soul around to have an argument with. I was still mad all through the concert. When that was over, and I was called on for a speech, I got my inning. I concluded my speech by saying:

"The next time I play Brighton, I hope to see our American flag wave over some important building and not the lavatory!"

Well, I guess the Stars and Stripes are flying from a lot of places of importance in England right now!

The next day was *Jahrzeit* (anniversary) of Pa's death. Sis and I drove down to London's East End to a poor little Orthodox *shule* to have *Kadish* (a prayer) said for our beloved and departed father. The *shule* was as old as Methuselah and filled with the air of sanctity that you feel in any house of worship that people have been praying in for generations.

Another who made us welcome was Ted ("Kid") Lewis, the fighter. I never knew an Englishman go nuts over Americans as he did. He and his wife, Elsie, took the boys and me all through the East End and to a lot of fights and introduced us everywhere. I'll never forget the tea party he and Elsie gave for four hundred boys from the free Jewish school in Petticoat Lane, at which I entertained.

It seemed as if every boat that docked at Southampton brought more and more American show people. All of them ultimately turned up in my dressing room at the Hippodrome Theatre, or for supper at the Metropole.

A few days later who should come along but Olsen and Johnson, the now famous *Hellzapoppin'* boys. I had known them for years in vaudeville. Now they had come over to try their luck in London. By this time practically the whole United States has seen these two crazy guys, so everybody can imagine the laughs and fun we had. Sis, Teddy, Jack, Olsen, Johnson, and I went around to shows, to cafés, to sights. We all went out to see Kid Lewis fight Frank Burns. The place was jam-packed and the crowds so quiet you could hear a pin drop. But the yells that went up after the knock-out were deafening. Afterward Olsen and Johnson put on a burlesque of the fight and I laughed so hard I damn near broke a blood vessel.

But the greatest time of all we had with the *Hellzapoppin'* boys was on Derby Day, when we all went to Epsom Downs along with Mr. and Mrs. Vogt, an English act, to try our luck with the horses. That was the greatest sight I ever saw in my life. Pouring rain, naturally, and the crowd on the road—Rolls-Royces, gypsy carts, taxis, hacks, delivery wagons, lemonade venders, sausage stands—sloshing good-humoredly through the mud. More than a million people were at Epsom Downs that day, from the richest to the poorest. Droves of bookmakers everywhere. Thirty horses in the Derby and everyone betting—from sixpence up. How we yelped when we backed the winner, Captain Cuttle. Boy, was that a day!

A few days later Olsen fell sick. He was up at Teddy's flat and he couldn't be moved out of the place for eight solid weeks. Teddy had to find another flat, and between the five of us we took turns in taking care of poor Olie. The damn flat was up three flights of stairs (no elevator), and I puffed and fumed every time I climbed up to it. One day Sis went up to do the cooking, and her stories of what went on with Chic Johnson thinking up the damnedest things to do for laughs were funnier than any of the stunts the boys pulled in *Hellzapoppin'*. One day when I went over there after work, Johnson was dressed up as a nurse. The next day, he was the charwoman. I'll never forget the day I went over to cook a hamburger dinner for Olie and found the Four Marx Brothers parked around the room, Al Herman, the black-faced comedian, and his wife, Madge, Bob Milo, Yvette Rugel, Teddy, Jack, Sam Joseph (the owner of London's foremost bookstore), who was Binnie Barnes's husband, Chic Johnson, and Sis—thirteen of them, all yelling for hamburgers. Olie, the sick man, was in stitches, me in the kitchen hysterical and making hamburgers for that gang. That was a night! The bobby on the beat came upstairs to find out what the disturbance was all about, and we gave him the time of his life!

Olsen and Johnson had bad luck that trip. They had had only a week or ten days over there before Olsen fell sick. London never did get to see the boys work, and so missed two great nuts. Olie and Chic are two swell fellows who plugged away for years. They struggled for over twenty-five years, and when they came into New York and took Broadway by storm with their show *Hellzapoppin'*, there was nobody in show business more deserving of success than they.

Our closing time was drawing near. A new show was going into the Hippodrome, and the Metropole was putting on a new revue. The papers publicized my last few weeks in London. Walter Wanger was at that time manager of the Rivoli Theatre in Whitechapel, in the East End. He came to ask me if I wouldn't play one week at the Rivoli before sailing for home. This house had a seating and standing capacity of five thousand; admission prices were tops—one shilling (twenty-five cents); other seats, sixpence (twelve cents). They had a 95 per cent Jewish audience. When the date came round I left my hotel in a taxi for the matinee, which started at two-thirty. When we got near the theater, we had to stop. The street was black with people, bobbies holding the crowd back. I asked the driver, "What's the crowd for? What's happened?" He didn't know. A kid jumped up on the running board and the driver asked him what was going on.

The kid said, "The Jewish actress, Sophie Tucker, is expected any minute!"

I was prouder of that than of anything that had happened to me in London.

In a minute the crowd recognized me and a cheer went up. The bobbies made way so we could get to the entrance. A big sign over the front of the house read: WELCOME, SOPHIE TUCKER, *America's foremost Jewish actress*. The theater was hung with flags—every sort of flag *except* the Jewish one.

I got out of the taxi, and I was mobbed. It took half a dozen bobbies to get me inside. The house was packed to capacity. What a reception they gave me! That welcome will always ring in my ears. I sang myself hoarse that week—six nights, six matinees—to about 50,000 people. They came from all over London. That week I played at the Rivoli I went to a lot of Jewish restaurants and met all the Jewish actors of London. They ran me ragged with requests for autographs, photographs—and touches.

During that time I met an old friend of Pa's, Professor Mallinx. He was a conjurer, and he used to do card tricks at our restaurant. It was years since I had laid eyes on him, but I recognized him the minute he was ushered into my dressing room. We sat there and talked about the past for an hour, remembering the nickels and dimes he used to give me to sing for him.

We had a big gala the last night of the *Midnight Follies* at the Metropole. The boys from Eton and Harrow had their party at the club that night, which added to the gaiety. Ethel Levey sang for me. There were flowers, speeches, gifts, and then "Auld Lang Syne," sung by everybody in the room —all on their feet, singing. I remember among the crowd that night Princess Helena Victoria, the Duke of Connaught, Lady Curzon, Mr. and Mrs. Benjamin Guinness, Mr. and Mrs. Robert Guinness, Major Bridges (the hero of the Battle of the Marne in 1914), Jascha Heifetz, Elsa Maxwell, Lord and Lady Allington, Lord and Lady Orsery, Lady Michelham and her party, and ever so many more. When they swung into "For She's a Jolly Good Fellow," I felt the tears come to my eyes. Is it any wonder I say "The British are regulars too"?

CHAPTER 20: *Everybody's Pal*

I CAME HOME BROKE. A swift run across the Channel to take a look at the night life of Brussels, Berlin, and Paris fixed that. But I had trunks full of gorgeous gowns that fairly screamed Rue de la Paix, and I had a complete stage setting of black patent-leather drops. I went for a lung ($1,000) for them. When the colored lights hit the drops, they turned all colors and glowed.

"The U. S. A. has never seen anything like them," I told the Boss, on landing. "Wait till you see me in my black gown and black-and-silver wrap I got from Lucien Lelong, with the spray of real black paradise in my hair. And the boys in their tails against those drops! Get me a date at the Palace, Boss! Give me two weeks to get some new songs, and I'll be in the big money again."

I'd already built up some terrific publicity on landing. The minute I saw the reporters and photographers come aboard, I rushed to my stateroom and got into a Paul Poiret royal blue suit trimmed in gray caracul. What a laugh when I barged in in front of the camera boys, leading the two German police dogs I'd bought in Berlin, and the boys saw I was wearing *pants!* Yes, it was Sophie Tucker, and not Marlene Dietrich, who introduced pants in the U. S. A. They got me into the headlines and the newsreels and were good for laughs any place. Yes, I beat Marlene to pants, but I've got to admit she beat me in them as far as looks go.

The Boss booked me into the Palace. *"Sophie Tucker direct from her European triumphs, with Ted Shapiro and Jack Carroll at the pianos."*

Smart billing now! I had to engage an electrician to work the special colors on my gorgeous patent-leather drops. But what a reception we got when the curtain went up: the two boys at the piano framed against those lovely "made-in-Paris" drops, and my entrance all in black and silver. Everything smacked of Paree. Was I proud! And was my Mollie proud as she stood in the wings!

"Now, honey, strut your stuff!"

One of the triumphs of that engagement at the Palace was the following letter from Mr. Albee—the one and only nice one I ever got from him in all the years I worked on his circuit:

April 5, 1923

My dear Sophie,

Notwithstanding you have regulated yourself and act into a Sunday-school class, now and then an old pal will show up just as you are shaking hands with the Prince of Wales and say, "Well, Soph, how's tings?"

One could not have a greater demonstration of the fine feelings of your present self than to be unstrung at the remark of your friends. To refrain, as you say, from swearing after you arrived at your dressing room, is the personification of your redemption from your hoop-la-high-da-do of years ago to your parlor entertainment of today. Marvelous change and very commendable, very commendable. What wouldst have me do?

Sincerely,
E. F. Albee

It was during this engagement in New York that Sime Silverman started to go to town for me. Sime's *Variety* was and still is the No. 1 vaudeville and theatrical paper. If *Variety* liked you, boosted you, you couldn't miss getting to the top. Your biggest booster was Sime himself if you had the stuff. What he did for Jimmy Durante will go down in the annals of show business. He saw a great talent and he saw to it that the whole world knew about Jimmy. Liberal, lovable Sime Silverman, the best-known figure on Broadway for years, with his curly chestnut hair and the one funny curl always out of order; a cigarette hanging from his lips at all times; his fingers yellow from nicotine; his low, rasping voice. A terrific personality. You never saw him go to a café, or any place, that he didn't have a gang with him. He and his wife, Hattie, and his son, Sid, all writing for *Variety* and making it the most powerful influence in American show business.

It was Sime who gave me the new billing "Madame Sophie Tucker," and Arthur Unger, Sime's writer in Hollywood, later labeled me "La Belle Tucker." Today I'm "Soph" to *Variety*. It was always Sime Silverman's idea to handle everything and everybody with humor. A swell idea for publicity too.

From my opening at the Palace in New York I went on to Boston, Phila-delphia, Baltimore, Washington, Pittsburgh, Cleveland, Detroit, and Chi-cago to show off the new act with my new billing—Madame Sophie Tucker. I was the cats! And I don't mean maybe.

I went out on the Orpheum Circuit to the West Coast. While in Chicago I signed on to do *The Pepper Box Revue* for Ackerman and Harris. They were my first bosses at the old Chutes when I played San Francisco in 1910. Featured with me in the *Revue* were Joe Phillips and George Le Maire—the same George Le Maire of the team Conroy and Le Maire, who gave me lessons in blackface make-up in my coon-shouting days. My contract was for ten weeks, to open in San Francisco after my vaudeville tour.

I finished the tour in Chicago and was much upset because Mollie was taken ill there. She could not walk up the stairs and was in great pain. The doctors looked grave and shook their heads. She was in no condition to travel, so I had to send her home. The parting after our being together so many years and through so many ups and downs broke us both up. I went West with a heavy heart, knowing I must look for a maid. I knew I would never find anyone to take Mollie's place. I struggled along, hiring somebody to help me weekly, and did the best I could until we started rehearsals in San Francisco. Then at the Curran Theatre I was lucky in finding another maid, who has been with me ever since.

After the *Revue* folded I thought I would go down to Los Angeles and loaf for a bit—something I hadn't done for a long time. I took a bungalow in a court on Westminster Boulevard in the midst of the movie colony, and went domestic in a big way. Will I ever forget the hamburger dinner I cooked for Fanny Brice and Aunt Jemima! How they laughed at the barren little bungalow after the elegant and luxurious homes of the movie stars! But I had fun with so many friends of earlier years in vaudeville coming out to Hollywood all the time.

Of course I was bitten by the movie bug! I started out to see if I had any chance in the silent films. The Warner Brothers, Harry and Jack, were the first victims I asked to make a test of me. They sent me out to make an outdoor farm scene. All I remember is the silver-back reflectors used, and that I was dressed in a gingham outfit and told to roll a big barrel up and down a hill. I looked as large as the Rocky Mountains. Worked a whole day on this test—and nothing happened. After I took a look at the rushes, I made up my mind I was wasting time hanging around the edges of Hollywood. I had neither beauty nor glamor to offer the screen. I went down to the Orpheum Theatre to see Harry Singer, then the manager there, and asked for some dates. I played the Orpheum tour back to Chicago, then more vaudeville in the East and so into New York.

Through the next two years I played steadily in vaudeville—back and forth across the country; the Orpheum Circuit and the Pantages and Sullivan-Considine circuits on the West Coast. My old friend, Marcus Loew, had just brought out these rivals of the Orpheum Circuit. I had built up a big following on the West Coast and made several trips, with longer stays than the other acts in the cities there. Sis and Amy Leslie went along with me on one of these trips—Son was already in California, living with Nellie V. Nichols, recuperating from sinus trouble. On the next trip Eva and Sadie Mandel, two of the four big *zoftig* daughters of the Mandel family who had the restaurant on State Street, Chicago, went along for the fun. We had a tremendous bill on that trip—the first real big vaudeville bill presented on the West Coast—Blossom Seeley and Bennie Fields, Frank Fay, Mosconi Brothers, Margaret Young, Jack Pearl, Emma Carus, Karyl Norman (the Creole fashion plate), blackfaced comedian Al Herman and his wife, Madge, William Haines (who made a nice place for himself in the movie world), a pair of fine hoofers, Jack Coogan and Eddie Cox. (Jack was the father of Jackie Coogan who was soon to spring into fame as the "Kid" with Charlie Chaplin.) Montague Love had a fine dramatic sketch, which landed him in the movies. Pola Negri, also on our bill, barely got over with the audience, but the movie scouts picked her for a type and she promptly skyrocketed to fame in the silent pictures. Handsome Clara Kimball Young was another performer on our bills who made the grade in Hollywood. These big bills were shown only in San Francisco and Los Angeles. The silent pictures were forging ahead so rapidly they were putting a dent in the vaudeville business. Theater managers were worried and were trying to fight the advance of the movies by putting on tremendous shows.

Helen Keller, with her teacher, Mrs. Macy, was on our bill too. She was a darling and full of fun. I got a great kick out of making her up for the show, dressing her. She would laugh, place her fingers on my mouth to read my lips, and howl with laughter at some off-color story or word I'd say to her.

There were parties at all San Francisco's wonderful eating places, but some of our best fun went on at Coffee Dan's, across the street from the Orpheum, where the performers would go for ham and eggs and laughs.

During my engagement in San Francisco, President Harding arrived there to stay at the Palace Hotel. During the days he lay ill, the whole city was tense, and his death plunged San Francisco into mourning. I had met President Harding a few months before, when I played Washington at Keith's Theatre. He saw our show and enjoyed the whole bill. We all met him afterward.

While still in San Francisco I had a letter from the warden of San Quentin Prison, asking me if I would entertain the boys there. I wired him that I would bring a few acts the next day, Sunday. I took Al Herman, Margaret Young, and Aveling and Lloyd. Teddy went along to play for us. It was a glorious morning when we took the boat across the Bay. The fields over in Marin County were ablaze with yellow poppies, blue lupin, and purple iris. We were all in high spirits until we came in sight of the high, ugly prison walls. Those walls made us all dry up. No more laughing, clowning for ourselves. We had to make the men behind those ugly walls laugh. Some job to put on the old phony smile when your heart cries for everyone shut up in that grim pile. We had lunch with the warden in his quarters, then we went into the hall to entertain the boys. It was a swell show we put on, and the prison walls rang with laughter, applause, and cheers.

After the show the warden asked me if I would see some of the boys who were sick and unable to go to the hall. The first one we met was Tom Mooney. Meeting him, talking to him, you knew he could never do such a diabolical job as bomb the Preparedness Parade. The warden pointed out one prisoner who had killed eighteen women. He looked the murderous type, sullen and greasy. He was in the house for killers and going to the chair. In the hospital, which was as clean as a whistle, were dozens of men in the wards or coming in and out for treatment. The warden said: "Miss Tucker, meet our trusty, Norman Shelby. Possibly you knew him as Kid McCoy."

For a minute I couldn't get my speech. "Kid McCoy? Of course I knew him! What's he doing here?"

"He killed the woman he was living with," the warden said.

Kid McCoy recognized me. He came toward me with outstretched hands, tears running down his face. "My God! Sophie Tucker! I'm happy to see your smiling face. I couldn't get away to the hall to hear you. I had a sick man I couldn't leave. What I wouldn't give to hear you sing again!"

The warden left us to reminisce, and we had plenty to talk about. Eighteen years ago Kid McCoy's Rathskeller, under the Martinique Hotel, at Thirty-first Street and Broadway, was one of New York's well-known spots. Many a night I went there and Kid McCoy would let me sing for the crowd and leave with twenty to thirty dollars pick-up money—all in silver dollars, halves and quarters—thrown on the floor while I was singing. Then Kid McCoy was in his heyday, a pugilistic success, and I was struggling to find my way in show business. I never knew he was in trouble, or doing a stretch. Life is funny. You're on top one day, down the next.

I was ready to leave. The whole afternoon had been very trying; to keep smiling to all the boys, with a kind word, a joke, a laugh for each one. The warden stopped me. He asked me to come to one of the hospital wards. "There's a man here who knows you very well—a very sick man. He heard the boys talk of the show you brought down. Won't you please come over to see him?"

The man lying in the bed was nearly sixty years old. I knew him well. He was Herman Roth, the lawyer, once prominent in New York. I was suddenly sick at the pit of my stomach. "May I have a chair, Warden, please? Sure, I know Herman. He is a friend of mine. A great friend to the profession. Many times I have asked his help for fellow artists in trouble. And he took care of them all without a fee." I asked Herman what had happened that put him in San Quentin. He told me that Barbara La Marr had had him railroaded and sent there. I could hardly sit there without crying. His pallor, his cough scared me. It broke my heart to see him there, thousands of miles from his home and family in New York, left to die alone in prison.

"Keep your chin up, Herman," I said. "I'll do something for you if I have to spend my last cent."

We got back to San Francisco about six that afternoon. I had just two hours before my train left for Los Angeles. I jumped into a taxi and drove out to my friend Chief Dan O'Brien's house. I told him about Herman. "I don't know anything about the case. All I know is that he was a friend of the actors. Now he is sick; dying alone—miles away from home." I made Dan promise to make every effort to get Herman out of San Quentin and sent home to die. A few weeks later Dan called me to tell me Herman was on his way East. And the letter Herman sent me before he passed away made me feel that the friends I had made in California, such as Dan and Governor James Rolfe, were real friends and always willing to help when called upon.

Now here's something which may be coincidence, though I think not. I'll always believe that my visit to San Quentin that day, and what I was able to do for the boys there—especially poor Herman—brought me a prompt reward. That night I left San Francisco on the Lark at 8 P.M. instead of our earlier train. Our train had just pulled out of Santa Barbara, we weren't fifteen minutes out and away from the station, when the earthquake, which damaged Santa Barbara's railroad station and town, occurred. None of us heard the rumble as the train was going pretty fast, but the conductor came by to tell us what had happened. Gosh, did I say a prayer of thanks!

I enjoyed my stay in Los Angeles that trip. The town was full of people I knew. Friends from old days in vaudeville now making careers in pictures. I got to know a number of the movie celebrities. I went out to the studios to watch them work. Aside from the celebrities, every studio seemed to have any number of beautiful girls who had to be taught to act. I used to look on and listen in amazement. The director with his megaphone, tearing his hair out, bursting blood vessels, shouting: "Go to the door! Open it. Look out. Be surprised. *Surprised,* damn it, *not happy!* Close the door." Hours and hours spent teaching gorgeous-looking creatures how to open and close a door, how to look surprised, horrified, happy. I kept wondering why the studios went through so much hell, but I had to be satisfied with the same answer from every director I asked why they bothered with such and such an actress: "She is a gorgeous creature."

How those gorgeous creatures took gas when the talking pictures came in. We were out at Warner Brothers Studio one day when Belle Bennett was making *Stella Dallas.* I had known Belle when she was in vaudeville years before. I admired and liked her immensely. I was particularly fond of her brother, a handsome boy of seventeen, who was there in Hollywood with her—a swell kid in every way. The boy was taken ill and rushed to a hospital. Belle was on the set, worried and sick at heart, as she told Mrs. Upright, one of her and my intimate friends, and me that day. But true to the code of the profession, she was carrying on. Mrs. Upright and I were watching her, full of admiration for her work, when the message came that she must go to the hospital at once. Mrs. Upright and I took her there. We were met by the doctor and a nurse. They told her she must be brave, that her brother was dying. It was only a matter of a few hours.

"Brother?" she cried. "He's my son! My son! I must tell him before he goes that I am his mother! He never knew me as Mother—only as Sister Belle!"

What passed between that swell kid and Belle that afternoon no one living will ever know. He died in a few hours. Meanwhile, the studio kept calling her to go on with *Stella Dallas.* What a trouper Belle Bennett was! In one week she was back at work. *Stella Dallas* was finished. It was a great picture. Had there been Academy awards at that time, Belle Bennett would have won the Oscar.

What made *Stella Dallas* the best picture of 1925 wasn't the director, or the publicity department, or the Warner Brothers Studio—it was Belle Bennett, the mother for one hour only—something only her intimate friends knew.

I was still playing around Los Angeles, having fun, when a wire came from the Boss to say he had booked me to play the fashionable Kit-Kat Klub in London. I hopped East and sailed to keep the engagement in August 1925. I followed Ted Lewis and the Dolly Sisters after their long and successful engagement there.

I looked forward with delight to returning to London where I had made so many friends and had such success three years before. Sis went with me again, and my good friend, Mrs. Sim Kracko, of Chicago. Ted Shapiro was my pianist, Jack Carroll having left the act when he got married a few months before. I now had a one-piano act, but I had a lot of swell new songs and I was confident I could not only repeat the success I'd had in 1922, but do better.

The Kit-Kat Klub was in the Haymarket next door to a cinema. You entered from the street into a fair-sized lobby, checked your things off at one side, and made a grand entrance down a wide staircase into a huge room done in white and gold, with luscious red hangings. Settees ran around all four sides. No matter where you sat, you saw everybody as they entered. The bandstand faced the staircase, and a spacious balcony ran all around the room. The balcony was a rendezvous for the professional people. It was only on the balcony that Klub members were permitted in street dress; no one could dance on the floor unless he was in dinner clothes. I had them build a platform for me in front of the bandstand so I could see everybody in the place and everybody *could see me easily*.

The Kit-Kat Klub was a membership club, with an entrance fee of a guinea. It was very swank, but I noticed many more Americans in every club, café, restaurant, and theater than there had been in 1922. Stockbrokers, salesmen and their wives—proof of America's postwar prosperity. They were welcomed everywhere as good customers; on the noisy side, but free spenders.

At the Kit-Kat Klub Brooke Johns and his Oklahoma Collegians, featuring Goody Montgomery, a very fine dancer, opened with me. Brooke Johns was a big handsome six-footer, who had a fine band and was very popular in London. Later on he left the band business and became a country gentleman, living outside of Washington, D. C.

Opening night was sensational. The ovation the crowd gave me lasted at least six minutes and warmed my heart. The manager, Colonel Jones, and Mr. Poulson, the maître d'hôtel, had told me earlier in the evening that there were a lot of important people in the room, including Lord Louis and Lady Mountbatten, Viscount Castlerosse, who was on the *Daily Express,* the Marquis of Donegal (the Walter Winchell of the *Sunday Dispatch*), Lord Beaverbrook and party, Lord Napier Allington and party (good old "Naps"), Lady Loughborough, the Duke of Manchester and party, the Honorable Mr. and Mrs. Richard Norton, and Lord and Lady Port Arlington. There were also many of the professionals, Ethel Levey, Alice Delysia, Tallulah Bankhead (then having a great success in *The Green Hat*), Beatrice Lillie, Gertrude Lawrence, Ella Retford, Leslie Henson, Mel Gideon, Maisie Gay, Barry and Gertie Lupino, and my own intimate friends, such as the Cohens, were out in force.

The biggest thrill of the evening was when His Royal Highness, the Prince of Wales, came in. He sneaked in on the balcony, as he wasn't dressed and he came only to hear me sing. I kept trying to spot him up there, but I couldn't. I wondered how he was going to take one of my new songs, "I'm the One the Prince Came Over Here to See," which, of course, was a play on his recent visit to the United States. The prince didn't object to it. In fact, as I learned later, he was the one who laughed the loudest. But the London County Council *did* object. One of its members spoke to the manager and I was asked to eliminate the number from my routine from then on. The story got into the press, which went to town with it. Across England and America and across the whole British Empire went the flash:

SOPHIE TUCKER SPOKE OUT OF TURN IN HER SONG ABOUT THE PRINCE OF WALES.

There was such a stew about the incident, and so much unfavorable publicity, it nearly killed off my contract at the Kit-Kat Klub. Finally, I went to Lord Beaverbrook about it. I said, "Can't you make the folks over here understand I didn't mean any offense to the prince? We can say things like that in my country. I'm an American. I didn't know I couldn't say it over here." Lord Beaverbrook saw my point. He ordered the story killed in his papers, and the fuss blew over.

My engagement at the Kit-Kat Klub was originally for eight weeks. Then the contract was extended for an additional ten weeks. It called for doubling in the music halls. One of these where I played a long run was the Alhambra Theatre. I'll never forget when I came into the Alhambra to do my first performance. There was the orchestra leader seated in a huge, comfortable armchair directing his show. He had no idea of jazz, and Ted and I used to laugh to see how he gradually woke up to the new American rhythm, getting more and more interested each day, until by the end of the first week of my engagement he was doing his directing on his feet. He became one of the greatest jazz enthusiasts in London. It was at the Alhambra that Gracie Fields made her London debut on the bill with me. She has a great talent, a great flair for comedy, and was a very big success.

In 1925 London was sporting a new type of rendezvous—small, intimate places, each with its own crowd. The most celebrated of these, the Forty-three Club, was owned and run by Mrs. Merritt, whose daughters later married into the nobility. The Forty-three Club was like our speak-easy joints. The only difference was that it was decorated with women, more women, and again more women. And the sky was the limit.

The café at the Piccadilly was another popular night spot. I doubled there awhile and then I went over to help in *Charlot's Revue,* in which Jack Buchanan, Beatrice Lillie, and Gertrude Lawrence—three great artists—were appearing. I went to pinch-hit for Maisie Gay, the leading comedienne, who took sick, and I only filled a gap in the *Revue,* coming in just before closing time and singing a few songs. I couldn't have done much more considering that at the time I was averaging over forty songs a day. André Charlot was very much worried as to what he would pay me, so I told him that I was just helping out a fellow artist and he could send me a bunch of flowers. I was repaid by the paragraph that appeared in the *Sunday Referee:*

A ray of sunshine (and some ray) fell across my path, however, when Sophie Tucker came along from the Alhambra to strengthen the show. Sophie would prove a veritable tower of strength to any show. She is a very remarkable artist.

After playing the Alhambra I doubled at the Holburn Empire Theatre; also at the Coliseum. There was one week when I played the following theaters without missing a performance: the Coliseum, matinee and night show, in a legitimate play called *The Monkey Talks.* It was a French comedy of circus life and I appeared as a singing clown in the prologue of the show, doing a straight dramatic bit and singing four songs. From the Coliseum I went on to double at the Piccadilly Hotel cabaret; then to do my bit in *Charlot's Revue;* and from that on to the Kit-Kat Klub. That was the most hectic week I can recall in my entire experience in show business, doing different numbers and wearing different clothes in four shows a night. I was drawing top salary now.

Hanan Swaffer paid me a great tribute when he said in the *Daily Express:*

What Mistinguette is to the little Parisian midinette, so Sophie Tucker embodies the very spirit of American sentimental and syncopated emotion. In England we have Marie Lloyd; in Paris they have Mistinguette; Sophie Tucker is no less a triumph for America.

I've already spoken of Tallulah Bankhead and what a sensation she was in London. I went to see her show and she gave a brilliant performance. It was there that I first learned about the "Gallery First-nighters"—a club of men and women, about one hundred strong—who went to every first-night opening. When they liked you personally, no matter how bad the show was, they made you a riot. I've never seen such a demonstration in any theater in the whole U. S. A. as they gave that night at *The Green Hat*. Leslie Bloom, the president of the First-nighters, was a great friend of the Cohens and I had met him at their home. He gave me a dinner at the club rooms and I welcomed the opportunity of making friends with a very powerful crowd. At that dinner I put my foot in it. Between two of the courses I asked Ted for a cigarette. He lit it for me, and at that moment Leslie Bloom sprang to his feet and proposed a toast to the King. I didn't know till later that the rule was no one smokes until *after* the toast to the King, which marks the conclusion of the meal.

I was getting to know a lot of professionals. In the theater, British show people are very conservative and stand-offish at first. They never speak to you unless you speak to them first, but after you get to know them they are friendly and great fun to work with. And what a memory they have for old favorites. I'll never forget going to see George Robey in *Sky High* a couple of nights after we landed and before my opening at the Kit-Kat Klub. He welcomed me from over the footlights and the whole audience greeted me.

But another experience I had later on during that stay in London was still more remarkable. Fred Lonsdale was putting on *The Last of Mrs. Cheyney,* starring Sir Gerald du Maurier and Gladys Cooper. Ina Claire came over to see the show to take it back to America, where she made a great hit in it. I was invited to the opening, and I told Mr. Lonsdale I would be a little late, but I had asked at the theater to be put on earlier in the bill so I could get to the première. A première in London is a sight worth seeing. By the time I drove up to the St. James's Theatre it was eight forty-five, and I was sure the show would be on. I rushed in and sneaked up quietly into Lady du Maurier's box, where she, her two daughters—one of them Daphne, who wrote the 1940 best seller and sensational picture, *Rebecca*—and Ina

Claire were seated. No curtain up as yet, but the house was applauding. I looked down from the box to see what was happening. I spotted a few friends in the audience and waved to them. The house was applauding madly now, so I applauded too. There was a roar of laughter. I kept on applauding, and turned to Lady du Maurier.

"What's holding up the show?"

"You are, my dear," she replied. "The audience has recognized you. Until you bow to them and acknowledge your reception, the curtain won't go up."

Well, I damn near fell out of the box. Then I turned quickly, bowed, threw kisses, waved right and left, and yelled: "Go on! Start the show!" Fancy a performer in the United States walking into a theater to see a show and holding up the curtain! But that's London—when they like you.

The Kit-Kat management had a place called the Café de Paris at Bray-on-the-Thames, which was very popular on Sundays. I was compensated for my extra day's work there. The management would send a car for me to the hotel at 11 A.M. After a twenty-eight-mile ride through the beautiful English countryside I would get to Bray for lunch on the lawn which sloped down to the river. The tables were set under colored umbrellas; all the guests would be in sport clothes. After lunch, parties would split up and go out on the river in punts and canoes. (Not me. I stuck to the motorboat.) Cocktails, from six to seven-thirty; dinner at eight. Dinner was served inside and outside on the terrace. After dinner, about 10 P.M., I would entertain. There was a small orchestra of two or three pieces and everything was very informal. It was like a house party. And I would sing for an hour or more. After a time or two the place was so crowded I said: "Come on. Everybody get a cushion and sit down on the floor. Get comfortable." Sitting on the floor became the thing after that. I didn't intend to start a custom; it was something that just happened. It was here, at the Café de Paris, that I introduced the "blackboard" and taught the British folk a great many of our popular songs. I had the chorus of each song painted on a canvas and would have it set up like a blackboard in a schoolroom, and make everybody join in the choruses with me.

And everybody means *everybody*. Every Sunday the Café de Paris was crowded with nobility, theatrical people, swells. I got a great kick one night when my fiancé, Al Lackey, was there having dinner with me. While we were dining, His Royal Highness, the Duke of Kent, came over and spoke to him, thinking he was Lou Holtz. Mr. and Mrs. Jesse Lasky were our guests that Sunday night.

Yes, I had a new love affair by this time. I'd met Al when I was working at Reisenweber's. He used to come there with four or five Philadelphia boys. They all worked out of a brokerage office in Wall Street. They were all great fans of mine, the boys. Never any women at their table. I would pass their table, say, "Hello, how are you?" but I didn't know one of them by name. One night Lou Clayton, of the Clayton, Jackson, and Durante trio, was at the table with them. That night I did something I very rarely did at the café. That was to dance. I stepped out with an out-of-town friend of mine and as we passed the boys Clayton started to rib me about dancing with one of them. I kidded him back. For some reason—I'll never know why—I picked out one of the boys and said, "I'll have the next dance with you." That was how I met Al Lackey. He was a swell dancer, and I love to dance. Night after night he and the boys would be at Reisenweber's and I'd get a dance. After my show they would go on to other late spots, or upstairs to our Paradise Room, and I would be invited to go along. Sometimes Al took me out alone, and we had a lot of fun. I was eight years older than he but in spite of the difference in age it was love right from the first. And so the big romance of my life got started.

The first time I went to London Al cabled me he was coming over. He came and stayed several months. When I was playing around the United States, we were together whenever it was possible. Al was a great help to me. He had a number of irons in the fire, but no steady job. We kept hoping things would work out so he would be in a position for us to marry. I'd had one experience of being married to a man who made less money than I made, and I knew what that situation did to romance. I wasn't going to repeat it, no matter how much I was in love. When I went to England in 1925, Al came over again, so we could be together.

Brooke Johns left for America and Isham Jones came into the Kit-Kat Klub with his orchestra. This meant rehearsals again on top of all the other work I was doing. I kept changing songs every week at the Klub and at the theaters where I played constantly. I had three outstanding song hits that season. In the theater it was my "Yiddisha Mama," which Jack Yellen wrote for me. I sang it in English and in Yiddish, and the song was tremendously popular, not only with the Jewish public but generally. The phonograph records of it have had an enormous sale. From that season, whenever I have gone to England, my "Yiddisha Mama" is one of the songs the audience always demands. It is identified with me every bit as much as "Some of These Days." In the Klub my most popular numbers were "Nobody Loves a Fat Girl" and "Me and Myself." The popularity of these two songs was due to that thing I discovered early in my career in show business—that an audience enjoys hearing you make fun of yourself. At our Sunday nights at Bray and on other nights at the Klub the crowd would shout for me to sing "Me and Myself."

ME AND MYSELF*

WORDS BY RAYMOND B. EGAN. MUSIC BY RICHARD A. WHITING

I read of married folks who don't get along.
I know of all their little troubles.
I hear of people finding romance all wrong,
And agree to disagree.
They have a barrel of care,
But I'm in no hurry to share

Chorus

Cause,
I get along with me and myself.
Me gets along so well with myself.
No one to lie to, say hello or good-by to;
So I'm happy, sez I to myself.

Getting in late and getting in wrong,
Trying to make your alibis strong,
Makes you grow older
With a chip on your shoulder;
I live and love it, but there's not enough of it,
Just to spend it and end it with somebody
No one, but me and myself.

Recitation

I want to take this opportunity to tell you folks that
Me and myself are real pals.
I wake up every morning, fresh as a lark,
No one around swearing about a collar button; take my little exercise, skip over
    to the mirror and say:
Greetings, Sophie. And the mirror smiles back and the day is started right.
Then at breakfast, when there's only one piece of toast left,
I don't have to grab for it. Myself sez to me:
Soph, old girl, finish the toast. You must be hungry.
And I say to myself: I don't mind if I do. No arguments at all.

Then when I find that I need a lot of new clothes
I don't have to run over to any fat old tyrant in Oxford bags
And call him Darling when I'd like to kill him.
Myself sez to me, Soph, old thing, you need a lot of new clothes.
And I say to myself, you're right, old thing!
And I go out and buy just what I want.
No questions asked.
Then when the first of the month rolls round,
The first of the month when the bills clutter up the vestibule,
The first of the month when every wife is humble,
What do I do? I open them up boldly. I show them to myself.
Myself sez to me: Soph, old top, send them over to your gentleman friend.
He'll take care of them!

Chorus
That's why I get along with me and myself.
Nothing goes wrong with me and myself.
I live and love it, but there's not enough of it,
That's why I'll hurry and worry about nobody
No one but me and myself.

Just picture getting an audience of British swells warmed up to sing that song with you. They changed some of the punch lines—"fresh as a lark" to "fresh as a daisy," "collar button" to "collar stud." Funny, those Britishers couldn't say "at all" quick and brisk like I do. I'd make them say it over after me. They would try, but they got all tied up, and then the fun would start. When we came to "no questions asked"—well, you can guess how they said *"ahhsked."* I'd stop them.

"Is that how I say it?"

"No!" they would yell.

"All right! Now, how do I say it?"

And then all together: "Aaasked!"

As fast as I introduced new songs, I gave them away to British performers; so many were giving impersonations of me, and I had great fun teaching them the numbers. I was very proud when Alice Delysia asked for some of my songs. Ella Retford was the first British star to give an impersonation of me, and I made her do it one night at the Kit-Kat alongside of me.

It was at the Kit-Kat that I introduced Binnie Barnes to her own people. Ted had been palling around London with Sam Joseph. Binnie was Sam's girl, whom he later married. Binnie was then playing around the smaller clubs in London. Ted thought she had something, and started grooming and rehearsing her. After he had her set he asked me to give her a chance at the Kit-Kat. I did, and she was a big hit right from the start. From that she went on to her success in America in the movies.

My coffee parties were getting very popular in London. The first time I was over there I found I just couldn't drink what the Britishers call coffee. So when I went back in 1925 I filled one compartment in my trunk with Maxwell House coffee (I should get a nice check for this plug). Anyway, I toted pounds of Maxwell House coffee and dozens of tins of Carnation condensed milk to London. I took along my own percolator, had the connection changed for British current, and after that I had my coffee the way I liked it. All the Americans I knew in London knew this, and a lot of my British friends too. Often I would serve ten to fifteen people in my sitting room. Whenever we ate in the hotel dining room, the page boy would bring the percolator of coffee from my room to the table. That would be a signal for every American in the room to bring over his cup and ask for a drink. I guess I was living up to the billing they gave me in London that season: EVERYBODY'S PAL.

Naturally, there were a lot of benefits going on and I played them whenever I was asked. They were swell publicity for me, of course. At that time I didn't know the value of the AP service, and I didn't have a personal publicity man. I did my own job. I saw to it that every newspaperman and -woman I knew in the U. S. A. and Eddie Darling got clippings every week from all the British papers that wrote me up. My paper bill was over two pounds (ten dollars a week), including the stamps for postage, but I figured it was important to keep the press at home in the know. The prestige I was rolling up in London should be good box office for me when I played vaudeville houses in the United States again.

I had opened at the Kit-Kat on August 31, and I went right on there and played the music halls until New Year's Eve. In addition to the shows and the café work and the benefits, there were any number of parties at private houses at which I was asked to entertain. These were at the fashionable houses in London. The smartest of all the parties was also the smallest. There were only eight guests. This was the party that Lady Loughborough gave for the Prince of Wales at her house in Talbot Square. During the evening I was sent for to sing for the prince. His equerry, Captain Alastair MacIntosh, came and escorted me to Lady Loughborough's. Alli later married Constance Talmadge and has been a figure around New York for some years. That night I took Sis and Fred Almy along with me to the party.

Fred had just brought the American Rodeo over to London, and Lady Michelham was busy falling in love with him. That special intimate little party at Lady Loughborough's was as informal and full of fun as a party of college kids over here. I sang all the songs the prince called for. He loved playing the ukulele. He got me to teach him my song, "Ukulele Lady." That same night I taught him the Charleston, then all the rage in the United States. Ted Shapiro was very, very popular now at all the house parties. The Prince of Wales had Ted with him many times alone, to play for him.

It was just before Christmas that we got word from home that Ma wasn't well, and it would be best for Sis to go back. For many years Ma had suffered from diabetes. She was told if she watched her diet carefully she would live to a ripe old age. She did this religiously. For years she had kept up marvelously and gotten every bit of enjoyment out of my success and out of what she was now able to do for her pet charities.

Sis caught the first boat for home, and I pitched into a few weeks of extra heavy work, what with all the Christmas festivities and private parties and benefits.

The first cables I got from Sis, after she got home, were reassuring. I snatched a few days' holiday right after New Year's and ran over to Paris to get some clothes and have some fun with Jennie and Rosie Dolly, who lived there. But I was back at work again in London inside of ten days. I had been signed up by Mr. Julian Wylie to star in one of his revues. I planned to do this directly I finished my contract at the café, so as to be ready to rehearse and open early in February. Then came the cable that was handed to me at the Alhambra Theatre during the matinee on a Wednesday. I knew before I opened it the message would be either "Come home at once," or "Mama is gone." My fingers turned to thumbs and my heart stood still. There were just four words. "Make first boat home."

There was no boat until Saturday. I called Harry Foster and the managers of the theater and the Kit-Kat and told them: "I'm closing Friday night, sailing Saturday morning," and gave them my reason. They objected, told me I couldn't break my contracts—that I'd have to fulfill them. My answer was: "The hell with you and your contracts! My mother comes first. I'm doing what we do in my country. You can always get success, money, but you can't get another mother. I'll make up my contracts on my next trip over. But I'm leaving on Saturday, and that's final."

God alone knows how I managed to do my shows at the theater and at the Klub through Wednesday night, Thursday, and Friday. But the show went on. I'm trouper enough not to fall down on that tradition. The Kit-

Kat advertised my farewell night on Friday. I never went through a performance with such a heavy heart. What nearly bowled me over was the crowd that packed the place to say good-by to me. There were royalty, nobility, theatrical managers, producers, the leaders in the theatrical profession, and hundreds of friends that I had made during my two London seasons. All so friendly, all so kind, all so eager to let me see that they were feeling for me, and no matter what it was I was going home to I could count on their affection and support. There were tears in my eyes when we came to "Auld Lang Syne" and "She's a Jolly Good Fellow."

But I couldn't leave them like that. That's not show business. No tears at work. I gulped down the lump in my throat and started to call on all the performers in the room—Cissie Loftus, Alice Delysia, George Grossmith, Hilda Glyder, Ethel Levey, Ella Retford, Heather Thatcher, Lew Hern, Eddie Chester, Fay Marbe. I introduced Fay to the British public that night, which was the night before her opening at the Café de Paris.

What a gala night! What I did at the Metropole in 1922 I did on a bigger scale. Now I dared take liberties with my British friends. I was standing on my platform in the middle of a bower of flowers and three enormous double magnums of champagne (I gave one to Ted, who clasped it to his chest all the rest of the evening) when I looked over toward the staircase. A party was just coming in, very late. I thought: I know that little fellow. He's an American. Then I saw his face, and I nearly whooped.

It was Irving Berlin, whose marriage to Ellin Mackay had filled all the papers in America and in London. After the marriage they had ducked the press and came over to England. That was all anyone knew. They had given the reporters the slip and kept in hiding until that night.

"Hello, Irving," I sang out. And then, "Ladies and gentlemen, introducing America's foremost song writer and my old friend, Irving Berlin!"

Poor Irving looked as if he didn't know what the hell hit him when there was a terrific welcome of applause. Then up he came, sat down at the piano, and, like old times, Irving played and I sang his old numbers.

And that was how I left London.

CHAPTER 21: *My Yiddisha Mama*

SOUTHAMPTON in the pouring rain. Bitter cold. Everybody hurrying to get out of the raw January fog and aboard the big luxurious *Leviathan*. It seemed to me I couldn't wait for her to pull away from the dock and nose out through the Solent toward home. It was a beastly crossing all the way.

It seemed as though the sky and the sea were taking their color and mood from my feelings. I spent my time in bed, hugging my prayer book and making trips to the wireless room to receive and send messages.

As always aboard ship, a concert was arranged, and all the performers aboard—there were quite a lot of us, including Rudy Valentino—were expected to take part. I knew I'd have to entertain though I never felt less like it in my life. There was some relief in the fact that, due to the terrible weather and so many of the passengers being seasick, the ship's concert was postponed twice. Finally, the date was set for the night before landing in New York.

By that time I was about all in from anxiety and the delay which the bad weather had caused and the radio messages I had had from home. I knew there was no hope of Mama getting better, and I was desperately afraid I wouldn't get home in time to see her before she passed away from us all. I thought about that time in Chicago when I'd had the wire telling me about poor Pa. I hadn't been in time then either. It seemed as if I couldn't bear it if I were too late this time.

I wasn't going to the concert. I was alone in my stateroom, which I shared with Mrs. George Claire. She was Tommy Dawes's sister and the mother of those two beautiful British artists, Johnnie and Wynne. There was a knock on my door.

"Come in," I said, and my heart gave a thump, thinking it might be a steward with another radiogram.

In came Rudy Valentino. He wanted to know if I was coming up to the concert.

"I can't sing tonight, Rudy dear. My heart is too heavy. I couldn't sing, even if I wanted to. You'll have to tell the passengers to excuse me, and explain to them why."

Rudy shook his head. "I know it's tough," he said, "but if you could make it, it would be a grand gesture. And it would mean a lot to every-body—such a miserable crossing, with people sick and panicky."

"I can't," I said.

He went away disappointed. Poor Rudy, so real, so unaffected. Success hadn't gone to his head. How many times we recalled the days when he felt he was lucky to earn fifty dollars a week as a ballroom dancer at Reisen-weber's.

I tried to read, but I couldn't concentrate. The ship was pitching badly. Everything rattled. The toilet articles fell off the dressing table. I began to feel worse and worse. Frightened. I suppose the other passengers were feeling that way too. I thought, "You're not doing anybody any good, or your-self either, brooding down here all alone. If you can do anything to cheer up the rest of the crowd, that's the best thing you can do for yourself and for Ma. That was what Rudy and Kitty Claire were trying to tell you."

I dressed quickly and ran up to the lounge. Not easy to do when the ship was throwing me from one side of the staircase to the other so the stewards had to keep me in balance. Up in the lounge I faced a sea of anxious faces, everybody holding onto their seats for grim death, chairs sliding all over the place. A lot of people had given up trying to keep in chairs and were sitting on the floor. Every time the boat rolled, you'd hear gasps and now and then a scream. Rudy was acting as master of ceremonies. He spotted me the minute I got to the door.

"Hooray for Sophie!" he hollered. "I knew she would come up and sing for us!"

Rudy and Teddy came down to the door and guided me to the piano. Just as I got there the boat listed again. I tried to hold myself up against the piano. Then the piano started sliding. It took Rudy and Ted and six stewards to keep it and me from smashing through the wall of the lounge. It was Rudy Valentino who suggested lifting the piano off the platform and setting it on the floor, with six stewards sitting around it, bracing it in place. Nobody could think of a way of bracing me up too. People were laughing now. It was funny, because while I was singing I was sliding around all over the place. I boomed out:

"The damn truck horse can't even stand up!" So I sat down on the floor and gave a show that way.

I shouted out whatever funny things I could think of to say. After all, what was important was to keep those hundreds of people from getting panicky. I sang all the songs I could remember—all that were funny and sure to get laughs. Rudy Valentino was sitting on the floor beside me.

"Please go up to the wireless room," I begged him, "and see if there is any message for me. It's been several hours since I've had any word from home."

He went. And I went on singing more songs, watching the door all the time for Rudy to come back. He'd been gone so long. What was keeping him? I'd been singing for over an hour.

"Listen, everybody, this is my last song. No more."

I looked toward the door. There was Rudy coming down the lounge. One look, and I knew. His face was a dead giveaway.

"Rudy!" I yelled. "My mother! She's gone!"

224 SOME OF THESE DAYS

That's all I remember of the concert. I didn't have to read the message, which Teddy gave me later, "Ma passed away."

All that night and all the next day the storm kept up. There would be no landing for us within twenty-four hours. The boats behind us had been warned to turn back to avoid the path of the storm. A British freighter, the *Antinoe,* was sending out an SOS. What hope had she against the mountainous waves which the mammoth *Leviathan* couldn't plow through? All I could think was, "We're more than a day late now. It will be impossible for us to make up any of the time. I won't be able to see my angel before they put her away." Orthodox families do not embalm the dead; they are buried the next day. That seemed the bitterest drop of all.

Brother Moe was at quarantine to meet me, and we caught the first train to Hartford. Teddy went with us and Kitty Claire.

I'll never forget, when we got to the street, seeing the sidewalk and road in front of the house black with people—all crying. They were Mama's poor. "She's gone. We've lost our best friend. Who'll give us food and coal now?" they wailed.

I ran up the stairs to Ma's little "nest" as she used to call her home. The stillness was terrible.

"Mama!" I cried, "I'm home. I've come back to see you!"

Sis and Phil came to the head of the stairs.

"Yes, Sophie dear, Ma is still here. She's waiting for you. She made us promise not to put her away until you came home."

My darling yiddisha mama knew what it would mean to me if I couldn't see her again, and, knowing that, she was willing to set aside her Orthodox beliefs. There was nothing that she could have done that would have showed me how much she loved me and how well she understood my love for her.

Several years before she died, when she was with me in New York, she said one day that she wanted to have her will drawn. I told her it wasn't necessary. She had only to tell me what she wanted done and I would promise her to take care of everything. "All right," she said; "the next time I come to New York we will do it." She never brought it up again, and I decided she had forgotten about it. After she was gone, we found her will. She had gone to a next-door neighbor and asked the neighbor's daughter to write down her instructions, what she wanted done with her possessions: her jewelry to Annie; her fine bedclothing to be divided between Annie and Phil. She was careful to explain in the will that if Moe had been married she would have left him some of the bedclothing. Her wearing apparel and mink coat to her friend, Mrs. Ettie Greenberg. "And to my daughter,

Sophie, who gave me everything, nothing because she don't need anything."

It was more than three months before I felt fit to work again. I went down to Atlantic City with Sis. When I began to feel that I could sing again, I sent word to Ted and to the music publishers to send their men and their latest songs down for me to hear them. I knew I'd have to get back to work, and I knew the only way for me to do this was to have some new songs and work up some new ideas. Down came Lew Brown and Ray Henderson, of the writing team of DeSylva, Brown, and Henderson. Bud DeSylva later left the combination and produced those two terrific Broadway hits, *DuBarry Was a Lady* and *Louisiana Purchase*. Lew Brown's *Yokel Boy* was a hit in 1939. I remember they brought me some swell songs, and I picked their hit number for 1926, "I'd Climb the Highest Mountain."

After consultation with the Boss, we decided that I should appear at a few benefits, to get my bearings, before he booked me for vaudeville dates, and he thought, after all I had been through, and considering the long time I had been out of the country, it was a good idea. The first was a benefit at the Manhattan Opera House for the Jewish Theatrical Guild, in which I hold a life membership. It was my first appearance in New York after the big success I'd had in London, which the papers over here had made much of, and after Mama's death. The audience showed their feeling for me by giving me a deafening welcome. What was terrible was that I stood there paralyzed. It seemed as though my feet just wouldn't move. The footlights, the faces, the applause scared me worse than I had ever been scared in my whole life. I felt my throat close up. I don't know how I got to the piano. When I did, I hung onto the side of it as though for dear life.

Somehow I managed to sing, but it was a mechanical Sophie Tucker. I might have been wound up like a doll. I couldn't smile. I couldn't be funny. I couldn't feel myself. I could only thank the audience and beg forgiveness, hoping I would soon find myself so that I could entertain as I used to do. Teddy led me off the stage. I couldn't have found the entrance myself. I was one mass of jitters. I got back to the hotel, and for weeks I couldn't leave my bed. Now I'd lost my self-confidence. I'd had stage fright before, but never anything like this.

"Darling, you mustn't give way like this," the Boss kept telling me. "You must pull yourself together."

And then, finally, his plea was: "Please do this for me."

I could see how grieved and worried he was, and that hurt me more than anything. I'd always been so proud of his faith in me. I couldn't let him down now. "All right, Boss, I won't let you down. I'll keep trying!"

For several weeks I made myself play all the benefits the Boss asked me to play—one for the survivors of the S.S. *Antinoe,* the freighter which had sent out the SOS in the storm; one for Eddie Cantor's Lake Surprise Camp; the Newspaperwomen's Ball; the New York Rotary Club; the Actor's Equity Show.

A message came from S. J. Kaufman of the Green Room Club that they were giving a get-together to welcome to America Jack Buchanan, Beatrice Lillie, and Gertrude Lawrence, who were with *Charlot's Revue,* then playing in New York, and Jack Hulbert and Cicely Courtneidge, who were playing in their own revue, and would I come to the party? I said I would get there in time for the show and to sing a few songs that they had heard me do at the Kit-Kat Klub in London, but I couldn't join the party, as I hadn't been well enough to go out socially. S. J. Kaufman introduced me to the gang and I walked on the little stage to a heart-warming ovation. There in the front row were those familiar faces I used to see in London, calling "Hello, darling!" "Good old Soph!" It ought to have bucked me up, but it did just the opposite. I went to pieces again. I couldn't put any life into the lines of the song. I was simply terrible, and I couldn't do anything about it.

Next morning I called the Boss and told him what had happened. I had a feeling I was done for as a performer. I'd tried, honestly, to make a come-back, and I hadn't been able to control my nerves. The Boss came over to the hotel that evening, and we had a long talk. He said he felt the only way for me to get my self-confidence back would be for me to work in a café. He believed working in close contact with the audience would cure me.

"All right," I said, "I'll try it, Boss. I'll do my damnedest!"

At that time the big cafés at which headliners used to appear weren't flourishing. The Prohibition Era was in full swing. The small speak-easies were popular. After looking the field over, the Boss decided he would open a café for me himself. He got in touch with John Steinberg and Christo, my Reisenweber captains, and a deal was made. A place was found on West Fifty-second Street, between Broadway and Seventh Avenue. It would seat four hundred, and there the Sophie Tucker Playground was opened in March 1926. Our opening night was a riot. According to one reporter:

After five years' absence from Reisenweber's, Sophie Tucker's debut at her Playground Wednesday evening was the scene for the heaviest first night in Main Street cabaret history. The frenzied shouts and cheers came from the throats of the town's most front-paged. Over five hundred celebs sat down in the same place, at the same time, peacefully—a Broadway record.

Mayor James J. Walker did the honors on opening night. Among the many celebrities, some of whom entertained, were Wilda Bennett, Carl Hyson, Belle Baker, Lew Brice (Fanny Brice's brother), Ann Pennington, Jack Rose, Joe Frisco, Willie Howard, Charles Purcell, Fowler and Tamara, Al Herman, Bea Lillie, Jack Buchanan, Gertrude Lawrence, the Duncan Sisters, Harry Richman, Yvette Rugel, Ben Bernie, and many more. Texas Guinan came over from her place, the Three Hundred Club. Freeman Gosden and Charles Correll, a piano and singing act, newcomers from Chicago, appeared at the Playground and later became the sensation of the air waves as "Amos and Andy."

One thing everybody seemed to enjoy was being in a roomy café after months of speak-easy two-by-four joints. It was a relief not to be crowded into a garage or a stable.

Well, the Boss had been right about it. Working in a café turned the trick for me. I began to get back my old assurance. I felt it flow back into me like new blood in my veins on that opening night. Maybe it was having my own place to work in, feeling the responsibility for the success of the venture into which the Boss had put his money. On that opening night, after the fun started, I kept remembering days in our restaurant back home in Hartford when I had entertained for the customers and felt it was up to me to bring in business.

Sophie Tucker's Playground was a hit right from the start. Fanny Brice called me up to say her maid told her that Sophie Tucker had given up the stage and had opened a playground for children!

Before many weeks I was my old self again—hitting on high. We were doing a big business. Eddie Elkin and his band gave out the popular music, with Morton Downey as soloist. They were big favorites, as well as Allan White's Collegians. Yes, we had loads of laughs and fun at the Playground. I'll never forget the night Jackie Osterman insisted on getting up on the floor. Jack Rose tried to stop him.

"Let him alone," yelled Frisco. "Maybe he'll flop."

And the night after Al Jolson had his tonsils removed and I announced from the floor that Al was doing fine, Jack Rose yelled, "I offered him a million dollars for the one with the mammy song in it!"

Yes, everybody came to the Playground. A lot of British friends who came to New York, came there to see me—Lady Loughborough, my old friend Cupie, Lady Michelham, Lord and Lady O'Shaughnessy among them. At the same time we had a new audience—the bootleggers! Most of these were foreign-looking, the men flashily dressed. Liquor was always plentiful at their tables. But they were well behaved, and they showed respect for me in that they would always check their guns. On most nights you could count as many as fifteen guns in the coat pockets of our customers in the Playground's checkroom.

At the Playground one night I got the shock of my life. Eddie Cantor and George Jessel came up for an evening of fun. I had helped Eddie at his benefit, so he came to do a turn for me. We had a big crowd that night, and Eddie and Georgie were in great form. They were the masters of ceremonies and I was busy going from table to table, meeting the customers. I caught Eddie saying: "And now, ladies and gentlemen, we are going to introduce a young fellow—a dancer. This is his first appearance in public. His mother is a very well-known performer and he has asked us not to mention her name, as he wants to make good on his own. After he dances, if you like him, I'll tell you who he is."

Just then I was called to the office. I was busy there for several minutes. When I came out I stood at the rear of the room. Out on the floor, dancing a mile a minute, was a kid. "Gee," I said to John Steinberg, "he looks a lot like my son Bert!"

I moved up closer to the floor. "My God, it is my son!" I yelled. "Eddie! Georgie! Bert! What are you doing here?"

The house was in an uproar by now. "It's Sophie's son!" "Isn't he a fine-looking boy?" "A good dancer too." Then tremendous applause.

I was stunned. I had no idea Son danced, or knew anything about show business. He had been in military school since he was six years old. He was now about fifteen. I never permitted him to hang around the theater or club where I was working. And his visits backstage were very few and far between. I had always been against his going into show business. I told him so many times, when, as a youngster, he said he wanted to be an actor. "No," I would tell him, and explain that as long as his grandmother was alive that was out of the question. I had given Ma my solemn promise. Never, as long as she lived, would anybody else in our family go into show business. My being in it was enough for her.

Oh sure, I was pleased that Bert had put it over, and I couldn't help admitting he danced well. But, when we got home, I laid the law down to him. "No show business for you until you finish your education!" However, I softened up and promised to send him to a dancing school to learn some routines. I also promised that at the proper time I would groom him and set him sailing on the ocean of show business if his heart was still on it when that *time came*.

For years the N.V.A. (National Vaudeville Artists) had maintained a club for vaudevillians in West Forty-sixth Street, New York City. The association charged only small dues, but money to support the club was brought in by all-star vaudeville shows, balls, benefits, and ads in the various programs that all successful artists were compelled to take. Mr. E. F. Albee headed the association. The club did nice work, but that work didn't reach out far enough. My Boss, William Morris, was the real instigator of a very wonderful charity for vaudeville performers. He had spent years at Saranac Lake, recovering his health. Through his efforts and the generosity of his wife and her sister Ella, a lodge at Saranac was opened and maintained, to which performers could go for a health cure at very little cost. The gratitude of the profession to William Morris for this benefit gave the N.V.A. directors the idea to open a sanitarium at Saranac which would be available for all their members. Immediately a drive was started to raise funds for this project, and at every vaudeville theater in the country money was collected. Special shows and attractions were put on to draw contributions from the patrons.

At the Palace Theatre, New York, the N.V.A. made the best showing and the biggest collection. In addition to the regular Palace bill, headliners and acts playing in the other theaters throughout greater New York would come to the Palace for one performance—gratis—to help the drive. Never in the history of American show business has there been anything like N.V.A. Week at the Palace!

Eddie Darling rang me up at the Playground and asked if I would give my services for one performance during N.V.A. Week, which was Easter week. He told me I could come at any time and at my convenience. I said I would gladly do so, but, inasmuch as my work at the Playground kept me every night until 4 or 5 A.M., I would have to go on at a matinee. I arranged with Eddie for a Tuesday afternoon. It was agreed that as soon as I got up I would rush to the Palace, and he promised to put me on the minute I got there, so I could do my turn and get back home and rest for my night's work.

It was just 3:45 P.M. when I showed up at the Palace on Tuesday. Eddie Darling came backstage as soon as he was notified I was there. Elmer Rogers, the manager of the Palace, told me Eddie had given instructions that I was to be put on as soon as I arrived. He said the act before intermission was on and I would follow this act. This was all right with me, of course.

Working at the Playground every evening and night, I never got a chance to see any of the shows in town. I wasn't on to who or what was playing at the Palace that week. It wasn't until I got to the theater that I learned that

Nora Bayes was the headliner. Right away I thought, that's swell! Between the two of us at this matinee we are sure to make things hum and there will be a big collection.

I had no idea Nora's act closed intermission. Usually top headliners were placed second from last, or one before closing.

I was seated near the entrance of Nora's dressing room, waiting for the act to finish that I was to follow, when I saw Eddie Darling dash madly across the stage—as if he was going to a fire. Nora's maid and Elmer Rogers were right on his heels. Eddie didn't stop for me. He rushed straight into Nora's room, leaving the door open. Nora's voice came out to me, clear and sharp:

"I tell you she does not go on ahead of me! If she does, I will leave the theater!"

I heard the arguing back and forth, Eddie protesting, telling her I was there just to help the N.V.A. drive, that I was giving my services for just that one performance. Nora kept on protesting:

"I tell you I will leave if she goes on ahead of me!"

I pushed into the crowded dressing room.

"Nora dear, please don't get upset. Eddie asked me to help the N.V.A. drive. That's why I'm here. I just woke up, and I came right over to sing a few songs. You know I wouldn't deliberately hurt you or your act. If you feel that my going on ahead of you does that, I will go on right after intermission. Another half-hour of waiting won't kill me."

It could have been fixed that way, of course, but for something I didn't know until Eddie told me long afterward. Mr. Albee had had it in for Nora for some time. He wanted to discipline her, bring her to heel the way he handled so many performers. Eddie Darling, who knew Albee like a book, hadn't wanted him to get wind of the trouble Nora was making backstage. But some busybody carried the news to Mr. Albee in his office upstairs. Down came the command: Miss Tucker was to go on as arranged. Nora Bayes could take it—or leave it. Nora left it—and the theater. With all our pleadings—Eddie Darling, Elmer Rogers, and I—Nora flounced out. Robert Emmett Keane, who was acting as master of ceremonies during N.V.A. Week, had to go out in front and tell the audience that Nora Bayes left the theater because of me.

I hadn't played the Palace for almost a year, and the audience gave me a grand reception. Still, I felt sick at heart over the whole business. How grand it would have been if Nora had stayed on. She could have brought me out, introduced me. The repartee from the two of us would have been a riot. But no. I left the theater immediately I finished, went home and back to bed to be ready for work at the Playground that night.

I was having dinner when Eddie Darling called me. Would I go on that night at the Palace and for the balance of the week—as headliner? He said Mr. Albee would not accept Nora's flouncing out of the theater, especially at a time when money was being raised for her fellow artists.

"Mr. Albee will not permit her to go on tonight," Eddie said. "She walked out of her own volition. He refuses to accept her excuse and says she cannot come back and play the Palace again."

I couldn't let Eddie down, and besides it was a big feather in my cap to be asked to headline the Palace bill in that important week. For the balance of the week I doubled there with the Playground. Once again, as a result of an unhappy experience, came financial success for me. Up to this time I had always had trouble with the Keith office when it came to salary. I was always fighting for what I thought I should get and not getting it. Nora Bayes got top money in vaudeville. When the Keith office asked me to take her place, I felt I could demand the big salary they paid her. I did, and I got it. I played the Palace two weeks, with great shows.

One of the acts on the bill was Jack Benny, billed as a monologuist and doing a violin solo. He took his violin work very seriously. I remember how frightened he used to be before going on the stage; and look where he is now and what he is doing in show business—thanks to radio!

There was something very touching about Nora Bayes. After that big scene at the Palace you'd have thought the next time she met me she would have been ready to claw my eyes out, but not a bit of it. She was as sweet as though there never had been any trouble. She never mentioned it, and I saw her many times before she died.

I was talking all this over with Eddie Darling, preparatory to writing the story of that episode at the Palace. It was Eddie who told me about Mr. Albee wanting to discipline Nora and doing so to the extent of giving orders she was not to go on at the Palace again. Eddie told me something else about Nora, which I have his permission to tell here and now.

It was some years after that N.V.A. Week that Nora rang up Eddie and asked him to come to see her. She hadn't been very cordial to him when they met, but now she was like her old self. He found her looking ill and tired. She said she had not been well and was going out of town the next day to rest up. She said to Eddie:

"There is one thing I want to ask you to do for me, Eddie."

He thought she wanted a booking at the Palace, and he started to explain that Mr. Albee had given strict orders . . .

But Nora went on. It wasn't a booking at the Palace she asked for. She wanted Eddie to promise her that he would get out the big photographs of her that used to be put up in the lobby when she was the headliner. She wanted him to promise her that he would put them up in the lobby early the next morning: "Just as if I was playing the Palace." He could take them down before the matinee, but she said she wanted to know, when she drove past the Palace the next morning, on her way out of town, that her pictures were there.

Eddie promised. He had some misgivings the next day for fear that Mr. Albee would come in, see the pictures and raise hell. But the pictures were there in the lobby, and for all anyone knows Nora Bayes drove by while they were there—or perhaps got out of the taxi and walked into the lobby and saw them.

Just a day or two later Nora Bayes was dead, following an operation.

It was soon after that N.V.A. Week at the Palace that one night Jack Rose came up to my apartment to dinner. While he was there, he was taken sick. I had a lot of trouble getting him to agree to go for an X ray, but finally I got him to the Polyclinic Hospital. He was told he would have to be operated on. A finer, funnier fellow than Jack never lived. Everyone in show business loved him. He made big money, but he spent it all—most of it he gave away. I had known his folks in London, and their home was always open to me when I was there. I felt I wanted to do everything I could for Jack. I told Al Woods, who was fond of Jack, what his condition was, and that there was no money on hand to pay for the operation. Al Woods said he would call up Dr. John Erdman and have him do the operation.

"Don't worry," he told me; "I'll take care of it."

Next I went to see J. J. and Lee Shubert, who were also very fond of Jack. They told me they would give me the Winter Garden for a benefit the next Sunday night, all the proceeds of the show to go to Jack Rose.

Next I rushed over to Al Jolson and got him interested. Between the Shuberts, Al Woods, Al Jolson, and me, the following show was booked for the Winter Garden that Sunday night. Reading over the list of performers, I would say that there never was such an array of stars giving their services to help a fellow performer who was in need.

Clayton, Jackson, and Durante	Al Jolson
Moran and Mack	Harry Richman
The Three Ritz Brothers	Joe Frisco
Sid Silvers	Jack Osterman
Phillips Family	Dennis King
Sylvia Froos	Harry Delf
Van and Schenck	Julius Tannen
Ben Bernie and Orchestra	George Raft
Rita Owen	Jack Repper
Bob Nelson and Harry Link	Belle Baker
Phil Baker	Vincent Lopez and Band
Willie and Eugene Howard	Jimmy Savo
J. C. Flippen	Jack Pearl and Harry O'Neal
Brennan and Rogers	Sallie Fields
Borah Minnevitch	Georgie Jessel
Sophie Tucker	Janet Winters

Before the night of the show I had seen Jack taken up to the operating room at the hospital and brought down again. Dr. Erdman had sent for me to come to his office, and told me the truth about Jack—"Give him everything his heart desires. Yes, it's cancer. Make him as comfortable and as happy as you can for the little time that he has left."

I didn't tell anyone what Dr. Erdman had told me, but I sent immediately for Jack's mother and sister to come over, only praying they would be in time to see him before the end.

The night of the big show I was in the hospital with Jack. Al Jolson had sent over a radio and wired it up so that Jack could hear the show. I sat with him until half past ten, when it was time for me to go over to the Winter Garden. "What do you want me to sing, Jack?" I asked him. "And what do you want me to tell the audience and all your friends who will be there?"

"Tell them all I thank them from the bottom of my heart—and you who have been like a mother to me. Please sing 'My Yiddisha Mama' for them. Before you sing it, here's a letter I wrote my mother. Read it to the audience and then mail it to her."

When I got over to the Winter Garden, it was about ten fifty-five and the show was going great guns. The house was rocking with laughter. I thought: I won't go back just yet. They all know I've been at the hospital. I'll only put a damper on the show if I walk in now. I'll time myself. At about eleven-fifteen they will have had plenty show and I will go on.

I walked over to the corner drugstore and had a cup of coffee. I sat there

at the counter killing time. Then back to the theater, and backstage. I heard
Al Jolson say, "Sophie should be here any minute." He spotted me standing
in the entrance. "Here she is! Sophie has just come from the hospital. We
have collected nearly twelve thousand dollars."

A hush went over that enormous house as I walked out on the stage.

"Yes, dear friends, I've come straight from the bedside of the most beloved
boy in show business, to bring you his message. Here it is: 'Tell them all I
thank them from the bottom of my heart.' He gave me this letter that he has
written to his mother in London. He asked me to read it to you and then
to sing one song for you—his request. Before I read the letter I want you
all to know that I have sent for his mother and sister and I expect them here
Tuesday morning. Here is Jack's letter:

"DEAREST MOTHER AND DAD,

They are giving me a benefit tonight because I am a very sick boy, a very
foolish boy because I didn't take care of myself. If I get well, dearest folks, I
promise I will come home and make up for everything. My beloved friend and
your friend, Sophie Tucker, has been like a mother to me, a real Yiddisha
Mama, and while she is singing this song tonight at this benefit for me, my
thoughts, my love are with you. God bless you both.

Your loving son,
JACK"

Yes, I sang "My Yiddisha Mama" at 11:30 P.M. at the Winter Garden
after a terrific show of laughs. Jack had asked for it and he got it. And maybe
he was a great showman as well as a homesick boy, because there is no doubt
that that song bowled the audience over. It was the climax of the show.
People said there wasn't a dry eye in the house. I went home and to bed, not
to leave it till Tuesday, when I went to the boat to meet his folks.

Four weeks later Jack passed away. Gone was a great performer and a
wonderful friend.

CHAPTER 22: *A Good Show Is Hard to Find*

SUMMER SET IN. As New York loosened its collar and pushed its hat back,
several big cafés opened up for business in the West Fifties. Trade at the
Playground started to slide. The Boss and I decided to close up; better get
out with a small loss than risk our shirts. All the time we ran the Playground, no liquor was sold on the premises. After all, the real object of
Sophie Tucker's Playground Café was to get me back into shape for work.
Now that I was raring to go, the Playground had fulfilled its purpose.

The Boss booked vaudeville dates for me again. Things looked pretty good. Then I heard that Rufus Le Maire was going to produce a three-star-name revue to open in Chicago that summer. I thought this would be a fine thing for me to get into if I could get to Le Maire and try to make a deal with him.

Rufus Le Maire had been the Shuberts' head man for casting and producing their successful revues for several years. Now he had decided to step out for himself and put on his own show, *Le Maire's Affairs*. He was a brother of George Le Maire. I had known him a long time. Rufus came with a deal, but first he took me over to the theater to watch rehearsals. He had already signed Ted Lewis and his band and Lester Allen, the very funny little comedian. The rest of the cast was swell and there was a gorgeous-looking chorus. Rufus showed me the costume designs. Everything looked good. I told him I would talk it over with the Boss.

I gave the Boss my impressions of the show. "Okay," he said, "if it looks that good to you, I see no reason why a deal can't be made." He sent for Rufus.

Al Lackey was made manager of the show in return for my getting my friend Mr. Al Lefcourt to loan me money to take the show to Detroit.

We opened in Detroit to a smash hit, then went into the Woods Theatre in Chicago. That was in mid-July, and we stayed there until the first week in December, doing a gross business of over three hundred and fifty thousand dollars. I introduced two great songs, "When the Red, Red Robin Comes Bob, Bob, Bobbin' Along," which was an immediate hit, and "The Turkish Towel." The minstrel scene, with Ted Lewis and band, and entire company, was a sensation. It wasn't only that the show was a success with the public, the company got along so well together. Lots of laughs on and off the stage for five months, and not one argument or cross word in the entire company.

When we knew we were a success, and sure to have a long run in Chicago, the parties started. Ted Lewis and Adah were the first with theirs, at the Hotel Sherman. Next, Lester Allen gave a costume party at the Congress. I kept my costume a secret from everybody, even from Al. I had rented a pirate's outfit, with a big hat, boots, dark wig, and mustache. It took me hours to get ready, particularly getting used to the boots, which didn't fit and hurt my feet. I wouldn't allow anyone to escort me to the party, which was at its height when I got to the Congress Hotel. I strolled in, went up to the bar, ordered a whisky straight, drank it down, ordered a second, and passed out of the picture. When I came to I saw John Price Jones, dressed in bath towels, doing a burlesque of my "Turkish Towel" number in the show.

Georgie Jessel was there as Rip Van Winkle, with a long white beard he kept tripping over. Ted Lewis was dressed as a Japanese girl. He had such a fine make-up that he went into the ladies' room and nobody screamed. We all left the party to go to the Frolics Café to see Joe E. Lewis, who had just started in business. By this time my feet were so sore, with blisters on both heels, that I pulled off my boots. When I was called on to entertain, I went out on the floor of the Frolics Café in my stocking feet.

Then it was my turn to give a party in the grand ballroom at the Sherman. Everybody came in rompers. There were about two hundred guests, as I had many friends in Chicago, and all the professionals playing in town were invited. Mayor Thompson was the guest of honor. The hit of the evening was made by Frank Behring, manager of the Hotel Sherman, who rode in on an enormous white horse. Shrieks went up from the crowd and a cry of, "I hope he doesn't . . . !" And the horse did, promptly!

Queen Marie of Roumania came to Chicago during our run there. We all hoped she would come to see the show, and an invitation was sent to Her Majesty. But she sent a gracious letter of apology, and we had to be content that night with Al Capone and a party of twenty. I have never seen so many bodyguards filling the boxes and all over the theater.

Rufus had given my son, Bert, a job in the show. Son carried one of the signs in the minstrel parade, up and down the aisle and onto the stage. Everybody backstage used to kid Bert. They tried out all the old show-business jokes, even to sending him out to the different theaters to find the key to the curtain, until Bert got wise to them.

At this time Paul Ash had set up a new kind of show business at the Oriental Theatre, giving amateurs and everybody a chance to go on the stage. One day Son came to me and told me he was all set to go with Paul Ash—"If I make good, Ma, I hope to be on my own." He had ten days in which to get ready for his opening, and I went to work to groom him. I had seen him rehearse a nice soft-shoe dance, and he also did the Charleston very well. Still, those two dances wouldn't make an act. I got hold of a writer and had him write an opening song to lead into the soft-shoe dance. After this, Son said he would like to give an impersonation of me singing the "Turkish Towel" number, which I was singing in *Le Maire's Affairs*. He sang it for me, and I must say he gave the best impersonation of me I ever saw anyone do. We worked over his act, and I ordered a smart Eton suit for him, in which he looked very well.

When the Thursday came on which he was to appear I called up Amy Leslie to go with me to the Oriental to catch Son's act. There was no publicity about it. Son had told Paul Ash not to introduce him as my son, as he wanted to make good on his own. Amy and I got to the theater while the picture was on, so it was possible for me to find a seat and not be recognized. I was wearing dark glasses anyway. When the show started, I began to get the jitters. Every time Paul Ash introduced a kid, my heart jumped up into my throat. He had a bunch of clever youngsters, Ginger Rogers, Milton Watson, Sy Landry, Johnny Perkins. After two or three, it was Son's turn. When he came on, I slid down in my seat, more scared than I have ever been in any theater. "Hold my hand, Amy," I whispered. He must not make his entrance as a fresh kid and "know it all!" But he didn't. He came on smiling, quiet, like a little gentleman. Over to Paul Ash, shook his hand, and thanked him, then faced the audience and started his introductory number and soft-shoe dance. That got over nicely. He accepted the applause just the way I would have had him do.

"And now, ladies and gentlemen, I will give you my impression of that popular song, the 'Turkish Towel' number, as sung by my mother, Miss Sophie Tucker."

There was a buzz of excitement through the house. People began turning around, trying to find me, but I was so low in my seat I was practically invisible. Son had to wait for the audience to quiet down, then he gave his impersonation. The house ate it up. By this time I noticed that his hands were trembling and his legs were getting shaky. He still had his big Charleston number to do. But he pulled himself together. Before I could say "Jack Robinson" he was into his dance, his legs flying. Now he's through. He runs off the stage—a terrific hit.

Paul Ash called him back and complimented him. Poor Bert, his legs were shaking so hard he could hardly walk. As for me, I had about broken Amy's arm. Then I heard him yell, "Ma! Where are you, Ma?" I flew out of my seat and ran down the aisle toward the stage.

"I'm coming, Son, I'm coming!" I had him in my arms. The audience was cheering. I could feel Bert trembling all over.

"Did I do all right, Ma?" he whispered.

I told him: "I'm proud of you today." And I told the audience: "For the fourteen years that I have been coming to Chicago you've accepted me in everything I've had the pleasure of bringing for your approval. Not once have you ever let me down. Today Sophie Tucker, the mother, gave you her son, and you accepted him, for which I am deeply grateful. May you all live to enjoy the pleasure and thrill of your children as I have today with my son."

Son left *Le Maire's Affairs* to go on his own, and with this warning from me: "You are primarily a dancer. That means continuous rehearsing—always getting new routines. If you do songs, new ones must go in the act. There are four and five shows daily in the theaters you are booked to play. You will need rest. You can't do any running around. Take care of your health, first, last, and all the time. If you pay attention to what I say now, you'll make a success of show business. If you don't, I give you less than two years and you are finished."

I would give that same advice, and I have given it, to any youngster today who is starting out on his own.

After a long run in Chicago, Rufus decided to take the show on the road and into New York. First stop, Cleveland, where we cleaned up forty thousand dollars. Cincinnati, thirty thousand dollars. Christmas week was split between Columbus and Dayton; result, thirty thousand dollars. We played Pittsburgh New Year's week and cleaned up forty-two thousand dollars.

In Washington, Rufus decided to make a change in the cast for the New York opening, three weeks off. He said the change was advised by the New York ticket brokers, who had come to Washington to see the show and make a buy for the New York opening.

When Rufus got that far, I butted in. "Your show has been going over eight months, playing to phenomenal business. Don't, don't! tamper with the success. Every city has loved it. Think of our long run in Chicago! Take your advice from the box office and don't pay any attention to the brokers."

Ted Lewis and Adah, Lester Allen, Bill Halligan—all begged him not to make any changes.

During this discussion none of us had any idea that the only change advised by the brokers, and decided upon by Rufus and his brother George, was to replace *me!* Then it came out. I was told that the brokers said I wasn't B. O. in New York. The way Rufus put it, "As a singer, you're all right, but as an actress, you stink." He then announced that he was going to get a great comedienne, Charlotte Greenwood, for the opening, and Peggy Fears for the singing lead. I gave him my two weeks' notice and left the show after our first week in Boston. We made forty thousand dollars that first week. Then Charlotte Greenwood came in. The show was pulled all around, sketches changed, new costumes—an output of about twenty-five thousand dollars. They played the second week with Charlotte Greenwood, and the receipts took a terrific drop. Lester Allen passed the news on to me. They played a week in Newark and then went into New York, where *Le Maire's Affairs* got only fair reviews. In six weeks the show folded!

Well—that's show business. I shrugged my shoulders and went back to vaudeville. Then the Shuberts sent for me to go into the Winter Garden with their revue, *Gay Paree,* and to take it on the road. Apparently the Shuberts didn't agree with Le Maire and the New York brokers. Shuberts' *Gay Paree* featured Chic Sale and Ben Bernie and his orchestra. Oscar Levant, of "Information, Please!" then played the piano in Bernie's band. And George Raft did his dance specialty, the Charleston, in the act.

I was so thrilled to have a chance to play on Broadway that I splurged on new clothes. Two handsome outfits! One of black sequins, with a high back collar, called for large drop earrings, which I didn't own. I hurried to a novelty jewelry store, bought a pair of imitation-diamond earrings for five dollars, and mixed them up with my good stuff. On opening night, at the party after the show, the comment I heard over and over again was not praise of my four hundred dollar gown or my work or Irving Berlin's new song hit, "Blue Skies," that I introduced that night. It was "Sophie, your earrings are the most gorgeous things I've ever seen on a stage!"

Well, maybe Rufus Le Maire and the brokers weren't so far wrong. *Gay Paree* lasted two weeks at the Winter Garden then went on the road. We played Chicago for three months to good business, then the Shuberts decided to send the show on a tour of one-night stands and I was replaced by Rita Gould. I figured I would treat myself to a much-needed vacation, but no sooner did I get to New York than the Boss called and said Eddie Darling wanted me for the Palace, with the Riverside, Royal, Alhambra, and Brooklyn houses to follow.

I held out. "I'll go if my salary is boosted again." The Boss said he would make a try. "It's July, remember—hot weather . . ."

Then Eddie Darling called me himself, with the usual bickering back and forth. I said I'd planned a vacation. I'd rather wait till fall and play the Palace later, but Eddie was stuck. He hadn't been able to get his show set. I was needed, and so I got the salary I asked for.

Anyone would think I would have had enough of revues by this time to stick to vaudeville. But when Earl Carroll made me an offer to go into his *Vanities* that September, I fell for it like a ton of bricks. I signed up to start rehearsals at once; break in at Staten Island for one week and then open at the Music Box in New York. The Boss made a nice deal with Carroll as to money, but there was some doubt about the billing because Carroll had signed Joe Cook to star in the show. I went up to see Carroll, whom I had known when he was a song writer. Now, as a producer, he had changed a lot—tall, thin, pale-faced, long, thin hands working a mile a minute. He said there was nothing he could do about the billing unless Joe Cook and I decided between ourselves. In other words, Carroll passed the buck. Al Lackey, who had gone along with me—he was acting as my manager—asked Joe if he was game enough to gamble, toss a coin. Heads, Joe would get first billing; tails, I got it. I had my usual luck at gambling and lost.

Carroll had promised me several great comedy sketches, but rehearsals were awful. Not one funny sketch! And the days were flying. Joe Cook didn't depend on Carroll. He always had his own great acts, and with his prize stooge, Dave Chasen, who today has one of the finest restaurants in Hollywood. I had a few great songs, a lovely wardrobe, and some promised comedy scenes. When Carroll finally threw me in a few homemade scenes, they were godawful! I decided, as all of us in show business did, that Carroll was strictly a producer for the gal end of it. He picked the show girls and chorus girls, gave his individual attention to their numbers and their costumes. That's all he was interested in, putting over *the most beautiful girls in the world*. But as to laughs, sketches, talent, Carroll would never spend money for this sort of material.

There is no getting around the fact, Earl Carroll could pick girls. Suzanne Bennett, who was in the show, and is now Lady Hubert Wilkins, was the dancing partner of the Prince of Wales at a private party given for him at the Lido by Josh Cosden. Flo MacFadden, the present Mrs. Jack Haley, was a dancer in our show. Another of the girls, Beth Vane, married Walter Douglas, the WMCA executive. Of the others, there were Kitty Ray, Dolores Costello and her sister, and Joan Crawford, then called Lucille LeSueur. Joan was spotted there and called to Hollywood.

We broke the show in over on Staten Island. Joe Cook was very funny, only his sketches were too long, and there were too many of them. With all the girl numbers, I was crowded down to a spot for a few songs. The show was fair. To cap it all, Carroll insisted that I lead a number with the girls on a spiral staircase. Thirty beautiful girls in the number, and he stuck me on top of the staircase to make the picture complete. Never having won a beauty prize, you should have seen me leading this chorus of beauty! By the time I got to the top of the staircase, I was so out of breath that I couldn't sing a note. And by the time I got down, I was dizzy, watching myself so I didn't fall. I called up the Boss. "Nothing will happen, as far as I'm concerned, in this damn show. Carroll is set with a real nude show and going the limit. The coppers will throw me in jail as a Madame, so get me out!"

Ten days after we opened in New York I left Earl Carroll's *Vanities* with a sigh of relief. Back into vaudeville for Sophie Tucker. And glad to get there! I played the Pantages Circuit at five thousand dollars a week. On that trip I introduced Jack Yellen's song, "Mama Goes Where Papa Goes," using a prop gun. I sang the song in English and then did a Jewish parody of it. Later on I taught Cissie Loftus to do an impersonation of me singing this song when we were both playing at the Palace in New York. I stood beside her during the number, and the act was a riot. Cissie did the impersonation at the Coliseum in London and I went on with her there.

Early in 1928, while I was playing engagements in the West, came a wire from the Boss, saying he had booked me back to the Kit-Kat Klub during the London season, which, of course, is the late spring and early summer. I made preparations to go. Sister Annie was living alone in Hartford, where she had a job at the Connecticut Furrier Company. I wrote her and asked if she would like to go along with me to England again. Back came a letter. Jules Aronson had asked her to marry him, and what did I think of it? I thought well of it. I'd always liked Jules, and I was sure he could give Sis the happiness she was entitled to and needed right now. It was over a year and a half since we had lost Ma, and with the boys away—Moe was in business over in Brooklyn—that left Annie alone. I remembered my promise to Ma, made years ago when I was just starting out in show business. I had promised that Annie, who was then raising my son for me, should have the grandest wedding any girl ever had. Now I would make good on that promise.

Annie set the date for March 31. As soon as I got back to New York, Brother Phil and I started with the preparations. Annie came down to shop for her trousseau, and day and night we were on the go. I engaged Chalif's Rooms on West Fifty-seventh Street for a real kosher wedding and supper, such as Ma would have had. Cantor Rosenblatt was singing in New York and I rushed over to arrange for him to officiate at the ceremony with Rabbi Aaron. Two hundred invitations were sent out to all the relatives in Boston and Detroit, the close friends of the family, Ma's old friends in Hartford, the *mishpocha* in Brooklyn and New York, and a lot of my personal and professional friends. Railroad tickets were sent off to those who couldn't afford to come so far. Hotel quarters were engaged to put up the family, relatives, and friends. Nearly every stage dress I had was sent to those who needed a fine dress for the occasion. During the ceremony Sime and Hattie Silverman came up to me. "My God, Sophie," said Hattie, "I see the Palace Theatre represented in all your gowns!"

The excitement grew every hour as the wedding time approached. I was over at Chalif's all day, overseeing the decoration of the little *shule* where the canopy stood, decorated with palms and flowers. Then checking on the supper arrangements, the seating at the tables, the food, wine. . . . Then back to the Park Central Hotel to get dressed in a lovely tan lace outfit. By that time I was trembling as if I were the bride myself.

Sister Annie in her white lace wedding gown looked beautiful. How I wished Ma and Pa were there with us to see her. She was escorted to Chalif's by Phil and his wife, Leah, Moe, and me. Phil wouldn't buy a dinner suit. He said he didn't believe in spending money for clothes he never wears, so he rented one for the evening. The bridegroom was escorted by his parents. We all met in the lobby at Chalif's.

Eddie Elkins and his orchestra struck up the Wedding March, and the bridal procession went into the *shule* for the ceremony. I was the matron of honor. I was taking the place that Ma, if she were alive, would have had. As I stood under the canopy near Annie, tears blinded me. I sent up a prayer of thanks to God for making this evening possible.

After the ceremony the fun started with supper and was kept rolling by Mr. William Morris, Sime Silverman, Herman J. Weisman (he was my school chum in Hartford, a prominent criminal attorney in Waterbury, Connecticut, and close friend of our family), and Jack Yellen. Annie's boss, Sam Cantrowitch, was there, and after a few drinks he insisted on making a speech about how sorry he was to lose "Hene," as he called her. "Ladies and gentlemen," he began. No sooner had he started than Al Lackey and Harry Lenetska gave him a hot foot. "God damn it!" He put out the hot foot and started again. Another hot foot. After three or four of these attempts, he exclaimed: "To hell with Hene!" and sat down. The wedding party kept up until daylight and continued until sailing time.

CHAPTER 23: *The Last of the Red-hot Mamas*

THE WEEK BEFORE SAILING for London I played the Palace in New York again. I was billed as "SOPHIE TUCKER, THE LAST OF THE RED-HOT MAMAS!" This was the first time I carried this billing, which was to become so closely associated with me that it has persisted through all the years since that season when I introduced Jack Yellen's song hit, "I'm the Last of the Red-hot Mamas." I took the song and the billing to England with me after the Palace had approved them.

It was grand coming back to London to find that I was still remembered.

Grand having all kinds of people, starting with the customs inspectors at the docks at Southampton, say, "Hello, Soph!" "How are you, Soph, old top?" or "Good old Soph!"—all of these lines from my song hit "Me and Myself" that I had sung in the cafés and British theaters when I was over there the last time. Even the bobbies in London knew me and grinned a welcome, besides the autograph seekers and fans who knew I was arriving and packed the railroad station to welcome me.

I had sailed a week ahead of time so I could have a little fun and also take a look at the shows in London before opening at the Kit-Kat. A new variety theater, the Palladium, had opened up and was very much in vogue. Two great scouts, George Black and Val Parnell, were at the head of it and were responsible for putting on wonderful shows. I dropped in to see Gracie Fields and a new comic who had sprung up, Max Miller. I found lots of new night clubs doing business in London besides the Kit-Kat: Quaglino's, Ciro's, the Embassy, the Mayfair, the Berkeley, Café de Paris, Grosvenor House, Dorchester House, and the Café Anglaise, where Morton Downey was then singing. I found American performers playing in nearly all the swank cafés. London was terrifically gay and jazz mad. They'd certainly caught on to the new American rhythms since my first visit six years before.

The Kit-Kat was no longer run as a membership club. It was a restaurant now, under the direction of Sir Walter Gibbons and managed by Robin Humphreys and Monsieur Poulson. There was a ten-dollar cover charge for my opening night, April 30. Just as I was getting ready for the opening, two American visitors dropped in to see me—Mr. and Mrs. John Balaban, of the Balaban Katz theaters in Chicago. I invited them to come along to the opening. They demurred at first, since they had no dinner clothes with them. They had just flown in from Paris and their trunks were coming by express. My Niece, Sadie, who had gone over with Al, Ted, and me that trip, and friends, who knew the Balabans, and I scurried around and fitted them out to go to the Kit-Kat. I got a table for them close to the little platform I used. I went into my dressing room and stayed there until I was ready to go on, making a real Tucker entrance—in great form, great voice, gorgeous outfit, new jewelry. Yes siree! I was damn proud of myself that night! And pretty damn careful. Every song had been gone over with Harry Foster and the managers of the Kit-Kat. I didn't want any more trouble with the censors or the London County Council.

If I got a kick out of being recognized and welcomed by the customs inspectors, the railroad guards, and the London police, it was nothing compared to the thrill of the greeting I got that night from London's upper crust

when I walked down the staircase to the strains of "Some of These Days."
"Welcome, Soph, old girl!" "Hello, Soph!" I wasn't nervous or frightened.
My heart sang. I called back: "Hello, everybody!" "Glad to·be back!" "Glad
to see you all!"—shaking hands here and there as I waded through the tables
up to my platform. I could see the Balabans eating it all up. Well, that
wouldn't do me any harm when I went back to play their theaters in
America.

The write-ups in the press were all I could ask for. To quote the *Bystander:*

Soph, this one calls herself, as she pours a bucketful of Tuckerisms over our
delighted heads. She is not young, nor slinky; she will admit to the deficiency
of both with a disarming frankness. But she tells us, and the whole gamut of
stark satire is uncovered in the saying that she has a kiss like a hungry mosquito.
Whatever she says, the assembled world roars with delight at the sound of her
voice. And well it may, for if ever there was a woman who earned her weekly
salary, it is the incomparable Soph. . . .

A few days after the opening I had a visit from André Charlot to ask
whether I would be interested in helping the Sunday Play Society and do a
bit in one of Maurice Baring's Greek plays. Roland Leigh, now director for
Warner Brothers, was directing it.

"What the hell can I do with a Greek play?" I demanded. "Why pick on
me?"

"Come on, Soph, it will be great fun if you do."

I finally said I would, and found myself up to my neck rehearsing daily
the part of Xantippe in the play *Socrates*. I was the old boy's scolding wife
and played opposite Mr. Edmund Brean. God knows why they picked on
me for the part. My outfit was a Grecian robe of flowing white crepe with a
wide gold kid belt, a leopard skin over my shoulder, and flat gold sandals.
For thirty years I had worn high heels, and those sandals were a torture to my
dogs. By the time Sunday arrived, I was limping and cursing myself for
ever getting into such a business.

Well, the play was on. The house packed. My cue came, and I went on
to a terrific reception. I hadn't gone three feet when the sandals made me
stumble. Under my breath (I thought!) I exclaimed: "Those goddamn
sandals!" The house caught it and broke into a whoop. My Grecian draperies got in my way and tangled up my knees. I couldn't, for the life of me,
think of my opening lines. All I could remember was that I was to scold
Socrates for getting home late. It made me think of my experience years ago
in burlesque. There was Socrates in his dirty outfit. So I boomed out:

"Socrates, you're twenty minutes late. *And you need a lot of new clothes.*" The last was one of the punch lines from my song "Me and Myself."

Well, that just broke up the Greek play. From then on it was an ad-lib show—full of laughs—and I guess everybody, including the press, was relieved.

My contract with the Kit-Kat was for eight weeks, but it was extended to run sixteen weeks. Meanwhile, I doubled at the Alhambra, the Palladium, and a number of other variety theaters in and around London. And all the time I was entertaining at benefits for every sort of thing from Queen Charlotte's Hospital birthday party at which Her Royal Highness Princess Louise, the King's aunt, cut an enormous birthday cake with one hundred and eighty-four candles to mark her grandmother, Queen Charlotte's, birthday, to the annual ball of the Oxford University Debating Society. Lady Keeble was hostess of the ball and sent a car to the Kit-Kat for me. I finished work at the club at twelve-thirty and drove to Oxford, arriving there at 3 A.M. I kept thinking: this is one place I never expected Sophie Tucker to get into. But I found the ballroom packed with boys and girls waiting for me, and we kept the fun going till the sun came up.

One of the benefits at which I was asked to help was for the Sir Douglas Haig Memorial, which was sponsored by the Duke and Duchess of York, now King and Queen of England. They came to the Alhambra Theatre to see me work. There was great excitement in the house when they were seen to enter the royal box, and delight when they laughed and applauded the show from start to finish. One night the duke and duchess came to the Kit-Kat with a party. I was using my blackboard there, with the choruses of the songs painted on it. I would call on all the men in the room to stand up and sing the chorus with me; then the men and women together. An old stunt, but always good. The night the duke and duchess were there, when I called on the men to stand up and sing, the men in the royal party were timid at first about rising. The duchess said: "Sophie said to stand up. Do what Sophie says." The whole room cheered their good fellowship.

England was getting back on her feet after a long period of hard times. The Exposition at Wembley was drawing big crowds. It seemed as if everybody wanted to have fun. The Kit-Kat and the Café de Paris, down at Bray, where I worked every Sunday, were running high.. Show people from America and from France kept passing through. One of these was Maurice Chevalier. I was sick in bed at the Savoy, with a very bad head cold, and a trained nurse was giving me inhalations of benzoin when Al Lackey came in, bringing Chevalier to meet me. It would be hard to imagine a less romantic setting—me under the steam tent and Chevalier firing questions at me about American audiences. He had just signed to make his first trip to America and he wanted pointers from an old hand like me.

Several years later Chevalier gave an interview to the *Daily Herald,* which I clipped and pasted in my scrapbook, marked with a big red star. Chevalier said:

Playing London at the moment is an actress to whose performance I personally owe a great deal. Just after the war I used to pay hurried visits to London fairly frequently. I would write Tom Hearns, my present manager, what were the best shows to see. He always met me at Victoria Station with a carefully compiled list of good shows. But whenever possible I scrapped the list and went to see Sophie Tucker. "Why," asked Tom on the first occasion, "do you choose Sophie? What has she to teach you?"

"Everything," I replied. There were scores of prettier actresses on the London stage and many with nicer figures, but there was no one who could put a song over like Sophie. Others relied to a degree on their beauty. Sophie relied on her brains and her art. She won. She made every man in the stalls think she was singing especially to him. I told Tom Hearns then that the actress who could hold her position as Sophie did had a lot to teach everybody who cared to learn. That is still true.

Chaliapin was singing in London and drawing big crowds. I met him one night at the Savoy. "Sophie dear," he boomed in his million-dollar voice, "with my voice and your personality what I couldn't do!"

The Exposition at Wembley was attracting important people from all over the continent. Sooner or later they would turn up at the Kit-Kat or for Sunday dinner at Bray—Indian princes with their retinues, ambassadors, and government officials, such as Prince Potenziani, the governor of Rome, and his daughter Princess Myriam. I got to know them quite well. The prince loved to hear me call him "Guv'nor." Hell! I didn't know what else to call him. I wish I knew where those two grand people are today.

After sixteen weeks at the Kit-Kat I contracted to go to the provinces—Leeds, Glasgow, Liverpool, Manchester, Birmingham, Brighton. I took my own road show out and went on sharing terms. That meant I played the house on a percentage. I paid the acts, and the balance was my own. I engaged about eight acts. I was now in business as the Sophie Tucker Enterprises, Ltd. In Leeds, which is a very big Jewish center, we did a hell of a business, and the hit of every bill was "My Yiddisha Mama."

Tallulah Bankhead was breaking in her show, *Her Cardboard Lover,* with Leslie Howard that week in Leeds. She did a grand job of it too—she and Leslie.

All in all, my touring the provinces was a big success financially. I had only one setback: in Manchester. The theater there refused a percentage deal and offered me a weekly salary, but I insisted on a percentage. I had been told that the Manchester Handicap was to be run that week, and I figured on doing big business with the crowds up for the race. Ultimately, the theater managers came round and signed up. On the day I opened a black fog settled over Manchester and all that week it was as dark as night, even at noon. Business was terrible, and no wonder. The theater managers wore a broad grin, realizing what my obstinacy had done to keep them out of the red. I barely made enough that week to pay the performers, and had to wire the London office for money to carry on. Fortunately, the fog didn't extend to the next town we were booked into and from then on we made money.

The tour was a big feather in my cap and great publicity. I made new friends, filled many pages of my address book, and came to London for my last week at the Holborn Empire.

I went back to London two years later to play in the musical comedy, *Follow a Star,* at the Winter Garden Theatre. A great deal happened to me and to those I loved during the two years I have skipped over. One of the things that happened was my marriage to Al Lackey. We had waited and put it off, hoping for a time when he would be established in some business of his own, but it seemed as though that time would never come. We loved each other very much and wanted to be together, so I said to myself, even though it was against my better judgment, why wait? Why let money interfere with two people's happiness? Besides, Al was acting as my personal manager. He was a lot of help to me. He was smart about show business. And so we were married.

Some of the things that happened during those two years I'll tell you later, since they were all a part of the last days of vaudeville. They were years in which the changes in show business, which had been coming along ever since the public developed a taste for motion pictures, suddenly swept away the entertainment world which most of us old-timers had grown up in. They were years full of headaches for everybody in show business.

I had plenty of headaches myself as well as heartaches, especially in the last weeks before I sailed for England in June 1930. I played a week at Loew's State Theatre in New York just before sailing and the time between shows I spent at Mollie's bedside. I lived in the theater and in the hospital. One night

I rushed up to see her after my second show. The nurse met me in the hall. She said Mollie was asking for me, waiting for me. I went in and sat by her bed and held her hand—so thin and wasted now. She lay so still under the white covers. After a bit she looked up at me and smiled. "Patsy," she said, "don't ever let down. You're one in a million. I love you." Her eyelids dropped tiredly. There was a little sigh—and Mollie was gone. She took a piece out of my life when she went.

We sailed on the *Ile de France*. Jack and Sylvia Yellen went along. Jack had been engaged to write the lyrics for *Follow a Star*. We had a good crossing, with lots of performers and artists aboard, including Norma Talmadge and Walter Damrosch. Between us we put on a fine ship's concert, but during the concert, while the ship was sailing smoothly and I was seated talking to the captain and Mr. Damrosch, something queer happened to the machinery. Jack Yellen was on the platform, as master of ceremonies, announcing the next act, when suddenly the *Ile de France* listed way over to one side. All the chairs and tables started sliding. Women screamed. The captain made a quick dive for the engine room. Mr. Damrosch grabbed me. "Quick! get up on the platform. Quiet these people!" The ship was still lying far over on her side and it was all I could do to walk to the piano. It seemed as if the boat would never straighten up again. Teddy started one of my numbers, and we swung into a show that we carried on in response to nods from Walter Damrosch until the ship's crew got the *Ile de France* on her keel again.

Paul Murray was producing *Follow a Star,* and starring Jack Hulbert and me. The book was by Douglas Ferber, with music by Vivian Ellis. Jack Yellen was to write special numbers and take care of my dialogue. The cast included Alfred Drayton, Claude Hulbert, Betty Davis, Archie Baskcomm, and Irene Russell. I had some handsome clothes, but Paul Murray and Hulbert insisted their costumer make my clothes for the show. I'll say they were stunning. A black cloth suit with a long coat trimmed with luxurious white fox; a beige afternoon frock trimmed with blue fox; a white panne velvet evening gown studded with brilliants and with a coat trimmed in ermine. The whole show was very smartly dressed.

During the weeks of rehearsals I had a chance for some fun with old friends, like the Cohen girls and Sim Rose, and I could accept some of the invitations from notables. The tennis matches were on. I remember going out to Lady Sophie Wavertree's at Sussex Lodge where I met and entertained ex-King Manuel of Portugal and his mother—both tennis fans— Prince and Princess Arthur of Connaught, and the champions, Bill Tilden,

Cilly Aussem, the German champion, Jacques Brugnon, the Australian tennis expert, and Christian Boussos, the French tennis king.

There was a very clever Englishman, Douglas Bing, playing at the Café Anglaise in London. The town was wild over him, and no wonder. Never have I seen such an artist, and what songs he had! I guess I was his steadiest American customer.

The first night we were in London the Yellens and I went to see Gracie Fields at the Palladium. Gracie spotted me from the stage and called on me, with the whole house egging her on, until I had to stand up and sing "Some of These Days." Ted wasn't along, so I sang without accompaniment.

We opened the show in Manchester. I'll never forget the welcome the Jewish Community Center gave me on our arrival there. It was pouring rain, of course. Dress rehearsal was called at the theater Sunday afternoon, and we never left the theater from then until Monday at 6 P.M. We had just time to go to the hotel, freshen up, and get back for the eight-thirty opening curtain. Bess Lonergan, writer for one of the American newspaper syndicates, the Cohen girls, Sim Rose, and Madame Suzanne came down to Manchester as my guests for the opening. I was scared stiff. This was the first time I had played in a musical comedy in a good many years, and I wasn't at all sure how the British audiences would like me in a show, playing a part. I still remembered Rufus Le Maire's verdict: "You're all right as a singer, but as an actress you stink!" However, during rehearsals the show had shaped up well, and Paul Murray and Jack Hulbert kept assuring me I was all right and had nothing to fear.

Well, Manchester agreed with them. We played all week to sellout business, and the press went to town for me in a big way.

The Manchester Guardian said:

It is not a style to suit everyone, but the Palace audience last night unmistakably relaxed on her ample bosom.

The show played the provinces four weeks before we came into the Winter Garden Theatre in London. If only the show had stayed the way it was when we opened in Manchester it would have been, I think, a smash hit in London.

But once again, as with Rufus Le Maire's *Affairs,* I saw a good show taken to pieces and badly put together, even after it had proved itself to be good. This happened in Glasgow, where Paul Murray fell ill. Jack Hulbert made all the changes himself, and the show that was brought to London was not a good one. Jack is a great artist, but that does not necessarily imply the cleverness of a producer. He never asked me if I thought this was good or bad. Several times I had to bite my tongue and remember I was a stranger and I had to be tactful. I was playing my first part in the show, and I couldn't afford to voice my opinion. Still it went hard with me to see a good piece of property butchered and to see family relationships and heart affairs affect a whole cast. The London *Press* welcomed me in headlines: GOOD OLD SOPH BACK AGAIN! and SOPHIE GETS RED-HOT WELCOME!

Hanan Swaffer actually liked the show, and said of it:

Sophie Tucker brings the house down. Sophie Tucker, making her London debut as a musical-comedy star, scored last night an enormous personal triumph. The first act of *Follow a Star,* full of novel ideas, is one of the most interesting I have seen in a musical show for a long time. Although the second is not so good, it is a clever show.

But it was Sophie Tucker's night. She is the wife of the world's worst conjurer, who discovers in a New York cabaret that he is an English baronet. So Sophie has to enter English society as Lady Bohum. We see the maternal Sophie, resplendent and sunny, skating over all the ice of swell manners, daring, saucy, and pert, and yet the most womanly of women underneath it all.

Betty Davis, a girlish newcomer, is charming and sweet. Jack Hulbert and his brother, Claude, have some good dances. The world's best. But it was Sophie's night. She proved, when she stepped out of the play, toward the end, and sang seven or eight numbers, with Ted Shapiro at the piano, that she was the cleverest artist of her kind in the English-speaking world.

She sang about how fat she was, told women how to make love—"Lonely Wives, You Should Worry," she chanted, "that's what God made sailors for"— and she sang about her size, and how red hot she could be, and how cruel she was. Nobody believed it, but it brought down the house. Beautifully gowned in white, with her golden hair shining, and with her face beaming with sauciness, Sophie held the house for number after number, daring, challenging, and yet so attractive. *Follow a Star* with Sophie is a splendid entertainment. Sophie is the star to follow.

While playing at the Winter Garden I opened the Kit-Kat restaurant again and doubled there. When my birthday came round, the Kit-Kat management gave me a party with a huge birthday cake. I sent invitations to all my friends in London to come to help me serve the cake to the customers. It was the first time anything of this sort was ever done in a public restaurant in London, and the people who were there that night enjoyed it enormously. The cake was served by Cicely Courtneidge, Irene Russell, Ivy Tresmand, Peggy Wood, Clarice Mayne, Janet McGrew, Hilda Glyder, Binnie Barnes,

Stephanie Stephens, and Erin O'Brien Moore. Marie Burke and the girls put on a show, too, which turned it into a gala night.

One of the pictures previewed in London that season was the Marx Brothers' *Cocoanuts,* and C. B. Cochrane brought the boys over to make a personal appearance at the same time. What a difference from 1922, when they first played the British music halls and how the British audience went wild over the boys and the picture! Sir John and Lady Milbanke gave a party at Quaglino's for Elsa Maxwell, Lady Ribblesdale, Mrs. Richard Norton, Mrs. Dudley Ward, Sir Adrian Bailey, Miss Grace Edwards, Lord and Lady Brownlon, Douglas Bing, Mr. Archie Campbell, the Marx Brothers, and me. Elsa was in great form that night, and as for the Marx Brothers, they had the crowd in stitches.

The show closed just before Christmas, which gave me a chance to run over to Paris and to keep a date with Jennie and Rosie Dolly. The Yellens left for home, but my hubby came over to spend the holidays with me, and we went down to Jennie's château at Fontainebleau.

I had an idea that a château was a simple little country house, and that was what I was expecting as we drove down from Paris through beautiful country. All the way along the road high iron or wooden fences hid the houses from our view. Finally, we drove through a huge estate into a magnificent courtyard. There was a big fountain in the center all covered with snow. You entered a long hall with marble pillars, then went into a huge living room with french windows opening onto a terrace overlooking the grounds of the château. The biggest Christmas tree I had ever seen, trimmed and weighed down with gifts, stood at one end of the room. The house was magnificent throughout. I went on tiptoe after Jennie, "ohing" and "ahing" at everything she showed me. Antique furniture, priceless crystal and china, furniture covered in Louis XIV petit point, bedspreads of handmade lace. A château to the Dolly girls, but a palace to me! And it had all the modern touches as well as the antique beauties: plenty of luxurious tiled bathrooms, and a kitchen with every modern American household device. Jennie and Rosie went into the kitchen to fix a Hungarian goulash the way their mother used to make it. It was a marvelous Christmas—the most wonderful I remember.

Jennie and Rosie Dolly had made a fortune in Europe and they lived up to it. Jennie's home in Paris was as luxurious as her château at Fontainebleau, and her salon on the Champs Elysées was the most exquisite shop in Paris to buy anything from baby clothes to luxurious furs. The walls were hung with fine paintings and etchings, and there was a little cocktail lounge for the patrons. The rugs in the dress salon had *Jennie Dolly* woven into the pattern.

Rosie didn't go in for these luxurious things as Jennie did. The two girls so different in temperament adored each other.

It is one of the things in life I could never understand that Jennie Dolly, who would give the shirt off her back to anyone who asked for it, should have had the deluge of misfortune that wrecked her fortune and her career, but not her spirit. First, the automobile accident in which she was nearly killed, the operations by the greatest plastic surgeons in France to restore her face. A fortune spent to save her life. After two years a new Jennie Dolly came to America, her wealth dissipated, her fabulous jewels confiscated by the French Government. Later Jennie came to Chicago and married Ben Venissky. All her friends hoped she was going to have happiness after so much trouble and suffering, but I guess happiness was not for Jennie. She left Venissky and took her two adopted daughters to Hollywood to put them in pictures. I was playing in the Orpheum Theatre in Los Angeles that week, and she rang me up to tell me she was coming down to visit with me —"just like old times." That was one night. The next day, when I woke up, they were crying the extras with the news that Jennie Dolly had committed suicide. Fanny Brice and I, who were the Dolly Sisters' oldest friends, stood by Rosie in her tragic loss. Rosie had married a Chicago man, too, Irving Netcher. Jennie's passing away cemented the tie of friendship between Rosie and Irving and me, a friendship which increases with the years.

While I was in Paris that trip I went to Jennie to make some striking gowns for me. I told her and Rosie that I'd had an offer to play the Empire Theatre in Paris early next March, and that I had asked a stiff price of seven thousand dollars, American money, not French, for the two weeks' engagement.

"But no artist—American or French—ever got that kind of money in Paris!" the girls exclaimed.

"Well, kids, your Sophie will get it if she plays there," I told them. I didn't explain that I had asked the stiff price on purpose, so the manager wouldn't book me, as the idea of playing in Paris scared me stiff.

CHAPTER 24: *The Last Time I Saw Paris*

YOU CAN'T be in show business steadily for over twenty years and not get wise to a few things about yourself and about audiences. I figured that I knew something about how to entertain Americans. God knows that if I didn't know it by this time, I never would. My experiences in England, playing the theaters and cafés, had taught me something about what goes over with the British customers. But what did I know about French audiences? Not a damned thing.

On my first trip to Europe, back in 1922, Sis, Jack, Ted, and I had taken a flying look at Brussels, Berlin, and Paris. We had sampled the night life in those three capitals. I'll never forget a play we saw in Berlin, with the most wonderful acting I have ever seen anywhere and a story that still haunts me. After the show we went around to a few of Berlin's hot spots—magnificent dance halls, marvelous food. At Pelzer's I swam in their big bowl of caviar. Gosh, I kept thinking, how Pa would have enjoyed this. But aside from those swell and high-priced places the one word for Berlin's night life was "rotten." The Europa and the Café Vernon were "nude" palaces—vulgar, dirty. The less said of them the better. Yes, everywhere you went you were struck by the cheap morale of Berlin and the number of "fag" joints. There was no time of day or night that you didn't see men dressed as women. On the streets and in every hotel lobby were men and women hustling. And there was nothing discreet about the way they sold their wares.

On that trip we went on from Berlin to Paris, which was then swarming with Americans and working overtime to keep the spenders amused. We hit all the high spots—Maxim's for lunch with the Dolly Sisters, the Folies-Bergère to see Mistinguette, then at the height of her popularity. I'd been compared and contrasted with her so many times, I was crazy to see her work. She was very good, but the rest of the show was only fair to my way of thinking. However, the scenery was gorgeous. It was that night that I copied down the name of the designer, who was programmed for staging the revue, and made inquiries where to find him. The next day I ordered from him two handsome patent-leather drops which I took home with me, as I have told in a previous chapter.

I had never seen so much nudity on the stage as at the Folies-Bergère. Apparently, that was what put the show over with the French customers. The show girls and the *demimondaines* (plain hustlers in our country) who packed the big barroom of the Folies were beautifully groomed, chic, smart. You could see those French gals knew their stuff.

At that time the New York Bar was the most popular American rendezvous in Paris. Les Copeland used to sing there—his specialty was the old, old songs of Chinatown. Les came from San Francisco's Barbary Coast and he made the songs he brought from there popular with Americans and Britishers who flocked to Paris. After Les Copeland, the New York Bar carried on with two singers from New York's East Side—Tommy Lyman and Roy Barton. Their great stunt was singing the barroom ballads of the Gay Nineties.

But the great night spot in Montmartre, back in the Twenties, the place that people fought to get into, was Zelli's. Zelli was an American, and he built the success of his place in Paris on what he had learned in America about running a successful saloon. He always greeted the customers at the door and called most of them by name as he shook their hands. Then he would tell the waiter to conduct them to the royal box. A great bull artist, Joe Zelli. He knew his Paris and he knew his international society. The fizz water I had there made me very happy, and I put on a show for the customers that should have been worth something more than just the headache I woke up with the next morning.

But even if I had been around Paris, what did I know of it except what it had to offer to tourists? I didn't know what French people were like inside, what would make them laugh or cry, or what made them mad. But I knew enough to know a continental audience was different from a British or an American one.

I'd had one experience playing a Saturday night at Ostend, Belgium, right after my engagement in London in 1928. Ted Lewis and his band had played there at the Casino and were a riot. I thought I could do what he had done, but, boy, oh, boy, did I flop! Did I lay eggs in Ostend! About fifteen hundred people packed the room to hear the big American artist. No one understood a word of what I sang. I sang song after song, and all the time the noise and chatter were terrific. A few applauded, but the rest didn't know what the hell it was all about. After I finished work, the manager sent word for me to come to his office for my money—one thousand dollars. He gave me a French check. "Nothing doing, mister," I told him. "I want American money." He told me it would take some time before he could do that.

"That's okay," I told him. "I'll be in my room. Send it up."

"Why don't you go into the gambling room?" he suggested.

"Thank you," I said. "I've already given it the double-O. I'm taking American money back home!"

Upstairs in my room, Carl McCullough, who was along with me, and my niece, Sadie, and I got into a pinochle game while waiting for my money to be delivered. The boat for London left at 5:30 A.M., and we had to catch it because I had an engagement for Sunday night. Four-thirty came, and no money. That's when I began to raise hell. At five-fifteen the money was handed over, and boy, did we streak it to the boat!

That experience at Ostend didn't make me feel too sure of French managers or of my ability to win and hold a French audience. When I found that the two managers of the Empire Theatre, Messieurs Varno and Dufré, hadn't balked at the price I asked them for a two weeks' engagement—seven thousand dollars—I made up my mind I was in for it. All through the winter weeks, while I was playing in and around London and the British provinces, I kept worrying about what was going to happen when I played Paris.

If only the Boss had been there to give me a steer!

My first worry was about the French house orchestra. French orchestras simply couldn't play American jazz. All the smart dancing places in Paris employed some American musicians. The Paris City Council had passed a law that 50 per cent of the musicians in every orchestra employed in a café had to be of French nationality. In some of the places the manager would have the French musicians keep quiet while the Americans played the jazz the customers wanted. I made up my mind that as soon as I got to Paris I would engage a five-piece band to play for me. Teddy was busy a week before the opening rehearsing five boys. I gave a lot of thought to what songs I would sing, and I made up my mind to use only melodies and rhythm songs, choosing those which I had recorded in London and the records of which had had a good sale in France.

It was Edwina Mountbatten who advised me to sing my theme song in French as well as in English. She and the Earl of Sefton made a translation of the chorus of "Some of These Days" and taught me to sing it. It took me weeks to memorize it, but I got it down pat. When I told the Dolly Sisters I was going to do this, they approved of the idea. It took me almost another week to train myself to call the Empire Theatre "Om-peer." But that pronunciation made a big hit with Messieurs Varno and Dufré. Having finally agreed to my price, they couldn't be nicer or more cordial to me than they were.

For weeks, before I opened in Paris, Jennie and Rosie Dolly were busy building up publicity for me. I don't think there was a single American, living or visiting in Paris, that the girls didn't call up, write, or wire to be at the opening to put over Sophie Tucker. This included the American ambassador and the entire staff at the Embassy. Maurice Chevalier, meanwhile, got busy with the press, who went to town for me.

When I got to Paris I found my suite at the Claridge filled with flowers and the exciting-looking boxes containing the clothes Jennie had made for me. There was another big box from the girls—with love—which they sent

around to my dressing room at the Empire. It was full of the craziest assortment of things you ever saw—soap, towels, perfume, make-up, and a roll of
toilet paper.

"Ha, ha," I laughed, when I came to this, thinking it was one of their
jokes.

"There is nothing to laugh at," Rosie came back. "You'll soon find that
the most useful present anybody can give you in a French theater. Have you
taken a look at the toilet yet, Soph?"

I hadn't, but after Rosie tipped me off, I prowled around until I found the
toilet. There was only one—for men and women. I'll bet no one had cleaned
it since Bernhardt played that theater. And just as Rosie said, the management provided no toilet paper. In France, every performer has to carry his
own.

I had the jitters when I walked on the stage at rehearsal. Every board
creaked under me. I had visions of a cave-in. But there was a marvelous stage
crew, who all seemed very friendly, even though not one of them spoke a
word of English.

On my opening night, when I heard my introduction played, I stood in
the entrance holding onto the scenery. I had a godawful feeling. Not about
my looks. The clothes Jennie Dolly had made me were beautiful and as chic
as anything a Paris audience ever saw. Just the same, I was plumb scared of
facing those French people. Teddy was on the stage. He had the band in
hand. The house gave him a good reception. I thought to myself, don't be a
damn fool. The Dolly Sisters are out front. They won't let you down. Sing to
them. Don't see anybody else.

With that I walked out onto the stage. To my surprise, the house gave me
a rousing reception, cheers. I looked out at the audience. There in the front
row were Jennie and Rosie, Maurice Chevalier, and, as far as I could see,
rows and rows of American faces. I thought, where in hell are the French
people? I looked off at the side. Standing along a balcony that seemed to run
around the whole orchestra were Frenchmen with their caps on and no ties;
French gals, all standing up, leaning against the railing. In London these
people would be sitting in the pit or in the gallery. In an American theater,
they would be upstairs in the balcony. Here the whole lower floor was a
beautiful sight—everyone in evening dress, the women wearing exquisite
jewels. I could see to the third row in the first balcony, which was packed
with nice-looking French people. The gallery was jammed. I could make out
a blur of faces. That's where the French people were who had come to give
the American *chanteuse* the once-over. They were the people I had to think

about—they and the gang with caps on leaning against the railing, sizing me up.

I sang song after song, still with my eyes and my heart on the galleries. When I swung into "Some of These Days," the house went wild. Then I sang the chorus in French, and it brought a terrific laugh and applause from all over the theater. There were calls for "encore," but I had rehearsed only five songs. I saw the ushers coming down the aisle with basket after basket of flowers. Fifteen of them were handed up over the footlights to me. What I couldn't get over was that the cards on the baskets of flowers bore names of people I'd never heard of. Then I found out that every single basket had been sent by Jennie or Rosie. The girls were determined to put me over with the Paris audience if they possibly could—just like their loving loyal hearts.

Of course every night isn't an opening night. The test comes later in the week. That's when you find out whether or not you are GOOD. The next few days went smoothly. The press was good, and the French people kept turning out. I think they decided I had personality and they appreciated that I was an artist. But the trouble was that they wanted me to sing in French, and all the French I knew was the chorus of "Some of These Days."

On Thursday night the audience started calling to me to sing in French. I tried to explain that I didn't know or understand French. The nicer people in the house tried to quiet the roughnecks. I'd been up against tough gangs in the small-time houses back home and I had my own way of handling them. I'd found out that I could win them over to my side by calling out to them. But here again the language was the barrier. There wasn't one damn thing I could do with that French gallery gang.

On Friday night the house had quite a lot of French Jews. Several notes had been sent back to me, and the managers also told me there were a great many requests for me to sing "My Yiddisha Mama." I was leary of this. I told the managers they would have to leave it to my own judgment as the act went along.

I went out to do my regular program. Again there were the calls to me to sing in French. And after every song someone in the audience would call for "Yiddisha Mama." Immediately the roughnecks would shout "no!"

I was in a hell of a fix and perfectly helpless as the audience fought back and forth—something I had never seen or heard of in any theater.

I finished my routine, singing the chorus of "Some of These Days" in French. I had made up my mind not to sing "My Yiddisha Mama." Then came more shouts and calls for it. Teddy shot me a questioning look.

I thought—and it was one of the stupidest blunders I ever made—so many have asked for it, I ought to sing it. I'll explain why I'm singing it. The song itself will touch everybody in the house.

I explained, and then sang the song in English. Everything was all right until I started the first sentence in Yiddish. Then up went "boo!" from all over the house! The boos were answered by a yell from the Jews and cries to be quiet. The others yelled back to the Jews. They didn't want the song.

The noise was so great I couldn't hear my own voice, nor could I hear Teddy at the piano. I thought: in a minute there'll be a riot. Quick as a flash I turned to Teddy and said, "Switch!" Before the audience knew what the hell was happening I was singing, "Happy Days Are Here Again."

My God, I only hoped they were!

While the house was still in an uproar I was off the stage. The American press ran headlines on the story: SOPHIE TUCKER HISSED OFF PARIS STAGE!

Well, it was great publicity, and my agent, Paula Gould, was right on the job to make the most of it.

I finished my engagement at the "Om-peer," being careful not to make any more changes in my standard program. That was the first and last time I played a Paris theater. I went back to help open the American Legion building there, Pershing Hall, when the American Legion held its convention in Paris that summer. All that spring and summer I played the variety theaters in the British provinces and the British seashore resorts. I had been away from the United States for over a year, and working all the time.

When I finished the tour, I was glad to join my husband in Switzerland, where he had gone to visit Mr. and Mrs. A. J. Balaban. There is one thing about working as hard as a performer works on tour, when you get a chance for a vacation you make the most of it. Al and I didn't miss a trick in Switzerland or in Venice. But the high spot of our trip was Vienna. All my life I had wanted to see that city of which I had heard so many stories and which is so famous in the world of show business. Poor Vienna, so pitifully changed, everybody said, since the world war and still managing to be gay and hospitable.

Something happened in Vienna which I like to think of in connection with that experience at the Empire Theatre in Paris, when the audience booed me for singing "Yiddisha Mama." Al and I were out shopping. We passed a gramophone store and, for the fun of it, went in and asked:

"Do you sell Sophie Tucker's records?"

"Oh yes!" the saleslady said. "We have all of them."

"Which is the best seller?"

" 'My Yiddisha Mama!' " she said at once. "We've sold thousands of them. I'd venture to say, *gnädige Frau,* there isn't a home in Vienna that doesn't boast that record. Would you like to hear it?"

"Go ahead," I said; "put it on." As she brought the record from the shelf, I said to her, "What would you say if I were to tell you I am Sophie Tucker?"

She looked at me blankly. "I could not believe or disbelieve you, *gnädige Frau.* I have never seen a picture of Sophie Tucker."

"Put the record on," I said, "and I will sing with it."

She put the record on and started the machine. There was the introduction to the song and then I started the first line, "Of things I should be thankful for, I've had a goodly share . . ."

Her mouth opened in amazement. *"Gott im Himmel!"* she cried. *"Gnädige Frau,* you are she!" Without another word she ran into the street and began to call to the people passing by and upstairs to people on the balconies and at the windows of the flats. "Come quick! Come quick! Here is the Yiddisha Mama herself. It is Sophie Tucker!"

In less than five minutes the store was crowded and the street outside black with people. Policemen and newspapermen elbowed their way through the crowd to find out what was happening. There weren't any boos for Jack Yellen's song in Vienna. Instead, I had to sing every word of it for the most eager audience I have ever faced.

A few nights later, when Al and I were dining at the Coblenzaal, one of Vienna's famous restaurants built on a cliff overlooking the Danube, the marvelous gypsy music the orchestra was playing got into my blood. Al and I got up to dance, as we loved to do. When we came to our seats, there was a note at my place:

GNÄDIGE FRAU,
Make us all happy tonight. Please sing "Some of These Days."
AN ADMIRER

Standing in the moonlight, on a terrace in Vienna, singing "Some of These Days" to the music of a gypsy band, is the most romantic experience my life in show business has brought me. And "Of things I should be thankful for . . ." one is that I was permitted to taste some of the flavor of Vienna before its spirit was stamped out by the Nazi heel.

There were no Nazis on view in Berlin when we got there for a big July Fourth celebration for Americans at the Hotel Adlon. A gala dinner party was staged by the American ambassador, and I looked forward to appearing in one of my stunning Paris gowns. It wasn't until I started to dress for the dinner that I found what the marvelous food of Vienna, Budapest, Prague, and other vacation resorts had done to my figure. Not one evening gown fitted me any more. It was then six-thirty and every minute counted. I called the hotel housekeeper and showed her the gap in my white crepe gown, where the hooks wouldn't meet. What could she do about it?

She sent out for a sewing machine, then she sat down and ripped open the seams. We tore up one of the sheets on the bed and set a piece of white linen in under the arms of the dress. That's how I went to the American ambassador's dinner. I never left my seat. I didn't dare move around. I entertained from the dais.

It is a commentary on Berlin in the summer of 1931 that I was invited to broadcast a recitation of "My Yiddisha Mama." I had to recite the song, as I didn't have any music with me and Teddy wasn't along to play the accompaniment. It was "Yiddisha Mama" that the Berlin Broadcasting Company asked for.

That for the Paris mob!

"My Yiddisha Mama" was written for me by Jack Yellen and Lou Pollack. I introduced it at the Palace Theatre in New York in 1925 and after that in the key cities of the U. S. A. where there were many Jews. Even though I loved the song, and it was a sensational hit every time I sang it, I was always careful to use it only when I knew the majority of the house would understand the Yiddish. However, I have found whenever I have sung "My Yiddisha Mama," in the U. S. A., or in Europe, Gentiles have loved the song and have called for it. They didn't need to understand the Yiddish words. They knew, by instinct, what I was saying, and their hearts responded just as the hearts of Jews and Gentiles of every nationality responded when John McCormack sang "Mother Machree." You didn't have to have an old mother in Ireland to feel "Mother Machree," and you didn't have to be a Jew to be moved by "My Yiddisha Mama." "Mother" in any language means the same thing.

I scored a tremendous hit with "My Yiddisha Mama" in England. All over the continent this is the song which has always been identified with me, as "Some of These Days" is recognized as my theme song in America.

Several years later, after Hitler came into power and started the persecution of the Jews in Germany, I heard that my records of "My Yiddisha Mama" were ordered smashed and the sale of them banned in the Reich. I was hopping mad. I sat right down and wrote a letter to Herr Hitler which was a masterpiece. To date, I have never had an answer.

When Al and I sailed home from Cherbourg at the end of that summer I had something to look forward to: this was the meeting with my daughter-in-law, Lillian.

It seemed as if all the important family news was always being wired or cabled to me. I was playing in Manchester early that summer, and just getting ready to go on for the second show, when a cable was handed to me. I ripped it open and read:

JUNE 2, 1931

WAS MARRIED TODAY TO A FINE JEWISH GIRL LOVE SON

I didn't have a chance for any reaction to this news because my introduction was being played. I went on, still clutching the cablegram inside my chiffon handkerchief, and all I could think of while I was singing was if only I could have been with Son when he got married. And, like every mother, I guess, I thought how young he was to take a wife.

Before I knew it I started telling the audience about the cable and Son getting married. It was good that I told them. I got it off my chest and felt better. And I could sing "My Yiddisha Mama" when the audience called for it with my heart in every line.

The Boss had booked me to play the Paramount theaters in New York and Brooklyn. I had a new moniker now—the "International Favorite." Georgie Jessel and I headlined the bill, and we did a fine business, but I noticed that a great change had happened in American show business during the four-teen months I had been in Europe. There was no getting around it, the movies had a death grip on vaudeville. It was extraordinary how the public had changed. They had become very blasé about entertainment. Whereas Americans used to arrange to spend an evening in the theater for a treat, now they seemed to go to the theater just to kill time. With the newspapers and motion-picture magazines telling the public the private lives of stars, a lot of the illusion and glamor of the stage were gone. The public knew too much about all of us. When they came to see us, they were more concerned with how many times we had been married or in the divorce courts and how many lovers an actress had than with what the show was like.

The theaters were full of children. At the first two shows in the afternoon the house would be full of boys and girls, slumped down in their seats, obviously bored with the acts and only waiting for the picture to come on. Kids and necking couples—those who started necking during the picture and kept it up when the show was on. It was worth something to try to untangle them to applaud your act. By the time of the last show, at 9:30 P.M., when you had your best audience, you were dead tired. Too tired to care whether they liked your act or not.

It was hell working in theaters the size they were building those days for the movie fans. Many times I would get right down in front of the orchestra pit so I could be close to the audience instead of singing miles away from them. Another thing, after the audience had been looking at a picture on a screen, a stage with just one or two performers on it seemed terribly empty. To get around this problem, Jack Yellen wrote a big production number for me, "Dance-hall Doll." I engaged a number of people to go on the stage with me to fill it up. Another song I dramatized in my bills at that time was "River, Stay Away from My Door."

I played across the country and in the cities of the West Coast. Changes everywhere. The Orpheum headliners playing picture houses in California didn't mean a thing any more. A picture name of any kind drew more business than I or any vaudevillian could do. If you were lucky to get a good picture, it meant a big week's business; a bad picture, and you starved to death. I was lucky to get Katherine Hepburn's first big picture, *Morning Glory*, at the Palace Theatre in Chicago. I went in on a percentage. Gone were the glorious days of the Palace vaudeville! They now ran four shows a day and only a few acts of vaudeville. Business was down as low as sixteen thousand dollars a week as compared to thirty-two thousand and thirty-five thousand dollars weekly receipts before the days of the picture theaters. I went in on a percentage and I finished up that week with eighty-five hundred dollars for my cut. But I wasn't responsible for the business. It was a great picture that drew the crowds. They publicized two Hartford girls at the Palace that week—Katherine Hepburn and Sophie Tucker. The mayor of Hartford sent a wire of greeting so we could publicize it. I sent off several wires to Miss Hepburn, asking her to send me a message for publicity for her picture and for me. I had to find out that most of the picture stars have no time and no interest to do things like that—the very things we vaudeville performers found out long ago piled up B. O. I was brushed off completely. I worked like a horse all that week. I didn't depend upon the theater's publicity budget. I engaged a personal publicity man and I spent over one thousand dollars for extra advertising. Oh well, I walked out with a bundle.

After being away from the Palace Theatre in New York for nearly three years, I played my first date there again in February 1932 with a fine bill— Bill Robinson, Smith and Dale, Jack Whiting, the Four Golden Blondes, Bernice and Emily. Prior to this bill the Palace had Lou Holtz for ten consecutive weeks, who did a record-breaking business. Lou could have stayed on ten more weeks if he hadn't demanded more money. So I came in and did only a fair week's business.

But I was back home at the Palace—the only theater left in New York that wasn't playing pictures. The demonstration by the audience at my opening performance gladdened my heart. It made me feel that the New York public still wanted real vaudeville. After months playing picture houses, it was like old times. The show around me looked like old times too. I tell you it felt good just to walk in the alley, to hang around backstage and talk to Morris, the doorman, Bill, the stage manager, all the boys. Ed Sullivan's article in the *Evening Graphic* sums it up much better than I can do. What he said for me was said for every performer in vaudeville:

BACK HOME

There was a world of meaning in the remark Sophie Tucker let drop at the Palace the other night. "I'm glad to be back here," she said simply. "Returning to this theater is like coming back home to me." Watching one of these grand veterans of vaudeville returning to such a theater as the Palace always sort of chokes me up. It's like watching a Dempsey or a Johnny Dundee crawling through the ropes in the twilight of their careers and going into action with colors flying. That's what I thought as Sophie Tucker came out on the Palace stage Sunday night. It was the return of the queen to the domain which she had ruled for years.

With her clean-cut jaw thrust out at almost a belligerent angle, Sophie came out on the Palace stage and went into action directly. There was no fencing and no sparring around for time. Here was a grand veteran of vaudeville, obeying vaude's dictum: "Make it fast and snappy, and make it good." No tiresome speeches, no coy mannerisms. "I'm Sophie Tucker," she seemed to say, "and here's what I've got." Her lower lip slipped out and put a twist to the lyrics as she sang, for the mannerisms of a Tucker belong to her alone. Looking at her, I wondered what thoughts were in her mind. Here she was, back in the Palace again after three years. Perhaps glamorous sections of her career were conjured up as she trod the familiar boards again and looked out into the orchestra over the bald dome of Lou Forman. There was no hesitancy in her movements. These veterans don't scare easily. She hit that first song and "went to town" on the second. She went into her third song, and the house came down.

Only then did Sophie Tucker relax. "I'm glad to be back here," she said simply. "Returning to this theater is like coming back home to me." Vaudeville performers all over the country knew what was in La Tucker's heart. For the veterans can read between the lines of even so unadorned a statement as she vouchsafed. And probably the audience got it, too, for the applause was staccato as Sophie Tucker, with mascara staining her eyes in suspicious fashion, walked off, with the roar of a Palace crowd again in her ears.

Backstage, the talk flew round that the Palace would soon go into a grind policy—four shows a day with pictures. The gloom was so thick you could cut it with a knife. We all had the feeling that now that E. F. Albee, the czar of vaudeville, was dead, even the Palace wouldn't hold out much longer against pictures. You know how people used to try to help a horse pull a load up a hill by sitting forward on the seat and working with him? That was the way every actor on the bill worked that week at the Palace. As though he could keep New York's only vaudeville theater by his efforts. I worked that way myself.

On Wednesday night I was standing center stage singing my fool head off when I happened to glance off at the side entrance. Bill, the stage manager, was beckoning to me. I paid no attention. I went right on with my act. A crowd gathered at the entrance. They were all beckoning to me to get off the stage. Then they pointed overhead for me to look up. I looked and saw a tongue of flame shoot out in the flies. Fire! I thought: I can't leave the stage now. I've got to tell the audience to leave quietly so there won't be a panic. The house was packed.

"Take it easy, folks. Don't run. Give everybody a chance to get out."

The front and side doors of the theater were open and the draft spread the flames above me. I was dressed in a gown covered with bronze sequins. If a spark fell on it, it would go up in a blaze—and me with it. I stood there singing and praying no spark would drop. Then I was yanked off the stage by the property boy and the steel curtain came down.

That was the famous fire at the Palace. Most of the damage was up in the flies and in the orchestra pit. Very little damage out front; only a few mink coats singed. The newspapers ran headlines:

RED-HOT MAMA BURNS UP PALACE THEATRE!

and

SOPHIE'S SONGS SO HOT, THEATER BURNS UNDER THEM!

CHAPTER 25: *Command Performance*

THE grand and glorious days of the Palace ended with the fire. The Palace was never the same again. When it reopened it was on the four-a-day grind policy. No pictures as yet but there was no longer any thrill in playing there.

It was just another week's work. All of us knew it wouldn't be long before pictures would crowd vaudeville out of its last stand in New York.

Up on the sixth floor of the Palace Theatre building, where Eddie Darling had his office, the atmosphere wasn't the same. You didn't see the bookers and the agents and the big executives of show business hanging around there any more. It was about as cheerful as a morgue. Nobody said it, but everybody knew that soon the elevators wouldn't stop at the sixth floor any more.

The years 1931 and 1932 saw the death of American vaudeville. Albee was gone, and the Orpheum Circuit of houses closed up one by one. No more routes of forty to forty-five weeks. In July of 1932 Florenz Ziegfeld died, though his name will never die in show business. Many of the ideas he launched are still going strong and piling up B. O. But the greatest loss of that year, not only to me personally but to the whole of American show business, was the death of my boss, William Morris. The whole theatrical world mourned him as a great man, not only in his profession but in all the human relations. To me, there never was anyone to equal him, or even stand beside him. I am not alone in my judgment of William Morris. For many years, and while American show business was running on high, there was hardly a show put on Broadway that its producers didn't seek his advice. And that went for the Metropolitan Opera House as well as for the ten-twenty-thirt's.

It took me months to realize that the Boss was gone and our close friendship of many years was over. So many little things that happened in those years came back to me and made me feel as though I wouldn't be able to carry on, especially in the tough times we were having, without his counsel and direction. America was sunk in the depression. The bottom had fallen out of show business and nobody knew what would happen next. How many times of late years the Boss had said to me, with a worried little frown, that he was afraid Abe Lastfogel would leave the office for a big contract in the movie field, and how could he carry on without his Abe, as he called him.

"Abe will never leave you or the office, Boss," I told him a dozen times.

Black as things looked in show business, the Boss had faith that things would right themselves before long. It meant everything to him to believe that the William Morris Agency, which he had founded and built up to the most important theatrical agency in the country, would carry on after he was gone. The Boss counted on Abe and on young Bill Morris to develop the work he had started. Show business might be in for a lot of new turns, but he expected Abe and young Bill to keep up with them and to keep ahead of the game.

For years everybody in show business used to say that the Boss's foresight was terrific. Well, he wasn't wrong about Abe Lastfogel or young Bill, as things have turned out. Abe Lastfogel, who started his career in show business as the Boss's office boy, has been called by the government to direct the shows which the U.S.O. puts on for our soldiers and sailors all over the world. And young Bill is making the William Morris Agency as great a force in show business in these days of radio and coming television as it was in the days before vaudeville turned up its toes and died.

All these changes made me do a lot of thinking. I found I wasn't doing a big business any more in the theaters. A lot of the pictures were bad and the public was getting tired of them. They stayed away from the theaters unless there was a five- or six-star bill in addition to the picture. The picture stars were coming in to take a fling at the theaters and pulling down fabulous salaries. The public ran to see what their idols looked like in the flesh. There wasn't a picture star who invaded the theater who got less than twenty-five hundred dollars a week for appearing there. The top salaries ran up to ten thousand dollars a week. Appearing is about as much as any of them did. Very few of the glamor girls and boys of the screen knew anything of the stage or could entertain an audience. They could pack the picture houses once around, but they could never play a return date, as they had nothing new to give. They laid eggs in every theater and they hurt themselves and the whole of show business by these attempts. The theaters still had to play real vaudevillians to give the audience the laughs they came for and which, God knows, they needed plenty of in those days when the banks were crashing all around us. All this ran into enormous sums.

I can tell you it hurt like hell to have to step down for the "no-talent" stars of the movies after you'd spent sixteen years plugging away to get to the place where you were a headliner and commanded big money.

I had a taste of this back in 1932, when I was asked to play the Capitol Theatre in New York. They had booked a headliner, Lilyan Tashman, who was billed as the best-dressed woman in pictures. I had known her as a Ziegfeld chorus girl, and one of the best. She was booked to headline the Capitol with Jack Benny, Jack Pearl, George Olsen and band with Ethel Shutta. A few months before I had played and headlined the Capitol at my salary of forty-five hundred dollars. They couldn't pay me forty-five hundred dollars this time, with the big bill, and they couldn't headline me, but they needed me on the bill that week. Would I agree to go on for thirty-five hundred dollars and share billing with Tashman and the other stars?

I tried to figure out the right thing to do. Of course thirty-five hundred dollars isn't "tin." If this combination of a show is a hit, it ought to be good for six weeks' work. I'm still in the good graces of my public and B. O., even at the picture houses, or they wouldn't be after me.

I figured I'd get Jack Yellen to give me a few good new songs. I was out to make myself the outstanding hit of the bill, but the billing was the problem. Tashman's contract was for sole billing. George Olsen and his band and Ethel Shutta were headliners too. Jack Pearl had been starred in musical comedies, so he called for headline position. God knows I'd been a headliner for so many years, I'd lost count. (Jack Benny never headlined any bill back in those days, so nobody worried about him!) I had the whole Morris Agency tearing their hair, trying to figure out a way in which I could have my position as a headliner without breaking the contracts of the others on the bill. The Boss—it was only a few months before he left us—pointed out that if I would give in, all the others would follow, and this would mean weeks of work for everybody and the biggest show on Broadway.

Jack Yellen phoned me, "Go into the Capitol, Soph. I've got two great songs for you. Sing them, and close with 'Some of These Days.' Don't sing any more. Tie the show up. Grab your dough and forget the billing."

I figured Jack and the Boss were right. I said I'd do it. Out I went to buy a few handsome gowns, as I had the best-dressed gal on the screen to compete with, and Ethel Shutta was no slouch herself when it came to dressing. On the bill Lilyan was headlined. I followed. Then came Jack Pearl, Jack Benny, and George Olsen's band with Ethel Shutta. For two weeks we murdered the customers, doing over one hundred and thirty thousand dollars business. With the same line-up we went to the Paradise Theatre uptown, then over to the Metropolitan Theatre in Brooklyn, breaking all records in those houses. We would have gone on playing in the same formation in every big theater in every key city across the country, but poor Lilyan fell ill at the end of the third week and was rushed to the hospital. She died shortly afterward. When we finished at the Capitol, Lilyan, Benny, Pearl, Olsen, and Shutta chipped in and gave me a beautiful, huge brown suède handbag with a card that meant more than the gift: "For Sophie. Still the tops in show business and a regular gal."

To make this success I gave up my position as a headliner, the thing I'd worked sixteen years to establish. I didn't do it willingly, or easily, or gracefully. I did it because I felt I had to, and somewhere around in the back of my mind there was a feeling that just as it had been good business to give up the big money I had made at the German Village to take twenty-five dollars a week in small-time vaudeville and good business to leave vaudeville for a smaller salary when I went to Reisenweber's, it would be good business in the end for me to meet the new conditions in show business even more than halfway.

Show business is changing all the time. If you want to stay with it, you have to change with it. Performers who refused to do that have been stranded all along the way. The old-timers such as myself—W. C. Fields, Fanny Brice, Eddie Cantor—who are still going strong today, owe our prestige to the fact that we were smart enough and flexible enough to change as show business has changed.

One of the changes that came about in those years and which has had a tremendous and far-reaching effect on show business in this country was the increasing popularity of cafés. As I looked over the field, I decided to build up the café work. I went to it and kept busy for twenty-five to thirty weeks in the year, giving only ten to fifteen weeks to theaters. When the Chicago World's Fair opened, I was playing at the "225" Club in that city. I opened there in April and played straight through until August. It was a small club, seating not more than one hundred and twenty-five people. The show consisted of four acts, including me. Joe E. Lewis came in for a run with me and we put on our "Stormy Weather" duet, which was a riot. There was I, standing in the middle of the floor singing the song with all the voice and heart I could put into it, and there was Joe behind me in a yellow raincoat and hat, with an umbrella and his stooge standing over him pouring buckets of water on him.

The cafés were paying me top money now. It was a lot of hard work and expense to pull down that salary. I had to have new gowns all the time and new songs because, in order to make a season's work at a café, you had to play return dates and have something new for the old customers all the time. I lived by schedule. Every night after work, at 3 or 4 A.M., I would put in an hour or two studying new songs before I went to sleep. Every afternoon from four to five Ted and I would rehearse. It was a full day. Living like that you don't have much time, or energy, for a personal life, and mine wasn't too happy.

I played the cafés back and forth across the continent. Joe Moss's Hollywood Restaurant was the big noise on Broadway, with Rudy Vallee and his orchestra. I went in there for six weeks with a great show. The Hollywood

Restaurant was a showcase with beautiful girls, many of whom found their way from there out to Hollywood and pictures. The Hollywood was the nearest thing to the shows that made Ziegfeld famous. During the winter months the Florida cafés opened up and did a whale of a business. I booked to play two weeks at the Hollywood Country Club in Florida in the winter of 1934 and stayed six weeks doing good business. But there, as everywhere, I had to compete with the crooners who were coming in strong, and with the name bands which radio was making famous all over the country. Radio had become the big medium. If you were lucky enough to get a radio contract, you were made. I made several trips to Mr. John Royal at N.B.C. and with the big shots at C.B.S., but the old stalling game was handed out to me the same as to hundreds of others. I just couldn't get a contract. Radio wouldn't have Sophie Tucker! That made it tough for me, but it wasn't the only obstacle that had been put in my way since I had started in show business. I'd overcome most of the others. I didn't see any reason for letting radio put me out of business.

Paula Gould, who was doing my publicity, and I put our heads together and thought up all the stunts we could to keep my name before the public. At the same time the news of my divorce from Al Lackey broke in all the papers—which didn't hurt me in the café business. Just the same, I wasn't of any value in the theater any more and I knew it. I didn't kid myself any. When the café business began to drop off, I called Abe Lastfogel on the phone: "Book me in London, Abe. I'm stale. Can't do business here." He called me back a few days later to say he had booked me for eight weeks at the Café de Paris in London, and to double in the theaters there. I was due to sail on the S.S. *Manhattan* on the first of May 1934. Thank God for the British!

I began to feel better the minute we sailed, and I went on feeling better every day. Just knowing that there was a welcome for me in the British theaters did that for my spirits. But there was no holding me down on the third day out when a radiogram from Harry Foster was handed to me. It informed me that I was selected to sing at a command performance for Their Majesties, King George V and Queen Mary, at the Palladium Theatre on the same night of my opening at the Café de Paris. What a night's work was laid out for me! Three opening performances on May 9: at the Holborn Theatre, at the Café de Paris, and the command performance at the Palladium.

Only one thing dampened the pleasure of my arrival at Southampton. I couldn't understand why my pals, the Cohen girls, Madame Suzanne, and

Sim Rose, weren't at the pier to meet me. It was the first time they had failed to be there. I worried all the way up to London. When we arrived at Waterloo, Harry Foster was there to meet me, and there were the Cohen girls and Madame Suzanne, but no Sim. Their faces told me, even before they spoke, that Sim Rose was gone. She had been buried a week before I arrived. It was the first break in our little circle, and I missed Sim every day I was in London.

With less than a week to go to my opening I had plenty to do. George Black, the manager of the Palladium, wouldn't give out definite information if I would or would not appear at the command performance, and the press made a lot of it. One of George Black's publicity stunts. One day the report was that I was in; the next day, the story came out that Sophie Tucker was too hot for Their Majesties to take! Great publicity! I engaged Jack Oliphant to do personal publicity work, to keep my name in the papers in London and in America. I knew all that was very important.

On the night of the ninth I opened at the Holborn with a grand bill. The house gave me an enthusiastic welcome. I gave them "Stay At Home, Pappa," "Lord, You Made the Night Too Long," "Louisville Lady," "He's Tall, Dark, and Handsome," "My Extraordinary Man," and, of course, "Some of These Days." I finished my two shows at the Holborn, getting more and more excited every minute. After all, a command performance in London is—a command performance! I had sung for Their Majesties, King George and Queen Mary, once before. That was the first season I played in London in George Robey's *Round in Fifty*. One of the acts of the revue was selected for that season's command performance, and it happened I was in it, and sang my two numbers, "Dapper Dan" and "When They Get Too Wild for Everyone Else, They're Perfect for Me," and got laughs and applause from royalty. Then I had appeared as part of a cast of the most popular revue in town. This time I had been selected as an individual performer to entertain Their Majesties.

After the second show at the Holborn, I freshened up and drove over to the Palladium Theatre. It was a rainy night, but all around the theater the street was black with people, waiting for a glimpse of the King and Queen. It was as much as I could do to get to the stage door. My appearance had been timed almost to the second. I had hardly a chance to powder my nose before I heard Jack Hylton introduce me and then my music being played. With hardly time to realize that this was the event of a lifetime, I went out on the stage.

You might think a command performance would be very stiff and ceremonious. There wasn't anything stiff about the welcome the house gave me that night. From all over that huge, crowded theater came applause and voices calling, "Hello, Soph!" "Welcome home, Soph, old thing!" "Glad to see you back."

That damn near did me in. I couldn't open my mouth. I stood there, my hands and my knees trembling, my legs ready to cave in. I bowed and bowed, and kept shutting my eyes to keep the tears back. It wasn't the King and Queen in the flag-decorated royal box, it wasn't that enormous audience —all in evening dress—it wasn't the stage entrances packed with all the other performers, all smiling, applauding, and cheering, it was the idea that these people loved me and wanted me and weren't too high-hat to let me know it.

The house quieted, and I sang the two songs which had been selected by the royal chamberlain—"Louisville Lady" and "Some of These Days." Maybe I ought to explain for American readers that the royal chamberlain selects the acts for a command performance for Their Majesties. He passes on all the material which will be used and, with the manager of the theater, is responsible for arranging the bill. It is usual to have one command performance made up of all British acts from the popular shows and variety houses in London once every year during the court season. The proceeds go to a home for aged actors and actresses at Bernsworth, near London.

Both songs had great arrangements, and I was at the top of my form. I had selected a lovely white lace ensemble with coral and diamond jewelry. My bracelet had a dozen coral balls dangling from it, and in my nervousness I kept fumbling with it until one by one they dropped off. By the time the first song was over, I was stepping on the balls. I had followed the Four Mills Brothers, American colored entertainers who used a microphone. The boys were the first colored act to appear at a command performance, and they introduced the microphone to the London stage. The mike was left standing on the stage, so when I kept slipping on the coral balls, I grabbed the mike and hung on for dear life. It made a funny piece of business, and the audience laughed. After my second song I left the stage, but the house called me back. I bowed and bowed. I knew I couldn't sing an encore—only the two songs which the chamberlain had selected. I looked up at the royal box. King George was smiling broadly. Queen Mary, looking so regal in a silk coat of peacock blue embroidered with Chinese dragons, smiled at me encouragingly. With them were the Princess Alice, Countess of Athlone, and the Earl of Athlone. I thought to myself, I will curtsy to them. I know how to do it. They and the audience will be pleased if I do. I took a graceful pose, started to put my right foot back, and go down. I was all right for a second, then my heel got caught in the lace. I straightened up, ready to start again. This time I was just about to get down when I felt my knees begin to wobble. "Better not try it," I said to myself. "If you miss, Sophie, you'll wind up sitting flat on your fanny. And what then?" So I straightened up, gave Their Majesties a good American salute, and left the stage, while the royalties and the audience howled with laughter.

After being worked up to such a pitch of excitement, it was a good thing for me that I had to go on to my opening at the Café de Paris. Otherwise, I would have exploded. As it was, it took me nearly an hour to get from the Palladium to the Café—a five-minute taxi ride at other times. But the command performance had brought out the crowds and the autograph seekers.

The Derby was something to remember that year. The Cohen girls and I placed our bet on some nag and we were sure we had a winner. The night before the race the Rajah of Rajpippla invited me to his house at Windsor where he was giving a big party in honor of his horse Windsor Lad, who was running in the Derby.

"Did you bet on my horse, Sophie?" he asked me.

"No. I've made my bet already."

"But you must bet on Windsor Lad. He can't miss. Here, bet twenty pounds on him, with my compliments."

I took the rajah's money and hurried to the phone and called the book-maker. The price on Windsor Lad was down from 15 to 7-to-1. "Okay," I told the bookie. "I'll put a hundred pounds on Windsor Lad."

I'd been betting on horses for years, but I never made such a big bet in my life. The way I figured it, if the rajah can give me twenty pounds, he must be damn sure his horse is going to win.

We all drove out to the Derby the next day. I didn't dare tell the Cohen girls I had a hundred pounds on Windsor Lad. They would have thought I had gone potty. All I told them was that the rajah had given me twenty pounds to put on his horse. Boy! oh, boy! did I ruin my pipes shouting for two nags! I remember Lady Oxford (Margot Asquith) stood beside me during the race and seemed rather bored by the whole proceeding. When Windsor Lad romped in, I damn near had heart failure. Seven hundred pounds, thirty-five hundred dollars, wasn't a bad take.

It was during that engagement in London that I met the great artist, Elisabeth Bergner, who was playing there in *Escape Me Never*. I went to see the Wednesday matinee and was so stirred by her performance that I sent a note back to her dressing room: "May I come back and meet you?" Back came the usher with the message: "Miss Bergner will see you after the next act."

Backstage, a nervous mite of a girl, who looked only about fifteen years old, came toward me. "Are you Sophie Tucker?"

"Yes, that's me."

"But I pictured you so differently. From your 'Yiddisha Mama' record I had a different idea of you. I carry that record with me wherever I go. There isn't one of us in Germany who hasn't this record of yours."

That girl, so gifted, was then a refugee. She had been ordered out of Germany and everything she owned had been confiscated. Even though she was adored in London, and was the sensation of show business there, she grieved for her homeland and suffered from being an exile. When she came to America, to play *Escape Me Never,* I was on tour. When I got back to New York, a month or so after the play opened, I wired her that I was coming to see the show. She stationed her manager to watch for me and bring me back to her dressing room, where I found two great artists, Katharine Cornell and Marlene Dietrich, paying her tribute.

Playing in Glasgow, I was told that Helen Keller was living in Strathpeffer with her teacher, Mrs. Macy. I got busy with the press to help me locate them, and wired them both to come to Glasgow to spend the day with me. We had so many memories to talk and laugh over from the days when we both played the Palace Theatre and I used to make Helen up for her act. They came to my matinee that afternoon. How the audience cheered when I introduced them! Helen understood every word I said by placing her hands on my lips, and I was able to repeat her replies to the audience. I remember the day before they arrived Peter Dewar, of the famous whisky-making firm, who was fishing in Scotland, rang me up. I told him about my guests, and he sent me a thirty-pound salmon for lunch. We fed the hotel help and everybody at the theater.

After playing the provinces I got back to London and planned to take a rest and a brief trip to the continent before sailing for home in time for the High Holidays with my family. Dr. DeKoos, who directed concerts in Holland, came to see me and asked me to take on a week-end engagement at Scheveningen, the fashionable summer resort near The Hague.

I laughed and shook my head. "The Dutch people would never under-stand me!" Then, when he kept on urging me, I said quickly I would go for a thousand dollars. I made the price stiff so he wouldn't play me, but he agreed to it without a murmur. I signed up for a Saturday-afternoon concert at the Kursaal and a supper show in the café in the same building. I was flattered that Dr. DeKoos would engage a roughneck like me for one of his concerts. He had booked Caruso, Alda, Jeritza, and other operatic stars.

What nearly floored me when I got to Scheveningen were the meals, especially breakfast, where you were offered a basket of twelve different kinds of bread, several kinds of jelly and jam, and an assortment of cheeses that I've never seen in any restaurant anywhere else in the world. And I've been around some. Luncheon began with seventy different hors d'oeuvres followed by chicken, beef, potatoes, vegetables, more cheeses, fruits, and nuts. Only the Dutch can put away meals like that. I used to think I was good when it came to eating, but they had me stopped. It's a perpetual wonder to me how those people are surviving on Hitler's war rations.

By Saturday afternoon we were all ready for the concert. There was a very fine Dutch band to play selections and solos, to be followed by Ted and me. The program was arranged as follows: orchestra selections of three numbers, then Tucker and Shapiro, seven songs. Intermission. Orchestra, three selections, then Tucker and Shapiro, seven more songs. About a two-hour show. I was in grand voice, as I had rested nearly a week, and I was happy about my gown, a lovely white satin fringed dress with which I wore diamond and ruby jewelry. But, just the same, I was nervous, because I was positive no one would understand a word I said. I remembered my experience in Paris, and I didn't count on being a success with a continental audience anywhere.

When my music was played, I went on and was given an almost deafening reception. It was a rainy afternoon—a real downpour—so the house was half empty. But everyone in the hall was standing up and applauding. I was flabbergasted. I turned to Teddy. "What's it all about? Are they kidding me?" He shrugged his shoulders. Neither of us could understand it. Well, I thought, there's something screwy here.

Finally, all were seated. I thanked them for their reception and started my first song. To my amazement, those Dutch people missed nothing. They laughed at every gag, every catch line. They caught onto everything I did. After the seventh song there was such a demonstration of enthusiasm that I couldn't believe my ears.

During the intermission I changed to a lovely light blue crepe, with a full skirt and a sheer bodice studded with blue stones. With this I wore diamonds and sapphires. Again an ovation when I went on, and applause after every song. By the end of the program I was tired, and gave the cue to Teddy and the orchestra for the last number. When I finished, bowed, and left the stage, a riot broke loose. "No! No! Don't leave! You haven't sung 'Yiddisha Mama.'" I had to go back and give it to them. Then for half an hour I held a reception on the stage and everyone in the audience came up and shook hands and told me—in *English*—how much they had enjoyed the concert. Dr. DeKoos kissed me on both cheeks; he was so thrilled over the success of the concert.

"Wait a minute," I said to him. "There's something I can't get through my head. Outside of a very few people who may have seen me in London, and those who know my phonograph records, nobody in Holland knows who I am or what I can do. How, then, could I rate an ovation of seven minutes?"

"Dear Miss Tucker, if you could understand Dutch, you would have heard the words the entire audience let out in one gasp at your entrance: 'My God! she's a white woman!'" It seems the Dutch thought from my phonograph records and my syncopation and deep voice that I was a colored star. The Dutch shopkeepers advertised my records: "By the American Negro Singer —Sophie Tucker."

I had quite a different experience singing in the café that evening. It was a large room, seating about five hundred, and everyone there was beautifully dressed. The women were jeweled and wore long evening gloves— something we had discarded quite a few years earlier. At the afternoon concert I had sung melodic and rhythm songs; for the café I selected hot ones. The first songs went over fairly well and brought laughs. The men applauded lightly. The women, however, just patted their hands quietly. Gosh, I thought, they're a stiff lot tonight! This is going to be tough. What a difference from the afternoon audience!

A few more songs. They laughed a little heartier; the ladies tapped a little harder. But that was about all. I turned to Teddy.

"This is the last one. This bunch is too cold for me. I'm a flop."

I finished and left the stage. I had my wrap on and was ready to leave the café when Dr. DeKoos came flying back.

"Why, Miss Tucker, you can't leave! The people are sitting there waiting for more!"

"Waiting for what?" I asked. "They don't applaud."

"Oh," he said, "I told you this afternoon that you would find the evening audience different. These people are the '400' of Holland, and it is not customary among them for ladies to applaud. Only the men do the clapping. But they do like you."

"Okay, Doc, I'll take care of them."

Out on the stage I went. I looked around at the bunch. "I understand from Dr. DeKoos that you like me. Is that so?" Applause and titters. "Well," I went on, "in my country, if we like an artist, we let her know it. I've got plenty more songs, and I can stay out here for hours, but you can't sit there and just tap your fingers and keep me guessing. Now, then, if you want to have some fun, and if you really like me, then let me hear the applause and we will all have a swell time!"

I nodded to Teddy to get to the piano, and we went to work on that bunch of Dutchmen. We made the gals peel off their gloves, and by the time I finished with them, they were as free and easy an audience as any I'd sung to on Broadway.

CHAPTER 26: *A Good Schnuck*

WHEN WE GOT BACK to London I found a message from the owner of the Hotel Martinez in Cannes, asking me to come there to sing at their annual gala for the war veterans. They already had a bill of all the leading French stars, he said, but they wanted to add me for an American touch. It would be a touch, all right, I decided as I wired him my acceptance. I'd do my damnedest to roll up a tidy sum for the veterans.

All this meant swell publicity for me, especially as I was to be the guest of the French Legion, and Jack Oliphant made the most of it. He had worked up some good stunts which kept my name in the British papers; the best of them a story about me rescuing a child from being run over in the street. That kind of publicity sounds silly to people outside the profession, and that kind of publicity wasn't necessary in the days before the motion-picture stars got all the headlines and the sensational write-ups. Vaudeville performers used to be able to stand on their own performances, but in late years we have had to follow the lead of Hollywood when it comes to publicity. There's just one thing a performer can't afford: to let the public forget about her. You're on the shelf if the public thinks you are.

So it was the Blue Train to Cannes, and a grand welcome for me on the station platform. Those Frenchmen certainly did it up brown. I felt like a king's mistress in the magnificent suite they gave me at the Hotel Martinez! Those were the big days on the Riviera, when Cannes was full of free spenders having fun before the big storm broke over their heads. The house for the gala was sold out; nearly ten thousand dollars was raised that evening I was set to close the bill on which I was the only American performer; a grand show, headed by Mistinguette, Mayol (the George Robey of France), Gaby Morley (the French Gertrude Lawrence), and about ten other stars, whose names were too difficult for me to catch.

Before the show two important jewelers from Paris, with shops in Cannes, came to see me. They asked me to wear their jewels to give a plug to their business. I had some very nice pieces of my own, but they looked like dime-store stuff beside the sapphires and diamonds Arnold Ostertag offered me to wear with my blue gown. I told the other jeweler, Jack Van Cleff, that I would display his emeralds and diamonds the next night if any affair came up.

The show was very long, and I only wished I could have understood all those fine French actors. I tell you it meant a lot to me after an hour-and-a-half show to be introduced to a marvelous reception. The audience was a very cosmopolitan one, with a lot of Americans. After the show I was called on to make a speech, which gave me a chance to plug Ostertag's diamonds, of which I was sporting about fifty thousand dollars worth. So I thanked him publicly for entrusting this beautiful jewelry to my keeping; and then I told the crowd if they would all go to the Plantation Café I would be there and would entertain them until morning. It was 9 A.M. when I tumbled into bed next day, after a breakfast of onion soup. Some night's work! I had my chance the next night to do something for Jack Van Cleff, because the director of the Casino asked me to give a gala night there. I said as long as it wasn't for charity they would have to pay me one thousand dollars. The price was right, and I strutted my stuff in a white satin gown with Van Cleff's emeralds and diamonds.

I loved the Riviera. The sky and the sea were so blue; the white villas looked so clean in the sunshine, the big pines so stunningly dark. The flower beds jammed with flowers of all colors were like jewels. Everybody was out for a good time and, as far as I could make out, the sky was the limit. I kept running into people I'd met in London, and Americans from all over the U. S. A. It was certainly old-home week for Sophie Tucker. I would have liked to have stayed on for several weeks, just to amuse myself, but there was a cable from the Morris office in New York, notifying me that they had booked me into the Chez Paree in Chicago for six weeks and then back to the Hollywood Restaurant on Broadway. I had to go home and back to work.

It was swell coming home to work and the knowledge that I was wanted by my own people. No matter how long you are in show business there is never anything boring about that. But this home-coming had something extra about it that will always make it stand out in my memory. This was the Beefsteak Welcome Dinner which the American Federation of Actors gave me shortly after my arrival in New York in the first week of November. About fifteen hundred of our profession and their friends came to the dinner which was held in Mecca Temple.

On the dais with me were Eddie Cantor, then president of the A.F.A., Ralph Whitehead, the executive secretary, Bugs Baer, "Uncle Dan" Frohman (who scared us all by having a heart attack as soon as he finished his speech, but in a quarter of an hour he was all right again and back in his seat and the fun went on), Joe Laurie, Jr., Harry B. Warner, Rabbi Tintner, Jack Benny, Judge Aaron J. Levy, C. F. Zittel ("Zit"), Walter Huston, William Morris, Jr., Abe Lastfogel, Elias Sugarman, George Burns (of Burns and Allen), Joe Penner, Harry Hirschfield, and William Wineberger.

Bugs Baer wrote an introduction for the menu which had a photograph of me:

BAER FACTS

The picture shows Miss Tucker as she looked in 1914 and from then on. Sophie hasn't changed a bit, except husbands. The last of the Red-hot Mamas started her singing career telling her lawyer about her ice-cold papas.

She just got back from England, where she gave a command performance before the King at Windsor Castle, which is now four a day.

The Queen was there, of course. Sophie never broke up a home in her life.

The King was delighted. He said, "That was the first voice I ever heard with a stucco finish."

He didn't know that Sophie had been singing that way for thirty years and hits a ripe pumpkin with a bed slat to get the key.

In this panoramic view, Sophie is shown in the role of an innocent little country girl in Rube Bernstein's Bathing Beauties.

That's five kings in Sophie's mitt. They had new deals in those days too. Sophie played "La Belle Madame" in Rube's show which had a triumphant tour of three years on Staten Island on the old Hoss-and-buggy Circuit. In those days, Sophie was very proud of her waistline, which can plainly be seen in the picture. She modeled for the Murray Hill Tent and Awning Studios.

Sophie tells us that she sat up all night and made that costume herself. No matter what she does, we always like to meet a little girl who taught herself. We went all the way down the river in a tug to meet Sophie on this trip, but the captain of the liner decided it would be better to unload Sophie right on the wharf.

This little affair is a home-coming party to Sophie, a great gal and a brilliant performer. We could have held it in Chicago, Los Angeles, Paris, London, or a thousand other towns. For, when you get as good as Sophie, no matter what town you are in, it is "Home."

I was all set with an after-dinner speech which Jack Yellen wrote for me and which I had carefully rehearsed, but when the time came to stand up and deliver it, I was so fussed I couldn't remember a word. I had to fumble for the lead sheets and try to read it, and I made a hell of a job of that, too, between trying to manage them and the stylish long-handled tortoise-shell lorgnette that Edwina Mountbatten—who always uses a lorgnette—had given me for a bon voyage present when I left England and I wanted to show off.

"Mr. Toastmaster, Ladies and Gentlemen, Friends—my very, very dear friends. There probably is some way of expressing what I . . . what I feel . . . that is, what I . . .

"Oh, hell! I should have broken this speech in at Jamaica. It's no use.

"I knew this would happen, so help me! I haven't been so nervous since my first bridal night. I'll have to read it. If I can read. (Business of putting up lorgnette.) How do you like that? Tucker with a lorgnette. *Derlebt!*

"A duke gave me this in London. It didn't do him a damn bit of good either. . . .

"But really, seriously, I wish I knew how to tell you how happy you've made me. You know, you must know that I appreciate this with all my heart and soul. But I'm just no good at this sort of thing. Give me a piano and some dirty catch lines and I'm all right. But this! Well, really, it's too much.

"I can only tell you that this is the biggest moment of my life. *And I've had some moments!* I swear to you that not even the command performance before the King and Queen *meant as much to me as tonight does!*

"To have you make all this fuss over me, receive me at the boat and come here tonight with all these people who really are somebodies, and pay me all this tribute, honestly I don't feel that I rate it.

"There is a story somewhere in the Talmud about two rabbis who were walking through the market place in Jerusalem, and one said to the other: 'Rabbi, show me in this crowd someone who you think is destined for heaven; who is sure of a reward in the world to come.' The rabbi looked around the crowd of merchants, learned men, pious men, and pointed to two actors, comedians. 'These two,' he said. 'Those actors are destined for happiness in the world to come.'

"The explanation for the rabbi's statement is that it was because the actors lived to make others happy. And we do. After all, that's the only real excuse for living.

"And tonight you've made me happy—happier than I ever thought I could be. I hope Rabbi Tintner will forgive me for muscling in on his territory. Just for that, if he wants to, he can get up and sing 'Some of These Days.' "

Yes, it's perfectly true. The approval and the affection of the members of your own profession are a greater reward and more soul-satisfying than just popularity with the public and big money. There are some performers who go over big with the public and are in the big-money brackets, but who have never stood well with their own profession. I've always been sorry for them. And I mean *sorry*—not envious. Because, when it's about 5 or 6 A.M. and the crowds have melted away and you're left alone to wipe off the make-up and take off your corsets and go to bed—and to bed *alone*—there's a lot of comfort in knowing that the men and women who work in show business have a respect for you and are fond of you. It takes away some of the lonesome feeling that overwhelms every woman who hasn't got a husband and kids around her, more times than she likes to admit. Money in the bank and plenty of bookings ahead don't cure that kind of heartache. But knowing, as you stretch your tired body out between the sheets with a sigh of relief, that you've done a good job, and the members of your own profession think you have, and say: "Oh, Sophie's a good *schnuck!*" goes a hell of a long way.

The American Federation of Actors had been organized by Ralph Whitehead in 1932, starting with a handful of vaudevillians and café entertainers. Eddie Cantor was president. Up to the time it was formed, vaudeville performers were still looked down on by other members of the profession in pretty much the way that all actors used to be thought of by the so-called respectable people not connected with the stage. A lot of us felt it was high time we had some kind of union which would assure vaudeville performers of some security and respect. The A.F.A. was the first concerted move made by actors to lift the status of the vaudeville performer and, if only for that reason, it deserved the support and encouragement of everyone in the profession. There was another reason why some such organization to protect the interests of entertainers was needed just at that time. Like every performer in the big cafés, I noticed an increasing racket in the number of benefits, political rallies, et cetera, that entertainers were expected to appear at for nothing. For example, when I opened at the Hollywood Restaurant in New York, that winter of 1934–35, I played my first week to capacity business. The second week I averaged ten different affairs the manager expected me to play besides the few benefits I was personally interested in. That week business at the Hollywood Restaurant fell off. The third week there were again eight to ten outside engagements I had to keep—no pay in them for me, of course—and business at the Hollywood fell off still more. On the fourth week still demands to appear at various affairs for nothing and no business at the restaurant. I had to take a cut in salary in order to keep working and give the place a break.

I called up Ralph Whitehead, executive secretary of the A.F.A., and told him he must find a way to put a stop to this racket. Theatre Authority, Inc., was the result of Whitehead's work in this direction, and for a while did a good job. The benefits were curtailed and our actors' charitable organizations profited by them as Theatre Authority, Inc., demanded 10 per cent to 15 per cent of the take, to be used for the actors' charities. Later, however, those running Theatre Authority, Inc., fell down on the job and the benefit racket boomed again.

During that season I kept plugging away at cafés. I played the House of Morgan Club in New York City. On the same bill with me were Edgar Bergen and Charlie McCarthy. Of course this was before they went on the air and became world famous. After I saw Bergen's act, I knew it was a wow, and I made up my mind, right then and there, if ever I played London again, I would see to it that Bergen and Charlie went with me. I knew they would be a sensation in England.

That season everybody in show business was out to get a radio contract. Radio had come to the fore just the way the picture business had done during the Twenties. Radio was where big money was being made and big names. Everybody said, "Get on the air and you're made!" I made several attempts, but I had no luck landing a radio contract. It looked as if I was going to have to keep on playing the cafés indefinitely. Paula Gould, who was handling my publicity, and I went into a huddle. "Look," I said to her, "it's going to be tough this winter. You've got to think up some stunts to keep Sophie Tucker's name in the papers." Paula suggested that I try to get some dates at a café in Hollywood. She reminded me that I might land a picture contract that way. The next day I called Abe Lastfogel and asked him what café I could play in Hollywood.

"There's only one. The Trocadero. But they don't pay your prices."

"Try them, anyway," I said. "See what you can get me. I've got a hunch it may lead to something."

My hunches have generally been one hundred per cent good. The Boss used to trust them, and Abe had caught the habit. But while they generally worked out all right in the end, most of them cost me a pretty penny on the side. This one ran true to form. The best Abe could get for me for a week at the Trocadero was one thousand dollars. When I paid the commission to the office, 10 per cent to Jack Yellen, Ted's salary, three railroad fares to Hollywood and back—not to mention hotel bills at a swank hotel out there and some new gowns to impress the movie moguls—I was going to be well in the red. Just the same, I felt the trip was worth it. There comes a time when you've got to spend money—yeah! and a lot of it—to make money. I could go on playing at the cafés and pile up profits, but show business was changing and I knew I ought to change with it. If I could get into pictures or on the air, I would be opening up new business for myself, which is what an entertainer has to do. And so I went to Hollywood.

Billy Wilkerson, the owner of the Hollywood *Reporter,* owned and ran the Trocadero. I'll hand this to him: he put over the greatest opening night for me I've ever seen anywhere. Phil Olman and his band were playing there. The night I opened, the Trocadero was packed. Every picture star and every important executive in the movie industry was there. I said to myself: "This is your chance, Sophie! If you don't put it over tonight, it is your own fault and nobody else is to blame."

I sang myself hoarse, and when the parade of flowers started and Irving Berlin and Fanny Brice came out on the floor to congratulate and kiss me, it was all I could do to make my little speech. I didn't mince matters. I told the crowd that the reason I came out to the Troc on a sacrificing salary, at big expense, was because I hoped I could find a place in the movies.

Well, business was so good the Trocadero kept me over a second week. Billy Wilkerson did everything he could to sell me to a studio, and on the day after my opening L. B. Mayer sent for me to come out to the MGM Studios to see him. I never heard a man rave as he did about my work. He said he was sure he could find a place for me in pictures. And I left feeling I was made. It had been worth while playing my hunch and Paula Gould's. I told L. B. Mayer I would stay around Hollywood for a while to give him time to get together with his producer, directors, and writers. There was no doubt in my mind I would soon be launched in the movies.

While I waited for that to happen, I ran to every party that every movie executive gave, hoping to get into their good graces. My friends gave parties for me to meet important people. I gave a few parties myself. Benefits piled up. I turned nothing down. I hung around three weeks, four weeks, five weeks—still no telephone call from MGM. At the end of six weeks I called the Morris office in Hollywood to book me a few theater dates. I couldn't sit around for months, doing nothing but wait. I would go nuts. The office arranged dates in San Francisco and Los Angeles and I played them. Then I came back and notified Mr. Mayer I was on hand. Did he have anything for me? The answer came back: "Sorry. Not right now." I hung around for another few weeks while my hopes got fainter and fainter. Then I said to myself: "To hell with pictures, Sophie. Forget them!" I packed up and caught the first train out of Hollywood for New York.

So, it was back to the cafés for Sophie! That winter I played the Hollywood Country Club in Florida for eight weeks and had the excitement of seeing my namesake, Emil Schwartzhaupt's filly, Sophie Tucker, run at Hialeah. She won the purse that afternoon and paid twenty-two dollars and fifty cents for two dollars. I told myself this was a good omen.

All the time I was looking around for new ideas. The more I looked over the entertainment field, the more clearly I saw that the big-name bands were making the biggest hits of anything in show business. They were getting the work in the leading hotels all over the country. I decided to get in on this field. After all, I'd had my own band with my Five Kings of Syncopation. When I told Abe Lastfogel about my idea, he was against it, but I was stubborn. We argued it out, and then I left the Morris office, after having been with them for nearly twenty-six years.

The Music Corporation of America was the leading booking office for bands. I got in touch with them, and in April went out to Chicago and rehearsed for three weeks with the band the M.C.A. organized for me—fifteen boys, including Ted Shapiro, and a girl singer, Dale Sherman. We played dates in the Midwest—Kansas City, Chicago, Cleveland, Detroit—but the stunt wasn't a success. I lost money every week. No sponsor offered me a radio contract. The M.C.A. were not successful in booking the act into the hotels my heart was set on. I learned that Abe Lastfogel was a lot smarter than I was.

After the month of August at the Piping Rock Café in Saratoga, I knew the band act wasn't going to last very long. The M.C.A. at this time was setting up an office in London and I booked through them at Grosvenor House for six weeks, to open the last of September, with an option of four more weeks, and to double in the theaters. M.C.A. also handled Edgar Bergen, and I got them to book Edgar with me. It was the first time I ever played London away from my own office and from Harry Foster, who had always looked after my bookings in England.

Going over, aboard the S.S. *Normandie,* I had my first transatlantic telephone call. The B.B.C. wanted me to do a radio program and offered forty pounds. I cabled back my price was two hundred and fifty pounds, whereupon the *Daily Mail* telephoned me to ask why I refused the B.B.C. offer. I told them I didn't need two hundred dollars that bad. Later on the B.B.C. raised the ante to one hundred pounds for a program, and I gave it to a charity.

My opening night at the Grosvenor House made me feel good all over. There were a lot of familiar faces in the room and everybody—the fashionable people and the professionals—treated me as though I had come home to my own. That season the London County Council found fault with one of my songs—"I Picked a Pansy in the Garden of Love"—and I had to eliminate it from my program. The song "My People" was my big hit that season in the music halls.

London was different that fall of 1936. There was an uneasiness in the air. Everybody knew and everybody whispered about Mrs. Simpson and her divorce, even though the newspapers didn't print a word of the news that was on everyone's tongue. As the fall drew on toward winter, the anxiety around Buckingham Palace deepened. People were taking sides and nobody knew just what the King was going to do or what Baldwin or the Archbishop of Canterbury had up their sleeves. That was the first season that I played in London that I didn't entertain some members of the royal family. The court was still in mourning for King George V.

The Lord Mayor of London wrote me and asked if I could do something to raise money for the King George V Memorial Fund. This was a great honor, of course, and I knew it would be a big job, but I decided to tackle it. I called in my accountant, Jack Reubens, for advice and help. He was very enthusiastic about the idea, and soon he lined up a list of important personages as patrons.

It was arranged to give an all-American show at midnight on December 10 at the Coliseum Theatre. Every American stage and screen star then in England would be asked to take part. The British stars, headed by Leslie Henson, were to sell programs and act as ushers. The tickets were priced from three guineas (fifteen dollars) up to eight guineas (forty dollars).

After Jack Reubens had the committee signed up and all arrangements made for the theater, I left town to play a few weeks in the provinces. While in Manchester I received a cable from Abe Lastfogel—Abe had forgiven me for my obstinacy about the band. After all, I had been honest with him, telling him I knew I had made a mistake and the figures proved it. Abe sent word that Hollywood had tumbled to my sex appeal. MGM wanted me! At last! Abe had signed me with their studio to do *Broadway Melody of 1937* with Eleanor Powell and Robert Taylor.

That cable was one of the thrills of my life. To think that L. B. Mayer had kept his word and come through with a movie contract! Well, maybe my hunch about playing the Trocadero in Hollywood hadn't been wrong. And maybe my feeling that L. B. wasn't conning me when he complimented me on my work wasn't wrong either. When you go along for a good many years as I have, you get to sense a right guy from a wrong guy. You get so you can size up people for what they are. You know the handshake of a regular feller, and you don't fall for the slimy-fish handshake. You're on to the quiet guys and the talkative ones who say a lot and yet say nothing at all. I had trusted L. B., only I didn't have the patience to sit on my fanny in Hollywood and wait for him to come across.

I got busy with cables to Jack Oliphant in London and Paula Gould in New York to step on the publicity. I canceled further dates in England, as I had to report in Hollywood on January 2, 1937. Back in London, from the provinces and a week of one-night stands in Holland, where the audiences called for "Some of These Days" and "My Yiddisha Mama," and seemingly couldn't get enough of either or both of them, I rolled up my sleeves and started in to work on our all-American show. Ann Harding and I had a date to meet the Lord Mayor to discuss and make the final arrangements. All the American performers were notified and called to rehearsal. Some of them I went to see personally. Only two American performers turned me down. When I called on Lupe Velez, who lived in Mayfair, she refused to see me. ZaSu Pitts, who was staying at the Hotel Savoy, sent down word she couldn't see me either. After these two slaps in the face I felt a little timid about facing the next star on my list—Marlene Dietrich. When I got to her apartment I asked the boy at the desk to please call and ask Miss Dietrich whether she would see Miss Sophie Tucker, who was down in the lobby. Such a pleasant voice came over the phone: "Send her up immediately."

And there, when I got out of the lift at her floor, was Marlene herself to welcome me. She took my arm, insisted on my taking off my hat and coat, and seated me in a big chair by the open fire. With one kick of her world-famous legs she pushed a footstool under my tired dogs. Tea was brought in and Marlene waited on me, insisting that I have my hot drink first and then she would talk about the show.

Marlene liked the idea of the show and agreed to help. While I was there, Doug Fairbanks, Jr., came in and I enlisted his help too. At rehearsals they were real troupers, Marlene especially. She would be there on time, willing to sit in the cold theater for hours, waiting her turn, eating a sandwich, drinking coffee from a paper cup. At that time Marlene was not an American citizen. The rehearsals were a lot of work, but a lot of fun too. The laughs we had watching Edward G. Robinson, Ben Lyon, Monte Banks, Allen Hale, and Jack Whiting rehearse their sketch! The three Diamond Brothers, Laura La Plante, June Clyde, and I did a burlesque of the old Florodora Sextette. We had three American bands, led by Roy Fox, Jack Harris, and Harold Gibbons. As we lined up the acts, it looked as if London had never seen such a show.

Meanwhile, as the night of the show drew nearer, the clouds over London darkened. The British papers were very circumspect, but the news was pretty general property that King Edward VIII was considering abdicating. One American gal had upset the traditions of British royalty. There was a question as to how popular Americans were going to be in England and whether an all-American show, under the circumstances, was a good idea.

On Wednesday, December 10, the B.B.C. announced to listeners to keep tuned in, as at any minute the news would be broadcast whether His Majesty would go on the air to verify or refute the rumors of his abdication.

I was playing that night at the Chiswick Theatre. From there I went by taxi to the Metropolitan for my last show. I left the taxi and was entering the stage door when I was struck by the fact that the street and the alley were deserted. There was no usual crowd hanging around to say hello or to ask for autographs. Suddenly I became aware that all of London was still. It was like a clock that had run down. It scared me, and I hurried into the theater. The show was on and the house was packed. But everybody was under a strain. In the dim corners backstage members of the stage crew gathered, whispering. The acts waiting to go on stood quiet in the wings. One of the women was crying. That was how I knew the King had abdicated.

I had my own anxious moment as I waited my turn to go on. I was the only American on the bill. How would the audience receive me? How would they feel tonight about Americans? My heart was in my throat as I went out onto the stage. I heard Teddy play the introduction—twice, then a third time—and it seemed as if I couldn't find my voice. I guess the audience sensed my feelings. Anyway, a voice called from the gallery: "Carry on, Soph, old girl! Carry on!" The whole house picked it up. As I swung into my opening number, I could feel that great British public carrying on like the great people they are.

My act over at the Metropolitan, I changed my costume and made a dash for the Coliseum—for the big midnight show. The theater was sold out. We made twenty thousand dollars that night for the Memorial Fund. Everybody, outside of the royal family, showed up. At the Coliseum, the atmosphere backstage was tense. Maybe it was that which made our American performers outdo themselves. It seemed as if they were determined to give the best that they had to give, as if to make up a little for what one American had done.

At the final curtain call, when everyone was on the stage, Michael Bartlett stepped down in front to sing "Auld Lang Syne." He followed this with "The Star-Spangled Banner." I don't suppose our national anthem was ever sung to an audience under such peculiar circumstances, but the British took it. As the last note died away Michael turned to me:

"Darling," he said, "shall I sing 'God Save the King' now?"

(Backstage there had been a lot of discussion whether it would be proper to sing "God Save the King" that night when England's king had just announced his abdication. I had asked some of the British folks what we should do. Some said we should sing it and some said no. I had meant to go out front and ask the Lord Mayor, but there had been so much to do backstage I didn't get to it, and here was Michael Bartlett asking me if he should sing it. It was up to Sophie Tucker to decide.)

The orchestra leader's eyes were fixed on me for the signal.

"Go ahead, Michael," I said. "Go ahead, leader."

To that waiting silence that filled the theater Michael's voice struck up firmly: "God Save Our Gracious King!"

Thousands of voices took it up—voices that choked, that broke down in the middle of the lines, and started off key. In the wings, where the stage crew crowded, they were singing, and men and women were crying. The tears started to trickle down my make-up.

The curtain was held, and the Lord Mayor came down to the stage from his box to receive the check for four thousand pounds which Ann Harding presented to him on behalf of American performers in London.

CHAPTER 27: *I Crash Hollywood*

I GOT EVERY DROP of satisfaction out of that trip to Hollywood, with an MGM contract in my pocket and their publicity staff on the job to make news out of my arrival there. Maybe if I hadn't gone through some heartaches over getting into pictures this contract wouldn't have meant so much to me. And then, too, I remembered not only the times I wanted to crash Hollywood and hadn't, but the time back in 1929—which I have saved till now to tell about—when I made my first picture, *Honky Tonk,* for Warner Brothers.

That contract, too, was offered me during a successful run in London. I had gone out to the Coast with trunks full of new Paris clothes and the feeling I was riding on air. The welcome the Warner Brothers gave me at the station, with flowers and a crowd of friends and a brass band, didn't deflate me. I was still elated after my first day in Hollywood when I climbed into bed, along toward morning, got myself comfortable, and started to read the script of *Honky Tonk.* I read it through from cover to cover, and my jaw dropped down on my chest. I couldn't see Sophie Tucker anywhere in the picture. I went over the script a second time, fighting my way through the flowery language. Could anybody picture me saying, "I shall be waiting, my dear, overlooking exquisite gardens from the french windows, watching the golden horizon"? *Derlebt!* I reached out an arm and grabbed the phone.

"Hurry, operator, and get Mr. William Morris in New York. And get him quick!"

When he answered, I began to jabber. "Listen, Boss, I've just finished reading the script, and it is godawful. It isn't me. I must not make this picture! Every bit of success I've built up will be killed if I do!"

"But, darling, you have a contract!"

"Contract or no contract! I can't do it!"

"You can't walk out on it," came the Boss's order. "Wait till you see the Warner Brothers. Have a talk with them. I'm sure they will change it and everything will turn out all right."

I had to be content with that. The next day was Sunday. I had an appointment at the studio Tuesday morning. In the meantime, I was to open at the Los Angeles Orpheum Theatre. The Boss had booked California dates for me before starting on the picture. He was shrewd enough to believe this would help to make the picture a success. It would give the Warner Brothers' staff a chance to see me do my act, and this was bound to be of value when we came to shoot the picture. All that Sunday I kept thinking I must put over a big hit at my two shows on Monday. Everybody from the studio must see the greatest act in my career, then they would understand why the script they handed me would have to go into the junk heap and a new one, that featured the real Sophie Tucker, be substituted for it.

We had a great show at the Orpheum that week, and I did my damnedest. I felt sure the studio gang would all be out in front. I'd show them what I could do. Harry Singer, the manager of the Orpheum, came back to my dressing room.

"Well, Sophie, this is your last date in vaudeville. I sure hate to see you leave us."

I didn't say it, but what I thought was: last day, hell! After the script I read Saturday night I'll be back in six weeks!

The press went to town for me.

". . . That tiny ton of personality plus—speaking of Sophie Tucker—is back in town. That's why the Orpheum was completely sold out early last evening—an unheard-of event since the new house opened. Seventeen baskets of flowers went over the footlights. Probably no performer since Bernhardt has received such an ovation over the Orpheum footlights. . . ." "The indefatigable, incomparable Sophie Tucker is back again. And how! After knocking them dead over in Europe, she panicked a packed house yesterday. . . ." "Sophie introduced herself as the last of the Red-hot Mamas. Say not the last, but none better! She leaves the stage this week to cool off in the talkies. . . ."

Wouldn't you have thought that would have told them something over at the studio? After reading the notices Tuesday morning, I felt sure the Warner Brothers would listen to me about the script. I'd known the Warner family from way back in the early days, when I used to play Youngstown, Ohio. Mother and Dad Warner were very kind to me. Whenever I played Youngstown, I had a standing invitation for a *gefüllte-fish* supper at their home on Friday night. After stuffing ourselves, Dad Warner and I would play pinochle.

Sam was the Warner brother I knew best. When he married Lina Basquette they stopped off in Minneapolis on their honeymoon to visit me. How Sam worked to put over the Vitaphone Talkies. His death was a great loss to the picture industry. Well, I thought, while riding out to the studio, Harry and Jack would surely see the point of my argument. They're great showmen, and as businessmen they aren't going to pay Sophie Tucker's price and not get Sophie Tucker value out of their money.

Out at the studio everything was very grand and all the executives— Jack Warner, William Koenig, Darryl Zanuck, writer of *Honky Tonk* and producer, Graham Baker, coauthor, Lloyd Bacon, director—welcomed me enthusiastically. I started to thank them for their flowers and said I hoped they enjoyed my performance at the theater.

JACK WARNER: "Shame I missed it, Soph. I was at dinner and couldn't get away."

DARRYL ZANUCK: "Funny, I've never seen you work in my life. I tried so hard to get down, but just couldn't manage it."

GRAHAM BAKER: "I saw you work years ago. I must go down to the Orpheum to see you."

LLOYD BACON: "My God, Sophie, I haven't seen you perform since you first sang the 'Grizzly Bear' back in 1909!"

I looked at them, and I was completely speechless. After a bit, when I got my breath, and started in to argue, I found I was up against a blank wall. I could see they put me down as one of those temperamental vaudeville dames who was trying to teach the motion-picture industry how to run its own business. I went home—sick at heart and sick at my stomach. Repeated phone calls to the Boss in New York, asking him to get me out of the contract, didn't do a thing. If only there had been a clause in the contract "script subject to approval." But there wasn't. I was in for it. I did manage to get the studio to send for Jack Yellen and get him and Milton Agar to write some numbers for me that would be more my kind of thing than what was originally in the script of *Honky Tonk*.

Naturally, all this fussing and fuming didn't make me too popular with the executives at the studio. Getting up at 6 A.M. was a tough job for me, who was used to going to bed about that time. And the work was hard—harder because I was unhappy. Trained as I had been in show business, I couldn't believe a picture could be good with no rehearsals. In vaudeville we rehearse an act or a new song for weeks. Break them in. Take out bad spots. Add good ones. That was how I was used to working. In the studio I discovered a new technique: one scene taken at a time, not more than four or five lines to a person. While they were setting the scene and the cameras were being arranged for shooting, the director and actors would be off at one side studying and rehearsing their lines. When the cameraman said "Ready," the scene was shot. One man, the director, looked on, approved. And that was that! If he didn't approve, the scene might be taken over a few times. But he was the only critic to be pleased. No one else had any idea what it was like, and you didn't have a chance to improve a look or a gesture. And while this was going on and the picture was being made in pieces, the publicity department was starting its propaganda to sell the picture, featuring the great ability of the star and cast, the warm, human, dramatic story, the cleverness of the writers and the directors. When I got an earful of this, I asked myself can the studio fool the public? Can a smart publicity department make the public like something just because they are clever at selling it?

Well, the picture was shot, and so was Sophie Tucker. There was nothing to do but to lie around, waiting for the preview. I just wished I could kid myself into believing the picture was as good as Jack Warner, Zanuck, and Lloyd Bacon said it was. I kept trying to pin Lloyd down about it. (I had known his father, Frank Bacon, the great star of *Lightning,* and his mother, Jane, a grand soul.) But all I could get was a pat on the back. After the morning rushes you always got "they were great" when you came to work the next day.

The Warner Brothers gave several big parties to introduce their new picture star. The parties were very elegant, but I kept wishing they would give a party for their old friend, Sophie Tucker, instead. In all the eight weeks I went in and out of the Warner lot I never met one of their stars and never saw the inside of a star's home. I wasn't made a part of the movie colony. It bothered me a bit at first, then I realized that at that time all the silent picture stars were feeling pretty panicky. Nobody knew if he was going to be any good in talkies. There was a revolution going on in the picture business and everybody in it had the jitters.

Well, the time came for the preview. My hubby, Al Lackey, Jack Yellen, Agar, and I started for the Westlake Theatre, Los Angeles, to see it. In those days they didn't have the splurges at previews they have today—the big arc lamps, the motion-picture cameras, the loud-speakers, and a master of ceremonies to announce the stars as they drive up. When we drove up to the theater, standing on the curb were the Warner Brothers, the directors, writers, actors, and everybody from every department. There were "hellos" and good wishes, and we all trooped inside, filling the house. When the announcement of the picture was flashed on the screen, everybody applauded. Then came the names of the cast, with applause for each one; the names of the authors, applause; producers, applause; directors, applause. Applause for the assistant directors, song writers, and the cameraman. Nothing but applause before the picture got going. I wondered what the picture would get after it was finished.

I slid down into my seat. I was just a novice at the motion-picture game. I knew I knew something about show business and vaudeville, and it seemed to me the rules of that game must apply to pictures too. If they did, and I knew those rules, then this picture was sure to be a flop.

I came on the screen. Yes, I looked very nice for a big woman—no wrinkles, no bags under my eyes, lovely clothes, hair smart, feet and ankles neat, jewelry the McCoy—no paste! Personality natural in everything I did. But as scene after scene was played, I kept thinking—if only I had been properly rehearsed, if only I had had a chance to break that in, I would have played it and I would have sung the number so much better.

Well, the picture was over at last, and the house went wild with applause. Applause from the Warner Brothers' Studio crowd. To Zanuck, "Swell job." To the Warners, "A great picture." To Bacon, "Best direction yet." To me, Warner Brothers' new star, "Colossal, sensational." I looked at all of them and I said just two words: "It stinks!"

I climbed into my car and went home and phoned the Boss. "Listen carefully, Boss," I said over the wire. "I worked hard all these years to make the name of Sophie Tucker a success. Now I've got to roll up my sleeves and start over again. I've got to overcome this stinkeroo picture or I am finished in show business!"

Next day I called up Jack Warner and asked when *Honky Tonk* would be released. He thought in about two or three weeks. This just fitted in with a plan I had made. I called up Harry Singer and asked him to arrange to play me a week in San Francisco and a week in Los Angeles before I went East. I promised to have a new act ready. And I reminded him that he would get the benefit of all the picture ballyhooing.

Jack Yellen wrote a production number for me around the theme song in the picture—"I'm Doing What I'm Doing for Love." It was the biggest production number I had ever had, and I had to engage half a dozen people to help me in it. Jack also fixed up some of the other songs from the picture that were tame, making them hotter for the stage.

I opened in Los Angeles first to a smash hit; then I went to San Francisco and on to the Palace in Chicago, doing great business. It wasn't until after *Honky Tonk* was released that my headaches started. The first town I played after the picture was shown was Rochester, New York. I had always been a big box-office attraction in that city, but that week the receipts went down. In the next town it was the same, and it was like that in every place I played where *Honky Tonk* had been shown. The press panned the story and my acting—and they were right about both. They liked the singing, they liked me personally, but that didn't save the picture or make me a picture star. The only satisfaction I got out of *Honky Tonk* was betting Harry Warner five hundred dollars the picture wouldn't play over two weeks in New York. *Honky Tonk* was taken off before the two weeks' run was over, and I collected my bet. To get the taste of *Honky Tonk* out of the public's mouth, the Boss started negotiating with London for me to go back there to play in Jack Hulbert's show *Follow a Star*.

Honky Tonk was a flop in America. When I met Jack Warner in London, in 1931, he told me that *Honky Tonk* was still making money for him in England, on the continent, in Africa and Australia, on the strength of my popularity. For years I got fan letters from all over the world. My favorite came from Port au Bain, Algiers:

I saw your beautiful self in the cinema play *Honky Tonk,* and I wish to tell you that I think you are the most beautiful lady I have ever seen. Your generous proportions appeal to me more than I can say.

I am a very rich man, and have an old, splendid house in Algiers, with eighteen rooms, and much silver and gold. If you will do me the honor to come to Algiers, I shall make you the favorite of my harem, give you your own chamber, with bath and many lovely gowns and shawls. I also have a pet monkey which I shall be honored to present to you.

Cordially,
SHEIK-ABEL-REY

To this I replied:

Very much flattered with your letter but I'm afraid my husband, Al Lackey, might not like the idea.

This, as I have explained, was my first venture in Hollywood. Do you wonder that I looked forward to my next adventure in 1938 with some misgivings and a great deal of hope?

This time I had a house in Hollywood. There were six of us—hubby and I, Ida Cohen, my English friend, who took over the job as housekeeper, Emma, my maid, my niece, Sadie, who drove out with a friend to see California, fell in love with it, and stayed on with us, and the cook. Al and I were still together in those days. We had our "ups and downs" and our "ins and outs," but I wanted to make a go of my married life if I could. God knows if you are in show business it's a hard thing to achieve a successful marriage. You are always having to pack up and move somewhere else when your married life requires you to be there on the spot. You are always having to go to the theater to put on a show when your husband wants you to sit down and listen to him talk about his business. And, if he has a business and works at it all day, he's too sleepy to pay attention to you when your work is finished around 2 or 3 A.M. and you feel like having supper and a game of pinochle—and a little loving. I thought when we went to Hollywood: "Now is the time to establish a home!" And for five months I really did have one.

Hollywood was full of old friends who welcomed me with parties. It seemed as if everybody I'd ever known in show business, from the earliest days, was out there on the West Coast making a picture. And when I went round to the MGM studios, it was like old-home week. There was Sam Katz (of Balaban and Katz), the producer of *Broadway Melody,* in which I was to play. There was L. B. Mayer's secretary, Ida Koverman, a swell gal whom I've known from the Orpheum days in San Francisco. There was Eddie Mannix, a big lovable Irishman who used to be the bouncer at the old Palisades Park in New Jersey and would keep our crowd in order when we went there of an evening for fifty cents' worth of fun. There were Harry Rapf, reminding me of the fights he and I used to have over billing when he was producing and booking on the Keith time; Benny Thau, whom I'd known when he worked for Eddie Darling in the Keith booking office of the old Palace Theatre building in New York. Benny used to run downstairs to the theater to get a line on all the acts, then hustle upstairs to report to the chief. There was John Considine, Jr., the son of my old pal John, Sr., of the Sullivan-Considine Circuit, and young John's wife, who had been Carmen Pantages, and whom I'd known when she wore rompers. There was the writer Edgar Allen Woolfe, the bushy, redheaded kid who showed me his first script when I lived in New York in the same hotel with his mother and dad and who had been lots of fun to be with in London. There was Billy Grady, the casting director—I reminded him of how he and Maggie, his wife, had hauled me over to Brooklyn one time to see the new "blessed event" in their home. In those days, Billy worked for Max Keller, a prominent booking agent. There was Eddie Buzzell, as fine a vaudeville performer as we ever had, and now a director. There was Dolly Tree, who had dressed my first show in London, *Round in Fifty,* in 1922. And there was Mary Garden, whom I met for the first time though I had carried the billing, "The Mary Garden of Ragtime," for several seasons after Jack Lait gave it to me in 1909. There was Robert Z. Leonard, director, who had never failed to come backstage and say "hello" to us vaudevillians every time he went to see a show; Jack McGowan, who had written a part for me in *Broadway Melody;* Edgar Selwyn, whom I used to pester to death to put me in his shows; Albertina Rasch, whom I hadn't seen since 1926, when she put her dancers in our show, *Le Maire's Affairs;* Arthur Freed and Nacio Brown, two boys from Tin Pan Alley whose songs I always liked to plug; and Gus Kahn, also from Tin Pan Alley. Gus and Grace Kahn taught me their first song hit in Chicago years back.

It was like getting home to the old crowd of the days before vaudeville ended. The only thing that was strange was the place, and what an amazing place the MGM lot was. A city in itself, with its rows upon rows of buildings. The executive offices lined up on one side of the main street. There was the bustling, humming publicity department; the wardrobe department with its millions of dollars' worth of merchandise; the music department; rows of offices for script writers, producers, directors, and their assistants; the dramatic school, headed by Phyllis Laughton; the photograph galleries; the foreign publicity department; the sound studio headed by Douglas Shearer (Norma's brother); the make-up department; the scenic department. There was the doctor's office, the dentist's office, the barbershop, the shoe-shine parlor, and the commissary where over five hundred people were fed at one time. And, moving around this city, hundreds of technicians of every kind— extras, writers, gag men, cameramen.

No wonder, I thought, people go nuts over Hollywood. There never was anything in show business on such a scale as this.

The cast of *Broadway Melody* was headed by Eleanor Powell and Robert Taylor. Binnie Barnes played in it, and Judy Garland. Roy Del Ruth directed the picture. It was a story of show business, and when I read the script I was terribly enthusiastic about it. I was determined that my second picture should be a success. And, remembering some of the things I thought were wrong with *Honky Tonk,* I tried to keep from making the same mistakes all over again. After all, I told myself, I am a singer of songs—not an actress. I had heard Laura Hope Crews was a wonderful coach, so I called her up and asked her to coach me. For weeks I went every day to Santa Monica and Laura worked with me to get me ready for the picture.

When we began to shoot, I found that the original story had been rearranged considerably to build up Robert Taylor's part. The first day I worked with him was in the backstage scene in which I had to sing "Some of These Days." Believe it or not, I was so excited by the idea of doing a scene with Robert Taylor that I fumbled and forgot the lines of my theme song!

Buddy Ebsen, George Murphy, Eleanor Powell, and Judy Garland were all vaudeville troupers like me. All of us were eagerly hoping for a break in pictures. Eleanor Powell was a tireless worker and a great dancer. It seemed only yesterday that she was just a hoofer on a vaudeville bill with me. Judy Garland was so eager and so determined to get ahead in pictures that it made me proud to work with her. One day I was told that Willie and Eugene Howard had been signed on to play a few scenes with me to give the picture the true feel of vaudeville. Strange as it seems, in the twenty-six years that I'd known the Howard Brothers, up to our work in *Broadway Melody,* the boys and I had played just one vaudeville date together. That was at the new Palace Theatre in Chicago. Of course we had played a few benefits together. The laughs and the fun we three had on the set, working in the boardinghouse scene!

And all those scenes on the cutting-room floor at the finish of the picture!

After our first day's work on the picture I was, naturally, very eager for L. B.'s comment and criticism. A few days later he called me into his office to tell me I looked lovely, my face was kind, my work with Judy was motherly, and he was greatly pleased. In return for these compliments I threw my arms around him. Then I ran home and phoned Abe Lastfogel the good news. L. B. often asked me over to his home for Sunday brunch, served out on the patio in front of the swimming pool. There would be twenty to thirty people—everybody of any importance in filmland. The food was the best I have ever eaten anywhere—always finnan haddie, a favorite dish of L. B.'s, among other things. After brunch he would have a concert and then pinochle and bridge games. L. B. is a champ at pinochle, and how he loves to beat everybody he plays with—which he usually does. He took me on a few times, but he was too good for me.

I'll never forget the day I drove out to the studio in the Chevvy I'd rented. As we drove in the gates there were L. B., Sam Katz, Harry Rapf, and Eddie Mannix in a huddle. I got out of the Chevvy and L. B. greeted me: "Is that your car, Sophie?"

"Yes sir," I said.

"You an MGM star riding around in that rattletrap!" And to the chauffeur, "You go to the Packard Company and get your missus a better-looking car!"

"Hold on, L. B.," I yelled. "I'm one gal on this lot that won't buy a car or a home out here until I find out how good you think I am in this racket!"

They started to shoot *Broadway Melody* in January and we finished early in April. Then came weeks of waiting while the cutting room was busy with their scissors. I hadn't any idea how much of my part was going to be left in or what chance I stood of doing another picture. I was drawing down the salary on my contract. But hell! I'm not used to hanging around doing nothing—and being paid for it! I began to fret. I couldn't find out where they were going to have the sneak preview. When I heard that they had taken the picture down to San Diego, there wasn't time for me to make the trip there. I bet I never closed an eye all that night wondering how it was going over with the audience. I was the first one out at the studio the next day to get the report, and the first man I bumped into out there was Roy Del Ruth. I was almost afraid to ask him. "How was it, Roy?" He smiled and said: "You were great!" Then Sam Katz came along and added: "They laughed and applauded every time you came on the screen. When was the last time you played San Diego?"

"I haven't played there in over eight years."

"Well, they remembered you all right. You were great!"

I stood there like a fool, looking at the two of them, blinking back the tears, not able to say a thing. It began to look as though I had launched myself on a career in pictures. And this, after thirty years in show business! I felt so good about the future I started to branch out. I bought a new car and I rented a lovely fifteen-room house in Beverly Hills. No house is considered fit for occupancy unless it has a swimming pool, and this one had a forty-by-sixty-foot pool, surrounded by tall trees, with dressing rooms and shower baths and everything just as you see in the pictures. Two or three times a week we had dinner parties, not for the movie moguls or important visitors, but for my old trouper buddies—the friends I'd known in vaudeville. They were the ones I wanted to be with and wanted to share my home with. I never ran my home Hollywood style, but more the way Mama had taught me. Friends were welcomed there at all times for a good home-cooked meal and a game of cards. My Sunday luncheons were mostly for children—Judy Garland and Freddie Bartholomew would bring their friends and the gang would have a swell time in the pool.

Still, I wasn't working, which was something strange for me. The publicity department had sent out word that Sophie Tucker would be built up by the studio to take over Marie Dressler's stories and her parts. I shook my head over this, and I begged L. B. to curb this sort of publicity. "Listen," I told him, "for over twenty-five years I've worked to build up the name of Sophie Tucker, and now your publicity department think they can turn me into a Marie Dressler. Marie left a name and reputation that belong to her alone. I'll never be anything but Sophie Tucker. Build *me* up for pictures!"

But the publicity had already gone out over the wires and my clipping bureau was sending me hundreds of clippings, from papers all over the country, in which I was played up as the next Marie Dressler. One day at lunch in the commissary on the lot I was asked to join Ida Koverman, who was entertaining Gloria Swanson and Frances Marion. Frances Marion had been a great friend of Marie Dressler's. I heard her tell Ida:

"Sophie is the one to play *Mollie, Bless Her.*" This was the story of Marie Dressler's life. The next thing I'd heard was that L. B. had bought the story, and the news in the press was that Sophie Tucker was to do the life of Marie Dressler. It struck me that it was a mistake to hammer me into the public's mind as a second Marie Dressler before *Broadway Melody* came out.

In the years I've been in show business there have been dozens of performers billed as the second "this" or "that." All of them died by the wayside. You can't be successful on someone else's reputation or name! No publicity department can bamboozle the public into accepting, as genuine, something that is fake.

I have great respect for Marie Dressler as a performer. I never knew her in the heyday of her success on Broadway. I met her first in London as Mrs. Jack Dalton, when I was entertaining at the Kit-Kat Klub and she was kind enough to compliment me on my work. The next time we met was in Philadelphia, where I was headlining Keith's theater. Marie Dressler had booked a two weeks' engagement at the Walton Roof in Philadelphia. She came backstage to see me and asked me to advise and help her, as she was petrified about playing in a cabaret show—something she had never done before. When I finished my show that night, I rushed up to the roof and took over the show there, introducing Marie to the night-club audience. For a whole week I was on the job, and she was a big success. However, she didn't like café work. It was out of her line entirely. But a great artist is great any place, any time, and I kept telling her so. Marie finished the Philadelphia engagement and the next I heard of her she was in pictures, where she was rolling up an enormous success.

After the news from San Diego I couldn't wait to see *Broadway Melody*. There was a preview at Long Beach, to which all the cast and staff from the MGM studios were invited. I should say there were about five hundred of us. The rest of the audience was very friendly to the cast as we came in, and when the names appeared on the screen, there was a lot of applause. But when the picture began, and scenes I remembered making were missing, I began to feel jittery. I felt as though the best of me had been left on the cutting-room floor.

"What do you think of it, dear?" Al Lackey kept whispering to me.

And I whispered back, "It stinks, if you ask me!"

Al had a lot of sense about show business and I could see that he agreed with me that for all I'd been told the San Diego preview was such a hit the picture wasn't good, and I was only fair. It was okay for Eleanor Powell and Robert Taylor. For them it was just another picture. Judy Garland was the only one in the whole cast in whom I saw great possibilities. I said so to L. B. and to everyone on the lot: "Judy, if carefully handled and groomed, will be the big MGM star in a few years." My predictions were right!

Now it remained to be seen how *Broadway Melody of 1937* would hit the general public. I wanted to get away from Hollywood for a while, because hanging around there and not working got on my nerves. Abe Lastfogel got me bookings to play Chicago and Detroit and then Piping Rock, Saratoga, for the month of August. I made only one personal appearance with *Broadway Melody*—that was in Albany. The audience gave me a warm reception, but I didn't like the picture in Albany any more than I liked it in Long Beach. It didn't seem to me that my career in pictures was breaking just right. However, I had been ordered to report back at the studio after the Saratoga engagement to make a second picture, *Thoroughbreds Don't Cry*.

The cast included Mickey Rooney and Judy Garland. Another boy's part in the picture was to have been played by Freddie Bartholomew, but the part was given instead to Ronald Sinclair, a little Australian boy new to pictures. I didn't particularly like my part. It was a part any fifty dollar character actress could do better than I. Producer Harry Rapf kept telling me: "Here's your chance to be another Marie Dressler." If he had that in his mind, I knew I was sunk. I was to play a straight character part—no singing—and the studio dressed me in Marie Dressler's dresses. I wasn't very hopeful of *Thoroughbreds Don't Cry*. But the picture was made, and then came the weeks of waiting, going out to the studio every day, hoping to hear the good news: "I've got something for you, Sophie!"

After four months of waiting I found myself getting irritable. When I entertained at benefits, I didn't feel that I was holding my audience. My songs weren't funny. It seemed to me that my work was strained. I knew what it was—the movies were getting me down. What I needed was to get back into my own hard-working two-a-day world. I called Jack Yellen and Abe Lastfogel to come over to my house, and I told them: "I can't stay out here any more and wait for MGM to come through. I'll go nuts sitting around doing nothing. Sure I'm collecting my weekly check every Friday, but, boys, I've been a check collector for over twenty-five years and I can still collect them. Jack, you get me some new songs. Abe, you book me East —at once. I'll get the hell out of Hollywood before I become one of the has-beens in show business."

Abe was worried about the contract, which had twelve more weeks to go. I told him: "To hell with the contract! MGM will be just as happy to get rid of me as I shall be to get away." And I was right. L. B. Mayer came through, paying me up in full—with no worries about lawsuits. I left Hollywood with fifteen scrapbooks, loaded with the greatest publicity I've had in all of my years of show business—the movies did that for me.

CHAPTER 28: *And That's Show Business*

PLAYING a fifteen-week engagement at Ben Marden's Riviera on the Jersey side of the George Washington Bridge during the summer of 1938 made me feel that I was back in my stride. I said to myself: "Now is the time to get into a musical comedy to open on Broadway in the fall."

To show how my hunches work out: I was coming out of my hairdresser's one day, on Sixth Avenue near Fifty-fifth Street, when who should I run into but Harry Bestry. Harry is a booking agent who works only on shows. I told him I was ripe for a musical comedy. "Get busy, Harry. See what you can do for me."

A few days later he called to ask me to meet him in Vinton Freedley's office. Freedley had a comedy he was putting on. We talked about it, but the part didn't just fit me. I left, hoping something more in my line would turn up later.

What did turn up was Cole Porter at the Riviera. I could see him watching my performance. Maybe, I said to myself, something is up. Then several nights later there was Cole Porter again. I began to feel goose pimples down my back. Then nothing happened for several weeks. I finished my engagement and went down to Atlantic City for a rest. Just when I was beginning to get philosophical about my hunch, there was Harry Bestry on the phone telling me to get back to New York to hear the new score Cole Porter had finished for Vinton Freedley's comedy, especially a couple of numbers especially for me. If I liked them, we could talk business.

The show was *Leave It to Me,* in which William Gaxton and Victor Moore starred, and in which lovely Mary Martin sang her famous number, "My Heart Belongs to Daddy."

The first time I saw Mary Martin rehearse I predicted she would be the outstanding hit of the show. She had so much on the ball—eagerness, charm, real ability. She just couldn't miss. Everyone in the company was crazy about her. We all grieved for her when the wire came announcing her father's death—a piece of sad news I had to break to her. She took it like a real trouper, keeping back the tears in obedience to the first rule of show business: the show must go on.

Leave It to Me was a success from the start. There was not one bad notice in the press. So, after twenty-nine years of working, hoping, trying, flopping, trying again, I made my first hit in a Broadway success. And, boy, did it feel good! The show played from the first week of November to the end of

July 1939. Then we went on the road. Through the following winter we toured the South in the worst cold weather they had had down there since Grant took Richmond. It was tough going, like the early days of trouping; the train jumps in the early mornings, the dirty, drafty dressing rooms, the eating places we would gather in for supper after the show. Tough, but I reveled in it. This was show business as I had known it long ago, and it suited me a lot better than plush-covered and chromium-plated Hollywood.

The hard work on the tour helped me to forget some of the unpleasant experiences connected with the big fight that had centered around the A.F.A. (American Federation of Actors) and which had come to a head and burst just about the time *Leave It to Me* was finishing its run on Broadway.

At the time I was president of A.F.A., which meant that I was in the fight up to my neck.

The A.F.A. was the first union especially for vaudevillians after the organization known as the White Rats, which was formed around 1905, and which had only a short existence. What had interested me in the A.F.A. from the start was that it was organized by vaudevillians for vaudevillians. Ralph Whitehead, himself a vaudevillian, started it and became executive secretary. Among its presidents were Eddie Cantor, Fred Keating, and Rudy Vallee. I was elected to the presidency in 1938—the first woman to hold the office.

You cannot grow up in vaudeville, as I did, without realizing that every variety artist should belong to a union. For many years the variety artist was the butt of the inequalities in show business. He had to travel long distances, playing one-week engagements and at a salary which kept him living in cheap, uncomfortable actors' rooming houses. Not infrequently his act would be canceled after the first show, which left him high and dry for the rest of the week. The personal preferences and prejudices of the theater managers could interfere with his act and cause arguments and scenes backstage that upset the performer before he went on, making him give a bad performance. I've told some of my own experiences along these lines. The crowded, unsanitary conditions backstage in many of the showiest theaters were shocking.

For years, whenever a bunch of us vaudevillians got together, we would talk about these things and argue over what vaudevillians could do to get a better break in show business. Everyone agreed that vaudevillians needed a strong union of their own. But everybody admitted in the next breath that variety artists, as a rule, made bad union members. The successful ones were always on the road and could not attend regular meetings of their union. We weren't like the legit actors who remained for a whole season on Broadway.

Some of us—and I was one of them—felt that the variety artists' union should be so organized that it would benefit its own members when any of them got into a tight spot. All of us have known what it is like to be out of work, to need money for an operation, or to have your teeth fixed, or your hair dyed so you can get a job. Most of us have felt that awful *gone* feeling at the pit of the stomach when you haven't got the money for that week's room rent, or for train fares to the next town where you believe you can get work in a café. I believed that a percentage of the actor's union dues should be set aside to form a fund to take care of emergencies such as I have pictured. It seemed to me that the actor who paid his dues to his union was entitled to relief from that union when he needed it.

I held these ideas long before I was elected president of the A.F.A. and they influenced me greatly in all that I did for the association while I was in office.

The A.F.A. was one of the organizations included in the 4As, which is the parent body of all the actors' guilds. Frank Gilmore was then president of the 4As.

Early in 1938, before I came East to open at Ben Marden's Riviera, a series of articles appeared in the Hollywood *Reporter* which implied that Whitehead was not managing the affairs of the A.F.A. properly. Membership in our organization was increasing steadily; it was now over fifteen thousand, with eighty-five hundred members in good standing. We had opened our federation to include circus performers. Whitehead reported that there had been some discussion among the officers of the 4As over this.

"Has the 4As ever returned the per capita tax on these members?" I asked Whitehead.

"No," he said.

"Have they ever asked if the tax paid them on our membership fee comes from circus performers, vaudevillians, or night-club entertainers?"

He assured me they had not.

That seemed to me to put us in the clear.

That summer the World's Fair opened in New York, which meant a lot of work for entertainers and a lot of business for our office. Meanwhile, the articles in the Hollywood *Reporter* kept appearing, hinting that the business affairs of the A.F.A. were not what they should be. I began to get letters from members demanding to know what about it. When I came East to open at Ben Marden's Riviera, I had a long talk with Whitehead. I was convinced of his honesty and I could not see that the A.F.A. was doing anything wrong. However, I did not like the adverse publicity we were getting, so I suggested to Whitehead—and he agreed—that we request the 4As to examine our books. I felt that for us to take such action would prove our good faith, and when the investigation showed that our affairs were all in order, as I was sure it would, that would give the lie to the annoying attacks in the Hollywood *Reporter*.

The investigation was started. For months during that winter and spring the accountants retained by the 4As were busy with our books. Meanwhile, I was doing eight shows a week at the Imperial Theatre in *Leave It to Me,* café work, and a twenty-six-week engagement in radio. One afternoon I went to the races. I came back to my hotel around six o'clock to get ready for the show and found a message to call Whitehead. There were also several slips with the message that Eddie Cantor had called me at twelve-thirty, at one-thirty, and later in the afternoon.

I called Whitehead. He said the investigators had handed him their report at eleven that morning. I told him to bring it round to my dressing room that night after the show. Then I rang up Eddie. When I got him he said:

"Sophie, I'm talking to you like my own sister. Get out of the A.F.A. Get out at once."

"Why?" I fired back.

"Because if you don't, you'll be in the middle of a rotten mess. Whitehead is under suspicion of misusing the A.F.A. funds. Resign, and do it *quick.*"

"Where did you get this information from?" I asked.

"Never mind where I got it. I'm telling you what to do." He added that he had called Harry Richman, our vice-president, and had told him the same thing: "Resign."

I hung up, and then I went down to the theater for the show. After the last act Whitehead came round to my dressing room with the report. The first paragraph read: "There were no discrepancies"; though later on there was reference to "misuse of funds."

From my telephone conversation with Eddie Cantor I figured that the stories going around town were probably a lot worse than the report, and that the best thing to do was to call a meeting of the A.F.A., present the report, and thrash the whole business out then and there.

I was determined to have as large a representation of our members as possible at that meeting. We set it for midnight, which would allow most of them to get there, and we arranged with the Hotel Edison, where we held it, to serve coffee and sandwiches so no one would have to stop to eat supper before coming to the meeting. For five nights before the meeting I went out after my show with some members of our A.F.A. office staff and we made every important night club on Broadway, in Greenwich Village, Brooklyn, Queens, and out at the fair to notify as many of our members as we could reach, and to make them promise to come to the meeting.

The night of the meeting was terribly hot. Maybe that had something to do with the tempers of those who came. The room was packed. On the platform sat Ralph Whitehead, Rudy Vallee, Joe Howard, Frank Fay, Milton Berle, Morton Downey, Aunt Jemima, Bill Robinson, Harry Richman, and I.

When I stood up to read the report of the 4As' investigators someone in the audience gave me the bird. I was prepared for that. Jack Gould of the New York *Times* had warned me several days before that a man whom Whitehead had once befriended and helped out of his own pocket had organized a gang of "ferrets" to break up the meeting.

The "ferrets" started on me. I tried to read the report, with the sweat pouring down my face and back, while the hecklers razzed me. Meanwhile, photographers who had been tipped off that there was going to be trouble at the meeting kept snapping away at us on the platform. Once, when I took my handkerchief to wipe the perspiration from my face and my glasses to see to read, a camera snapped me. Next day there was my picture in one of the papers with the caption: SOPHIE TUCKER WEEPS AT MEETING.

I never was further from tears in my whole life. I was too mad to cry. Fighting, cussing mad.

Finally, I saw there was no use going on with the meeting. The "ferrets" had staged one of the worst riots I ever saw anywhere. I turned to Harry Richman and told him I was going to call for an adjournment. I hardly got the words out of my mouth before the "ferrets" started a free for all with the members who wanted to hear the report. Then someone put out the lights. What began as an open meeting of the A.F.A. finished as a brawl in which the police had to be called in.

Worse than the newspaper stories of the meeting, some of which were headlined SOPHIE TUCKER GETS THE BIRD, and SOPHIE TUCKER CHASED OFF PLATFORM BY ANGRY ACTORS were stories published in the press and circulated generally that the books of the A.F.A. had been taken over by Mr. Thomas Dewey, then district attorney of New York City. This publicity, which was untrue, did the cause of the vaudevillians a great amount of harm. I am able to state unequivocally that these stories were false because of the following letter addressed to my attorney:

Office of the District Attorney
New York County,
New York City.

June 22, 1939

Abraham J. Halprin
170 Broadway
New York City

Dear Mr. Halprin,

This will acknowledge receipt of your letter of June 22. You are correct in your statement that *no* books or records have been seized by this office or anyone subpoenaed or examined.

If it shall at any time become necessary to examine any of the officers or employees of the association which you represent, or the books and records thereof, I shall be glad to take advantage of your kind offer of co-operation.

Yours very truly
(*signed*) Robert H. Thayer
*Assistant District Attorney
in charge of Indictment Bureau.*

However, true or false, the harm was done to the A.F.A. The 4As revoked our charter and organized a new Guild of Variety Artists to take the place of the disgraced A.F.A. Some of us objected to this procedure; we felt that the A.F.A. had been wrongly condemned, and that it had not been given a fair chance to state its case. Consequently, we refused to disband the A.F.A., and so requested a new charter from the I.A.T.S.E. (International Alliance of Theatrical Stage Employees and Moving Picture Operators).

This move didn't please the 4As. The I.A.T.S.E.—often called the Stage-hands' Union—was very powerful. George Browne was then its president. It looked to me and to Harry Richman and to some of the others that we would strengthen the cause of the vaudevillians by becoming affiliated with such a powerful organization. But, as it happened, and soon came to light, Browne and a man named William Bioff were then racketeering in the I.A.T.S.E. The court started an investigation of their activities with much publicity, and that ended what remained of the A.F.A.

Harry Richman and I had been suspended by the Screen Actors' Guild, by the A.F.R.A. (American Federation of Radio Artists), and by Equity for joining forces with the I.A.T.S.E. But this suspension was soon lifted and Harry and I were permitted to go back to work.

You might think after these experiences that I would have lost faith in the value of a union for variety artists. On the contrary. I am convinced that the actor needs his union. But he needs to be an active, vigorous part of it. It isn't enough for him to carry a card—the way it is now, some of us carry a whole deck of union cards to prove our membership in all the various guilds. The actor must take part in the affairs of his own union to keep it working for his benefit and to prevent racketeers muscling in on him. The only actors' union that is of any use to actors is one which is run by actors and for actors.

Because of the many branches of show business today, the performer frequently carries several union cards and pays dues to several unions. This in itself is confusing and annoying. Too often the artist doesn't bother to attend meetings, even when he could; nor does he read his union newspaper. Then he grumbles: "What good is a union to me?"

There are a lot of abuses to performers that should be legislated out of existence, and which could be done away with if the actors' unions went to work on them. Take this business of late shows in cafés, when, frequently, there aren't more than a dozen customers in the place, and half of them are drunk or asleep. Another thing that should be done away with, to my way of thinking, is the custom of running six or seven shows a day in the motion-picture theaters. It doesn't wear out the films, but it sure plays hell with musicians, singers, entertainers. All entertainers should have one day a week off to rest. They would give better shows, and the customers would be just as satisfied.

I've said a lot about what it takes to stay in show business. Above all, the performer must look ahead. You can't grow stale or cling to a period. You must belong to your time. Show business is constantly changing. And there are a lot more changes right around the next corner. You can see some of them coming. Take this business of taking shows to the workers in war plants. There's no reason to believe that this is going to end with the war. One of the great powers of radio as entertainment is that it takes entertainment to the people wherever they are. It is quite likely that workers are going to demand that entertainment be brought to them where they work, and that we will have traveling shows, touring the industrial centers, playing during rest hours in big industrial plants, long after those plants have been converted to peacetime production.

The trouble over the A.F.A. is directly responsible for this book. Not that it was my original idea to tell the world the low-down on that. But this is how it happened.

When the publicity was at its height and its nastiest, I was working at the Versailles Restaurant in East Fiftieth Street. One night Ted Friend, of the New York *Mirror,* came over to my table.

"You know, Sophie," he said to me, "you should write a book."

"I've been writing a book for years," I answered back. "It's called *Horses That Owe Me Money,* and I haven't come to the end of it yet."

"Just the same, I mean it," said Ted. "You're an institution, Sophie."

"A lot of guys have called me a lot of names," said I, "but you're the first one ever called me that."

I might have passed up Ted's remark but for Louis Sobol coming along not ten minutes later. He dropped into the chair where Ted had sat. And the first thing he said was: "Sophie, you should write a book. Your autobiography. Now is the time for you to do it."

Well, as I figured it out later on, Ted and Louis are two smart boys. Maybe they've got something in that idea. Maybe Sophie Tucker has got something to say to folks that she hasn't said in her songs and her gags. I decided to buy a stack of yellow paper and some lead pencils and see for myself if I could take on a new act.

It has been a long, slow business, writing down everything I could remember; writing it by hand, usually late at night after I have come home from work, wherever I've been—in New York, Chicago, Hollywood, Florida. I've had no time off for writing. As a matter of fact, since I started on my book I've been kept working harder and steadier than I've worked in years. There has been my season on Broadway with George Jessel in *High Kickers,* a lot of work in cafés all over the country, and several pictures, including *Sensations of 1944,* and *Follow the Boys.*

From the beginning I have wanted this book to answer some of the questions beginners in show business ask me about how to get started, and how to make a success as entertainers.

From the days when I started headlining bills I have been asked how to get ahead in show business. Harry Richman's mother brought him—a kid in short pants—to play for me; Mama Dolly used to question me about what was good for her girls, and there was Minnie Marx and ever so many more. In this book, as I told my story, I have tried to stress those things that I know are vitally important; such as the obligation to be always on time. If you're in show business you can never afford to be five minutes late. When you're starting out, you've got to be on time or you'll be fired. After that it gets to be habit. The headliner is never late.

Be sure you look right. The performer never has any time off. There never

is a day or an hour when you can afford to slump. You never can tell whom
you may meet, who may come along, what opportunity may come your way,
And you've got to be ready for it. You can't afford to be passed over because
you didn't make up properly that day, or you were careless about your
clothes, or didn't keep the appointment with the hairdresser the day before.

Never let down on a show. Suppose there are only a handful of people in
the house; one of them may be a producer. You never can tell. Besides, the
artist learns about entertaining through such experiences, and no artist ever
knows all there is to learn.

I'll never forget the last show at the Palace in New York. It was ghastly.
Everyone knew the theater was to be closed down, and a landmark in show
business would be gone. That feeling got into the acts. The whole place, and
even the performers, stank of decay. I seemed to smell it. It challenged me. I
went out on that stage determined to keep my mind on the future—not on the
past. I was determined to give the audience the idea: why brood over yesterday? We have tomorrow. As I sang I could feel the atmosphere change. The
gloom began to lift, the spirit which had formerly filled the Palace and which
made it famous among vaudeville houses in the world came back.

That's what the entertainer can do. That's the power he has; and which
he can use when he knows how to use it.

One of the most important things to remember is that when you're on the
stage you're in character. Don't ad-lib. Don't be smart-alecky. You may think
you're being terribly funny, but it's ten chances to one the audience doesn't
think so. Comedy doesn't come as easy as all that. Most of it has to be worked
over, carefully timed, rehearsed, planned. It looks light and easy, but it only
looks that way because the comedian has rehearsed it until his technique
is perfect.

Be individual. Don't make yourself into a carbon copy of some other entertainer, or some glamor girl of the screen. One of the saddest things in show
business is the number of girls working in cafés in every town of any size
who look, dress, and sing just alike. You can't tell one from the other. And
not one of them will ever get anywhere in show business until she breaks
away from that pattern, until she sings something original, individual. They'll
go on clutching the mike, the way a Saturday-night drunk clings to a lamp-
post, singing into it the same monotonous song, and wondering why they
never get a break.

Making a success in show business calls for plenty of patience and for
tolerance. You can't afford to hold resentments or grudges. They interfere
with your work. And first, last, and all the time, it's your work that counts.

It isn't easy to be a successful entertainer. Not any easier than to be a success in any other profession. For entertaining is a profession. When you go into one of the professions you expect to make sacrifices and to work to get ahead. Doesn't a nurse have to study and work hard? Doesn't a teacher have to educate herself? Think of the years of work that go into the making of a physician.

We talk about "the profession," meaning the actor's. It's something to be proud of. It has a great, honorable tradition. It's worth working for.

Writing a book isn't easy. And neither is ending it. I was sitting staring into space, chewing on my pencil, with a blank sheet of paper in front of me, when who should come along but Louis Sobol.

"What's the matter, Soph?"

I told him I was trying to think up a way to end the book he had urged me to write.

"That's easy," said Louis. "End it this way:

—AND MORE TO FOLLOW."